❧ TED 621A/623 ❧

METHODOLOGY
FOR SECOND LANGUAGE DEVELOPMENT

REVISED EDITION FOR NATIONAL UNIVERSITY

Compiled by Peter Serdyukov, DPS, PhD and Robyn A. Hill, PhD

Taken from:

The Foundations of Dual Language Instruction, Fifth Edition
by Judith Lessow-Hurley

102 Content Strategies for English Language Learners: Teaching for Academic Success in Grades 3 -- 12
by Jodi Reiss

Strategies for Teaching English Learners, Second Edition
by Lynne T. Díaz-Rico

Custom Publishing

New York   Boston   San Francisco
London   Toronto   Sydney   Tokyo   Singapore   Madrid
Mexico City   Munich   Paris   Cape Town   Hong Kong   Montreal

Cover image: Courtesy of Photodisc/Getty Images.

Taken from:

The Foundations of Dual Language Instruction, Fifth Edition
by Judith Lessow-Hurley
Copyright © 2009, 2005, 2000 by Pearson Education, Inc.
Published by Allyn & Bacon
Boston, Massachusetts 02116

102 Content Strategies for English Language Learners: Teaching for Academic Success in Grades 3–12
by Jodi Reiss
Copyright © 2008 by Pearson Education, Inc.
Published by Prentice Hall
Upper Saddle River, New Jersey 07458

Strategies for Teaching English Learners, Second Edition
by Lynne T. Díaz-Rico
Copyright © 2008 by Pearson Education, Inc.
Published by Allyn & Bacon
Boston, Massachusetts 02116

This special edition published in cooperation with Pearson Custom Publishing.

All trademarks, service marks, registered trademarks, and registered service marks are the property of their respective owners and are used herein for identification purposes only.

Printed in the United States of America

4 5 6 7 8 9 10 V0CR 13 12 11 10

2009220180

NM

**Pearson
Custom Publishing**
is a division of

PEARSON

www.pearsonhighered.com

ISBN 10: 0-558-43937-3
ISBN 13: 978-0-558-43937-8

Learning Outcomes:

Upon successful completion of this course, candidates will be able to:

* Demonstrate graduate level written, communication and presentation skills, including APA formatting skills

* Demonstrate application of graduate level analytical and critical thinking skills

* Identify and describe distinct pedagogical, psychological, socio-cultural, political and legal factors that influence teaching and learning of English as well as academic subject matter

* Explain theories of first and second language development, how first language literacy connects to second language development, and factors providing access to the core curriculum to all students;

* Compare language theories and models; language variations; contrastive/ comparative linguistics; oral and written discourse; and students' linguistic development;

* Discuss the foundations and critical issues of bilingualism

* Explain the connection between first language literacy and second language development, relationship between native and second language "Basic Interpersonal Communication Skills" (BICS) and "Cognitive Academic Language Proficiency"(CALP), and utilize SDAIE techniques to develop students' CALP

* Identify and describe the most advantageous theories, technologies and practices of English Language Development that could be applied in the classroom

* Integrate Specially Designed Academic Instruction in English (SDAIE) and other methods of ESL instruction into their teaching practice

* Plan and design a lesson based on state adopted academic content standards that would incorporate a variety of efficient strategies and technologies, sequencing and differentiated instruction to accommodate students' special needs and teaching ESL across the curriculum.

* Apply the most effective classroom management strategies; create a positive climate for learning

* Use various assessment techniques, quantitative and qualitative methods of evaluation and assessment.

* Teach exemplary lessons in diverse classrooms for students of diverse cultures, ethnicity, races, languages, gender and individuals with special needs.

Contents

Chapters 1–11 taken from The Foundations of Dual Language Instruction, Fifth Edition, by Judith Lessow-Hurley.

• CHAPTER *14*

A SOLID START: BUILDING AND ACTIVATING BACKGROUND KNOWLEDGE   191

• CHAPTER *15*

$\mathcal{P}$RESENTING NEW MATERIAL: TEACHING THE LESSON   207

● CHAPTER *16*

$\mathcal{D}$ID THEY GET WHAT I TAUGHT? CHECKING COMPREHENSION   229

• CHAPTER *17*

*E*XTENDING COMPREHENSION: TEXTBOOK VOCABULARY
STRATEGIES 243

• CHAPTER *18*

*E*XTENDING COMPREHENSION: TEXTBOOK READING
STRATEGIES 263

• CHAPTER *19*

REINFORCING LEARNING: ACTIVITIES AND ASSIGNMENTS   283

Chapter 20 taken from **Strategies for Teaching English Learners,** *Second Edition, by Lynne T. Díaz-Rico.*

• CHAPTER *20*

$\mathcal{P}$ERFORMANCE-BASED LEARNING 309

chapter 1

Historical and International Perspectives

People from the United States are sometimes surprised to find that tourists or immigrants often speak, read, and write several languages. Around the world, bilingualism is more the norm than the exception. This is true now and was also true historically. This chapter will review the history of bilingualism and dual language education around the world and consider examples of the use of two languages at the present time in society and in education.

Societal Bilingualism

THE ANCIENT WORLD

Bilingualism was common in antiquity. Political and territorial consolidation and domination of one or more groups of people by others generally created situations in which conquered groups added the dominant language to their repertoire. Linguistic tolerance on the part of ancient conquerors favored linguistic diversity. Starting in the sixth century B.C.E., ancient Greeks, for example, penetrated and dominated large areas of the Mediterranean. While they preserved and promulgated Greek language and culture through schooling, they had no interest in replacing local languages with their own. With language shifts slow in the making, many individuals maintained the ability to function in more than one language (Lewis, 1976).

To the extent that formal schooling was available, education in more than one language seems to have been the norm in the ancient world. The need for dual language education may have been tied to literacy. The scarcity of written materials meant that a person who wanted to read widely had to read in more than one language (Mackey, 1978).

Education in Europe has always placed value on bilingualism and biliteracy, dating back to the fact that formal schooling was implemented on a large scale by the Romans throughout their empire and that all students were

1

> ## ℬilingualism among Jews
>
> Jewish bilingualism from ancient times to the present has received the special attention of scholars (Lewis, 1976). Hebrew was used for worship by Jews long after it ceased to be a mainstream Jewish language. Dispersed around the world, Jews have learned many languages, while simultaneously maintaining a home or community language. Although no longer widely spoken, Yiddish is perhaps the most familiar Jewish language to English speakers, because it is related to German. As you can see in the following list, many Yiddish words and constructions have entered English.
>
> *Bagel:* A bread, shaped like a donut, that is boiled and then baked.
>
> *Chutzpah:* Nerve or audacity.
>
> *Glitch:* An unexplained malfunction; usually refers to computer programs.
>
> *Klutz:* A clumsy person (adjective: klutzy).
>
> *Maven:* An expert; sometimes slightly pejorative—a know-it-all.
>
> *Schlock:* Cheap or badly made merchandise (adjective: schlocky).
>
> *Schmaltz:* Over-flowery sentiment (adjective: schmaltzy).
>
> It is interesting to note that there is still a significant population of Sephardic Jews who speak Ladino, a form of Spanish spoken by Jews of Greek, Turkish, and Syrian ancestry and written with the Hebrew alphabet. Spanish was carried to the Middle East by Spanish and Portuguese Jews exiled from Spain in the late fifteenth century.

schooled in Latin regardless of their first language. Latin as the language of schooling has persisted until relatively recently, until the rise of nationalism and the concurrent Protestant Reformation motivated the use of vernaculars for scholarship and education.

THE MODERN WORLD

Bilingualism is common in modern times in almost every corner of the world. In 1982, Grosjean suggested that only Japan and what was then West Germany could be classified as monolingual countries, and even at that time they had significant populations whose first language was not the language of the majority. In general, we live in a multilingual world.

There are many officially monolingual nations that house large linguistic minorities. This is especially characteristic of newly independent developing nations whose political boundaries do not coincide with linguistic boundaries and who have chosen a national language for unification purposes.

A number of countries are officially bilingual or multilingual, including Canada, Belgium, Finland, Cyprus, Israel, and Ireland. Note that official bilingualism does not imply that all inhabitants of a country are bilingual. Often only a small percentage of the population of an officially bilingual country uses both languages regularly. Official bilingualism means that more than one language may be used in transactions with the government or in the schools. Different countries develop different policies with respect to the languages they endorse.

Some countries may have many more languages than their governmental policies recognize. Hindi is the official language of India. It is the most widely used, spoken by nearly half the population (Kinzer, 1998). Yet, in addition to Hindi, 14 languages plus English are officially recognized in the constitution, only a fraction of the 200 different languages spoken on the subcontinent (Khubchandani, 1978). People in India generally speak more than one language, and may well have oral proficiency in five or six. As one author comments, "in spite of mass illiteracy, a societal type of bilingualism/multilingualism . . . has become the life and blood of India's verbal repertoire" (Sridhar, 1993).

It should be noted that the political dimension of language operates everywhere, and India is no exception. English speakers, generally members of the educated elite, number only about 5 percent of the population, and members of regional parties, in a challenge to the ruling party, have decried English as a colonial language and one which should not be used for public, official purposes (Kinzer, 1998).

China is a nation with enormous territory and diverse cultural groups that has many languages represented within its boundaries. In general, government support for Mandarin Chinese as a unifying national language, combined with tolerance for diversity, has favored bilingualism in mainland China. Following the return of Hong Kong to Chinese rule in 1997, however, the government decided to replace the use of English as the language of instruction in high schools on that island, mandating the use of Cantonese instead. This has caused considerable consternation in Hong Kong, where English is considered an absolute necessity for business success (Gargan, 1997).

In South Africa, dramatic changes in government have led to the recognition of nine African languages as official in addition to English and Afrikaans (National Public Radio, 1995). This is yet another example of the dynamic interaction of politics and language.

A discussion of bilingualism in the world would be incomplete without mention of Paraguay, which is unique. Guarani, the indigenous Indian language of Paraguay, is its national language, and it is also the first language of 90 percent of Paraguay's population. Spanish is Paraguay's official language, used in schools and for other government activities. Over half the population is bilingual, but Guarani, a cherished national treasure, is the language of choice for personal intimacy and poetry (Rubin, 1972).

MULTILINGUALISM IN THE UNITED STATES

When the U.S. Constitution was written, its authors made an affirmative decision not to establish an official national language. Recently, local initiatives have resulted in policies proclaiming the official standing of English. Nevertheless, the United States is a multilingual nation, with many indigenous Native American languages, indigenous Spanish, and the diverse languages of its many immigrant groups, which contribute to the nation's linguistic wealth. (Language policy in the United States is more fully discussed in Chapter 10.)

─Education in More Than One Language: An International Perspective

Societal bilingualism is common, and dual language instruction is practiced worldwide. Formats for providing education in two languages are as varied as the world's governments and their constituencies. The following are three cases where governments support more than one language through education.

CHINA

According to Jernudd (1999), China has 56 nationalities, and all but two of those have their own languages. Constitutional policy requires that China take steps to preserve its minority languages. Writing systems have been developed for many indigenous languages that previously did not have them. Media broadcasts are often aired bilingually, and political information is disseminated in a variety of languages (Fincher, 1978). China presently offers home language instruction to many of its ethnic minorities, with gradual introduction to Chinese in the second year of schooling. As you might expect, China's vast size, its uneven levels of development, and the number of ethnicities and languages within its borders hamper full implementation of its language and educational policies (Spolsky, 2004). Where implementation has been successful, however, Chinese authorities have reported an increase in achievement as well as improved attendance on the part of ethnic minority children enrolled in dual language programs (Jernudd, 1999; Wang, 1986).

CANADA

Since the passage of the Official Languages Act in 1967, Canada has been officially bilingual (English and French). The history of bilingual education in Canada is primarily the history of the struggle for equal status for French, which is the minority language. Canada has had notable success with its French–English immersion programs for anglophones (English speakers), which have provided a model for dual language instruction worldwide. (Immersion programs are discussed in detail in Chapter 2.)

Canada continues to struggle with the needs of speakers of so-called heritage languages, languages other than French and English used by indigenous or immigrant minorities. Dual language instructional programs have been established, some with the goal of transitioning children from their primary languages to English, and others with the intention of preserving or restoring proficiency in a heritage language. (For a detailed review of dual language programs for heritage languages in Canada see Cummins, 1984.)

Attempts are being made to preserve the few remaining indigenous languages, deeply endangered by federal policies that Pringle describes as "assimilationist and often brutal, with school-age children removed from their home communities to residential schools in which they were forbidden to speak their mother tongue (even when, on arrival, it was their only language) and were punished and humiliated for doing so" (1999, p. 82).

SWEDEN

Providing dual language instruction in an increasingly diverse world is not without its challenges. Sweden is an example of a country that has attempted to maintain a pluralist position in educating language minority students. In the second half of the twentieth century, Sweden, which had been fairly homogenous, experienced a large influx of immigrants, who currently constitute approximately 12 percent of the population (Boyd, 1999). Bilingual education is provided for immigrant children with the goal of enabling them to function fully in both Swedish and their home languages. Children receive all instruction in the home language, but its use is decreased until, by the fifth or sixth grade, instruction in all subject areas is bilingual ("Bilingual programs in Sweden," 1985). Boyd (1999) points out that as linguistic diversity in Sweden increases, it has become difficult to provide bilingual education for all language groups. Also, there is an increased need for well-trained teachers who have the skills to promote multicultural understanding and positive cross-cultural relations among their students.

The History of Dual Language Instruction in the United States

People are often surprised to discover that dual language instruction has been widely available in the United States since the beginning of its history as a nation. Immigration has been a constant in U.S. history, and languages other than English have been tolerated and even officially recognized from the outset. The Continental Congress, for example, published a number of documents in German to assure accessibility for the large German-speaking minority (Keller & Van Hooft, 1982).

THE NINETEENTH CENTURY

In the nineteenth century, non-English or dual language instruction was offered in more than a dozen states in a variety of languages including German,

Swedish, Norwegian, Danish, Dutch, Polish, Italian, Czech, French, and Spanish (Ovando & Collier, 1985; Tyack, 1974). Both immigrants and Native Americans made instruction in two languages available for their children.

Dual Language Instruction for Native Americans. Formal schooling was locally administered by Native Americans only insofar as the U.S. government allowed. Where locally controlled education was permitted, Native American communities often provided dual language instruction.

The Cherokees established and operated an educational system of 21 schools and 2 academies, which enrolled 1,100 pupils, and produced a population 90 percent literate in its native language. The Cherokee language had a writing system, created by Sequoyah in the early part of the eighteenth century (Foreman, 1938; Kilpatrick, 1965). As a result, bilingual materials were widely available, and by 1852 Oklahoma Cherokees had a higher English literacy level than the white populations of either Texas or Arkansas (Castellanos, 1983, p. 17).

The tribes of the Southeast were particularly successful in dealing with culture contact with Europeans, who called them the "civilized tribes" as a result. The European perception that the southeastern tribes were capable of self-government resulted in some measure of tribal autonomy in education. In addition, several of the southeastern tribes' languages had or developed writing systems, softening the dominance of English and facilitating the availability of dual language education. In general, however, U.S. government tolerance for Native American self-determination, education, and language was tied to political expediency, and those Native American school systems that were permitted to exist and survived the Civil War were eradicated in the latter part of the nineteenth century (Weinberg, 1977).

Dual Language Instruction for Immigrants. Immigrant Germans fared well in maintaining their language through dual language instruction during the nineteenth century. German patriotism in the Revolutionary War was highly regarded, and, therefore, German language and culture were accepted with tolerance. Also, despite the fact that Germans were a minority, they were heavily concentrated in the remote farming areas of the Midwest. As a result of their geographic isolation, they were not viewed as a threat by the rest of the population. Given that education was locally controlled and financed, their concentration enabled them to exert the political strength of their numbers on the schools (Liebowitz, 1978).

In response to political pressure from the German community, German–English dual language programs were instituted in Ohio in 1840, and by the turn of the century 17,584 students were studying German in dual language programs, the great majority of them in the primary grades. Dual language programs were also widespread in Missouri (Tyack, 1974). In 1880 German was taught in 52 of the 57 public schools in Saint Louis, and German–English programs attracted not only German children, but also Anglo-American children who learned German as a second language (Escamilla, 1980).

The Cherokee Writing System

"Sequoyah hit upon the great truth, and what to him was an original discovery, that enlightenment and civilization of a people would progress and develop in proportion as they were able to express themselves and preserve their ideas upon the written and printed page, and exchange these ideas, one with another, by this medium" (Foreman, 1938, p. 74).

Revered and honored by the Cherokee Nation, Sequoyah is known for the creation of the Cherokee alphabet. Its 85 characters, pictured here, represent all the sounds in the Cherokee language. In 1827, the Cherokee Nation published the first edition of the *Cherokee Phoenix,* a bilingual newspaper.

● The Cherokee Alphabet

D	a	R	e	T	i	Ꝺ	o	Ꝺ	u	i	v
Ꮖ ga Ꮹ ka		Ꮢ	ge	Ꮹ	gi	Ꭺ	go	Ꭹ	gu	Ꭼ	gv
Ꮎ	ha	Ꮄ	he	Ꭿ	hi	Ꮀ	ho	Ꮁ	hu	Ꮂ	hv
W	la	Ꮈ	le	Ꮅ	li	Ꮆ	lo	Ꮇ	lu	Ꮉ	lv
Ꮜ	ma	Ꮊ	me	Ꮋ	mi	Ꮰ	mo	Ꮄ	mu		
Ꮔ	na	Ꮕ	ne	Ꮑ	ni	Z	no	Ꮕ	nu	Ꮕ	nv
Ꮳ	hna	Ꮟ	nah								
Ꮝ	qwa	Ꮺ	qwe	Ꮝ	qwi	Ꮽ	qwo	Ꮾ	qwu	Ꮿ	qwv
Ꮚ sa Ꮝ s		Ꮞ	se	Ꮧ	si	Ꮦ	so	Ꮡ	su	Ꮢ	sv
Ꮥ	da	Ꮧ	de	Ꮧ	di	Ꮩ	do	Ꮪ	du	Ꮫ	dv
Ꮤ	ta	Ꮦ	te		ti						
Ꮝdla Ꮩ tla		Ꮭ	tle	Ꮮ	tli	Ꮯ	tlo	Ꮰ	tlu	Ꮱ	tlv
Ꮳ	tsa	Ꮴ	tse	Ꮵ	tsi	Ꮶ	tso	Ꮷ	tsu	Ꮸ	tsv
Ꮹ	wa	Ꮺ	we	Ꮹ	wi	Ꮼ	wo	Ꮽ	wu	Ꮾ	wv
Ꮿ	ya	Ᏸ	ye	Ᏹ	yi	Ᏺ	yo	Ᏻ	yu	Ᏼ	yv

Toward the end of the nineteenth century, anti-Catholic bias provoked by an influx of Irish immigrants spilled over onto previously tolerated Germans, many of whom were Catholic. Increasing immigration resulted in a wave of xenophobia that often targeted foreign languages. The large instructional programs in German gave the language a high profile, and the German language became a focus for the antiforeign feelings that flourished in the second half of the eighteenth century.

The onset of World War I brought anti-German feeling to a head, and a rash of legislation aimed at eliminating German language instruction caused the collapse of dual language programs around the country. At the turn of the century, only 14 of the 45 states mandated English as the sole language of instruction in the schools. By 1923, a total of 34 of the 48 states had English-only instructional policies (Castellanos, 1983).

THE TWENTIETH CENTURY

Two by-products of World War I, isolationism and nationalism, took their toll on dual language as well as foreign language instruction. Instruction in foreign languages was virtually eliminated in the period between the first and second world wars. Events in the 1950s, however, revitalized interest in these fields. The successful launching of Sputnik by the Soviet Union caused a reevaluation of education in general and inspired the National Defense Education Act (1958). Knowledge of foreign languages was perceived as essential to our national defense, so the act provided funding for foreign language study.

During the same period, the Cuban revolution (1959) brought a flood of educated Cuban refugees to Florida. In 1963, in response to the needs of the Cuban community, the Coral Way Elementary School in Dade County, Florida, was established. Coral Way offered dual language instruction for both Cuban and non-Hispanic children. The program served a middle-class population, was well funded from both public and private sources, and, unlike many subsequent programs, was neither compensatory nor remedial.

The nation was in the midst of an energetic movement favoring the expansion of civil rights, accompanied by a powerful affirmation of ethnic identity for minority groups. In that political climate, and with the success of Coral Way in the public eye, bilingual programs were quickly established in a number of states, including Texas, California, New Mexico, New Jersey, and Arizona (Ambert & Melendez, 1985).

In 1965 the Elementary and Secondary Education Act (ESEA) was approved and funded by Congress. The act was part of President Lyndon B. Johnson's War on Poverty, and its broad purpose was to equalize educational opportunities. The Bilingual Education Act, or Title VII of the ESEA, was signed into law in 1968. Title VII did not mandate bilingual education, but provided funds for districts to establish programs that used primary language instruction to assist limited English proficient children. In subsequent amendments to the act, funds were allocated for teacher training, research, information dissemination, and program support. (Title VII and other pertinent legislation are discussed in detail in Chapter 9.)

In addition, judicial action provided strong support for services for limited English proficient children. In 1974, the U.S. Supreme Court decision in

Lau v. Nichols held, on the basis of Title VI of the Civil Rights Act (1964), that children must receive equal access to education regardless of their inability to speak English. (*Lau* and other pertinent decisions are discussed in detail in Chapter 9.)

In 1971, Massachusetts was the first state to mandate bilingual education. By 1983, bilingual education was permitted in all 50 states, and 9 states had laws requiring some form of dual language instruction for students with limited English proficiency (Ovando & Collier, 1985).

In the three decades following *Lau,* lack of government support for primary language instruction, combined with strong reactions to the influx of immigrants, has weakened support for dual language instruction. California, for example, with a population of over 1,550,000 limited English proficient children at the present time, eliminated its mandate for bilingual education in 1987, and recently passed a proposition eliminating bilingual education entirely. Arizona and Massachusetts have followed suit.

THE TWENTY-FIRST CENTURY

The number and diversity of immigrants to the United States is on the increase and, amid ongoing and predictable controversies about language policy and immigration reform (see Chapter 10), informed and highly skilled responses are required daily from educators in every area and at every level. Dual language instruction models that emphasize bilingualism as enrichment for all students may broaden the public's understanding of education in more than one language. As we will see in the chapters to follow, that kind of approach is beneficial to individual students and to the nation as a whole.

Summary

Dual language instruction in one form or another has been available all over the world since ancient times. Countries in the world today may espouse one of many potential language policies, but in any case there are bilingual individuals in virtually every nation in the world. Dual language instruction is available in many countries in a variety of formats, depending on the population and the purpose.

Dual language instruction has been available in the United States since before colonial times. Nationalistic feelings that accompanied World War I limited the use of languages other than English in schools, but interest in foreign language instruction was revived after World War II. The success of bilingual programs established in Florida shortly after the Cuban revolution, combined with a political climate that favored ethnic identity and civil rights, inspired the implementation of dual language programs nationwide.

Questions to Think About and Discuss

1. Should the United States have an official language policy? If so, what languages should be recognized as official? What areas of public life should be governed (schools, courts, health care, etc.)?

Activities

1. Interview classmates or acquaintances born or educated outside the United States. Find out how many languages they know and how they learned them. If they attended school outside the United States, find out the following:
   - Was the language of schooling the same as the home language?
   - Were they required to learn more than one language at school?
   - Which languages were used for content instruction?
   - In their view, how common is bilingualism in the country they came from or studied in?

   Compare their language experiences to your own.
2. Dual language instruction was widespread in the nineteenth century. Look into the history of your area and find out if there were educational programs in more than one language prior to 1963.
3. Many languages are spoken in the United States. Make a language map of your area. Depending on where you live, you may want to map your city, town, or county. A rigorous demographic study may be impractical, but school district figures may be a good starting point. Churches that announce services in various languages may help you. Concentration of ethnic businesses is another clue.
4. Inventory the non-English media in your area. Include radio, television, movies, and newspapers. Check the local public library to find out the number and circulation of non-English materials.

Suggestions for Further Reading

Baetens, B. H. (1993). *European models of bilingual education*. Clevedon, UK: Multilingual Matters.

As the introduction to this book points out, there are useful lessons to be learned from European bilingual models. The articles included in this book describe a variety of language circumstances. The interplay of language, culture, politics, and education is more often than not ignored in American conversations about bilingual education. This book calls our attention to subtleties with which we might usefully inform our debate.

Crawford, J. (1989). *Bilingual education: History, politics, theory, and practice.* Trenton, NJ: Crane.

One of the more comprehensive overviews of issues related to bilingual education in the United States, this well-written book provides a detailed analysis of the history and politics of dual language instruction.

Edwards, J. (1998). *Language in Canada.* Cambridge, UK: Cambridge University Press.

Language has been a point of tension in Canadian history. Given the current political climate in the United States, this detailed account of language history and planning in Canada provides useful insights into the complexities of language planning in a multilingual society.

Kaufman, D. (2003, April). Letters for the people. *Language Magazine, 7,* 24–26.

A brief but informative article about Sequoyah, who developed the writing system for Tsalagi, the language of the Cherokees. Tsalagi was the first Native American language known to have a writing system, and this article is worth the attention of anyone interested in language. As an added benefit, the article would be worthwhile reading for middle and high school students as well.

Keller, G. D., & Van Hooft, K. S. (1982). A chronology of bilingualism and bilingual education in the United States. In J. A. Fishman & G. D. Keller (Eds.) (1982), *Bilingual education for Hispanic students in the United States.* New York: Teachers College Press.

A chronology of bilingual education in the United States beginning with the colonial period and ending in 1980 with the creation of the Department of Education Office of Bilingual Languages and Minority Language Affairs. There have been many political changes since this book was published that have had a dynamic effect on bilingual education. Nevertheless, it is an excellent historical record, and reminds us that bilingual education is not a new idea in the United States.

Kloss, H. (1977). *The American bilingual tradition.* Rowley, MA: Newbury House.

An analysis of language policy in the United States and its possessions and protectorates, this book is a classic history of bilingualism and bilingual education and is generally considered a basic source of information in this relatively unexplored area.

chapter 2

Dual Language Program Models

Simply stated, *dual language instruction* is an educational program offered in two languages. This definition is straightforward but lacks specificity. Dual language instruction can be offered in a variety of formats or models, depending on the goals of a program and the population it serves.

Some programs, for example, are designed to promote bilingualism and biliteracy for students. Others use a primary or home language as a bridge to assist students while they learn the dominant mainstream language.

This chapter will explain the concept of a program model and describe various types of programs currently in use in the United States. It will also present an overview of the competencies that teachers must have to provide instruction in dual language classrooms.

What Is a Program Model?

If you were to visit a dual language classroom you might note several features, including the functional use of each language and the methodology for distributing the languages in the curriculum. You would also notice the amount of time each language is used. In a particular classroom, you might observe that Spanish is used for instruction 50 percent of the day. Such an observation, however, takes on meaning only in the context of a program model. A *program model* refers to the span of language use and distribution toward a goal for a specific population, across the grades.

If, for example, the classroom you have visited is a Spanish–English bilingual kindergarten, it would be important to know whether the 50-50 time distribution of languages continues in first grade, or whether the use of Spanish diminishes as children progress, to 40 percent in the first grade and 30 percent in the second, so that children move toward a situation where no Spanish is used at all. Such a program model differs significantly from one where the 50-50 ratio is maintained throughout all grades and both languages are maintained and developed.

Dual language instructional models have been described in a number of ways, some far more complex than others. One theorist cross-referenced the learner, the languages, the community, and the curriculum to arrive at 90 different possible kinds of programs (Mackey, 1972). A simpler typology, based on philosophical rather than linguistic factors, distinguishes between assimilationist and pluralistic program models. Assimilationist programs aim at moving ethnic minority children into the mainstream (dominant) culture. In contrast, pluralistic program models are those that support minority languages and cultures (Kjolseth, 1976).

Transitional Bilingual Programs

WHICH STUDENTS DO TRANSITIONAL PROGRAMS SERVE?

Transitional programs serve students who are limited English proficient (LEP). For general purposes, we can define LEP students as those who have been determined to have insufficient English to function academically in an English language classroom where instruction is designed for native English speakers. Which students are actually designated as LEP may vary from state to state or even from district to district within a state, because tests and testing procedures are not uniform.

It should be noted that the labels we use are significant and shape and reflect how we respond to the world around us. *Limited English proficient* is a deficit-based term—it identifies students by what they can't do, and sets us up to consider serving them in a remedial or compensatory mode. Today, educators generally refer to English language learners, a serviceable and fairly neutral term.

WHAT IS THE GOAL OF A TRANSITIONAL PROGRAM?

The goal of transitional programs is to develop a student's proficiency in English. In a transitional program, the primary language is used for instructional support until students have reached satisfactory levels of English proficiency, usually as defined by a process involving test scores and teacher observations. Students are expected to move out of a transitional program when they are capable of functioning in an English-only classroom. In many programs, the expectation is that children will be ready to make the change after a period of approximately three years.

U.S. government policy tends to favor transitional programs—by far the most common models in use today. There are a number of problems inherent in transitional bilingual programs:

- They foster subtractive, rather than additive, bilingualism. (See Chapter 3 for a discussion of these concepts.)
- They are compensatory and do not involve the monolingual English-speaking community.
- Exit assessments may measure students' face-to-face language skills and fail to consider the specialized language skills needed for academic success. Placement in English-only classrooms on the basis of such programs can lead to academic failure. (See Chapter 5.)
- It is unrealistic to expect all children to master a second language in a three-year period.

TRANSITIONAL PROGRAMS: A LOT BETTER THAN NOTHING

In 1988, the California Association for Bilingual Education published *On Course: Bilingual Education's Success in California* (Krashen & Biber, 1988), a summary and analysis of data from eight programs across the state, including transitional programs. The Eastman Avenue School in Los Angeles reported an increase in the California Assessment Program (CAP) scores for students who participated in a carefully structured transitional program. More recently, a study that looked at the achievement of English learners over eight years and across content areas (CREDE, 2003) concludes that English language learners who attended mainstream programs with no primary language support "showed large decreases in reading and math achievement by Grade 5 when compared to students who participated in language support programs" (p. 3).

Ultimately, we have to think back to the concept of "program." Villarreal points out that effective programs must have enthusiastic leaders who are committed to supporting dedicated, qualified teachers. Effective programs, transitional or otherwise, provide a supportive climate and an instructional program that is both accessible and challenging, built on the linguistic and cultural resources of students, their families, and their communities (Villarreal, 1999). A carefully modeled transitional program that meets those criteria, while not the best of all worlds, offers meaningful support for English language learners and is undoubtedly better than submersion.

——*Language Maintenance Programs*

Language maintenance programs are pluralistic and promote bilingualism and biliteracy for language minority students. Maintenance programs may be the most effective means of promoting English proficiency for limited English proficient students because:

- Concepts and skills learned in a student's first language transfer to the second language.

- A strong base in a first language facilitates second language acquisition.
- Support for home language and culture builds self-esteem and enhances achievement (Hakuta & Gould, 1987).

In other words, maintenance bilingual education, which is additive rather than subtractive, leads to academic success and also facilitates the acquisition of English skills for the language minority student. (For further discussion, see Chapter 5.)

Enrichment Programs

Efforts were made in the late 1960s and early 1970s to provide dual language instructional programs for both language minority children and monolingual English children. The need, however, for language support for limited English proficient children has been overwhelming. In the face of limited resources and staffing, the response has been largely compensatory in nature. The tendency to view dual language instruction as compensatory education has eroded the political base necessary to assure services for language minority students and has denied access to bilingual education for monolingual English-speaking children as well.

Educators have begun to reconsider enrichment or two-way bilingual instruction, which provides dual language instruction for all students. Two-way programs are becoming increasingly popular in areas where magnet schools have been established to facilitate desegregation. Problems in implementing enrichment programs arise from a lack of qualified staff, constant pressure to meet the needs of increasing numbers of non-English speakers, and lack of community understanding and support for dual language instruction.

Immersion Programs

Beginning in 1965 with the now famous Saint-Lambert experiment, success in Canada has inspired a strong interest in immersion programs. In an immersion program all the usual curricular areas are taught in a second language—this language being the medium, rather than the object, of instruction. Immersion instruction should not be confused with submersion or "sink-or-swim" instruction, where non-English-speaking children are mainstreamed in English-only classrooms without assistance and expected to keep the pace. In an immersion classroom:

- Grouping is homogeneous, and second language learners are not competing with native speakers.
- The teacher speaks the child's first language and can respond to student needs.

- Children are not expected to function immediately in their second language and can express themselves in their first.
- First language support is offered in the form of language arts instruction.
- Instruction is delivered in the second language, but is carefully structured so as to maximize comprehension for students.

THE RESULTS OF IMMERSION: THE CANADIAN EXPERIENCE

The implementation of carefully structured additive immersion programs may provide useful educational services to both limited English proficient and monolingual English students in the United States. Results of research and evaluation studies of French early immersion programs in Canada indicate that students:

- Achieve at levels comparable to those of comparison groups who received all instruction in English.
- Fall behind comparison groups initially in English literacy skills, but catch up to and even surpass those groups once English instruction begins.
- Achieve higher levels of proficiency in the second language than students who study it as an isolated subject.
- Attain native-like receptive skills in their second language and, while their productive skills fall short of native proficiency, are quite capable of expressing themselves in the second language.
- Have heightened sensitivity to social and cultural aspects of their second culture (Cummins & Swain, 1986).

The Canadian experience with immersion instruction suggests that the model works best with children from a dominant language group who are not at risk of losing their first language since it is readily available in the environment beyond the school. In other words, immersion programs are most effective when they are linguistically and culturally additive.

IMMERSION PROGRAMS IN THE UNITED STATES

There are several immersion program models currently operating in the United States. Enrichment, two-way, and English immersion programs will be described in the following pages.

Enrichment Immersion Programs. These programs, like the Canadian programs that inspired them, immerse monolingual English speakers in a second language. The Culver City Spanish Immersion Program in California, started in 1971, is the oldest example of a replication of the Canadian model in the United States. Enrichment immersion programs have been used as "magnets" in voluntary desegregation efforts. Such efforts expand participation in enrichment immersion programs beyond middle-class white students to working-class and black students and provide opportunities for research on the effects of immersion on speakers of nonstandard varieties of English (Genesee, 1987).

Two-Way Immersion Programs. In these innovative programs, sometimes called *developmental* or *bilingual immersion programs,* monolingual English-speaking children are immersed in a second language alongside limited English proficient children who are native speakers of the second language. English is introduced gradually until it comprises about 50 percent of the curriculum. The model is actually a combination of maintenance bilingual instruction for LEP students and immersion instruction for monolingual English speakers. The strength of this approach is that it aims at additive bilingualism for all the students involved. The goals of a two-way immersion program are bilingualism and biliteracy for all students.

According to Thomas and Collier (1997), the following factors are present in successful two-way immersion programs:

- Students participate for at least six years.
- The ratio of speakers of each language is balanced.
- Languages are carefully separated.
- The minority language is emphasized in the early grades.
- Instruction is excellent and emphasizes core academics.
- Parents have a strong, positive relationship with the school.

The two-way immersion model was first implemented in San Diego, California, in 1975, and has been replicated nationwide. At River Glen Elementary School in northern California, a linguistically heterogeneous group of kindergarten children starts school each year in a classroom where Spanish is used 90 percent of the time and English 10 percent of the time. By fifth grade, English and Spanish are each used 50 percent of the time in class. The program at River Glen was started as part of a magnet school desegregation program and has been extremely successful in attracting an ethnically diverse student population.

Two-way immersion programs address an issue that has surfaced in research on traditional programs. In traditional programs, the teacher is the only native speaker in the classroom. Native-like language input is therefore somewhat limited, and students in interaction with each other tend to develop what might be characterized as a classroom pidgin of the target language (Higgs, 1991; Swain, 1991). Because two-way immersion classrooms mix students from both language groups, all students have many opportunities to interact with native speakers, which enhances their chances to develop native-like proficiency in their new language.

According to a directory published by the Center for Applied Linguistics (2007), as of November 2006 there were 338 two-way immersion programs in the United States. All programs pair English with another language, most commonly Spanish, which is offered in 316 schools. The other languages offered are scattered among French, Cantonese, Korean, Navajo, Japanese,

Mandarin and German. California has the greatest number of schools offering two-way immersion programs, but programs exist in 29 states and the District of Columbia.

A web search indicates that interest In Mandarin is surfacing in many areas. For example, Iowa, which does not appear in the CAL data as of this writing, is using newly available federal funds to begin two-way immersion programs in both Spanish and Mandarin (Iowa State University, 2006).

Bilingual immersion supports the primary language of language minority students, and offers an enrichment program to English speakers. Results of longitudinal studies indicate that students in these programs achieve high levels of bilingualism as well as high levels of academic competence in their subject areas (Lindholm & Molina, 1998). Another important outcome of two-way immersion programs is that students not only speak each other's languages, they learn to appreciate and respect each other's culture (Guido, 1995; Lindholm, 1994).

ENGLISH IMMERSION

Political pressure in the United States to move away from primary language instruction has resulted in experimentation with English immersion programs, sometimes called *structured immersion,* for minority students (see Table 2.1). One important longitudinal study of English immersion indicates that it is less successful for minority language students than bilingual education with native language support (Ramírez et al., 1991).

—Models and Realities: What Does Bilingual Education Look Like in Practice?

Description of program models doesn't always capture the reality of bilingual program implementation. In real schools, educators must deal with the realities of resources, staffing, and the variety of needs that children bring. A report commissioned by the U.S. Department of Education (Fleischman & Staples-Said, 1994) describes ten programs nationwide in districts that range from small to quite large, from rural to urban, serving children from a wide variety of backgrounds and languages.

The smallest of these, a southwestern rural district with a total population of 165, supports 31 LEP migrant farmwork students with an ESL pull-out program. The ESL teacher is Spanish-speaking and uses primary language to assist students in developing primary language literacy skills. The largest district described in the report is urban and located in the Southeast. The district's total enrollment is about 300,000 students, 15 percent of whom are LEP. Of the 45,000 LEP students, most are Spanish speaking, 12 percent speak Haitian

● TABLE *2.1*

*P*rogram Models, Goals, and Outcome

Program Model	Goal	Outcome
Transitional	Proficiency in L2 for language minority students (assimilationist)	Subtractive bilingualism
Maintenance	Bilingualism and biliteracy for language minority students (pluralist)	Additive bilingualism
Enrichment/Two-way	Bilingualism and biliteracy for language minority and language majority students (pluralist)	Additive bilingualism
Immersion		
1. Enrichment	Bilingualism and biliteracy for language majority students (pluralist)	Additive bilingualism
2. Two-way	Bilingualism and biliteracy for language minority and language majority students (pluralist)	Additive bilingualism
3. English immersion	Proficiency in English for language minority students (assimilationist)	Subtractive bilingualism

NOTE: L1 = first language; L2 = second language. For language minority students in the United States, L2 = English.

Creole, and a small number speak other languages. Where language concentrations make it practicable, the district offers primary language instruction in core curriculum classes. All LEP students receive English as a second language (ESL) instruction in a pull-out program. A newcomer program serves LEP middle and high school age students who need to develop primary language literacy skills to facilitate their transition to English.

Despite the very different qualities of all the districts described in the report, and the variety of populations they serve, all the teachers interviewed for the report expressed concerns about the need for support and understanding from their colleagues and administrators. Another area of concern was the need for services for parents who themselves do not speak English and are often undereducated as well as overwhelmed by the demands of working several jobs.

Teachers expressed similar concerns in interviews conducted by Lemberger (1997). Her analysis of eight teachers' narratives reinforces the idea that consistent leadership and administrative support are essential to program success.

Newcomer Programs

The challenges of providing appropriate schooling for second language learners are complicated at the secondary level by a number of factors. The structure of secondary schools themselves, with multiple course offerings and tracks, makes it difficult to offer a consistent program for second language learners without restricting choices of electives and limiting their high school experience. Also, even though older students with first language literacy learn English quickly, they may encounter difficulties with advanced high school curricula. For students who aren't literate, the challenge is clear, and materials and methods for meeting their needs are not readily available.

Beyond the demands of classes and assignments, newly arrived students who have had no schooling in their home countries and even those who have are likely to have little knowledge of the way we "do" high school in the United States. Think, for example, about the way bells ring to signal the change of classes. If you grew up and went to school in the United States, that probably seems quite ordinary—so ordinary that you probably barely notice it. If you didn't grow up here, and you were new to this country, daily procedures like the bells in a U.S. school might be perplexing, even overwhelming.

Finally, newly arrived students may have needs associated with the pain of leaving their home countries or adjusting to U.S. society. Some of them may be refugees, some may have left parents and other family behind, and some may have suffered the deprivations and horrors of war.

In an effort to help newly arrived students adjust to the experience and expectations of U.S. schools, some districts have created newcomer programs. Newcomer programs take a number of forms, from an orientation class to a freestanding school, but they generally attempt to assist students to:

- Overcome the trauma of relocation.
- Develop familiarity with the customs and culture of U.S. schooling.
- Develop English proficiency.
- Adapt to U.S. society in general.
- Succeed in their transition to mainstream schools.

Until recently, there was little research on newcomer programs, but the need for such programs and interest in them is growing. Additional information about newcomer programs is available on the web at www.ncela.gwu.edu and www.cal.org.

Also, schools must be responsive to the needs of language minority parents. Traditional forms of parent involvement may not be effective, and schools have to devise innovative, creative approaches to outreach and involvement. All the teachers in Lemberger's study expressed frustration with the limited availability of materials in both native and second languages. This is especially important because LEP students may not have access to many books at home (Krashen, 1997/1998).

It should be noted once again that many "programs" are not programs at all, lacking a consensual set of goals and consistent approaches to reaching them. Lemberger (1997) comments: "A teacher could never be sure that what she taught in one grade would be followed up by another colleague. Native language development might not be supported and built upon from year to year depending on whether the receiving teacher understood the value of maintaining and using the native language" (pp. 147–148).

Critics of bilingual education often overstate the extent of services to LEP students. Many LEP students, however, are not served by any program at all. The Council of Chief State School Officers reports (1990) that in 20 of the 48 states that responded to a survey on services to LEP students at least 25 percent receive no services. Four states responded that they fail to serve 60 percent of their LEP student populations. The report characterizes the current state of service to LEP students as "an abdication of legal responsibility as well as social responsibility" (p. 22).

Dual Language Instruction in Private Schools

Professional attention generally focuses on dual language instruction in public school settings. Despite current interest in two-way and enrichment programs, most address the needs of limited English proficient children. Bilingualism, however, is widely considered the hallmark of an educated person, and dual language instruction has found outlets in the private school arena as well.

Dual language instruction for privileged sectors of society has been available in the United States for quite some time. For example, Bryn Mawr School in Baltimore, Maryland, established in 1885, offers French, Latin, Greek, German, and Spanish as enrichment for students in kindergarten through fifth grade (Tomlinson & Eastwick, 1980).

According to one comprehensive report, there are approximately 6,500 private schools in the United States that provide some form of education in a language other than English. At the time the study was completed, the Jewish community accounted for nearly half that number, providing schooling in both Hebrew and Yiddish, but at least 108 languages were represented in private schools (Fishman, 1985).

It would be difficult to estimate the number of such schools at the present time, but there are revealing examples. For instance, the Association of Northern California Chinese Schools lists 84 member schools (ANCCS, 2003). Some of them enroll upwards of a thousand students. These are generally "Saturday" schools, offering Chinese instruction on weekends only. Note that children who attend these schools develop language and literacy in two languages. In other words, they actually receive a bilingual education—it just happens under more than one roof.

As part of a federal project on bilingual education, researchers made site visits to 24 private schools that had dual language instructional programs. They found that private schools use many of the same methods as public schools for providing dual language instruction. Despite the lack of innovation, private dual language programs are distinguished by their emphasis on the value of knowing two languages (Elford & Woodford, 1982). This emphasis appears to persist, even in the current political climate. For example, the International School of the Peninsula in Palo Alto, California, offers a full curriculum in both Mandarin Chinese and French to approximately 500 students, many of whom are American-born English speakers. In its mission, the school states: "We are committed to developing well-rounded individuals with a broad international awareness and the ability to communicate in at least two languages" (International School of the Peninsula, 2003).

Reports in the popular press indicate that demand for second language instruction has spread to include private preschools (Wells, 1986). The value placed on bilingualism by those who can afford to pay for private schooling raises an important issue: Why is dual language instruction desirable for a socioeconomic elite but undesirable for minority language groups? Despite the current lack of government support for bilingual programs and public misconceptions about their value, perhaps two-way enrichment programs will change attitudes about bilingualism and dual language instruction.

Bilingual Teachers

All too often lay people, and even some professionals, assume that bilingual teachers are teachers whose only qualification is that they speak two languages. That would be the same as assuming that an English teacher is any person who speaks, reads, and writes English! A good bilingual teacher, like all good teachers, has attitudes, knowledge, and skills that are particular to the students and the subject matter. What good teachers do, and what they need to know to do it, is the subject of ongoing conversation among professionals at every level.

Clearly, bilingual teachers need to be bilingual and biliterate in English and in the language of their students. But they need other competencies as well. They need to understand the nature of language and how languages are learned so they can create appropriate learning environments for second language learners.

In addition, they must understand their students' culture in ways that transcend surface culture and address the values and beliefs underlying the ways their students act in and out of classrooms. Understanding of culture, combined with awareness of the social contexts of their students, allows effective bilingual teachers to reach out and connect with the families and communities of the students they serve. Understanding the historical and political contexts of bilingual education and of their students supports teachers' abilities to advocate for their students' needs in a climate increasingly characterized by hostility toward newcomers and diversity.

Finally, like all teachers, bilingual teachers must be skilled at assessing students' needs, as well as planning appropriate goals, objectives, and activities to meet those needs and gathering evaluative data on an ongoing basis as students grow and change. Bilingual teachers plan and prepare in more than one language, and strive to meet multiple content and language objectives as students learn two languages through bilingual instruction. Currently, 44 states and the District of Columbia offer certification for teachers of English as a second language, and 28 certify bilingual teachers. Seventeen states require that teachers placed in bilingual classrooms have the appropriate certification (NCELA, 2007).

Summary

Dual language instruction may be transitional or maintenance-oriented. Immersion models have received attention recently because they have proven effective in Canada for teaching minority languages to majority children. A variety of immersion designs are currently being tried in the United States. Enrichment programs that provide second language instruction for monolingual English speakers are increasing in popularity. Dual language programs are available in private schools as well. Teachers who work in dual language instructional settings need specialized training in both bilingual and multicultural education.

Questions to Think About and Discuss

1. If you were going to build a program that served English language learners from the ground up, what would it look like? What outcomes would you try to achieve? To meet those goals, what kind of program model would you implement? What competencies would you expect teachers to have?
2. Consider your own teacher preparation program: Does it adequately prepare you to meet the needs of second language learners? If so, how, and if not, what experiences and expectations would you choose to add or improve?

Activities

1. Visit a public dual language instructional program. Interview a program administrator, a teacher, a parent, and a student enrolled in the

program. Find out what they perceive the goals of the program to be. Analyze the program design. Does the program model fit the goals that the participants envision?

2. Visit a private school that offers dual language instruction. What program model is in use? What are the goals of administrators, teachers, parents, and students in this school? Describe the student population of the school.

Suggestions for Further Reading

Cummins, J. (1989). *Empowering minority students.* Sacramento: California Association for Bilingual Education.

This book examines the relationship between minority students' experience of schooling and the sociopolitical context of education. Language and bilingual education are explored from the perspective of critical pedagogy, and programs that have been successful for language minority students are described.

Cummins, J. (1996). *Negotiating identities: Education for empowerment in a diverse society.* Ontario, CA: California Association for Bilingual Education.

Negotiating Identities is more a simple update of Empowering Minority Students. Cummins expands on the notion that bilingual education cannot be thought of simply in terms of language, and this book guides the reader to think about language and schooling in terms of power relations and the impact of social and political contexts on the relationships of students and their teachers.

Cummins, J., & Swain, M. (1986). *Bilingualism in education.* London: Longman.

This book explores the nature of bilingual proficiency and suggests that positive linguistic, cognitive, and academic consequences result from high levels of proficiency in two languages. Results of research and evaluation studies related to Canadian French immersion programs are described in detail.

Frederickson, J. (1995). *Reclaiming our voices: Bilingual education, critical pedagogy & praxis.* Los Angeles: California Association for Bilingual Education.

Critical pedagogy creates a classroom world wherein students can find their own voices, engage in creative dialogue, and transform their lives and their worlds. This collection of articles brings the reader into the conversation about critical theory and pedagogy tied directly to considerations of language, culture, bilingualism, and biculturalism.

Genesee, F. (1987). *Learning through two languages: Studies of immersion and bilingual education.* Rowley, MA: Newbury House.

An examination of immersion programs for majority students in Canada and bilingual programs for minority language students in the United States. A chapter on immersion in the United States details programs in California, Maryland, and Ohio.

Genesee, F. (Ed.). (1994). *Educating second language children: The whole child, the whole curriculum, the whole community.* Cambridge, UK: The Cambridge University Press.

This collection of articles links schools, families, and communities, and addresses the second language learner's experience in all those contexts, reaching beyond language to incorporate social and cultural dimensions as well.

Krashen, S., & Biber, D. (1988). *On course: Bilingual education's success in California.* Sacramento: California Association for Bilingual Education.

Following a summary of a rationale for primary language instruction, this book provides descriptions of bilingual programs in California that have been successful in improving student achievement.

Lemberger, N. (1997). *Bilingual education: Teachers' narratives.* Mahwah, NJ: Lawrence Erlbaum Associates.

The author interviewed eight bilingual teachers from a variety of backgrounds who teach in a variety of settings. The book includes the teachers' own stories, as well as an analysis of the issues and themes that emerge. No book to date better captures the on-the-ground experience of teachers in bilingual classrooms.

Office of Bilingual Bicultural Education, California State Department of Education. (1984). *Studies on immersion education: A collection for United States educators.* Sacramento: California State Department of Education.

The first section of this book presents an overview of major issues related to immersion programs. The second section includes descriptions of programs in Canada. Section three looks at immersion education in the United States.

Olsen, L. et al. (1994). *The unfinished journey: Restructuring schools in a diverse society.* San Francisco: California Tomorrow.

Using descriptions of a number of programs currently in place, this report shows how schools can effectively restructure to meet the needs of diverse student populations.

Skutnabb-Kangas, T. (1981). *Bilingualism or not: The education of minorities.* Clevedon, UK: Multilingual Matters.

Far more than a simple discussion of program models, this book provides an insightful analysis of bilingualism and the education of minorities from a broad political perspective. Included are discussions of bilingualism of children from a variety of language backgrounds, the neurolinguistic and cognitive aspects of bilingualism, the impact of social and educational policy on immigrant children, and a typology of dual language programs accounting for differences between majority and minority students.

Aspects of Language

This chapter will ask you to think critically about the nature of language. This may be difficult because language is almost invisible to us. We acquire language when we are very young and use it for a multitude of purposes every day. But, unless we have a scholarly interest, we rarely stop to look at it.

Textbooks on linguistics or communication disorders provide detailed introductions to the concept of language. This chapter will not investigate language in depth but is intended as an overview of various technical and academic ways of looking at language.

From a teacher's point of view, it is important to know what language is and how it works because language should be used in a planned way, much as we use other instructional materials and media. This chapter has two purposes, which will allow us to objectify language so that we can use it effectively for dual language instruction. First, we will define language and look at its component parts. By defining language, we will render it more visible and acquire the basic vocabulary necessary to discuss numerous aspects of dual language instruction.

Second, we will consider some of the common preconceived notions about language. We have strong emotional bonds to our language because it is the vehicle through which we convey our experience and culture. Therefore we need to separate basic concepts about language from attitudes that may interfere with our ability to use language as a classroom tool or to deal equitably with children whose language backgrounds differ from our own.

The Study of Language

The study of dual language instruction requires us to consider language from at least four different perspectives. *Linguistics* describes the structural aspects of language. Much of the basic vocabulary needed to discuss language acquisition and language proficiency comes from the field of linguistics.

Psycholinguistics deals with the relationship of language and the mind. Psycholinguists consider how language is acquired and how language is processed in the human mind.

Neurolinguistics is the study of language and the brain. Neurolinguists try to figure out how brain development and function and language ability are linked. For example, neurolinguistic researchers have sought evidence that will prove or disprove the so-called critical period theory that the brain changes during puberty in ways that make language learning harder after early adolescence than before.

Sociolinguistics is the relatively new and exciting field of inquiry that investigates how language works in society. Sociolinguists study the language dynamics of everyday interactions between people. If you have ever considered dialect differences or the manner in which people alter their speech when addressing a superior or a member of the opposite sex, you have made sociolinguistic observations.

Planning and delivery of effective dual language instruction are based on theory, research, and practical applications from all these areas of language inquiry.

What Is Language?

The American Speech-Language-Hearing Association defines *language* as a complex and dynamic system of conventional symbols used in various modes for communication and thought (American Speech-Language-Hearing Association, 1983). Let us take a closer look at this definition.

A system is organized, governed by rules, and works toward a purpose. Automobile engines and the digestive tract are examples of systems. Language is a system—it is ordered and purposeful. The essential purpose of language is communication. A careful focus on the purpose of language dispels many unfortunate attitudes people have about languages and, concomitantly, about each other. Also, as we shall see, understanding the basic purpose of language is useful for understanding how languages are acquired and provides important insights as to how languages should be taught.

Language is an orderly combination of conventional symbols. The symbols are the words we use to label the objects, actions, and ideas that we perceive in our reality. These symbols are conventional—that is, we assign a socially agreed-on symbol to objects and ideas so we can talk about them. We all agree on a name for a particular object or idea for purposes of communication.

In English, for example, we use *chair* to identify a common object used for supporting us in a sitting posture. A Spanish speaker refers to the same object as *silla*. It's altogether arbitrary: no matter what you call it, you can still sit on it. The concept of the arbitrary nature of symbols used in language becomes important when we start to investigate bilingualism. As we shall see, bilingual people have a strong understanding of the arbitrary nature of the symbols of language, which enhances their problem-solving skills.

Subsystems of Language

Breaking language down into its subsystems facilitates understanding of how it works and provides us with some of the vocabulary necessary for discussing language acquisition, language proficiency, and second language instruction. Language is generally considered to have five fundamental subsystems.

THE PHONOLOGICAL SYSTEM

The phonological system is the sound system of a language. When we hear speech, we perceive phonemes, the smallest distinguishable units of sound that carry meaning for us in our language.

It might seem as though we ought to be able to hear the distinctions between all the sounds that humans produce, but that is not the case. Each language makes use of only a small number of the wide range of possible sounds that human beings are capable of uttering and discerning.

For example, in English it makes a significant difference to you if someone *pats* you on the head or *bats* you on the head. But in some languages, the sounds that we write as *p* and *b* are heard as identical, a phenomenon easier to understand if you consider that both sounds are produced using the same parts of the mouth in the same fashion. The only difference is that the initial sound in *bat* includes the use of voicing, while the initial sound in *pat* does not. Not all languages distinguish between voiced and voiceless sounds, which sound distinctive to native English speakers. For speakers of languages that do not distinguish between these sounds, English words such as *ban* and *pan* or *bay* and *pay* sound alike.

Sign languages, not having sound systems, have an equivalent system known as *cherology*. Cheremes are the smallest units of gesture that are distinguishable and carry meaning to a speaker of sign (Wilbur, 1980).

THE MORPHOLOGICAL SYSTEM

The morphological system is the system of how words are built. Morphemes are meaningful units, which can sometimes stand alone as words, but often appear in combination with other morphemes. For example, the word *girl* has one morpheme, which carries the meaning of a young female human. *Girls* has two morphemes. The second morpheme, *-s*, indicates the concept of plural. *Girls* is a single example, which sidesteps more complicated morphological issues, such as the relationship between *man* and *men*. A complex analysis of the theory of morphology is out of place here. However, it is important to know that words are built systematically, much as sentences are.

SYNTAX

Syntax refers to the structure or architecture of sentences. It is common but inaccurate to think of syntax as grammar. Syntax, however, is descriptive rather than prescriptive. For example, "I don't have a pencil" is recognizable to a native speaker of English as an acceptable sentence. On the other hand, "A pencil don't have I" sounds awkward. It does not conform to the generally accepted patterns or rules of English.

On the other hand, look at the sentence "I ain't got no pencil." A native speaker of American English knows that it is an English sentence and conforms to English syntax. Nevertheless, we have a tendency to judge "I ain't got no pencil" as incorrect English. It is not standard usage, and its use would be ill-advised for a formal situation such as an employment interview. From a purely descriptive standpoint, however, it fits into basic English sentence patterns. Despite the fact that it may make schoolteachers shudder, it is used in classrooms countless times every day, and, from a syntactical point of view, it works in English.

In sum, *syntax* refers to the rules that govern a language. *Grammar,* on the other hand, has a prescriptive connotation—it looks at whether or not a particular construction conforms to a language standard. We shall analyze the meaning of standard language later in this chapter.

SEMANTICS

Semantics is the study of meaning. Semantics was considered the purview of philosophers until fairly recently. Modern analyses have led linguists to conclude that while meaning and structure are inextricably connected, syntactical analysis of language is insufficient to explain meaning (Hayes, Ornstein, & Gage, 1977). One area of inquiry in semantics is the study of words. Words can be analyzed with reference to their denotations. Earlier in this chapter, we talked about conventional symbols, and we agreed that *chair* refers to a piece of furniture used for sitting. *Chair,* however, can denote several things, depending on the context. In a committee meeting, for example, *chair* may well denote the person who organizes the meeting, or the action of leading the group.

Words also have connotations that supplement their denotations. While the words *Asian* and *rice-eater* may refer to the same individual, they have very different connotations. *Asian* refers to a person's geographical or cultural origins; *rice-eater* has pejorative connotations far beyond an observation on dietary habits.

The subtleties of denotations and connotations are a minefield for second language learners. Good dictionaries provide information about semantic distinctions, but there's still room for error. David Sedaris (1997), in a humorous essay about learning French, tells how he decided to learn ten daily words and practice them while doing errands in a small town in Normandy. "Out of the five translations for a given English word, I would manage to write down and memorize the most bizarre and obsolete. This was the case with the word 'glove.'" In an attempt to converse with the butcher about the weather, Sedaris remarked "It is brisk this evening. . . . Perhaps I should wear the heavy steel mitts worn by medieval knights as they rode into battle" (p. 71). In other words, Sedaris selected the word *gauntlet* from the options offered in his French dictionary. The difference between *glove* and *gauntlet* is semantic.

In addition to analyzing the dimensions of particular words, semantics studies phrases and sentences and analyzes different kinds of ambiguities. For example, the sentence "They were hunting dogs" has structural ambiguities. Thus, two differing meanings are represented with the same surface structure of language. Advertisers often take advantage of ambiguities. An advertisement for Toyota comments, "People drive us" (*New York Times Magazine,* 1997, p. 31). Two advertising messages are cleverly packaged in one short phrase. One tells us that people drive these cars (they're popular, people like them), and the other suggests that the company is motivated to serve people and meet their needs. That's semantics!

As language users, we daily sort out many different and ambiguous meanings. Our intuitive understanding of semantics enables us to tune into correct meanings by relying on linguistic context.

PRAGMATICS

Pragmatics is not an internal linguistic subsystem, such as phonology, morphology, syntax, and semantics. Rather it is the system of the use of language in social contexts. Language use is determined by the function of an interaction and by the relationship of the people involved (Bloom & Lahey, 1978). For example, "I now pronounce you man and wife" has no meaning if uttered by a child in play, but significant consequences when stated by an appropriate official during a wedding ceremony.

In language, one form may serve several functions. "It's ten after five" may be a response to a direct question. It may also be a way of suggesting to people that they have arrived behind schedule. Uttered in a particular context, it may mean "We're going to get stuck in rush hour traffic!" Conversely, one function may take many forms. The question "Can we begin?" and the hint "We're running short on time" both serve the same function.

Native speakers intuitively understand pragmatic systems. If someone asks, "Can you tell me the time?" a native English speaker, acting on knowledge about language and social context, knows that it is inappropriate to answer yes.

IMPLICATIONS FOR TEACHERS

Understanding the subsystems of language provides teachers with insights into the challenges that face second language learners who are learning English. For example, an analysis of the phonological system of English shows that there are actually about fifteen vowel sounds in American English, represented by various combinations of letters. No wonder it's a challenge for speakers of other languages to learn to read and write English!

On the other hand, morphological analysis can be helpful for some students learning to read. Spanish speakers, for example, can benefit from thinking about cognates. Spanish uses lots of Latin-based words for ordinary conversation, whereas English uses the German-based variety for day-to-day conversation, saving the Latin-based words for "best." Think about this: In casual English, it's likelier that I "met" you on the way to the store than that I "encountered" you. Students whose first language is Spanish may have less trouble understanding the word *encounter,* because the everyday Spanish word is *encontrar.*

There are many published programs for teaching reading and second language. Teachers need to select from among them and also tailor them to the needs of specific groups and individual students. A good understanding of the way language works is an important tool for evaluating different approaches as well as for using them effectively.

Written Language in a Computerized World

Email, bulletin boards, and chat rooms have added a new dimension to written communication. Acronyms are often used as a kind of shorthand. Emoticons, symbols made of letters and other keyboard symbols, express feelings that might not come across otherwise. Below are some common acronyms and emoticons that you may come across when you communicate in cyberspace. The list is hardly exhaustive, and like all language forms, is constantly evolving and changing. For an in-depth look at how language is evolving in the computer age, read *Language and the Internet,* by David Crystal (Cambridge University Press, 2001).

ACRONYMS

BTW	By the way	LOL	Laugh out loud (also lots of love)
CUL8R	See you later	LTNS	Long time no see
FOAF	Friend of a friend	OTOH	On the other hand
FTASB	Faster than a speeding bullet	ROFL	Rolling on the floor laughing
GGN	Gotta go now	SOP	Standard Operating Procedure
HHOK	Ha ha, only kidding	TIA	Thanks in advance
IMHO	In my humble opinion	YWSYLS	You win some, you lose some

EMOTICONS

: -)	A smile, happy, funny	: - I	Disgusted
: - (	A frown, sad, unhappy, bad news	(:-&	Angry
; -)	A wink	: - o	Shocked, amazed

The conventions of emoticons are different in Japanese. Here are some examples:

(^^) (^0^)	Smile or laugh	(#^^#)	Turn red
(^_-)	Wink	(^_^;)	Cold sweat, nervousness
(^.^)	Kiss		

Other Aspects of Communication

Apart from language, communication is enhanced by paralinguistic ("beyond language") and nonlinguistic messages, which can be transmitted in conjunction with language or without the aid of language. Paralinguistic mechanisms include intonation, stress, rate of speech, and pauses or hesitations. Nonlinguistic behaviors include gestures, facial expressions, and body language, among others.

Paralinguistic and nonlinguistic behaviors differ from culture to culture and language to language. Such differences are often the cause of misunderstandings in cross-cultural situations. Students who wish to become proficient in a second language should pay careful attention to the nonverbal behaviors that pertain to the languages they are studying.

Language Attitudes

In the foregoing section we have treated language almost clinically. Remember, however, that in the introduction to this chapter we said that it is necessary to identify the attitudes or biases we have and separate them from basic concepts about language. Language exists in political and social contexts that must be understood so we can use language as an instructional tool and also respond equitably to students with a language background different from our own.

It is difficult to pinpoint attitudes we hold about language because the emotional bond we have to our native language is extremely strong. Søren Kierkegaard, the nineteenth-century Danish philosopher and writer, referring to the porridge his mother prepared for him when he was a child, reflected that no other porridge could ever be as flavorful. We can draw an analogy between language and Kierkegaard's porridge—no language ever seems quite as rich or evocative as our own.

In this section we will investigate a few of the commonly held attitudes about language.

ARE SOME LANGUAGES BETTER THAN OTHERS?

One prevalent attitude is that some languages or varieties of a language are more correct or better than others. For example, Spanish speakers are often asked if they speak Castilian. The Spanish word for Castilian is *castellano*. In Spain *castellano* refers to the regional dialect of the province of Castile. In parts of Latin American, *castellano* is used to refer to Spanish in general. The uninformed English speaker, however, who refers to Castilian generally means something along the lines of "the King's English"—a proper, high-class form of the language.

This attitude and many others can be dispelled by focusing on the fact that the primary purpose of language is communication. A Spanish speaker answering the phone in Argentina says *allo* (hello). Other Latin Americans pick up the receiver and say *diga* (speak). Mexicans say *bueno* (good or well). Mexicans joke about the expression, claiming that their phone system is so bad that any time they can get a call through is *bueno!* None of these responses is better than any other. Depending on where you are, there are many appropriate ways to answer a phone in Spanish. It makes sense to facilitate communication by responding according to local custom.

ARE SOME LANGUAGES MORE EXPRESSIVE THAN OTHERS?

One common attitude that people hold about language is that there are ideas or feelings that can be expressed in one language that can't be expressed in another. An expression of this bias is that some languages are less logical than others. In particular, people sometimes suggest that some languages are not useful for communicating about technology.

As Muriel Saville-Troike remarks (1982, p. 82), "While all languages may be inherently capable of serving all purposes humans may ask of them, specific languages evolve differentially through processes of variation, adaptation, and selection." In other words, as people in a society have a need to communicate in a particular way or about a particular subject, their language expands and adapts to meet their need.

For example, there are several cultures in the South Pacific that commonly use a large squash-like vegetable we call breadfruit for a variety of purposes. Breadfruit is used as a basic food, but also serves several ritual and ceremonial purposes. People in those cultures have many words for breadfruit that indicate its color, ripeness, size, and particular use. In the United States we rarely encounter a breadfruit, and the one name we have for it may not be familiar to you at all. Nevertheless, with some circumlocution and explanation, English can produce all the nuances necessary to talk about breadfruit.

Some languages borrow to meet expanding technological needs. There is a bias against borrowing, and some governments have even passed laws to limit loan words. According to an article in *Newsweek* (Doerner, 1987), the French government has established a secretary of state for francophone affairs, and judgments have been levied against companies that use English words in advertising in lieu of French equivalents.

Hebrew, however, is an example of a language that has borrowed extensively to meet the needs of modernization and yet has maintained its linguistic integrity. Preserved for centuries almost exclusively as a liturgical language, Hebrew came into everyday use with the creation of the state of Israel in 1948. Biblical Hebrew was, of course, incompatible with the demands of the modern world. It might be possible, for example, to create a circumlocution for *telephone* by saying "a way to talk to people at a distance through wires." But that would be cumbersome in real-life situations when you want to say, "Answer

Neologisms

Languages are constantly changing. At the lexical level, words become obsolete, and new words come into use. New words, or neologisms, are formed in several different ways. We make new words from old ones by adding prefixes and suffixes. For example, from *structure* we get *superstructure* and *infrastructure*. Our media-driven society acquired a suffix from Watergate and we've used it to describe any number of political scandals, thus "Monicagate." We also borrow words from other languages, which you know if you like a croissant with your latte. Back-formation, making verbs from nouns, is a common process that gives us verbs like "to impact," "to parent," "to incentivize." Back-formation seems to excite controversy among grammarians (Andrews, 2001), but it happens all the time.

Technology is evolving at an unprecedented rate, giving rise to a lot of new words, many of which derive from acronyms. So, for example, *laser* comes from light amplification by stimulated emission of radiation. *Modem,* from modulator-demodulator, isn't quite an acronym. It's more of a compound word, which is another way neologisms are made. *Cyberspace* and *infomercial* are new compound words that have quickly become familiar to us all. Sometimes we blend words (*motel* or *brunch*) or we shorten or clip words to make new ones. *Blog* is short for weblog, much as *ad* is short for advertisement.

Jeremy Bentham, a nineteenth-century British philosopher and social reformer, coined many words in his time that are in common use today. For example, Bentham gave us *international* and *maximize*. Bentham may be best known, however, for his auto-icon. On display in a cabinet at University College London as requested in his will, the auto-icon is Bentham's skeleton, dressed in his own clothes and topped with a wax head. Readers who want to know more about the auto-icon (and what happened to Bentham's actual head) can log on to www.ucl.ac.uk. To take a look at the very newest words in English go to www.logophilia.com.

the telephone!" So Hebrew borrowed the word *telephone,* and in Hebrew it sounds much like the English word.

At the same time, the Academy of the Hebrew Language attempts to coin Hebrew neologisms (new words) to keep up with modern needs and demands, without incorporating too many loan words or English derivatives. After some deliberation, the Academy settled on *tanuron* or "little oven" for toaster oven in an attempt to avoid the use of the English word *toaster* (Schmemann, 1996).

We have looked at only a few of the many possible attitudes about language. Linguists agree that all languages are linguistically equal and that every language is equally capable of expressing whatever its speakers need to communicate.

Attitudes about language persist because people feel close personal and emotional ties to the languages they speak. Mandy Patinkin, the vocalist, recorded an album of Yiddish songs. While doing so, he invited several

Yiddish-speaking friends to discuss translations and pronunciations. Describing the ensuing "friendly battle," he comments, "It became clear to me they were battling to preserve their ancestors' neighborhoods, the way the word was spoken on their parents' streets, their homes, their corners" (Patinkin, 1998). Such attitudes and emotions are understandable. A teacher who works with language minority students, however, must be aware of language attitudes as potential misinterpretations of the nature and purpose of language as a human endeavor.

—Language Varieties

STANDARD

The term *standard* has been used in the foregoing section, but it has not been defined. It is commonly assumed that there is a standard, fixed, and correct form of a language against which we can measure a given sample of that language. But the concept of an immutable and proper language form contradicts the very nature of language itself. As we have seen, language is flexible, responsive, changing constantly.

Students of language sometimes suggest that a language is a dialect with an army. That somewhat humorous assertion gets close to the truth about language variation. The term *standard* is elusive precisely because it has its roots in politics rather than in any basic truth about language.

Standard language is the language of the group in power. Formal attempts are made to standardize language. For example, Spanish is regulated by 22 language academies, the oldest of which is the *Real Academia Española* (The Royal Spanish Academy), created in Spain in 1713 by King Philip V.

The most recent academy was established in New York in 1987 in an attempt to protect Spanish from becoming anglicized (Chavez, 1987). The United States has the fifth largest Spanish-speaking population in the world, and Spanish is in constant contact with English. One result is words like *carpeta* (rug), *roofo* (roof), and *lonche* (lunch). Another outcome is the addition of words like *taco* and *burrito* to the American English lexicon.

Spanish, along with the other Romance languages, is itself the product of languages in contact. When the Romans conquered Iberia, speakers of indigenous Iberian languages learned Latin. They spoke it with an accent, overlaid grammatical structures from their native tongues, and sprinkled it with local words for familiar concepts and objects. That natural process formed the basis for what we know as modern Spanish.

Languages are dynamic; they change to meet the communication needs of their speakers. It is possible for a "language government" such as an academy to set a standard. However, the standard set is not as crucial as *who* is doing the setting.

DIALECT

Dialects are variations of a language used by particular groups of people. Regional dialects often have distinct vocabularies. A water pistol on the East Coast of the United States is a squirt gun on the West Coast. In Spanish, a peach is *melocotón* in Puerto Rico and a *durazno* in Mexico. Dialects may also differ phonologically or syntactically from place to place.

Regional differences in languages may reflect differences in language history. American English includes usages that sound archaic to the British ear and may well be remnants from colonial times. American English also includes a large lexicon of words borrowed from Spanish (McCrum, Cran, & MacNeil, 1986).

People often relate regional dialects to stereotypes. For example, in the United States, speakers of Bostonian dialects are sometimes considered "stuffy." Southerners are said to drawl and are considered lazy and slow moving. Such biases have nothing to do with the real nature of dialects or the people who speak them. Despite our biases, regional differences present few problems for native speakers. Humans are quite responsive to language and quite flexible in their ability to communicate.

Just as language varies from place to place, it also varies among different social groups. Social variations of language are sometimes called *sociolects.* Professor Higgins, in *My Fair Lady,* was well aware of the different responses people have to different sociolects when he undertook his project of turning a flower seller into a member of high society.

Any individual's particular speech, or *idiolect,* is influenced by both regional and social class factors. From a teacher's viewpoint, it is important to remember that language can vary for many reasons and stay conscious to the biases that may come into play when we are exposed to different varieties of language. This awareness will help us avoid prejudging a student's abilities based on our own perceptions of language.

PIDGINS AND CREOLES

Sometimes languages in contact produce pidgins. This happens when speakers of two different languages, compelled to talk to each other, develop a bare-bones code for communication. Pidgins can emerge in a variety of contexts for a number of reasons. According to Stockwell, "[Pidgins] have arisen typically in time of imperialism, slavery, plantation labour migration, war and refugee situations, and around trading ports" (2002, p. 18). Born of necessity, pidgins are limited and simplified languages, but they are systematic and rule-governed.

A pidgin is nobody's first language, but as soon as a new generation learns a pidgin, it becomes a creole. Creoles are generally far more complex and elaborated than the pidgins from which they evolve, since they have to serve the full range of their speakers' needs. According to Todd (2001), over

100 million people speak some kind of creole, including 5 million speakers of Haitian Creole and 5 million speakers of Afrikaans.

Gullah, also known as Geechee, is an American creole. Gullah developed in the nineteenth century from contact between English and languages of West Africa spoken by enslaved people. Today it is still spoken on the Sea Islands off the coast of South Carolina and Georgia. Many people in the United States are familiar with Gullah through the speech of Uncle Remus in Joel Chandler Harris's tales of Bre'r Rabbit. In 1995, the American Bible Society published a Gullah translation of the Gospel according to Luke, called De Good Nyews Bout Jedus Christ Wa Luke Write. You may be familiar with the following verse:

> 2:10. Bot de angel tell um say, "Mus don't feah! A habe good nyews. Cause ob dis nyews, oona gwine rejaice. All de people gwine rejaice tommuch." (American Bible Society, 1995, p. 10) (*2:10. And the angel said unto them, Fear not: for, behold, I bring you good tidings of great joy, which shall be to all people.*)

REGISTER

People use different varieties of language, depending on the setting, relationship between speakers, and the function of the interaction. A *register* is a situationally appropriate form of a language.

Sociolinguistic concepts such as register are important to consider when assessing language proficiency and providing second language instruction. A person learning a second language may have a good accent or control of syntax and still lack the ability to function in a variety of life situations. For example, you may have experienced difficulty if you learned a second language in a classroom setting and then attempted to enter into the quick give-and-take of an informal gathering among friends.

BUT IS IT SLANG?

The word *slang* is commonly used to refer, somewhat pejoratively, to nonstandard speech. Speakers of one variety of English, for example, may comment that speakers of another variety "speak slang." From a professional perspective, *slang* has a more precise meaning. According to one linguist, "One of the main defining features of 'slang' appears to be its ephemeral nature" (Wardhaugh, 1993, p. 165). In other words, slang is usage that is popular for a while and then fades away. In some cases, however, slang may become acceptable and enter common usage. In that case, it is no longer slang.

More Than One Language

Information about the number of languages in the world and the number of speakers of those languages is readily available. There is little data, however,

In Your Classroom
Teaching Students about Language

The study of language and its history is beneficial at every level. Entertain young students, build their vocabularies, and expand on social science lessons by engaging them in activities that consider the origins of words.

Many English words have their origins in other languages, and some even come to English several languages removed. Words travel as the baggage of trade and also of conquest. *Apricot,* for example, is a Greek word with "al" or "the" added as a prefix from Arabic. The word traveled to Europe with the Moorish conquest of the Iberian peninsula and found its way into English when the Gauls conquered the Anglo-Saxons in the eleventh century! The words below are a tiny sample of words in English from other languages. Use your own knowledge of languages and the dictionary to discover the languages of origin for these words. (Hint: They're organized in language groups.)

- Algebra, almanac, nadir, zenith, zero
- Dungaree, khaki
- Aria, piano, soprano
- Avocado, chocolate, guacamole
- Adobe, brocade, canyon, guerrilla

You may want to do this activity with your own students using words that have come into English from their primary languages. It's one way that monolingual teachers can value the languages their students bring to the classroom.

regarding the number of people in the world who are bilingual or multilingual. It would be difficult for a researcher to collect that information, since theorists have defined *bilingualism* in many different ways.

WHAT IS BILINGUALISM?

A strict definition of *bilingualism* suggests that a bilingual person has native-like control of two languages (Bloomfield, 1933). Yet while many of the readers of this book undoubtedly function in more than one language, probably few would claim native-like capability in each language in every situation. Discussions with multilingual people reveal that they make choices about language use that are affected by the setting and function of the particular interaction (Miller, 1983). People who function in two or more languages know that those who have equal and highly developed capacity in two or more languages are relatively rare and generally much admired.

Grosjean, in *Life with Two Languages* (1982), surveyed monolingual and bilingual college students to find out how they interpreted the term *bilingual*. He asked them, "If someone told you that X was bilingual in English and

French, what would you understand by that?" (p. 231). In this survey, both monolingual and bilingual students indicated that *bilingual* means speaking two languages, and high ratings were given by both groups for the description "fluent in two languages." Unlike monolingual students in the study, however, bilingual students gave a high rating to "regular use of two languages." In that regard, bilingual students agree with many modern theorists who tend to favor the idea that use of two languages, rather than fluency, is the hallmark of bilingualism.

CODE-SWITCHING

Bilinguals sometimes alternate the use of two languages from sentence to sentence, or even within one sentence. *Code-switching*, as this is called, may be misinterpreted by monolinguals as an inability on the part of a bilingual individual to speak either language properly.

Analysis by linguists and sociolinguists, however, has demonstrated that code-switching is a systematic and rule-governed language behavior. Within certain linguistic constraints, bilinguals may code-switch to:

- Fill a lexical need: *"Le puse al niño en el* daycare."
- Emphasize a point: "Get up now. *Levántate!"*
- Express ethnic solidarity: *"Andale pues;* let's get together soon."

Other reasons for code-switching may include the desire to convey emotional or personal involvement, to include or exclude someone from a conversation, and to assert the status of the speaker (Grosjean, 1982).

In general, a person who code-switches demonstrates linguistic creativity and sophistication. However, a second type of code-switching, called *regressive code-switching* (Gonzalez & Maez, 1980), occurs in children who are losing their first language and leaning on their second language to supply missing elements. This kind of situation raises a pedagogical issue: Should teachers code-switch in dual language classrooms, or keep the languages entirely separate?

Experts generally agree that teachers should restrict code-switching to the intersentential type. That is, teachers should switch languages only from sentence to sentence and not intrasententially, or within a sentence. They should, however, accept intrasentential code-switching by

The Poetry of Code-Switching

Soy un ajiaco de contradicciones.
I have mixed feelings about everything.
Name your tema, I'll hedge;
name your cerca, I'll straddle it
like a cubano

(ajiaco: stew; tema: theme; cerca: fence)

SOURCE: Gustavo Pérez-Firmat, in *Bilingual Blues*. Arizona State University, Tempe, AZ: Bilingual Press/ Editorial Bilingüe, 1995.

their students (Ovando & Collier, 1985). There is some evidence, however, that complete separation of the two languages of instruction is beneficial to the development of both (Cummins & Swain, 1986). Concurrent use of language in the classroom and other instructional approaches are discussed in Chapter 5.

BILINGUALISM: A HANDICAP OR A TALENT?

Research prior to the 1960s tended to support the notion that bilingual children did poorly in school, and bilingualism was generally regarded as an academic handicap. Later analysis of those early findings reveals that the studies were biased against ethnic minority students. Sampling techniques and statistical analyses were flawed, and investigators failed to take into account other variables such as social and economic factors. Also, tests were usually administered only in English.

The assumption that bilingualism was a handicap led to unfortunate practices such as punishing children for using languages other than English in school, even at play. Rejection of a child's language and, by implication, culture adversely affects that child's self-concept and chances for academic success. In retrospect, the bilingualism-as-handicap position can be seen as a self-fulfilling prophecy.

Despite suggestions that early research on bilingualism may have been methodologically flawed, there have been recent studies that support the conclusions of earlier work and show that bilingual children score lower on verbal tests of intelligence or academic achievement than their monolingual counterparts. Other studies, however, indicate that bilingual children perform better than monolinguals on tests of linguistic skills, divergent thinking, sensitivity to communication, and general intelligence. (See Baker, 2006, for a review.) How can we explain this apparent contradiction?

Quite simply, children can be enriched by knowing more than one language as long as they are *additive* rather than *subtractive* bilinguals. An *additive bilingual* has learned a second language in addition to the first, whereas a *subtractive bilingual* has gradually lost one language while acquiring a second. The distinction is significant from a pedagogical viewpoint because research indicates that children with high levels of proficiency in two languages show "positive cognitive effects" (Cummins, 1981, p. 39). In effect, children who come to school speaking more than one language, or who learn a second language in school, will benefit academically as long as both languages are nurtured and developed to the fullest extent.

The Ebonics Debate

In 1996 the Oakland Unified School District in northern California passed a resolution that identified Ebonics, sometimes called Black English or Black Vernacular, as a distinct language and proposed teaching students in Ebonics as a bridge to standard English. The debate that ensued about the resolution was startling both in terms of its ferocity and the inaccuracy of understandings on which it was based. It quickly became clear that the controversy about Ebonics and its use in schooling was fueled by deep and often unexplored feelings about race, ethnicity, culture, and language.

Ebonics, a term derived from the words *ebony* and *phonics,* refers to a variety of English sometimes also called Black English, Black English Vernacular, or African American Language. Ebonics has been a stigmatized variety of English, moreso perhaps than other varieties because it is associated with black people who have historically borne the brunt of racism and discrimination in American society. White America is often uncomfortable when Black America asserts its power, whether in the streets, the voting booth, or the public schools. Assertions about the validity of a particular language or dialect are often politically informed, as we shall see in Chapter 10, and it should not have come as a surprise to the authors of the Oakland resolution that the policy they promulgated was likely to provoke ardent responses across the political spectrum.

Dialects spoken by African Americans have historically been seen as deficient rather than simply different. In an article that is now a classic discussion of dialect and language bias, Labov (1995/1979) demonstrated that attitudes about what he called *Black English Vernacular* notwithstanding, it was clearly a communicative, and in fact, highly expressive variety of English. More recently, Williams (1991) has asserted that various features of what he calls *African American Language* can be traced back to languages brought to this continent by enslaved Africans. This ought not to be a radical notion, given what we generally know about languages, but is often received with skepticism by those who would deny African Americans any claim to a heritage that precedes their enslavement.

It should be noted that there are many forms of Black English. Many African Americans speak standard English, and many are bidialectal, using standard English in their schools and places of employment, and some form of Ebonics in their personal and community interactions. This should not seem unusual or startling, since we are all multidialectal.

Lawrence Block, in his mystery novel *A Walk Among the Tombstones* (1992), describes how TJ, a detective's street kid sidekick, tries to extract the number of an unlabeled pay phone from an operator. She refuses his request when he asks in Black English, so he calls another operator, and speaking standard English, successfully obtains the number. When Matt, the detective, expresses amazement at TJ's ability to switch back and forth, TJ muses "They two different languages man, and you talkin' to a cat's bilingual" (p. 116). TJ is dated, but he understands that for African Americans, like everyone else, the ability to use more than one dialect is an asset, not a liability.

Zora Neale Hurston was one of the first African American writers to capture the richness of black dialect on paper. In an essay describing Hurston's work, Claudia Roth Pierpont makes an eloquent observation about Black

English: "This is dialect not as a broken attempt at higher correctness but as an extravagant game of image and sound. It is a record of the unique explosion that occurred when African people with an intensely musical and oral culture came up hard against the King James Bible and the sweet-talking American South, under conditions that denied them all outlet for their visions and gifts except the transformation of the English language into song" (Roth Pierpont, 1997, p. 80).

Summary

Language is a system of arbitrary symbols used for communication. The field of linguistics describes the structure of language. Psycholinguistics investigates the relationship of language to the human mind, while sociolinguistics investigates how language varies as it is used in social situations. People have unfounded and emotional biases about language, but, in fact, all languages are responsive to the communication needs of their speakers and are equally suited for communication. Standards are arbitrary and determined by the dominant group in any society.

People who speak two languages may not use both of them with the same degree of facility in every situation. Sometimes bilingual people code-switch. This is not an indication of imperfect mastery of language. Code-switching can be seen as a sophisticated and expressive language strategy. Early research on school achievement suggested that bilingual students were at a disadvantage compared with monolinguals, but recent studies indicate the contrary. Understanding the nature of language and objectifying it as a tool are essential for teachers who work with second language learners.

Questions to Think About and Discuss

1. Read and analyze the following verse from the poem "Jabberwocky" by Lewis Carroll: What language is it written in? How do you know? What information does each subsystem of language give you for making that determination?

   'Twas brillig, and the slithy toves
   Did gyre and gimble in the wabe:
   All mimsy were the borogoves,
   And the mome raths outgrabe.

2. Identify the ambiguity in each of the following sentences and add words, a phrase, or a sentence to eliminate it.
   - John married Isabel.
   - The American history teacher is good looking.
   - Martha thinks she is a genius.

3. Read the following letter, which appeared in the *New York Times.* Analyze the author's language attitudes. Do the author's beliefs about language match up with the understandings you have about the nature of language?

> To the Editor:
>
> As a native of Japan, I am well aware of the importance of the Confucian ethic as an explanation for the academic success of Asian students. However, there may exist another reason why Japanese children, say at Sendai, can do better in mathematics. When I was tutoring my wife's granddaughter, who is a Caucasian, I was struck by the awkwardness of the English language for reciting the multiplication table.
>
> As an example, you must pronounce 4 × 4 = 16 as "4 times 4 is 16" in a rather unrhythmical way. We can say the same in Japanese, "shi-shi-ju-roku" with a singsong musical rhythm. We learn the multiplication table up to 10 × 10 in this fashion. Even after 39 years in this country, I revert to the Japanese method because of its ease.
>
> I can well imagine that the relative difficulty of memorizing the multiplication table in English may cause boredom and loss of interest in math for many youngsters in this country. Of course, math does not consist solely of such routine. However, this example demonstrates the subtle influence of language structure.
>
> Another possibility is the effect of the tone of the language. Japanese is rather imprecise but psychologically warmer than the more precise but perhaps drier character of the English language. This subtle difference may also cause different psychological attitudes in the learning process of youngsters.

4. A letter appeared in an advice column in a magazine aimed at young women. The letter writer commented that she would prefer to be called a *girl* or a *lady* than a *woman,* concluding "Women must battle patriarchy, but we must choose our battles." The response from the columnist suggested, "Ponder the following headlines:
   • Women battle patriarchy.
   • Ladies battle patriarchy.
   • Girls battle patriarchy." (Goldhor Lerner, 1993, p. 40).
   Do these three headlines sound different to you? Why? What subsystem are you working with when you try to answer these questions?

5. Working with your classmates, try to translate the following British sentences into American English:
   • My car needs work on the buffer, the windscreen, the bonnet, and the wings.
   • On the way home, could you stop at the chemist's and the news agent?
   • Take the lift. It's just past the pillar box.
   • I called the booking office, and they were out of stalls.
   • Run those through the franking machine and post them.

6. Which of the following assertions are true? Why or why not?
   • Italian is more romantic than English.

- Physics and mathematics cannot be discussed in Navajo.
- English is the most logical language in the world.
- Languages that have writing systems are more creative than languages that do not.
- The languages of primitive societies do not have complex syntactical systems.
- "He gots a hat" is not English.

7. According to an article in the *New York Times* (Speech Therapist, 1993), there is a speech therapist in New York who specializes in transforming people's accents. According to the article, "He teaches senators how to drop their regional accents when they are in Washington, and how to pick them up again on the campaign trail" (p. A10). Why would a public figure want to be able to change language varieties at will?

8. Slang is a form of language that is popular for a short period of time. In some cases, slang enters the language mainstream, and may become standard usage. The word *dis,* derived from disrespect, originated among African American young people, gained popularity among young people in general, and now appears in newspapers and magazines. Can you think of any other examples of slang that have moved toward the linguistic mainstream?

9. *Jargon* is specialized occupationally-related language. Think about your own employment. What kinds of specialized language do you use?

10. It is now possible to access translations on the World Wide Web. Computer translations, however, are far from perfect. An attempt to translate "She is having a bad hair day" into Italian, for example, resulted in "It is for you a defective day of hats, no?" (Kelley, 1998). What are the factors that make translation from one language to another difficult? Do you suppose it will ever be possible to render poetry from one language into another by computer? Why or why not?

Activities

1. Tape record a non-native speaker of English in an informal conversation. Analyze the language sample from a structural perspective: Does the speaker have a noticeable foreign accent? Is the speaker's syntax close to native standards? Apart from your observations about structure, how would you rate the speaker's overall communicative competence? Share your samples with your classmates. Discuss your conclusions.

2. Talk to people who speak more than one language about their experience and understanding of bilingualism. What do they think *bilingual* means? How did they learn their languages? Which languages do they use for different situations? What attitudes do they have about their languages? About bilingualism in general?

Suggestions for Further Reading

Bryson, B. (1994). *Made in America: An informal history of the English language in the United States.* New York: William Morrow.

You might be surprised to know that President Benjamin Harrison established a Board on Geographic Names in an attempt to standardize place naming in the United States. According to this entertaining book, Greasy Corner, Arkansas, Bugtussle, Texas, and others equally picturesque escaped this standard and are still on the map. Made in America *is a treat for language students.*

Crystal, D. (1997). *The Cambridge encyclopedia of language* (2nd ed.). Cambridge, UK: Cambridge University Press.

This book touches on everything you ever wanted to know about language in an entertaining format that includes maps, illustrations, and lists of every description.

Freeman, D. E., & Freeman, Y. S. (2004). *Essential linguistics: What you need to know to teach reading, ESL, spelling, phonics, grammar.* Portsmouth, NH: Heinemann.

All teachers are concerned about teaching reading and language arts to all their students. A solid background in the nature and dynamics of language is in many respects the most useful tool for effectively developing students' literacy. Essential Linguistics *provides that background at an appropriate level of depth for beginning teachers.*

Morris, D. (1977). *Manwatching: A field guide to human behavior.* New York: Harry N. Abrams.

An entertaining analysis of nonlinguistic communication, this colorfully illustrated book discusses gestures, eye contact, clothing, cosmetics, use of objects, and other human behaviors that transmit messages.

Nunberg, G. (2001). *The way we talk now: Commentaries on language and culture.* Boston: Houghton Mifflin.

A collection of essays on language most of which were aired over the last ten years on National Public Radio. Thoughtful and informative, these essays make the reader stop and take a new look at the language we use every day.

Tannen, D. (1990). *You just don't understand: Women and men in conversation.* New York: Morrow.

Gender differences are fascinating, and it's not surprising that this discussion of the ways that men and women use language was a long-standing best seller.

Wardhaugh, R. (1993). *Investigating language: Central problems in linguistics.* Oxford, UK: Blackwell.

An excellent overview of language and the theories about how humans learn it. Includes a glossary of basic terms.

Wolfram, W., & Ward, B. (Eds.). (2006). *American voices: How dialects differ from coast to coast.* Oxford, UK: Blackwell.

Written by well-known experts for a broad-based audience, this engaging book describes a multitude of American regional and social dialects. Short chapters describe the features of the many ways we speak English in the United States, and the occasional insertion of a regional glossary is both informative and entertaining.

Language Development

*I*n the period between birth and age four or five, children learn to express themselves with language. How they accomplish this impressive feat is not completely understood, although great strides have been made in the study of language development in the last 25 years.

A survey of the research in language development is an enormous undertaking. An understanding, however, of how children acquire language is essential for dual language curriculum development and instruction. This chapter will present a brief overview of first language development and second language acquisition theories.

First Language Development: Memorizing or Hypothesizing?

People often assume that children develop a first language by simply imitating what they hear around them; in fact, that was once the traditional view of first language development. According to the behaviorist view, for example, children reproduce language, or approximate imitations of what they hear, and are reinforced by rewards, such as attention or response.

Although such views were widely held well into the twentieth century, the notion that imitation and habit formation are the primary bases for language development is flawed. Imitation theory does not account for the creative capacity of language—the child's ability to produce original utterances.

The well-known linguist Noam Chomsky revolutionized thinking about language development in the early 1950s when he suggested that children are born with an innate capacity to develop language. Chomsky suggested that children have a built-in mechanism, which he called the *Language Acquisition Device*, or LAD, that preprograms them to develop grammar based on the linguistic input they receive. Today it's easy to create an analogy for Chomsky's model based on computers: think of the LAD as the operating system, and a particular language as software, installed incrementally as input is received.

Chomsky's view dramatically altered thinking about language development. Psycholinguists moved away from the traditional behaviorist idea that

47

language is developed through habit formation and began to consider the idea that children discover the organizing principles of the language they are exposed to. Recent theory has expanded Chomsky's original focus on syntax, suggesting that children make sense of semantic and pragmatic systems of language as well. Overall, however, modern theories agree that children develop language by hypothesis testing, or rule finding.

RULE FINDING

As we saw in the first chapter, language is a system, governed by rules at the phonological, morphological, syntactical, semantic, and pragmatic levels. The rule-finding approach to language development suggests that children develop hypotheses about the rules of their language based on the input they receive and then test those hypotheses by trying them out.

The evidence we have for children's rule finding comes from the "errors" they make when they apply the rules they have formulated. *Error* has a special meaning in this context. It does not mean *mistake,* but refers instead to the forms generated by applying rules that do not take irregularities or exceptions into account. Errors of this kind are called *overgeneralizations*. These systematic errors reveal the strategies the child is using to create language. The rules of the child's system can be inferred from the error patterns.

Some syntactical overgeneralizations may be familiar to you. English-speaking children quickly find the general rule for plurals: *Cat* becomes *cats,* *dog* becomes *dogs,* and so on. Having arrived at a way to construct plurals, a child will then say "I have two foots." *Foots* is an error resulting from a systematic attempt to apply the rule for plurals to all situations, without taking exceptions into account.

On the phonological level, English-speaking children notice that a word may have more than one syllable. They express that fact by repeating the first syllable or syllables (Ervin-Tripp, 1976). A small child, daunted by the word *refrigerator,* converts it to *freda-freda.* The child is saying "I can't quite manage it yet, but I know this word has more than one syllable."

In Spanish, the first-person form of a verb in the present tense results from dropping the infinitive ending and adding "-o" to the root. For example, *tomar* (to take) becomes *tomo* (I take); *comer* (to eat) becomes *como* (I eat). When you ask small children in Spanish if they know something, they often reply *sabo,* from the verb *saber* (to know). *Sabo* seems logically correct, but it is an "error" resulting from overgeneralization of a rule. The syntactically correct form is an exception to the rule. As children mature, they learn to use *sé.*

Children even overgeneralize at the semantic level of language. For instance, a young child may use the word *doggie* to refer to other animals, like cats and horses. In that case, *doggie* is an overgeneralization that refers to four-footed furry animals.

When children grasp the organizational principles underlying language, they can produce and understand novel utterances—things they have never heard or said before. Rules children generate sometimes produce language that differs from adult language. Child language, however, is neither haphazard nor an inept imitation of adult language. Child language is a system in itself—in fact, a series of systems, that gradually evolves into the adult form of the language.

First Language Development and Comprehensible Input

Chomsky originally proposed that LAD allowed children to make sense of the linguistic input they were receiving, even though that input was fragmented and confused.

Contrary to Chomsky's assertion, subsequent research indicates that linguistic input directed at children is in fact carefully organized (Macaulay, 1980). This reversal of thinking about linguistic input is important. It moves the focus for the study of language acquisition from the biological component to the social component, which features the child and the provider of linguistic input as active participants in language development.

CHILD-DIRECTED SPEECH

Child-directed speech is a phenomenon that has intrigued linguists and psycholinguists. Recent research has analyzed the special register used with children, sometimes called *child-directed speech, caretaker speech,* or *motherese*. In certain settings, it seems that mothers engage in a special kind of "conversation" with their babies while nursing them (Snow, 1977). Such a conversation might seem one-sided, with the mother doing most of the talking, except that mothers are exceptionally forgiving about what they will accept as a response. Initially, burping, yawning, sneezing, and other incidental sounds are acceptable to a mother as responses. Long before the emergence of the child's speech, these interactions between mother and infant apparently teach turn-taking, a basic skill in human communication.

One recent study compared the way Russian, Swedish, and American mothers talked to their children with the way women generally speak to other adults. The researchers noticed that mothers exaggerated vowels, slowed their rate of speech, and raised their pitch when they talked to their infant children. One possible explanation is that this kind of speech provides a model that is easy for babies to imitate. Mothers' linguistic modifications were similar across three languages, which suggests that these strategies may be universal (Barinaga, 1997).

Apparently, adults and even other children naturally modify their speech to encourage children's language development. Comprehensible input for children is provided through a variety of strategies such as:

- Speaking slowly.
- Using simple vocabulary—in short, simple sentences.
- Avoiding pausing before the end of a sentence.
- Exaggerating intonation and raising voice pitch.
- Repetition.

An instruction for an adult, for example, might be: "The cereal is on the second shelf to the left of the coffee." On the other hand, for a child the same instruction might take this form: "See the red coffee can? Up on the shelf over the blue dishes? Yes, that one. The cereal is next to it. Good, you got it."

THE SOCIAL AND CULTURAL CONTEXTS OF LANGUAGE ACQUISITION

Research on caretaker speech, or motherese, as characterized above, has generally focused on middle-class English speakers (Peters, 1985). This focus is shifting as we begin to recognize that language learning is inseparable from culture learning. In an analysis of language acquisition among the Kaluli of Papua New Guinea, Schiefflin (1985) remarked, "Every society has its own ideology about language, including when it begins and how children acquire it" (p. 531).

Kaluli people (Schiefflin, 1985) assume that infants are incapable of understanding, and they rarely address them directly except to use their names. It is assumed that children begin to speak when they use the single-syllable words for *mother* and *breast.* From that time on, children are instructed directly by their caretakers in how to respond to a third party. For example, if two children are playing, a Kaluli mother may instruct one to respond to the other, "Give me that," followed by the instruction, "Say like that."

Givón (1985) reports that the Utes, who are Northern Plains Indians living in the United States, discourage interaction between adults and children. In general, people are not encouraged to speak out in council until they have reached the age of 40 or 50. It is not surprising, therefore, that Ute children are expected to listen and not talk to adults. These children receive most of their linguistic input from other children.

In other words, language acquisition is a subset of the larger socialization process. It is a particularly important subset because nearly everything we do involves language. The primary knowledge a child learns through language is how to become a competent member of a particular society. The Kaluli and the Ute cultures illustrate that concepts about the nature of children, the nature of language, and therefore the nature of linguistic interaction vary from one culture to another, depending on values and beliefs.

INPUT MODIFICATION

It is interesting to note that as the child's language develops, the strategies and modifications of adult language providers change (Garnica, 1977). As children mature, adults reduce the number of special cues and hints they provide to facilitate communication. Adults are remarkably patient with tiny infants, accepting even the sounds of body functions as responses in conversation. We are more demanding of toddlers, but still tolerant of the limits of their language ability. The older a child gets, the more we expect a child's language to approximate the norms of adult language.

Awareness of the modification of input for new language learners helps us develop strategies for second language instruction and content instruction in the second language. Linguistic modifications made consciously as part of an instructional program can assist students to gain competence in a second language.

STAGES OF FIRST LANGUAGE DEVELOPMENT

Crying. Children all over the world move through the same stages of language development. At first, children cry to express dissatisfaction. Crying is not speech, but it does have elements of speech, such as intonation, pattern, and pitch. Recent experimentation suggests that infants use the fussy transitional period between quietude and crying to explore their speech organs and discover new sound possibilities (Campbell-Jones, 1985). Between the ages of two and four months, babies add cooing, an expression of pleasure or satisfaction, to their repertoire.

Babbling. At about the age of five months, babies begin to babble. Babbling children are exploring the potential range of speech production, practicing using their speech organs, and controlling them via the brain. The sounds made by a babbling child are not particularly related to the sound of the language that child hears. All normal children are born with the same organs for speech production, and all babbling babies sound much the same.

The quality of babbling changes, however, at about the age of six months, when children begin echolalic babbling. At that stage, a child seems to produce with greater frequency the sounds that are prevalent in the language the child is hearing. There are conflicting views about the function of echolalic babbling, but it seems to be a ruling-out process, where the child eliminates those sounds that are not meaningful in the native language and attempts to imitate those sounds that are (Sachs, 1985).

Telegraphic Speech. Around the age of one year, children can produce a one-word utterance, and, sometime in the second year, speech expands to two-word utterances. These early utterances generally refer initially to the appearance or disappearance of something: "All-gone milk" is a concept that has significance for very young children. Psycholinguists have attempted to identify the relationship between cognitive and linguistic development. In general, they have concluded that children have to grasp a concept, or at least a rudimentary version of it, before they can produce the language for it (Gleason, 1985).

The Origins of Human Language

Nobody is really certain how or when humans began to talk, but people have always speculated about the origins of human language. According to Crystal (1987), in the seventh century B.C.E., an Egyptian king sent two newborns to live with a shepherd who had strict orders not to speak to them. From the sounds they made, the king concluded that Phrygian was the first human language. Experiments of that sort have been reported throughout history, but the puzzle has not been solved.

Otto Jespersen, a Danish linguist who lived in the first half of the twentieth century offers an idyllic theory of how humans developed language:

> [T]he genesis of language is not to be sought in the prosaic, but in the poetic side of life: the source of speech is not gloomy seriousness, but merry play and youthful hilarity. And among the emotions which were most powerful in eliciting outbursts of music and of song, love must be placed in the front rank. . . . In primitive speech I hear the laughing cries of exultation when lads and lasses vied with one another to attract the attention of the other sex, when everybody sang his merriest and danced his bravest to lure a pair of eyes to throw admiring glances in his direction. Language was born in the courting days of mankind. (pp. 433–434)

Recently theorists have proposed the less romantic idea that human language evolved from primate calls (Pinker,1994), from grooming behaviors (Dunbar, 1996), or from gestures (Corballis, 2002).

Experts also debate when human language emerged. McWhorter (2001) suggests that human speech began about 150,000 years ago. Whatever its origins and whenever it developed, our complex communication code sets us apart from all other species. Lieberman (1998) eloquently concludes his book on the origins of language suggesting that "surely we must use the gift of speech, language, and thought to enhance life and love, to vanquish needless suffering and murderous violence—to achieve yet a higher morality. For if we do not, Eve's descendants will reach their end. . . . And no other creature will be here to sing a dirge or tell the story of our passing, for we alone can talk" (p. 151).

Meanings expand during the two-word stage, and children develop telegraphic speech. Telegraphic speech is abbreviated, or elliptical in nature, like the language used in telegrams. Children in this stage rely on gestures to elaborate what they mean. For example, "Daddy up" may mean "Daddy, wake up," "Daddy, pick me up," "Daddy, stand up," or any number of things, depending on the situation. After the two-word stage children move to a three-word utterance stage. As the child's utterances grow longer, reliance on gestures diminishes, and complex grammatical forms develop. Figure 4.1 illustrates the stages of language development.

ORDER OF ACQUISITION

The stages of language development are universal and progress from the simple to the complex. Remember, however, that what may be simple in one

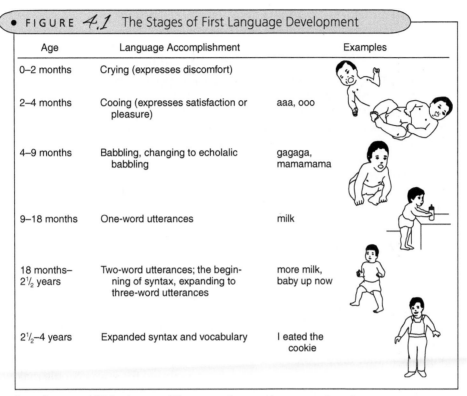

● FIGURE *4.1*   The Stages of First Language Development

Age	Language Accomplishment	Examples
0–2 months	Crying (expresses discomfort)	
2–4 months	Cooing (expresses satisfaction or pleasure)	aaa, ooo
4–9 months	Babbling, changing to echolalic babbling	gagaga, mamamama
9–18 months	One-word utterances	milk
18 months–2½ years	Two-word utterances; the beginning of syntax, expanding to three-word utterances	more milk, baby up now
2½–4 years	Expanded syntax and vocabulary	I eated the cookie

(Note that every child develops at a different rate. Ages are always approximate.)

language can be relatively complex in another. For example, in English, we can indicate that the book belongs to Mommy by saying "Mommy's book." In Yiddish, a highly inflected language, the construction changes to "the book of the Mommy," and the word for *Mommy* is altered to indicate that it has become an indirect object in the phrase. English-speaking children will learn to express possessive forms earlier than their Yiddish-speaking peers.

A normal child enters kindergarten with a vocabulary of approximately 8,000 words and an excellent grasp of syntax, which provide the foundation for the language and literacy development that will follow in school. This accomplishment provides a strong rationale for providing primary language instruction in the early grades. As we will see, it is logical to begin early skill instruction in that language, building on the conceptual and linguistic framework the child brings to school.

CHILDREN AS SOCIOLINGUISTS

Like adults, children alter their language to respond to the setting, the function of the interaction, and the relative status of the individuals involved. For example, children differentiate between formal and informal speech, possibly as the result of the emphasis adults place on politeness.

Children also assign different language characteristics to males and females. While most evidence of gender-related speech differences is anecdotal rather than empirical, we do know that there are societal stereotypes regarding language and gender. It has been demonstrated that as early as preschool, children participate in common stereotypical expectations about how males and females use language. For example, using puppets and role playing, researchers found that young children consider tag questions and indirect requests appropriate for females, and associate direct and competitive speech with males (for a review, see Warren-Leubecker & Bohannon, 1985).

Bilingual children develop a keen sense of the relative prestige of their two languages (Saville-Troike, 1976). Teachers must be aware of the relative status of each language they use in a dual language setting, so as to counteract the negative biases children may bring to the classroom (Legarreta-Marcaida, 1981).

Second Language Acquisition

How do people learn a second language? Do they rely mainly on transferring knowledge from their first language to their second? Or do they recapitulate first language development, sorting out the organizing principles of their new language as they are exposed to it?

Proponents of the transfer approach have analyzed the errors people make in their second language to see if they are the result of interference from the old habits of their first. Proponents of the developmental position look for evidence that learners engage in a rule-finding process as they acquire their second language. Understanding the process of second language acquisition is useful to dual language teachers because it can provide insights into ways to structure effective second language instruction.

Researchers in the area of second language acquisition have discovered that the process is quite complex because language learning is a multifaceted problem-solving activity. Much as they would approach any problem, people approach language learning using the information and abilities they already have. Using first language knowledge and skills may produce errors that resemble interference, but which are in fact evidence of a creative cognitive strategy for solving the new language puzzle. In other words, transfer of language information may be part of the process. In addition, evidence suggests that second language learners may also recapitulate the first language developmental process. The surface manifestations of that process, or the language they produce, may not resemble first language development at every stage because the learners come to the process with useful prior knowledge and cognitive maturity.

Given the many variables that might affect the process of second language acquisition, it is not surprising that researchers have launched their investigations from a variety of viewpoints. The following sections briefly discuss the possible effects of age, personality, and social setting on learning a second language. Remember, however, that these factors are artificially distinguished for study purposes. Our best understanding of second language acquisition indicates that the process involves an integration of psychological, social, and linguistic factors.

THE EFFECT OF AGE

It is generally assumed that children learn second languages better than adults do. Lenneberg (1967) lent credence to that notion when he proposed that a second language is best learned in the "critical period" between the age of two years and the onset of puberty. He suggested that the ability to learn languages is debilitated by the completion of a process of lateralization in the brain, when each side of the brain develops its own specialized functions. A recent study using a form of brain scanning has produced evidence that young language learners learning two languages use the same part of the brain for both, whereas older learners use a different part of the brain for their second language than they used for their first (Kim, Relkin, Lee, & Hirsch, 1997).

The critical period idea is intuitively appealing, but it should be noted that much empirical research has focused primarily on pronunciation. Some analysis suggests that children who learn their second language before puberty do in fact acquire native-like pronunciation, unlike adults, who usually speak a second language with an accent. Larsen-Freeman and Long (1991) summarize the research on the effect of age on second language acquisition, commenting "younger is better in the most crucial area, ultimate attainment, with only quite young (child starters) being able to achieve accent-free, native-like performance" (p. 155).

According to Bialystok and Hakuta (1994), younger is indeed better, but with an interesting twist that aligns nicely with the new neurolinguistic findings described above. They suggest that if in fact there is a critical period, it is less likely to be related to brain lateralization and the onset of puberty at adolescence, and more likely to be the period before the age of five. They qualify that notion, commenting that "one reason why children younger than five years old behave like native speakers is that they *are* native speakers" (p. 79). In other words, before the age of five or so, children are acquiring a language as a native speaker might, and are not really second language learners at all.

The comparison of adults and children and the focus on pronunciation obscure the real issue for educators. What is of interest to us is whether

---

$\mathcal{L}$earning a New Language

To tell you the truth, the hardest thing about coming to this country wasn't the winter everyone warned me about—it was the language. If you had to choose the most tongue-twisting way of saying you love somebody or how much a pound for the ground round, then say it in English.

SOURCE: The mother, in *¡Yo!* by Julia Alvarez. Chapel Hill: Algonquin Books, 1997.

younger or older children are better at developing the kind of second language proficiency they need for school. And the answer to that question is complex. Collier (1987) points out, "It depends. It depends on the learner's cognitive style, socioeconomic background, formal schooling in first language, and many other factors" (p. 1). Collier goes on to conclude, however, that it is safe to say that children between the ages of eight and twelve acquire a second language faster than children between the ages of four and seven, which may be related to cognitive maturity and first language competence. Children past the age of twelve seem to slow down, and that may be because the demands made of them in school are out of keeping with the level of language that they bring to bear.

THE EFFECT OF PERSONALITY

If you have been a second language learner you may have found on occasion that your ability to use the language is enhanced after you've had a glass of wine in a relaxed, informal setting. It may surprise you to know that researchers have also noticed this phenomenon and have actually studied the effect of alcohol on second language performance. This is not as silly as it may appear at first glance, because it would be useful for us to understand the role of personality factors like inhibitions in second language learning.

If you are a person who can easily shed your inhibitions, you may be willing to take some of the risks involved in trying out a new language. Other personality characteristics may also affect your ability to learn a second language. For example, if you are a person with strong self-esteem, you may be well equipped to withstand some of the embarrassment that naturally occurs when you make language errors. If you are naturally outgoing, you may be likely to become involved in situations where you can use and practice your new language and facilitate its development (Brown, 1987).

Some caution is called for here: In the first place, it is difficult to define personality traits. Even with operational definitions, personality traits are difficult to measure. Nevertheless, it seems clear that individual psychological traits have an effect on the ability to learn a second language.

THE SOCIAL FACTORS

Communication is at the heart of language, and the need to establish communication is a powerful motivation for language development. Therefore, it is essential to consider the nature of interaction between people in social contexts and the effects of that interaction on second language acquisition.

In first language development, for example, it has been noted that motherese, or caretaker speech, is often ungrammatical. In one well-known study (Brown, Cazden, & Bellugi, 1973), it was found that parents do not correct statements made by their children if they are grammatically deficient, but do correct them if they are untrue. In other words, parents are more concerned with the content of communication than with form.

Richard-Amato (1988) points out: "When the child says 'Daddy home' for the first time, no one labels this a mistake.... Instead it is thought of as being ingenious and cute and the child is hugged or rewarded verbally" (p. 36). Caretakers are delighted by a child's verbalizations and are anxious to promote interaction that may facilitate language development. Likewise, in situations with second language learners or speakers, native speakers may alter or modify their speech to facilitate understanding and response. This has been called *foreigner-talk*. In general, second language learners may do well in settings that emphasize communication.

One observer (Seliger, 1977) has noted that small children will participate in and appear to enjoy interactions that may be difficult or impossible for them to comprehend, which may function as a way of generating input. It is possible that the inclination to initiate and maintain interaction may be a strategy that distinguishes successful second language learners. In other words, some people may be better than others at creating situations that generate input, which brings us back to the question of the effect of personality on language ability and demonstrates the links between the social and psychological aspects of second language learning.

Integrative Models of Second Language Acquisition

Sufficient information on second language acquisition exists to enable us to formulate hypothetical models of the process. Models can then provide frameworks for additional research and coherent instructional programs. The sections that follow discuss two theoretical approaches to second language acquisition. These are but a small sample of the ways this process has been analyzed, but the two theories described here are useful because they integrate psychological and social considerations.

THE ACQUISITION–LEARNING DISTINCTION

Stephen Krashen (1981) has proposed a distinction between *language acquisition* and *language learning*. Language acquisition, in informal terms, is picking up a language—learning it unconsciously from the social environment. Language learning, on the other hand, is learning a language or learning about a language in a formal sense, for example, in a classroom setting. According to Krashen's theory, children develop language through acquisition, by understanding language that is a little beyond their capabilities, presented by language providers who communicate with the child in a modified form.

These small increments of language, available to the learner when they are embedded in comprehensible input, are particularly accessible in nonthreatening, low anxiety situations. Krashen refers to the affective component of language learning as an *affective filter,* a kind of emotional barrier to language learning that must be lowered if acquisition is to take place.

Krashen suggests that language learning is different from language acquisition in the following way: Learning provides a *monitor,* which allows the learner to correct language output. This monitor, however, is useful only when the learner knows the appropriate language rule, has time to use it, and is focused on form, as in writing. In this framework, acquired language is viewed as more important and more useful than learned language in the quick give-and-take of ordinary communication. According to Krashen, in real communication situations, second language learners most often use the language they have acquired, rather than the language they have learned.

The distinction between learning and acquisition, the concept of the monitor, and the role of affective considerations may shed light on some of the issues currently debated in second language theory. The theoretical distinction between learning and acquisition and the monitor construct provide keys to the process in general. Krashen's theory suggests that transfer errors, or errors that reflect first language structures, appear when an individual is relying on the monitor. To the extent that an individual functions in an acquired-language mode, "errors" will replicate developmental errors.

The model also suggests answers to questions about specific variables. For example, it addresses the concern about the relationship between age and the ability to gain a second language. In the short run, older learners seem to gain competence in a second language more rapidly than young children. The model suggests that they may be better monitor users. On the other hand, children outperform adults in second language in the long run. Krashen's theory suggests that children are less likely to rely too heavily on the monitor and are less prone to the anxiety that often accompanies second language learning. Similarly, individual variation in second language ability can be explained in terms of both individual ability to use a monitor appropriately and quickly and individual willingness to take risks and rely on acquired language.

Krashen's theory has gained tremendous popularity among classroom teachers and has led to the development of innovative methodology that moves significantly away from grammar-translation and other traditional approaches. (The natural language approach, based on Krashen's theory, is discussed in Chapter 6.) At the same time, Krashen has drawn fire from critics of the model (Ellis, 1988; Larsen-Freeman & Long, 1991) who suggest that it is flawed because:

- The concept of an unbreachable distinction between acquisition and learning doesn't fit with what we already know about subconscious and conscious learning, which seem to exist on a continuum.
- Krashen doesn't really tell us what goes on cognitively during acquisition and learning.

- We cannot empirically test either the acquisition–learning distinction or the monitor construct.

Finally, Krashen's model places more emphasis on the importance of input than output. In Krashen's view, hypothesis testing is an internal process whereby learners match up input with the knowledge they already have about the language. From his perspective, output is mainly useful insofar as it generates input. Swain (1985), however, has suggested that output is essential to language acquisition. Talking to someone in a new language requires the speakers to use all the language resources they have to come up with language the listener can understand—something that might be called "comprehensible output" (Swain, 1985, p. 249).

If we assume that both input and output are essential to language acquisition, we are led to consider the dynamic interaction between the language learner and the social environment. The next section describes a theory that places interaction in a central role.

LANGUAGE LEARNERS AND LANGUAGE SPEAKERS INTERACT

In 1979, Lily Wong Fillmore completed a study of ten early primary school children, in which five Spanish speakers were paired with five English speakers for an hour of daily play time. The Spanish-speaking children in the study used similar strategies to acquire English in varying degrees, but no one was more successful than Nora. Wong Fillmore remarks, "The secret of Nora's spectacular success as a language learner can be found in the special combination of interests, inclinations, skills, temperament, needs, and motivations that comprised her personality" (p. 221). "Nora put herself in a position to receive maximum exposure to the new language" (p. 222).

Wong Fillmore (1985) suggests that three components are necessary for an effective language learning situation:

- The learners.
- The speakers of the language the learner wants to learn.
- The social setting that brings learners and speakers together.

Once the learners and the speakers have been brought together, three types of interactive processes take place. First, there are social processes. In social processes, learners assume that the language used is relevant to the immediate situation, and speakers cooperate with that assumption. Second, there are linguistic processes. Learners use what they already know about language to try to make sense out of the linguistic input they receive. And third, there are cognitive strategies that learners use to figure out the relationships between what is happening and the language being used. Nora made maximum use of the strategies Wong Fillmore describes. It's important to notice that Nora, like other young children, did not have a language learning agenda. Rather, she wanted to make friends and play with other children, and learned English as a concomitant to social involvement.

Wong Fillmore also suggests (1991) that the ability of language learners to utilize strategies is affected by the social context. She emphasizes that all the factors are interrelated and proposes that situations involving contact with speakers of the target language and consequently the amount and type of input a learner receives may be related to the age of the learner.

For example, in the United States, young newcomers attend school, where they are likely to meet English speakers and to have classroom experiences that provide them with comprehensible input in English. Older immigrants, however, often find jobs where coworkers share their primary language, which limits their exposure to English. Also, older learners may find it harder than younger ones to get the kind of interaction they need to develop a new language. Young children can manage their social interactions with language that is not very complex. In fact, very young children often play happily together even though they may not understand each other's language. Adults, on the other hand, cannot participate fully in social interaction without the use of language, so beginning speakers are at a social disadvantage.

Wong Fillmore's model proposes that variations in language learning may result from a complex relationship of differences in individual personalities, cognitive abilities, and social skills, as well as from the social context itself. Wong Fillmore's analysis emphasizes the dynamic role of social interaction in second language learning.

Summary

Traditionally it was assumed that children developed language through imitation and habit formation. Chomsky revolutionized thinking about language development by theorizing that we can explain original utterances only by assuming that children have an innate language learning device that enables them to deduce the rules of syntax. Subsequent theorists have suggested that children apply this rule-finding approach to the semantic and pragmatic systems of language as well.

Theorists in second language acquisition ask whether second languages are acquired by transfer of first language knowledge or through a developmental process that parallels first language acquisition. Krashen distinguishes between language learning and language acquisition in an attempt to explain why some research produces evidence of transfer and other research substantiates the developmental process in second language development. Wong Fillmore suggests that learners make use of cognitive, linguistic, and social strategies during social interactions to acquire a new language.

First language development and second language acquisition theories will enable teachers in dual language settings to make decisions about methodologies for first language development and second language instruction.

Questions to Think About and Discuss

1. Think about the pedagogical implications of Krashen's and Wong Fillmore's theories of second language acquisition. In other words, based on their theoretical frameworks, how would you best organize your classroom to maximize second language learning?

Activities

1. Record an audio or video of an interaction between a child age one to three and the child's parent. Identify the strategies the parent uses to facilitate the communication. For example, how does the parent acknowledge the child's role in the conversation? Does the parent repeat what the child says? Paraphrase or elaborate on the child's contribution. Identify any strategies the child uses to maintain or prolong the interaction. What stage of language development has the child reached? Give examples that support your choice.

2. Visit a classroom and observe an English as a second language lesson. Note the materials and the methods. What assumptions are being made in this setting about how people learn language? For example, does instruction mainly consist of oral pattern drills? Completion of grammar exercises?

3. Interview an immigrant who is learning English as a second language. How does this person view the process of second language learning: Is this person taking classes or learning the language informally? Is the process easy or difficult? What is the most difficult part of the process? In this person's view, what factors have facilitated the process; that is, what helped the most?

Suggestions for Further Reading

Bialystok, E. (Ed.). (1991). *Language processing in bilingual children.* Cambridge, UK: The Cambridge University Press.

The articles in this book contain descriptions of original research on bilingual children's acquisition of language. The chapter by Wong Fillmore, "Second-language learning in children: A model of language learning in social context," is an excellent summary of her longitudinal research and the conclusions she has drawn from it.

Bialystok, E., & Hakuta, K. (1994). *In other words: The science and psychology of second language acquisition.* New York: Basic Books.

An update on second language acquisition theory that brings together a variety of perspectives, organized around language, the brain, the mind, the self, and culture as the "channels that jointly comprise the ecosystem of language learning" (p. viii). Discussions of research offer insights into the complexity of second language learning. This is an extremely readable book, enhanced by anecdotes and reflections gleaned from the authors' own experiences that allow the reader to connect research and theory to everyday experiences.

Brown, H. D. (1987). *Principles of language learning and teaching* (2nd ed.). Englewood Cliffs, NJ: Prentice-Hall.
An update of a well-known book on second language learning, this edition provides clear, concise explanations of theories of second language acquisition. The book is enhanced by the addition of an "in the classroom" section at the end of each chapter that highlights second language teaching methodologies.

de Villiers, P. A., & de Villiers, J. G. (1979). *Early language.* Cambridge, MA: Harvard University Press.
An easy to read, straightforward discussion of the course of language development, this book is enlivened by samples of children's language.

Gass, S. M., & Selinker, L. (1994). *Second language acquisition: An introductory course.* Hillsdale, NJ: Lawrence Erlbaum.
A detailed, comprehensive, multidisciplinary analysis of adult second language acquisition.

Gleason, J. B. (Ed.). (1985). *The development of language.* Columbus, OH: Merrill.
Ten articles that provide an overview of theory and research of first language development across the entire life span. The chapter on language in society (Warren-Leubecker and Bohannon) is an excellent summary of research regarding acquisition of the social rules of language.

Krashen, S. D. (2003). *Explorations in language acquisition and use: The Taipei lectures.* Portsmouth, NH: Heinemann.
Based largely on a series of lectures that the author presented in 2001 at National Taipei University in Taiwan, this book provides an excellent review of Krashen's theories, along with a discussion of comprehensible output and its role in second language acquisition.

Larsen-Freeman, D., & Long, M. H. (1991). *An introduction to second language research.* New York: Longman.
Just about everything you wanted to know about second language acquisition is included in this well-organized book, which explains second language acquisition research methods, describes and critiques prevailing theories, and discusses implications for instruction.

Lightbown, P., & Spada, N. (1993). *How languages are learned.* Oxford, UK: Oxford University Press.
Contains an overview of theories of first language development and second language acquisition, followed by a discussion of approaches to teaching second language that emphasizes the relevance of research to practice.

Miller, T. (2007). *How I learned English.* Washington, DC: National Geographic.
A fascinating collection of very short essays by Latino writers, scholars, and professionals describing their encounters and struggles with English. In the foreword, the well-known journalist Ray Suarez comments that if you have ever tried to learn a new language, "you will recognize yourself somewhere in these pages" (p. xiv).

Ventriglia, L. (1982). *Conversations of Miguel and Maria: How children learn English as a second language: Implications for classroom teaching.* Reading, MA: Addison-Wesley.
Based on analysis of children's conversations, this book analyzes second language acquisition strategies and presents classroom methods based on those strategies. Emphasis is on the importance of social context in second language acquisition.

chapter 5

Primary Language Instruction for Limited English Proficient Students

Amanda is a second-grade student in a private school in an affluent suburban area. Her father is a computer software engineer and her mother is an attorney. In school, Amanda receives instruction in her subject areas in English; she studies French as a second language. In second grade, French is also used for art and social studies as well as related cultural activities and events. As Amanda progresses toward sixth grade her French instruction will increase, and she will develop speaking, reading, and writing skills.

Lilia was born in the United States of parents who were born in Mexico and speak no English. Lilia attends second grade in a public school in an economically disadvantaged urban area. When she entered kindergarten, Lilia was assessed as limited English proficient. She is enrolled in a program that offers her subject area instruction in Spanish, accompanied by daily classes in English as a second language. In addition, Lilia receives social studies and physical education instruction in English and participates in schoolwide activities and assemblies where English is used. As soon as Lilia can score above the 37th percentile on a standardized achievement test administered in English, she will be placed in a classroom where no Spanish is used.

Few people question the value of additive bilingualism for English-speaking children. Amanda's friends and family are impressed by her ability to speak French, and many have expressed the wish that they had received a comparable education. But controversy surrounds the idea of providing public school instruction for limited English proficient students in their native language while they learn English as a second language. Lilia is expected, appropriately, to learn English. While she may maintain her ability to speak Spanish, it is unlikely that she will ever become fully bilingual and biliterate.

This subtractive bilingual scenario will not only limit her abilities in Spanish, but may have a negative impact on her abilities in English as well.

This chapter will present a five-point rationale for providing primary language instruction for limited English proficient children and will outline instructional approaches for implementing primary language support in the classroom.

A Rationale for Primary Language Instruction

TRANSFER OF CONCEPTS AND SKILLS

The construction of a rationale for primary language instruction can be approached from several directions. We will begin by responding to the often expressed criticism that classroom time spent in the primary language is wasteful. That idea is based on the assumption that languages are learned and maintained separately in the human brain. There is no evidence to support that model of language learning, which has been called the *Separate Underlying Proficiency model* (Cummins, 1994). In fact, research supports the opposite notion, or *Common Underlying Proficiency model* of language learning, which assumes that skills and concepts learned in one language transfer to another.

How Does Transfer Work? Reading illustrates a process where there is significant transfer of behaviors, skills, knowledge, and attitudes from one language to another. A detailed analysis of the skills and subskills that comprise literacy would be out of place here, but consider a few of the concepts that provide the foundation for reading. You may find it difficult at first to identify them, because reading is highly automatic for literate adults!

Look at Figure 5.1, and try to read the Hebrew word. You are given some hints about direction and about sound–symbol correspondence. As you worked out the word, were you engaged in learning to read? This exercise, using a language with an unfamiliar alphabet, has demonstrated that when you read in a new language, you apply literacy skills you already have to language-specific information.

Now consider some of the components of reading. Reading requires the understanding that print carries meaning. We develop this awareness in children through reading readiness instruction. Adults read to children, point out signs and other sources of information in print, label objects in the classroom, and teach them to read and write their names.

Other prereading skills include directionality, sequencing, and the ability to distinguish among shapes and sounds. Those skills are not language bound; they transfer, as does the knowledge that written symbols correspond to sounds and can be decoded in a particular direction and order.

● FIGURE *5.1* Reading a New Language

Hebrew may seem baffling to many of you because it uses an unfamiliar alphabet. Using the language-specific information provided, try to read the Hebrew word. After you have read it, think about the literacy skills you already have that helped you.

Language-specific information:

- *Direction*—Read Hebrew from right to left.
- *Sequence*—Some vowels are placed under consonants. Read the consonant first, and then the vowel.
- *Sounds and symbols*—Here are some correspondences that you will need to know:

שׁ = *sh*, as in *shoe*

ל = *l*, as in *lamp*

ם = *m*, as in *mouse*

ָ = *o*, as in *tonic* or *cot*

וֹ = *o*, as in *home* or *bone*

Try to read this word (turn the page upside down for the answer):

The word you read is *shalom*, which means "greetings," or "peace."

In addition to basic skills, reading habits and attitudes have a significant impact on an individual's ability to read. A sense of being a literate, capable person who can listen, concentrate, and complete a task transfers from one language to another (Thonis, 1983).

Reading is only one of the many areas where transfer from one language to another is significant. Content areas can be studied in any language, and the concepts are added to the common underlying cognitive store. From a pedagogical viewpoint, the message is clear. Instructional time spent in a child's primary language is not wasted. Skills, concepts, and knowledge acquired in one's first language will be readily available in one's second.

PRIMARY LANGUAGE DEVELOPMENT AND SECOND LANGUAGE ACQUISITION

Providing instruction in a child's primary language enhances acquisition of a second language. Unlike the notion of transfer, this idea seems counterintuitive, and yet it is a related concept, grounded in the Common Underlying Proficiency model.

Research has demonstrated (see Cummins, 1981, for a review) that older immigrant children, with substantial educational preparation in their own language, fare better in achieving second language proficiency than younger immigrant children. Evidently, the older children have a well-developed conceptual base in their primary language as a result of their previous schooling and literacy. Learning a second language, for them, is a matter of translating concepts and ideas that are already firmly established. They need only learn new labels, unlike younger children who face the more difficult task of having to learn basic concepts in a new and unfamiliar language.

For example, basic concepts involving spatial relationships are often reinforced in preschool or kindergarten as part of prereading and early mathematics. For small children concepts like *over, under, behind,* and *around* may be unfamiliar. Learning them in a new language is difficult. For adults, who have internalized spatial relationships, they are relatively simple. Learning them in a new language requires only learning new words for relationships that have long become conceptually automatic.

The apparent contradiction that instructional time spent in a first language facilitates acquisition of a second is resolved by the Common Underlying Proficiency model. If we think in terms of a bank or reserve of language, with all deposits adding to the balance, we see quickly that a child who is poor in one language will be poor in another. Primary language instruction is the easiest way to increase a child's language wealth.

STUDENTS NEED TO DEVELOP CALP

Earlier, we discussed the distinction between Basic Interpersonal Communicative Skills (BICS) and Cognitive Academic Language Proficiency (CALP), theoretical constructs developed by Cummins. BICS refers to the basic language skills necessary for communication in context-embedded settings, whereas CALP is the type of language proficiency needed to function in a classroom environment, where required tasks are context-reduced.

Students need to develop CALP in order to function adequately in academic situations. Relying on the ideas that concepts and skills transfer from one language to another and that students with a strong cognitive base will easily make the transition to a second language, the thesis that CALP should be developed in a student's first language follows.

Critics often suggest that language minority students should spend no more than three years in primary language programs. Cummins has suggested (1981) that it takes an average of five to seven years for children to develop

CALP in any language. Recent longitudinal research by Thomas and Collier (1997) reinforces that assertion. They analyzed approximately 700,000 school records from five school districts across the United States with large populations of language minority students. They conclude that in the absence of any primary language instruction it takes seven to ten years for a non-native speaker of English to reach native-like age and grade-level performance. Students who arrive in the United States with two to three years of schooling in their country of origin, in other words, with two to three years of primary language instruction, reach age and grade-level performance after five to six years.

Finally, the data indicate that students in high-quality bilingual programs need four to seven years to reach the performance level of native speakers. Clearly primary language instruction should be seen as more than a temporary vehicle for content coverage. For language minority children, primary language instruction is a tool for conceptual development that will enrich their ability to function in both first and second languages.

EFFECTS OF BILINGUALISM ON ACHIEVEMENT

It was suggested previously that early research in the field of bilingualism led to the conclusion that knowing more than one language was an educational handicap. Some recent studies, however, have indicated that bilingual children have greater cognitive flexibility and better language skills than monolingual children. This is logical, since bilingual children have more opportunities to play and work with language than do their monolingual counterparts.

Inconsistencies in studies on bilingualism have perplexed researchers for some time. The "threshold hypothesis" (Cummins, 1994) suggests that positive effects of bilingualism are associated with high levels of proficiency in more than one language. In other words, children who have acquired a high degree of proficiency in a second language while maintaining their abilities in a first show positive effects compared to those with partial or limited bilingualism. Once again, we are led to the conclusions that additive bilingualism has positive effects and that language minority children should be provided with instruction in their primary languages.

PRIMARY LANGUAGE INSTRUCTION AND SELF-CONCEPT

The notion of self-concept is intangible and complex. A person's self-concept is made up of an intricate network of factors, including:

- *Comparisons*—"How do I compare with other people?"
- *Perceptions of others*—"How do I think other people see me?"
- *Ideals*—"How would I be if I could be any way I choose?"

People develop their self-concept through the experiences they have with others. Some individuals have a particularly powerful impact on the self-concept of children. Parents play an important role in self-concept development, as do teachers (Amoriggi & Gefteas, 1981).

Children are natural sociologists and sociolinguists, well aware of attitudes in their environment regarding their culture and language. Children who perceive negative attitudes in the school setting toward their first language will become involved in subtractive bilingualism. Bilingualism is correlated to positive academic effects in situations where both languages have perceived value in the home and community (Cummins & Swain, 1986).

According to Thomas and Collier, the sociocultural context of schooling is an important factor in the schooling of language minority students. Two-way programs that encourage integration of native speakers of English with language minority students enhance the status of the minority language (Thomas & Collier, 1997). In order for bilingual programs to succeed, schools must promote the idea that the language children bring to school is prestigious and appropriate for use by educated people.

—Overall, What Does the Research Indicate?

There have been several attempts to evaluate the effects of bilingual programs on a large scale. Two well-known and often cited studies are a national evaluation of Title VII funded projects completed by the American Institute for Research (Danoff, Coles, McLaughlin, & Reynolds, 1977a, 1977b, 1978) and a study commissioned by the Office of Planning, Budget and Evaluation of the United States Department of Education (Baker & de Kanter, 1981).

Neither of those studies produced evidence favoring bilingual education, but both engendered heated controversy. Criticism has generally centered around research design and methodology. Two important factors call the results of the studies into question:

1. Many programs are labeled *bilingual,* but there may be a low degree of comparability among them. Immersion programs, as well as English as a second language pull-out programs, may be labeled *bilingual* by administrators seeking compliance with state and federal regulations, or researchers who fail to understand the distinctions. In some areas, shortages of adequately trained staff result in assignment of monolingual teachers to "bilingual" classrooms where primary language support may be limited or nonexistent.
2. An effective research design requires that programs be randomly assigned to sites and then evaluated. There are no studies where this condition, called *random assignment to condition,* has been met. Consequently, program evaluation results are difficult to interpret.

The Baker and de Kanter analysis, which was actually a synthesis of 28 smaller studies, has been reanalyzed and compared using statistical processes that control for differences in the nature of the data (Willig, 1985). The reinterpretation provides evidence that supports bilingual education and the use of the primary language in the classroom.

In a later article, Rossell and Baker (1996) analyzed 72 studies in an attempt to compare transitional bilingual education, defined as a program that develops literacy skills and teaches content areas in the students' primary language along with graduated ESL instruction, to three other types of the programs: *submersion* (or *sink-or-swim*), *structured immersion,* which offers instruction in English with primary language support "in the rare instances when the student cannot complete a task without it" (p. 10), and ESL pull-out. They concluded that transitional bilingual education was rarely better than regular classroom instruction, and never better than structured immersion.

Krashen (1996) reexamined all the studies analyzed by Rossell and Baker that could be found in the published literature, concluding that their overall study is seriously flawed. He points out that Rossell and Baker were willing to include studies about programs that were not spelled out in any detail, but merely called *bilingual.* Crawford also notes (1997) that Rossell and Baker ignore the use of primary language where it suits their purpose, lauding one successful program for its English-only approach, when in fact the use of English was supported with nearly a half day of primary language instruction. In other words, if a program worked, they chose to not call it a *bilingual program.*

Furthermore, Rossell and Baker started out with 300 studies and ruled out those they found methodologically unacceptable. Krashen suggests that several studies ruled out showed results that would support the use of primary language in a bilingual program model. Finally, Crawford (1997) points out that "Rossell and Baker relied heavily on program evaluations from the 1970s, when bilingual pedagogies were considerably less developed than they are today" (1997, p. 36).

Clearly program research on the benefits of primary language instruction for language minority students is inconclusive. The issues are further clouded by politics. The U.S. Department of Education has repeatedly questioned the value of dual language instruction and has taken steps to expand funding for English-only programs. On the other hand, a report published by the U.S. General Accounting Office (1987a) supports dual language instruction.

Basic research on bilingualism, however, leaves little room for doubt as to the value of primary language instruction for language minority students (Hakuta, 1985). In communities that show a high regard for two languages and in educational programs that encourage additive bilingualism, knowing two languages is positively associated with intellectual and academic achievement (Cummins & Swain, 1986).

If Primary Language Instruction, Then How?

Some experts have suggested that for limited English proficient students, primary language instruction should be carried out for as much as 70 percent of the school day in early grades (Legarreta-Marcaida, 1981) with English taught as a second language. As children master English, content instruction in English can be increased. A ratio of 50-50 English and other language through sixth grade sets the stage for additive bilingualism, which opens the door to academic achievement.

Given the obvious constraints of a school day, how is it possible to deliver instruction in two languages across the curriculum? Several methods have been proposed.

SEPARATION OF LANGUAGES

Languages may be separated by time, in alternate-day or half-day formats. In a team teaching situation, or when a teacher works with an aide, languages may be separated by person, with each person using one language exclusively. Languages may be separated by place, with rooms or classroom areas designated for particular languages.

Two-way immersion programs require that languages be separated by person, and often by place as well. Two-way immersion teachers are bilingual but early primary children often assume that their teachers speak only one language, even though teachers respond to students' questions and comments in both. It's possible that young children don't yet conceptualize receptive ability, that is, understanding a language, as part of "speaking" a language.

Languages may also be separated by subject. When languages are separated by subject, the ethnic or minority language is often used for areas such as social studies and art, with science and mathematics reserved for English. This is language stereotyping and should be avoided, because it damages the prestige of the minority language. Likewise, when languages are assigned by person, it is often the teacher's aide who speaks the minority language. Although skilled aides play a necessary and important role in dual language classrooms, a scenario where authority figures in a school speak only English, and only subordinates use the minority language, damages minority language prestige.

CONCURRENT TRANSLATION

Commonly used but not well understood, concurrent translation involves using two languages interchangeably during instruction. There have been several criticisms of this approach:

- Teachers often code-switch, assuming that they are engaged in concurrent translation. While code-switching is linguistically coherent, it is pedagogically random—that is, the switches a bilingual speaker may make in ordinary conversation do not necessarily meet instructional objectives for language development or delivery of content.
- In practice, concurrent translation often approximates direct translation; students quickly learn to tune out the language they don't understand, waiting for the information in the language they do.

- Concurrent translation can be strenuous and tiring for a teacher to implement. Two teachers, or a teacher and an aide, can implement the method, assuming the availability of sufficient staffing.
- Teachers often overestimate the amount of time spent using the children's primary language and, in fact, spend a disproportionate amount of time speaking English.

The New Concurrent Approach (NCA), developed by Rodolfo Jacobson (1987), suggests using a structured form of code-switching for delivery of content instruction. In Jacobson's method, language switches are carefully planned. There are no intrasentential switches, and all switches are made at the completion of a thought group. Planned switches are justifiable for:

- Conceptual reinforcement and review, to assure that all children have mastered the lesson material.
- Lexical enrichment, to give children the vocabulary necessary to discuss a particular subject in both languages.
- Appropriateness for curriculum—that is, ethnically related events or subjects may be treated in the appropriate language.

PREVIEW-REVIEW

The preview-review approach incorporates elements of NCA. In preview-review, content areas are previewed in one language, presented in the other, and reviewed in the first. This method may be particularly useful at the upper primary and secondary levels, where content materials such as science or social studies textbooks may not be readily available in minority languages.

Note that concurrent and preview-review approaches are appropriate for content instruction. Language development in either language and second language instruction should be delivered in the target language.

Cooperative Learning

Cooperative learning is a classroom management strategy that departs from traditional whole-class instructional formats and opens up opportunities for first and second language development. In cooperative learning, the class is divided into teams, whose members work together and rely on one another to learn concepts, solve problems, and complete projects (Kagan, 1986).

A cooperative strategy may be as simple as peer tutoring, where students assist each other with drills and practice for material such as spelling words or math facts. Or cooperative learning can involve teamwork to complete complex projects that require planning, research, and implementation.

There are more chances for students to communicate in a cooperative format than in traditional settings. In addition, the quality of communication is higher as students try to negotiate content-related meaning (Kagan, 1986; Long & Porter, 1985), because cooperative learning creates two-way tasks where each participant has information that the others need.

Cooperative learning models provide rich communication opportunities for limited English proficient students. For example, *Finding Out/ Descubrimiento* (Cohen, 1986) uses science and math content to teach critical thinking skills. Students are assigned to task groups with rotating roles such as facilitator, safety officer, and reporter. Groups work on problems in learning centers in areas such as optics, electricity, and water. Materials are provided in English and Spanish, and bilingual students serve as translators. Students can complete their activities working in either language.

Cooperative learning strategies do not involve explicit manipulation of language. Primary language use is permitted in cooperative grouping, but the strategy seems to promote acquisition of the dominant language— English. In that sense, cooperative learning strategies might be classified as a second language teaching approach. It is clear, however, that cooperative strategies produce more opportunities for content-related communication among students than a traditional, teacher-centered classroom environment. Thus they enhance academic learning. In addition, cooperative strategies motivate students and promote a positive affective climate. These qualities make cooperative learning particularly appropriate for a dual language classroom.

Summary

Program research provides evidence of the value of primary language instruction for language minority students, but is inconclusive. Basic research on bilingualism, however, provides strong support for the value of additive bilingualism. Primary language instruction is justifiable because:

- Concepts and skills learned in one language transfer to another.
- Primary language development facilitates second language acquisition.
- Students need time to develop cognitive academic language proficiency.
- Proficiency in two languages has positive effects on achievement.
- Primary language instruction enhances self-concept.

Primary language instruction can be offered in a variety of formats including:

- Separation of languages by person, place, time, or subject.
- Concurrent translation.
- Preview-review.
- Cooperative learning strategies.

Questions to Think About and Discuss

1. Imagine that you are going to create a primary (K–6) school from the ground up. Among its intended outcomes, this school has as a goal that all its students will be bilingual and biliterate by the time they finish sixth grade. Under ideal circumstances, what kind of program would you recommend? What is your rationale?

2. Following up on the first question, what kinds of programs would you recommend in middle and high school for students who graduate from your ideal school? Why?

Activities

1. Visit a classroom within a dual language instructional program. What language strategy does the teacher use in content areas? How does that fit the program model?

2. Monitor language use in the classroom during the observation period:
   - What percentage of time is each language in use?
   - What are the purposes for which each language is used? Which language is used for instruction in each area? What language is used for reinforcement and praise? For discipline? For instructions?
   - Are language switches purposeful? What purposes can you discern?
   - Are bulletin boards and other classroom displays bilingual?
   - Are materials available in both languages? Are the materials comparable in quantity and quality?
   - Which personnel use which language? How proficient are instructors and assistants in the classroom languages?
   - Overall, are languages assigned equal value in this classroom?

3. Develop an instructional unit in social studies, science, or mathematics that utilizes cooperative learning strategies.

4. Many parents, concerned that their children learn English as quickly as possible, are uneasy about the use of primary language in school. Prepare a PowerPoint presentation for a parent group that explains the benefits of primary language instruction.

Suggestions for Further Reading

Cummins, J. (1994). Primary language instruction and the education of language minority students. In California State Department of Education (Ed.), *Schooling and language minority students: A theoretical framework* (2nd ed.) (pp. 3–46). Los Angeles: Evaluation, Dissemination, and Assessment Center, California State University, Los Angeles.

Cummins's article sets forth a theoretical framework with an analysis of supporting research that provides a rationale for providing primary language instruction for limited English proficient students. This article, along with others in this new edition, also explores the social, political, and cultural dynamics of schooling for language minority students.

Gonzalez, A., & Guerrero, M. (1983). *A cooperative/interdependent approach to bilingual education.* Hollister, CA: Hollister School District.

This handbook provides detailed practical information about the jigsaw method of cooperative learning. Sample lessons, time lines, and record-keeping forms assist teachers in implementing the jigsaw process in their classrooms.

Kagan, S. (1986). Cooperative learning and sociocultural factors in schooling. In California State Department of Education (Ed.), *Beyond language: Social and cultural factors in schooling language minority students* (pp. 231–298). Los Angeles: Evaluation, Dissemination, and Assessment Center, California State University, Los Angeles.

A comprehensive introduction to cooperative learning strategies, this article overviews research results of cooperative learning with special attention to the outcomes of cooperative learning strategies for minority students. The article is particularly useful because it contains an overview of training models and resources available for teachers and schools.

Krashen, S. D. (1996). *Under attack: The case against bilingual education.* Culver City, CA: Language Education Associates.

This succinct book is a collection of articles previously published by the author that address commonplace criticisms of bilingual education. Krashen provides data to demonstrate that the students who appear to succeed without bilingual education often have what he calls "de facto bilingual education." Chapter 4, "Does Literacy Transfer?" supports the importance of teaching children to read in their first language.

chapter 6

Second Language Instruction

The term *English as a second language* (ESL) often evokes images on a continuum—ranging from a program separate from a dual language instructional model, involving high-intensity English training, to minimal "pull-out" instruction where limited English proficient children are taken out of their classroom to receive ESL instruction for a small portion of the school day.

Some people erroneously assume that there is a distinct difference between second language instruction and bilingual instruction. Second language instruction, however, is an integrated part of any dual language instructional model. Most dual language instructional programs target limited English proficient students and have an ESL component. However, programs that include monolingual English speakers now exist, and they provide an opportunity for them to learn a second language as well.

Language development is basic to schooling, and, as we have already seen, first and second language development can take place in the context of many models. Apart from language development through content instruction, approaches have been developed that focus on second language instruction *per se.* Specific second language methodologies will not be addressed in detail in this chapter, since that is more appropriate to a methods text. This chapter will briefly review traditional and innovative language teaching approaches.

A NOTE ABOUT TERMINOLOGY

Literature about language instruction sometimes refers to *foreign language instruction,* such as English as a foreign language (EFL), and also to *second language instruction,* as in English as a second language (ESL). Instructors generally use the term *second language* when it is a language widely used in the immediate social environment. A *foreign* language is one that the student is not likely to encounter in the social environment outside the classroom.

For purposes of dual language instruction it is convenient and logical to refer to *second language instruction.* Programs in the United States are generally geared to teach English to students with limited proficiency in that language. English is clearly a dominant language in the United States and is available in the general social environment. Many programs have two-way goals as well, intending either to restore ethnic languages to children whose families have lost them or to give children in general the opportunity to acquire a new language. Usually the languages offered are present to some extent in the United States, which is a multilingual environment. These languages can therefore be referred to as second languages.

Literature that refers to teaching EFL has information that is relevant and applicable to second language instruction. Regardless of the source of information, we will use *second language instruction* as an inclusive term.

Early Viewpoints on Second Language Instruction

GRAMMAR-TRANSLATION

It is common to hear someone say, "I studied French (or Spanish, or German) for years in school, but I can't speak a word." Many of those people were probably instructed with the grammar-translation method, which focuses on learning language rules and working with written texts. Seldom successful, the grammar-translation method is a remnant of the study of Latin grammar, which was highly valued in the Middle Ages. Medieval scholars, however, pursued the intricacies of Latin grammar for its own sake, not necessarily to gain proficiency in the use of Latin. It is likely that the skills they had in day-to-day Latin were gained through direct contact with the language in communicative situations.

As the use of Latin as a vehicle for everyday conversation declined, Latin texts were increasingly translated into vernaculars. The prestige, however, attached to the study of Latin and Greek persisted, as did the idea that the development of grammar skills transferred to other areas of thinking. Resistance to formal study of modern foreign languages continued until well into the eighteenth century, and the grammar-translation approach prevailed despite attempts to devise alternatives (Grittner, 1969).

THE SEARCH FOR ALTERNATIVE APPROACHES

Diller (1978) tells the fascinating story of Francois Gouin, a nineteenth-century Latin teacher from France, who decided to teach himself German. Gouin began by memorizing a German grammar book and 248 irregular verbs, an effort that took him ten days. Despite these efforts, he was unable to understand a word of spoken German. Convinced, however, that he was on the right track and only needed to broaden his knowledge, he set about memorizing 800 German roots. At that point, unable to engage in even simple conversation or to translate written German, he purchased a dictionary and proceeded to memorize 30,000 words in 30 days, an effort that all but destroyed his eyesight, but failed to make him proficient in German.

Imagine his surprise to find that his three-year-old nephew had learned to speak French during a three-month vacation in France! Focusing his attention on his nephew's accomplishments, Gouin developed the *Series Method,* which involves learning a new language through an ordered series of concepts that introduce new vocabulary and grammatical patterns.

Gouin's method was devised on the basis of limited information about language learning, since he focused exclusively on his nephew and never investigated children's language development strategies further. However, his insights about the need to provide real context for language teaching were brilliant, and his early efforts certainly demonstrate the lengths to which people have gone to master a new language.

Another nineteenth-century language instructor, Maximilian Berlitz, literally stumbled on his approach. Berlitz ran a small language school in Providence, Rhode Island. Incapacitated by illness, he hired a French instructor through the mail to teach his students. It was only when the instructor arrived in Providence that Berlitz discovered that his new employee spoke only French. With no alternative, he sent the Frenchman off to do the best he could. When he was sufficiently recovered to visit his school, Berlitz was astonished to discover his students happily conversing in French with far more skill than they had ever acquired before. Based on that revelation, Berlitz developed the *Direct Method,* an approach that immerses students in the second language (Simon, 1980). In the Direct Method, the student's first language is not allowed in the classroom. Materials are presented through a variety of media in an orderly progression, and grammar rules are taught inductively. Although Berlitz gets surprisingly little mention in scholarly discussions of second language instruction, he is a pioneer in immersion methods, and large numbers of students are enrolled in Berlitz schools around the world today.

Late nineteenth- and early twentieth-century attempts to replace grammar-translation with more effective means of second language instruction generally failed to gain popularity. The grammar-translation approach held sway until the onset of World War II.

Modern Approaches to Second Language Instruction

THE AUDIOLINGUAL APPROACH

World War II raised public awareness about the inadequacies of language teaching in the United States. Faced with a pressing need for personnel with skills in many languages, some of which had never been studied or codified, the U.S. Army developed a revolutionary approach to second language instruction that was called the *audiolingual method.*

The audiolingual approach is based on the assumption that language development requires habit formation and reinforcement. It involves students in language activities that include three components:

- Practice and memorization of situation-based dialogues.
- Drills to reinforce the major patterns in the dialogues.
- Conversation with a native speaker about the topic of the dialogue.

The audiolingual approach was successful and caught on rapidly with some modifications. Some deviations from the original format enhanced the methodology. For example, the original program focused exclusively on the development of oral skills. Teachers quickly found that written materials were useful—especially for adult learners who had often invented their own writing systems as an aid to memorization.

On the other hand, audiolingual approaches are sometimes implemented using the dialogue and drill components, while eliminating the conversation component of the original. In view of recent findings about second language acquisition, it may well be that the real communicative situations were an essential and productive aspect of the Army's method.

OTHER RECENT APPROACHES

New directions in thinking about second language acquisition unleashed by Chomsky (see Chapter 4), along with dissatisfaction about the state of language instruction, have led to the development of many new approaches to second language instruction. In general, second language instruction has moved away from the tight restrictions inherent in the audiolingual approach and now tends to focus more on the active involvement of students in the language acquisition process.

Modern approaches reflect the idea that language acquisition is a natural and creative process that involves the student in thinking in the new language. Production of the new language arises naturally when a student is ready to begin to speak. There are several new approaches that have caught the attention of dual and second language instructors. Some may be surprising, since they represent a departure from the language teaching most of us have experienced. These approaches focus on providing language instruction in nonthreatening environments and emphasize communication rather than correct form or knowledge of rules. The following brief descriptions will provide a flavor of recent innovative approaches to second language instruction.

Total Physical Response (TPR). Developed by James Asher, TPR is based on the assumption that a second language is internalized through a process of codebreaking similar to first language development and that the process allows for a long period of listening and developing comprehension prior to production. Students are given a period of several weeks or months during which they are not asked to produce language and need only respond to commands that require physical movement (Asher, 1982).

Suggestopedia. Developed by Georgi Lozanov, Suggestopedia relies on the assumption that it is possible to increase our ability to learn language by tapping the paraconscious reserves of the brain. Lozanov's method provides a rich acquisition environment; careful attention is paid to the affective dimension of language acquisition. Lessons take place in a pleasant and informal setting.

The culminating component of each Suggestopedia session is unique. Instructors, trained in psychology and art, read language selections in careful synchronization with musical selections. Students prepare for the session by engaging in relaxation techniques derived from yogic meditation and breathing exercises. These exercises activate the subconscious mind and allow students to tap reserves of super memory (Lozanov, 1982). While many aspects of Suggestopedia would be difficult to implement in the public school setting, innovative aspects of this approach have been incorporated into second language teaching programs with excellent results (Bancroft, 1978).

Counseling-Learning. Developed by Charles Curran, the Counseling-Learning approach is actually an instructional theory that is applicable to a wide variety of subjects. The approach suggests that basic precepts of counseling are broadly applicable to all learning situations. Curran chose to apply his thinking to language teaching, since it appeared to be an area where many techniques were unsuccessful. In addition, language teaching is a fruitful area for research because gains can be readily tested.

Counseling-Learning assumes that there are parallels between a counseling situation and an instructional situation. The learner, or "client," may feel threatened and insecure and may experience conflict and frustration. The role of the teacher or "counselor" is to empathize with the student (client) and to provide the learner with skills that will eliminate frustration. Students work in small groups and initiate conversations in their native languages, which are then translated by language experts who sit outside the circle. As students become less anxious and more proficient, conversations become more personal and more linguistically complex, and students require less translation assistance from the experts. Tape recordings of the sessions and brief sessions on points of grammar provide opportunities for review and clarification.

Curran's research indicates that students who attempted new languages with the counseling method made favorable progress when compared with students who participated in traditional college language classes (Curran, 1982).

The Notional-Functional Approach. Although TPR, Suggestopedia, and Counseling-Learning have been called *interpersonal approaches* (Brown, 1980) and reflect a strong concern for the importance of the affective variable in second language learning, the Notional-Functional approach considers the pragmatics of language. A Notional-Functional syllabus organizes instruction around the functions of language. Students learn appropriate communication strategies for a variety of situations. For example, a Notional-Functional syllabus might provide students with opportunities to learn to agree, argue, question, or compliment.

The Natural Approach. Stephen Krashen's theory of language acquisition (see Chapter 4) inspired the development of the Natural Approach (Krashen & Terrell, 1983) to second language teaching. The Natural Approach is of particular interest to instructors at the primary level, since it has greater practical applicability at the elementary level than many of the other new communication-based approaches, such as Suggestopedia. We will, therefore, outline the Natural Approach in some detail.

According to Krashen, language acquisition will occur when certain conditions are met. The Natural Approach (Terrell, 1981) meets those conditions by:

- Providing comprehensible input.
- Focusing on communication of messages.
- Creating low anxiety situations.

The Natural Approach assumes that speech emerges in four natural and distinct stages:

- Preproduction, when students communicate primarily with gesture and actions.
- Early production, when students begin to use one- or two-word utterances, or short phrases.
- Speech emergence, when students use longer phrases or complete sentences.
- Intermediate fluency, when students can engage in conversation and produce connected narratives.

Instruction in the Natural Approach is organized according to these progressive levels of language acquisition. At the outset the teacher supplies a lot of comprehensible input, but does not demand production from the students. As students progress, the teacher introduces new receptive vocabulary and encourages higher levels of language use. Reading and writing activities are incorporated into the curriculum when students have reached intermediate fluency.

The Natural Approach promotes basic proficiency and is particularly appropriate for primary levels. However, overreliance on approaches that do not explicitly address syntax may result in fossilization or the internalization of incorrect forms. As students advance in their second language, therefore, teachers generally supplement the Natural Approach with instruction in language arts areas such as reading, writing, and critical thinking.

Integrating Language and Content: Specially Designed Academic Instruction in English

Recently, educators have begun to understand that language learning is most meaningful when it is tied to content instruction. Snow, Met, and Genesee (1989) suggest that language development is facilitated when it is combined with content area instruction because:

- Cognitive development and language development are inextricably tied, especially for young children.
- School subjects are what children need to talk about in school, so content area provides both the motivation and the opportunity for meaningful communication.
- Tying language development to content area allows students to develop the kind of language that is used in school. (See Chapter 5 for a discussion of Cognitive Academic Language Proficiency.)

Increasingly, teachers are utilizing an approach called *Specially Designed Academic Instruction in English (SDAIE)* to assist second language learners in developing their abilities in English while they master the concepts and skills in the required curriculum.

SDAIE is particularly useful in situations that arise where primary language instruction is difficult or impossible—for example:

- Bilingual staff is unavailable to meet all students' needs, and/or
- The classroom contains students with a variety of primary languages other than English.

In general, SDAIE combines the important components of quality teaching with approaches based on second language acquisition theory. Properly implemented, SDAIE addresses all areas of instruction, including planning, classroom management, lesson delivery, and assessment.

PLANNING

Recent research (Short, 2002), demonstrates that teachers, even teachers with training in second language instruction, emphasize content and tasks over language. In SDAIE, however, language is seen as the vehicle for content, and vice versa. Consequently, teachers should plan each lesson to meet not only the curricular objectives related to content, but also to include appropriate language objectives. Met (1994) distinguishes between content-obligatory and content-compatible language objectives. *Content-obligatory objectives* are those that must be included to make a lesson comprehensible for students. So, for example, second language learners studying the Civil War need to be familiar with words like *enslavement, federalism,* and *emancipation.*

Content-compatible objectives are those that can be tied into the subject matter to assist students in language growth and development but aren't mandatory for students to understand the subject at hand. In the case of the Civil War, a teacher could, for example, emphasize the use of conditional phrases: "What would have happened if John Wilkes Booth had failed to assassinate the president?" Use of the conditional can be incorporated into almost any subject area and isn't required for students to learn about the Civil War. Based on an assessment of students' language development and needs, however, a teacher might want to include this content-compatible objective.

CLASSROOM MANAGEMENT

Classroom management is an important component of SDAIE. If we accept current analyses of the ways that students develop in their second language, we can assume that we need to provide safe, comfortable classroom environments and organize instruction to provide opportunities for students to interact around meaningful activities. Cooperative grouping, described in Chapter 5, is one useful approach. Buddy systems and peer-tutoring systems also allow students to try out their language in a nonthreatening environment while completing academic tasks.

LESSON DELIVERY

Sheltered English. One important methodology within SDAIE is *sheltered English.* In a sheltered classroom, English is used as the medium of instruction in the content areas, and teachers use strategies to encourage English acquisition through comprehensible input and contextualization. Such strategies might include:

- Slow but natural levels of speech.
- Clear enunciation.
- Short, simple sentences.
- Repetition and paraphrasing.
- Controlled vocabulary and idioms.
- Visual reinforcement through the use of gestures, props, pictures, films, demonstrations, and hands-on activities.
- Frequent comprehension checks.

Teachers in a sheltered English classroom maintain a setting with a low level of anxiety, stressing comprehension prior to eliciting production and emphasizing communication over correctness. Activities are selected that encourage hands-on, active engagement with the material, as well as social interaction among students.

Sheltered methodology responds to the idea that the language of classroom discourse (CALP) differs significantly from language used for everyday purposes (BICS). If students are asked to "list the factors that contributed to the Civil War," a teacher in a sheltered setting might review the words *list* and *factor*. As Corson (1995) notes, "Academic . . . words are mainly literary in their use . . . the words' introduction in literature or textbooks, rather than in conversation, restricts people's access to them" (p. 677).

Thematic instruction has particular utility in sheltered classrooms, because students encounter familiar language across several subject areas. Thematic instruction organizes teaching and learning around a key concept or big idea, allowing students to think critically and use oral language, writing, and reading across multiple disciplines or subject areas. One teacher in Santa Clara County organizes each school year around a single theme. In 1993, for a combination fifth/sixth/seventh-grade class, the central theme for the school year was titled "Kokopelli's Flute—A Song of the Southwest" (Perssons, 1993). The school year started with "Story of the Earth," in which students read, illustrated, and dramatized ancient myths, and culminated with a field trip to the Southwest, organized in great measure by the students themselves.

Students in sheltered settings should have an intermediate command of English and should be grouped within the classroom according to their English ability. It is important to remember, however, that it is not the objective of a sheltered classroom to provide remediation in subject areas. The subject content and objectives of a sheltered classroom should be identical to those of a mainstream classroom in the same subject.

ASSESSMENT

Assessment is a key part of any instructional approach. Genesee and Hamayan point out (1994) that when language instruction is integrated with content instruction teachers need to use a variety of assessment techniques that distinguish between students' language abilities and growth and their mastery of subject matter.

Standardized testing has traditionally been the backbone of classroom assessment of student achievement, but teachers are turning increasingly to what have been called *alternative assessment approaches*. One form of alternative assessment is performance assessment. In performance assessment, "a student completes an assignment alone or with other students, often in a content area, and prepares a summary or interpretation of the activity" (O'Malley & Valdez Pierce, 1991, p. 2), which is then evaluated by the teacher. Many teachers are now combining the results of traditional and alternative assessments into portfolios.

Portfolios allow students to present work in their native language, or in ways that are not exclusively language bound, such as photographs and videos. They help students track their progress in language development over time. Portfolios also allow parents of second language learners to see what

In Your Classroom
Instruction that Supports Second Language Learners

Strategies that support language development and scaffold content for second language learners require attention to all areas of instruction, including classroom management, lesson planning and delivery, and assessment. Based on what we know about how students learn a new language, here are some basic ideas to help you get started:

Language is best learned in a comfortable, low-stress environment. Students need to feel safe as they try out their newly acquired language skills. One simple way to create a secure environment is to establish routines. Routines allow students to know what to expect, even if they don't understand everything you say, and also provide an opportunity for them to begin to attach the language you use to what's happening around them. You can build your routines around the calendar and the weather. "Let's all bring our chairs and sit in a circle. Who can tell me what day today is?"

Language is learned through communication (i.e., real interaction about real events, tasks, needs that have meaning to the participants). Don't expect and certainly don't require a quiet classroom. Set up students' desks to facilitate conversation and create activities that require students to interact. Groups of four allow for pair-share and crosstalk.

Every individual has different abilities. Give careful thought to how you group your students. Consider students' language abilities and their social skills so that your groups have balance. Remember, all your students have strengths, and all your students are growing and changing. Groups don't have to stay fixed for a whole year. Regroup students as they develop their abilities, and create opportunities to utilize their strengths.

Not every language learner is ready to talk in class. Our receptive language abilities are generally greater than our productive abilities, and new language learners may be reluctant to express themselves publicly at first. Create opportunities for nonverbal responses. For example, young children can make "lollipops," with one green and one red side to hold up in response to yes /no questions. Create opportunities for verbal participation that don't create discomfort. Group recitation and group singing are fun for young children and allow them to practice language without discomfort.

Real communication is meaningful. Give your groups tasks that require interaction. For example, if each student in the group becomes an "expert" in one aspect of an assignment, and every student in the group needs to produce a paper about the whole assignment, everyone will be drawn into the conversation.

In all areas of learning, we build on prior knowledge. Thematic instruction allows students to use language they have already learned to address new tasks and solve new problems. If you are reading *The Very Hungry Caterpillar* (Carle, 1969), your students can count caterpillars, butterflies, and fruits. You can use the story as the basis for a science unit on caterpillars or on nutrition, a math unit on measurement ("How far can a caterpillar of a given length travel?"), or as a way to introduce concepts related to change. The possibilities are as unlimited as your imagination, and that's just one story and one theme!

Young students need to be taught to work collaboratively. Don't assume that students will naturally know how to function in a group. Engage your students in creating a safe learning community by developing rules for respectful interaction. Define roles and tasks for group assignments and monitor group interactions.

Modify your spoken language to make it accessible to new language learners. Speak slowly and clearly, and avoid idiomatic expressions.

Scaffold instruction with as many real experiences, demonstrations, and illustrations as possible. Especially for beginners, concrete objects and pictures are essential to understanding content and developing language.

Check for understanding in a variety of ways. It is ineffective with *any* group of students to ask, "Did you understand?" In general, people who don't understand aren't clear about whether they understand or not, so the question is not a useful assessment tool. Check for understanding by soliciting demonstrations of learning. Think of ways that new language learners can show you they understand by doing. For example, ask them to point to a location on a map or solve a math problem on the board.

their students are doing in school (Genesee & Hamayan, 1994; O'Malley & Valdez Pierce, 1992).

Literacy and Biliteracy

WHAT IS LITERACY?

Speaking to me, a student who was entering high school from eighth grade expressed surprise that he had to take a class in English.

"Why do I have to take English in high school?" he said. "I speak it already!"

"Because you've got to read Shakespeare, and where else will you do it if not in high school?!" I replied.

My reply was only half-joking: As a modern, literate society we share the assumptions, correct but usually unexplored, that language development continues through adolescence and young adulthood and that full language development includes literacy. Consequently, we require English speakers to take English in high school and through college.

In other words, literacy means more to us than simply mastering the ability to decode the written word. As one author puts it, "Literacy can be viewed . . . as the ability to think and reason like a literate person, *within a particular society*" (Langer, 1991, p. 11).

Furthermore, literacy has political implications. Since the earliest times of our republic, literacy has been seen as crucial to participation in a representative democracy. In a literate society, the ability to read is the key that unlocks the doors to the knowledge base of the culture of power and to the political system. Williams and Capizzi Snipper define *critical literacy* as the ability to determine "what effect a writer is attempting to bring about in readers, why he or she is making the effort, and just who those readers are" (1990, p. 11). In common parlance, a critical reader can read between the lines. It is not surprising, therefore, that the most repressive regimes in the world are the ones that offer the least opportunity for schooling or support for literacy.

BILITERACY

Often, when people discuss bilingualism and bilingual education, their attention is focused on the ability to speak a language. A preservice student teacher in a class on bilingualism once asked, "If children come from Spanish-speaking families, why do they need to study Spanish in school? Won't they learn it at home?" Children in Spanish-speaking households learn Spanish just like children in English-speaking households learn English.

But much as we assume that English speakers will develop literacy in their language in school, so speakers of other languages benefit from the language development that a school setting offers. And much as we expect an English speaker to be familiar with the great works of English language literature (abbreviated as "Shakespeare" in my reply to the eighth grader), or to write research papers and business letters in an appropriate format, so an educated Spanish speaker needs formal instruction to perform comparably in Spanish. Biliteracy, then, includes the development of the full range of understanding and skills appropriate for an educated speaker of two languages.

HOW CAN TEACHERS SUPPORT BILITERACY?

Theoretically, literacy is most readily achieved in a student's first language. Note that this generalization may not apply in American schools to speakers of some Asian languages such as Chinese. Mastery of the Chinese writing system is arduous, and youngsters may more readily learn to read in English, assuming that they have acquired some oral proficiency.

In general, however, as we have already seen, most of the concepts and skills that support our ability to read transfer readily from one language to another. Once we are literate in any language, we are literate. While we need to learn specific features of a new writing system, we don't need to learn to read each time we learn to read a new language.

Also, contrary to earlier thinking that students should not be introduced to reading in their new language until they are literate in their home language, it appears that bilingual students often become biliterate in both languages at about the same time and without the benefit of targeted instruction. De la Luz Reyes analyzed the work of four second-grade students who had been in bilingual classes from kindergarten on. Despite the fact that they each had only received literacy instruction in their dominant language, all achieved a

Several states permit automobile owners to create their own license plate numbers. Look at the following examples of so-called "vanity" license plates:

VET4ME	JANS BUG	AUIYQ
MOM ROX 2	XQQSME	EDUK8TR

You can probably read these license plates, and in some cases you may even know the make of the car or something about the owner. Think about how you are able to come up with this information. The letters and the sounds they make provide important clues, but clearly your ability to do so goes beyond graphophonic knowledge, the ability to connect letters and sounds.

You can decipher these license plates because you can draw on a reservoir of prior experiences and understandings about language (English in the examples above) and about the world. You know for example, what a license plate is, and that sometimes people use language on them in special and often playful ways. You know that sometimes letters or numbers on license plates stand in for syllables or entire words. You know that the plates often refer to the cars people drive, or the people themselves, and that cars have nicknames.

Reading is supported by our knowledge of content, our knowledge of meanings (semantics), and our cultural understandings. When you read in a second language, depending on your proficiency, you may not have the context knowledge that a native speaker has, so you may read more slowly and rely more heavily on graphophonic clues.

When you read with your English language learners or before you ask them to read on their own, spend time developing context. Students can read about new and unfamiliar situations. That's exactly what the world of reading is for. But you need to build a foundation for your students so they can extract meaning from the text.

You can support second language readers before, during and after reading a story with many different kinds of activities. For example, you can:

- Show students real examples of key objects that appear in the text and talk about them. Where realia are impractical, bring in good illustrations. If a story includes a guitar, maybe you can play the guitar for your students or you know a colleague or a student who can. That may not be practical, but you can always bring in a picture and a sound recording to share.
- Build a semantic web around key words in the text. Start with a word, and ask students to add meanings they associate with that word. Think, for example, about the words you might associate with *guitar*. As students build the web, they may suggest or you can add other related words that appear in the text.
- Build a cultural web. If your students come from different cultures, ask them to tell the class about stringed instruments from their cultures, or find examples and illustrations of instruments from the cultures represented in your classroom and beyond. For example, there's an enormous variety of stringed instruments around the world, including but hardly limited to charangos, ukeleles, balalaikas, ouds, sitars, erhus, harps, dulcimers, and kotos. Images and even audio samples of many of them are readily available on the web.
- Transform the genre: Ask students to act out a section of the story or text, perhaps using puppets, or to create a tableau, or "still" image from the text. Imagine a tableau of "The Cat and the Fiddle."

significant degree of biliteracy by second grade. De la Luz Reyes asserts that the children's "spontaneous biliteracy" was the result of "a learning environment that fosters and nurtures the learners' cultural and linguistic resources" (2001, p. 113). She also notes that the children's social play, which emerged in activities related to classroom activities, revolved around reading in both Spanish and English.

Riches and Genesee (2006) in their review of research on the relationships between first and second language and oral and written language conclude "L1 literacy does not detract from L2 literacy but rather contributes to and supports its development" (2006, p. 81). They further note that English language learners who are successful readers and writers use all the language tools at their disposal, using their knowledge of language in general and of their specific languages to help them make sense of text. This supports the concept of a reservoir of deep underlying language proficiency and suggests yet again that for academic purposes, bilingual is indeed better.

LITERACY AND THE SECOND LANGUAGE LEARNER

The process of becoming literate involves the construction and creation of meaning through text. Current theorists suggest this interaction with text to engage meaning is both cognitive and social (Hudelson, 1994; Riggs, 1991). Citing Goodman and Goodman, Riggs asserts that "in a literate society, using written language is as natural as using conversation, and the uses of written language develop as naturally as do the uses of oral language" (1991, p. 524).

Many of the strategies that teachers use to develop native literacy are useful for assisting students to develop literacy in a new language. Hudelson (1994) suggests that teachers create a print-rich environment, provide opportunities for collaboration, and organize instruction so that students engage literature in a meaningful way and write purposefully.

It is important to remember, however, that text is embedded in cultural and social contexts, which may be unfamiliar to second language learners. Escamilla (1993) points out that students can answer many conventionally structured comprehension questions by quoting directly from a text without any real understanding. Harman (1991) provides an excellent example of how this is possible with a nonsense sample text: "The three blugy chinzles slottled prusily on the flubbish werlies." By referring to the text, it is possible to answer the question "How did the blugy chinzles slottle?" (p. 144) without any real comprehension. Teachers of second language learners need to develop strategies for evaluating whether students have engaged the real meaning of a text.

HOW CAN SCHOOLS PROMOTE BILITERACY?

In the American context, the development of fully bilingual and biliterate students requires a rethinking of language education. First, we must promote

In Your Classroom
Using Technology to Teach a Second Language

As access to technology increases, teachers may want to mediate language instruction. Technology can:

- *Motivate:* Today's students are often familiar with contemporary technology, even at fairly young ages, and are often excited to work on classroom computers.
- *Use visual approaches:* Animations and videos are especially useful with young students who have not yet developed literacy skills.
- *Differentiate:* Use technology to provide individualized instruction or to provide activities for independent groups.
- *Provide input and monitor output:* As traditional language laboratories have done for years, technology can allow students to listen to their new language and record and listen to their own language production.

But while drill-and-practice on language skills may be helpful, it can easily devolve into mechanistic "drill-and-kill." Teachers should organize assignments and select software that encourage interaction and problem solving.

Research and literature on how to use technology effectively when working with English language learners is still emerging. One good resource for teachers is *Technology and Teaching English Language Learners,* by Mary Ellen Butler-Pascoe and Karin M. Wiburg (Boston: Pearson, 2003).

maintenance bilingual education for language minority students and enrichment language instruction for native English speakers. Then we must extend our programming to include secondary and postsecondary education. For example, all too often, native Spanish speakers have little opportunity to develop skills in reading and writing Spanish. Courses specifically geared for native speakers are offered at some high schools and colleges, but they are still relatively rare. Expansion of our efforts will no doubt require that educators promote understanding of the dimensions and value of biliteracy.

Summary

Dual language instructional programs include a component for developing students' proficiency in a second language. Grammar-translation approaches have dominated second language instruction for centuries, despite their ineffectuality in developing communicative competence. The audiolingual approach, first developed for military purposes, relies heavily on habit formation and has proven somewhat useful.

Theories about second language acquisition have led to the development of approaches that attempt to develop communicative competence. Total Physical Response, Suggestopedia, and Counseling-Learning pay careful attention to the need to address the affective variables in second language learning. Notional-functional approaches respond to the pragmatics of language and organize activities around language functions.

Krashen's theory of second language acquisition has formed the basis for the Natural Approach, which attempts to provide rich, comprehensible input to students in a comfortable environment as they move through the stages of language development.

Specially Designed Academic Instruction in English (SDAIE) combines second language instruction with content instruction. SDAIE applies to all aspects of instruction, including planning, classroom management, lesson delivery, and assessment. It is useful for intermediate second language speakers and as a bridge for students about to make the transition to all-English classrooms.

Literacy and biliteracy are important considerations in dual language instruction. Literacy must be defined as *critical literacy,* and students should have the opportunity to develop their critical literacy skills to the fullest extent in both their languages.

Questions to Think About and Discuss

1. If you learned a second language in school, how were you taught? Was the approach effective? Why or why not? As best you can remember and discern, did it conform to any theory of second language acquisition with which you are familiar?

2. If you successfully learned a second language outside of a formal school setting, what were the factors that led to your success in gaining proficiency in that language?

3. What kinds of approaches and programs are used in your school to teach English as a second language? How do these programs measure up to what theorists tell us about the ways children learn a new language?

4. What is the prevailing approach to literacy in your school? How are second language learners introduced to literacy? Is the approach successful? Why or why not?

5. How can teachers create learning environments that support literacy beyond a mechanistic, skills-based approach? In other words, how can teachers encourage students to engage with text and learn to love reading?

Activities

1. Visit a primary level and a secondary/adult second language lesson. What kind of assumptions underlie the kind of approach in use? To

what extent are these assumptions in keeping with current second language acquisition theory?

2. Investigate commercial language teaching programs in your area. What languages are taught? What approaches are used? How much do the courses or programs cost? How many students are enrolled in the programs?

3. Develop a lesson plan in social studies, science, or mathematics appropriate for a sheltered English setting. Include content-obligatory and content-compatible language objectives. Describe how you plan to contextualize the material. Be careful to maintain the level of the material in the lesson while modifying the delivery for intermediate second language learners. Include an assessment component.

Suggestions for Further Reading

Asher, J. (1986). *Learning another language through actions. The complete teacher's guidebook.* Los Gatos, CA: Sky Oaks Productions.
A handbook on Total Physical Response, this book provides background on how the approach was developed, documents its effectiveness, answers common questions about it, and provides a lesson-by-lesson plan for its implementation.

Blair, R. W. (Ed.). (1982). *Innovative approaches to language teaching.* Rowley, MA: Newbury House.
Blair divides language teaching approaches into three categories: the comprehension approach, approaches to a rich acquisition environment, and rich learning environment approaches. Within those categories, the book contains articles by a number of authors, including Asher, Terrell, and Lozanov. The introduction to the book sets the development of language teaching in a historical context and also contains a paper presented by Krashen at Brigham Young University in 1979 that is an excellent introduction to his theories on language acquisition. The book's bibliography is particularly useful because it contains references divided by teaching approaches.

Carle, E. (1969). *The very hungry caterpillar.* New York: World Publishing.
A children's classic, and a wonderful addition to any primary level classroom library, this book has been translated into many languages. Many teachers have used it in lots of ways, and a web search will provide you with excellent ideas and starting points.

de la Luz Reyes, M., & Halcón, J. J. (Eds.). (2001). *The best for our children: Critical perspectives on literacy for Latino students.* New York: Teachers College Press.
This book looks at the sociocultural, sociohistorical, and sociopolitical contexts of literacy. The third section of the book provides an overview of creative and successful instructional approaches that support literacy for Latino students by engaging those contexts in meaningful and powerful ways.

Echevarria, J., & Graves, A. (2007). *Sheltered content instruction: Teaching English language learners with diverse abilities* (3rd ed.). Boston: Pearson.
Following brief overviews of foundational information, this book has five chapters focused on classroom practice guiding teachers in strategies to shelter content to make it accessible to second language learners.

Freeman, D. E., & Freeman, Y. S. (2001). *Between worlds: Access to second language acquisition* (2nd ed.). Portsmouth, NH: Heinemann.

Combining descriptions of theory with practice and examples of student work, this book is useful to all teachers who want to support their second language learners. The book is particularly valuable because it speaks to the cultural and social contexts of second language learning and reaches beyond the classroom, showing teachers how to work with their students' families and communities. Appendices include bibliographies related to second language acquisition theory, methods of teaching, and resources for classroom use.

Hadaway, N. L., Vardell, S. M., & Young, T. A. (2002). *Literature-based instruction with English language learners.* Boston: Allyn and Bacon.

The emphasis on accountability has pressured many teachers into reductionist strategies for teaching reading. While these strategies may show immediate short-range gains on standardized tests, they do not necessarily develop students' literacy, construed in the broadest sense. Teachers will find this book useful in thinking about ways to develop reading around literature. This is particularly valuable for second language learners, because exposure to literature supports language acquisition.

Hamayan, E. V., & Perlman, R. (1990, Spring). *Helping language minority students after they exit from bilingual/ESL programs: A handbook for teachers.* Rosslyn, VA: National Clearinghouse for Bilingual Education.

This short publication enumerates and explains strategies that teachers can use to shelter their content-area instruction to assist their second language learners. The handbook provides detailed information about setting up and monitoring a buddy system that pairs second language learners with bilingual or monolingual English-speaking students.

Krashen, S. D., & Terrell, T. D. (1983). *The natural approach: Language acquisition in the classroom.* San Francisco: Alemany.

This book contains an explanation of Krashen's theory of language acquisition and develops the implications of the theory for classroom instruction. Several chapters are devoted to actual classroom activities for the implementation of the Natural Approach. The introductory chapter provides a historical overview of second language instruction, which provides the context for the development of this new approach.

Peregoy, S. F., & Boyle, O. F. (2005). *Reading, writing, & learning in ESL: A resource book for K–8 teachers* (4th ed.). White Plains, NY: Longman.

Providing clear directions for teaching reading and writing in English to English as a second language learners, this book includes activities and resources and addresses the daily concerns of classroom teachers.

Pérez, B. (Ed.). (1998). *Sociocultural contexts of language and literacy.* Mahwah, NJ: Lawrence Erlbaum.

Starting from the assumption that "Literacy is always socially and culturally situated" (p. 4), this book explores reading and writing instruction as they might be situated in a variety of cultural communities, and offers teachers perspectives and strategies to inform instruction in rich and productive ways.

Ramírez, A. G. (1995). *Creating contexts for second language acquisition: Theory and methods.* White Plains, NY: Longman.

This book is comprehensive, up-to-date, and useful. It includes a well-organized overview of current theory as well as useful directions for practice, with descriptions and examples of ways to teach listening, speaking, reading, and writing to second language learners. The book deserves special acknowledgment for attention to the dynamics of culture in second language learning.

Richard-Amato, P. A., & Snow, M. A. (1995). *The multicultural classroom: Readings for content-area teachers* (2nd ed.). White Plains, NY: Longman.

Following a collection of articles that define a theoretical framework and describe cultural considerations, this book addresses the specifics of classroom instruction in social studies, mathematics, science, art, physical education, music, and literacy development for second language learners.

Valdés, G. (2001). *Learning and not learning English.* New York: Teachers College Press.

The author follows four newly arrived middle school students through their English as a second language instruction, and through their experiences and perceptions, teases out the ways social and political dynamics affect the extent to which English language learners succeed, or more importantly, fail, despite their teachers' best professed intentions. As the author points out in this critical analysis (p. 155), "Individuals of good will are not aware that they have become instruments of dominant interests. They are seldom conscious of the fact that power is exercised both through coercion and through consent."

chapter 7

Aspects of Culture

$\mathcal{L}$anguage and its use in the classroom are natural foci for the study of dual language instruction. Language, however, is inextricably bound with culture, and cultural factors have an important influence on educational outcomes for all students.

The history of the United States has always been characterized by cultural diversity, but never so much as in modern times. The last part of the twentieth century has seen unprecedented numbers of immigrants coming to the United States. In addition, changes in immigration law in 1965 opened the door to newcomers from every corner of the world.

Nowhere is the impact of continued and varied immigration felt more than in the public schools. Each day, teachers attempt to meet the needs of children from many different cultural backgrounds. This chapter will attempt to clarify definitions of culture and provide examples of its characteristics and manifestations. In addition, this chapter will consider multicultural education and its relationship to bilingual education.

Culture and Population

American culture is difficult to characterize because it is made up of many complex and changing subcultures. In fact, complexity and change are at the heart of American culture. The demographics of the United States are in flux at the current time for a variety of reasons.

THE IMPACT OF IMMIGRATION

Compelled by war or famine or lured by the prospect of life in a new and exciting world, people have been immigrating to the New World since before the inception of the United States as a nation. In the nineteenth century, social, political, and economic upheaval caused an influx of people from all over Europe. The Irish arrived, having fled the potato famines. German and Scandinavian farmers were attracted by the farmlands of the Midwest. Chinese laborers built our transcontinental railroad lines. Italians, Poles, and Czechs, attracted by the opportunities for economic success and freedom from oppression, all made their way to the United States in the late 1800s.

The nineteenth-century wave of immigration swelled into the twentieth century, reaching a peak between 1900 and 1920 when numbers of Italians and Eastern European Jews flooded East Coast ports, and Mexicans, displaced by the Revolution of 1910, immigrated northward to the Southwest and California.

Reaction to newcomers was swift and often vicious. *Xenophobia* (a fear of things that seem foreign) and racism led to attempts to limit immigration. The Chinese Exclusion Act of 1882 was the first federal attempt to limit immigration by nationality. The 1917 Immigration Act excluded Asians, and the National Origins Act of 1924 established quotas for nations outside the Western Hemisphere (The Immigration Project, 1981).

In 1965, however, President Lyndon B. Johnson signed legislation that altered national immigration policy. Prior to 1965, immigration law favored ethnic groups who were already represented in the U.S. population. Johnson's legislation placed an annual limit of 20,000 immigrants for each country. As a result, people are entering the United States in significant numbers from all over the world. In 1984 the United States admitted 600,000 legal immigrants.

Official numbers do not appear to exceed figures of the early part of the century, but illegal immigration adds significant numbers, perhaps doubling official counts ("Growth of a Nation," 1985). Not only has the number of immigrants increased, but the diversity of newcomers has increased as well, with the flow from Europe decreasing and the influx from Latin America and Asia increasing.

OTHER DEMOGRAPHIC FACTORS

While steady and varied immigration has an undeniable and dynamic impact on our profile as a nation, it is not the only factor that affects the demographic picture. Differential rates of growth among various groups also have a significant effect on our population. The "baby boom" that occurred after World War II was primarily a white middle-class phenomenon, and the rate of growth in that segment of the population has since decreased significantly. People of color in the United States are younger than white people and have higher birth rates (U.S. Bureau of the Census, 1997).

The changing demographic and cultural situation in our schools means that all teachers will have to develop skills to work with children who fall into the following categories:

- *Language minority children:* These are children who have a person who speaks a language other than English in their homes. They may be bilingual or may speak only English. In either case, they are likely to have links to an ethnic minority culture.
- *English language learners:* According to the National Clearinghouse for English Language Acquisition (NCELA), there were approximately 5.2

million English language learners in public schools in the United States (K–12) in 2004–2005. While public school enrollments rose about 2.6 percent between 1994 and 2005, the number of English language learners grew by an astonishing 61 percent. Enrollments of student with limited proficiency in English are predictably high in certain states. California, for example, which enrolls approximately 10 percent of the nation's school-children, identified approximately 1.6 million English language learners in grades K through 12 in 2006–2007 (California State Department of Education, 2007). Other states with high enrollments of English learners include Arizona, Florida, Illinois, New York, and Texas. But enrollments are not limited to those areas, and increases in the English learner student population are large in places you might not expect. Georgia, for example, experienced an increase of 113 percent from 1999–2000 to 2000–2001. In the same period, Montana experienced an increase of 88.4 percent (Kindler, 2002). Looking at a longer time frame, in the decade between 1990 and 2000, 19 states experienced growth in limited English proficient student populations in excess of 200 percent (NCELA, 2003). Updated information about your state's student population is available from the National Clearinghouse for English Language Acquisition at www.ncela.gwu.edu. The website for the state department of education in your state is another useful source of up-to-date demographic information.

The school has traditionally been a gateway to mainstream culture for the diverse groups that make up American society. As the population changes, and indeed as our concept of mainstream culture is altered by the groups that enter it, teachers will need to develop a deep understanding of the nature of culture and the implications of diversity in the classroom.

What Is Culture?

Like language, our own culture is usually invisible to us. We tend to associate culture with things that are far away and exotic. A student of mine once commented, "I didn't know there was such a thing as American culture until I spent time in Central America." Away from home, amid people who operate under different assumptions, that student was able to perceive characteristics of her own culture. According to an old Japanese saying, "One sees the sky through a hollow reed." If we equate the sky to reality, then the hollow reed through which we view it may be likened to our culture. But what exactly is culture?

Definitions of culture abound in social science literature, and the search for a single definition can be perplexing and frustrating. As basic social science assumptions have changed over time, so have definitions of culture. The trend toward behaviorist thinking gave rise to definitions of culture that emphasized the observable patterns of behavior of a particular group. In the

1950s the thinking of cognitive psychologists influenced anthropologists, who began to conceptualize culture in terms of ideas and beliefs to the exclusion of observable behaviors.

One frequently cited definition describes *culture* as a system of standards for perceiving, believing, evaluating, and acting (Goodenough, 1971). Each culture has many complex and overlapping systems within which its members operate and through which they assign and extract meaning. When you encounter a culture different from your own, you try to figure out how things work (*cultural behavior*) and why they function as they do (*cultural knowledge*).

For our purposes, it is useful to accept a fairly inclusive approach to the concept of culture. One analysis (Arvizu, Snyder, & Espinosa, 1980) suggests that culture is "a dynamic, creative, and continuous process including behaviors, values, and substance learned and shared by people that guides them in their struggle for survival and gives meaning to their lives." Let us consider the components of this definition, that is, the characteristics of culture.

CULTURE IS DYNAMIC

Just as language changes over time to meet the needs of its users, culture changes over time as people adapt to changing circumstances. For example, people often think of Native Americans as people who live in tepees, wear feather headdresses, and hunt buffalo. That characterization might be historically accurate to a limited extent, but it no longer applies, despite pervasive media images to the contrary. While Native Americans today cherish and protect their traditional heritages, they are also likely to be part of mainstream U.S. culture.

CULTURE IS CREATIVE

The process of culture change is one of creativity. Each new environmental change results in a cultural adaptation. Old ways are replaced by the new in dynamic and creative ways. For example, economic circumstances in the United States have resulted in large numbers of women entering the wage-earning workforce. The result has been a change in our perception of family structure, in our belief system about the abilities of women, and in systems for caring for children outside the immediate family.

CULTURE IS CONTINUOUS

Changing circumstances produce new systems of action, belief, and perception, but the new systems contain traces of the old. Such traces are what we call *tradition*. Each successive generation passes on its cumulative culture to the next. Chinese Americans, for example, celebrate the Chinese New Year in the United States. While the traditional week-long celebration observed in

China is impractical in a modern U.S. setting, traditional foods are prepared and customs are still maintained.

CULTURE IS LEARNED

We are not born with our culture. A film called *Living on Tokyo Time* (Okazaki, 1987) tells the story of a young Japanese woman who immigrates to California and marries a Japanese American man in order to obtain legal immigration status. The movie recounts her experience and her surprise as she discovers that although her new husband looks like someone from Japan, he is unfamiliar with Japanese customs and even with Japanese food. Such characteristics as the color of our hair and eyes are genetically determined, but we learn our culture as we are socialized by the people and circumstances that surround us, in a process called *enculturation*.

CULTURE IS SHARED

Just as language is useful only if we agree on certain conventions, culture needs shared assumptions in order to function. Some of you, for example, may belong to an in-group or subculture that uses a particular handshake as a greeting. Members of that group rely on the handshake as a symbol for group membership and a way of opening a social interaction. Such a symbol is useful only if members of the group share an understanding of its meaning.

The assumption that culture is shared is operative even when a particular behavior or activity is not. For example, among mainstream Americans, people generally brush their teeth individually, in private. Despite the absence of others, we each usually brush our teeth according to shared culture knowledge about what to use and how to proceed, with certain shared assumptions about the value of dental care.

Every culture is extremely complex, and not every member knows all the systems and symbols involved. Conversely, most of us belong to more than one subculture and may be competent in the symbols and systems of several (Goodenough, 1971).

CULTURE IS A STRUGGLE FOR SURVIVAL

Each culture is an adaptive response to a particular environment. The symbols and systems of a culture evolve to allow a particular group to adjust to its circumstances. As mentioned before, we tend to have an inaccurate and stereotypical view of Native Americans, both as they are in the present and as they were in the past. Photographs, however, taken between 1896 and 1930 by Edward S. Curtis (Brown, 1972) reveal the astounding number and variety of Native American cultures that existed on the North American continent prior to European domination.

The hunting tribes of the Great Plains lived in tepees, which were made of readily available buffalo skins and easily transported in keeping with the tribe members' needs as nomadic hunters. Indians of the coastal Northwest, on the other hand, lived in reed houses and were skilled as fishermen. Each group developed a culture that met its needs for survival and responded to the resources and demands of its environment.

Culture and Language

The relationship of culture and language has been of interest to anthropologists and linguists since the early twentieth century. The debate centers around Edward Sapir's suggestion that speakers of different languages have different perceptions of the world; that is, language determines culture. This view, promulgated by his student Benjamin Lee Whorf, is sometimes called the *Whorf* (or *Sapir-Whorf*) *hypothesis.* The layperson's expression of the Whorf hypothesis is often stated in this way: "There are some things you can only say in Spanish," or whatever language the speaker holds dear.

One researcher (Chaika, 1989) has characterized language as "a mirror of its speakers' attitudes and ideas. A mirror reflects. It does not determine; it does not hold prisoners" (p. 295). As we saw in our discussion of the nature of language in Chapter 3, language changes and adapts to meet the needs of its speakers. While some languages may have more concise forms of expression for objects or concepts that exist in a particular culture, any language can express any idea that its culture requires. For example, Japanese has *wabi,* a word that describes the flaw that makes an object beautiful (Rheingold, 1988, p. 74). The German word *schadenfreude* describes the pleasure one person takes from another person's misfortunes. We don't have an English word for those concepts, but we can express the ideas. Actually, *schadenfreude* has been borrowed by English speakers and now appears in many English dictionaries. Apparently, while few of us might like to admit feeling it, the word for *schadenfreude* comes in handy!

The contemporary educational philosopher Neil Postman (1995) says that "we use language to create the world. . . . Language allows us to name things, but, more than that, it also suggests what feelings we are obliged to associate with the things we name. Even more, language controls what things shall be named, what things we ought to pay attention to" (pp. 83–84). The debate as to whether or not language determines culture or vice versa may continue, but it is inarguable that language and culture are inseparable, and learning a new language invariably entails learning a new culture.

In the motion picture *Born in East L.A.* (Marin & Macgregor-Scott, 1987), a native-born Mexican American is mistakenly deported from Los Angeles to Mexico. Trying to earn his way back to the United States, he takes a job with a *coyote* (people smuggler), teaching people English so they can blend in when they make their way across the border. His students are Asian immigrants trying to cross the border into the United States illegally. He quickly discerns what they will need to know in Los Angeles. He dresses them in bandannas, teaches them a "cool" walk, and begins their training in English with the words "*Orale vato*, wha's happenin'!" (Hey, buddy, what's happening?) It is clear from the outset that language learning must be accompanied by culture learning.

How Is Culture Manifested?

James P. Spradley (1972) commented, "The man in the street is a naive realist who lives in a world he can count on, a world he believes is much the same for everyone else" (p. 8). In other words, we usually assume that the qualities we perceive in the world around us and the meanings we assign to symbols and events are concrete and universal. On the contrary, people around the world have devised an infinite number and variety of social institutions, daily habits, and meaning systems in their quest for survival.

To get a sense of the vastness of the cultural enterprise we will look at a few of the many manifestations of culture. All of us are familiar with myriad examples of each culture area. Exemplification, however, sometimes leads to stereotyping. The examples presented here are meant to be illustrative, but may be somewhat oversimplified.

CLOTHING AND DECORATION

While we might immediately assume that the purpose of clothing is for protection against the weather, a closer look shows us that people use clothing for a variety of purposes such as gender differentiation, status display, and ritual.

For example, if you have ever planned a wedding, you know how much emphasis is placed on proper dress for everyone involved. In middle-class mainstream U.S. culture, brides often wear white. However, depending on the formality of the occasion or their previous marital status, they may wear another color and dress less formally. Attendants are carefully dressed, and the groom and his party must be attired in keeping with the nature of the event. Flowers are carefully selected and arranged. Stores even market mother-of-the-bride dresses, indicating that we have a particular cultural expectation of the bride's mother. Rites of passage and other ceremonial events require special dress and adornment that differs from culture to culture.

HOUSING

Again, it seems logical to assume that the purpose of housing is protection. As shelter, housing generally conforms to the resources and demands of each particular environment. Stone houses in New England are practical and serviceable in an environment with abundant large rocks in the soil and a cold climate. Such houses would be impractical and out of place near the equator, where the climate is always warm and humid, or for nomadic peoples who need shelters that can be dismantled and carried for long distances.

But housing, like clothing, serves purposes beyond the need for protection. A home may serve as a center for family or community life, and an analysis of housing often reveals social organization. Houses may also indicate status. For example, the President of the United States always resides in the White House for the duration of the term. While not necessarily the most opulent residence in the country, the White House has social and historical significance.

TIME ORIENTATION

Different cultures have different orientations to time. You may have encountered an overt reference to cultural time orientation if you have been invited to a party and were told that it would start at six o'clock in the evening *hora Latina* (Latin time). Such an invitation acknowledges the fact that in the Hispanic cultural context, a social invitation for six o'clock may indicate an event that will start no earlier than seven in the evening. If you were to appear at six, you would likely be the first to arrive and would find your hosts unprepared. Some people might suggest that Hispanics are not prompt or "have no sense of time." Such an ethnocentric view fails to understand that each of us knows when to arrive for a particular event within the context of our culture or subculture.

SPATIAL ORIENTATION

Each culture has its own patterns for the use of personal space. You may have noticed a proxemic pattern if you were born in the United States and have had a conversation with a person born in the Middle East. Middle Easterners have a different concept of appropriate distance from North Americans for nonintimate personal conversation, standing closer to each other than North Americans do. Such differences are often the cause of misjudgments and misunderstandings: one person assumes the other is moving in too close, while the other person judges the first as aloof or uncaring. Proxemic patterns also manifest themselves in architecture, arrangement of furnishings, and body language (Hall, 1966).

VALUES

Each culture has a frame of reference for identifying what is desirable or important to the group. The academic achievement of newly arrived Asian immigrants has led to speculation that their success is related to the Confucian value system and the value it places on scholarship (Butterfield, 1986). Without entering into a discussion of the merits of that suggestion, we note that it acknowledges the role of values in culture.

Values are harder to identify than the material aspects of culture, but they are of particular importance to teachers. All too often teachers acknowledge surface aspects of culture through ethnic heritage celebrations, classroom decor, and curriculum materials. While such acknowledgments of material or surface culture are worthwhile, they are not sufficient.

For example, it has been said that Navajo children from traditional backgrounds look down when they are addressed by a teacher. Teachers who fail to understand that the children are showing them respect within the context of Navajo culture often misinterpret their behavior and assume they are disrespectful or even sneaky. Mainstream American culture places a high value on direct eye contact, as manifested in expressions such as, "I looked him straight in the eye."

One teacher tells of his difficulty in trying to encourage Rosa, a Mexican American high school student in his remedial English class. In an attempt to express a genuine interest in her, he complimented her on a new hair style. Shortly thereafter, she began cutting class and finally revealed to a counselor that she thought the teacher was taking an inappropriate romantic interest in her (Wineburg, 1987). In that case, the values difference between Rosa and her teacher led to an uncomfortable and potentially serious misunderstanding. Misunderstanding of deep culture or value systems may result in discriminatory treatment of children from minority groups.

Bilingual Education and Multicultural Education

In practice, educators often refer to *bilingual/multicultural education*. Because the terms appear side by side, *bilingual* and *multicultural education* are erroneously construed as identical. The two are not one and the same thing, although there is a relationship between dual language instruction and multicultural education.

WHAT IS MULTICULTURAL EDUCATION?

Carlos Cortés, a leading exponent of multicultural education, begins his definition of *multicultural education* by describing what multicultural education is *not* (1990). He asserts that multicultural education is not the celebration of holidays or the inclusion of special history days or weeks in the curriculum, an approach that James Banks, another important multicultural theorist, refers to as "tepees and chitlins" and "heroes and holidays" (1977). Banks calls such approaches to multicultural education additive—they tack on bits and pieces to the existing curriculum, but they do not alter the basic structure of schooling. Cortés and Banks also agree that multicultural education is not the study of a particular ethnic group, although ethnic studies may contribute to multicultural education by generating the scholarship necessary to build an inclusive curriculum. Finally, multicultural education is not a compensatory program for students who are identified as "minority."

Multicultural education in its broadest sense entails educational reform or restructuring to empower students, provide all students with equitable

Letter from a Mother of a Native American Child

Dear Teacher:

Before you take charge of the classroom that contains my child, please ask yourself why you are going to teach Indian children. What are your expectations? What rewards do you anticipate? What ego needs will our children have to meet?

Write down and examine all the information and opinions you possess about Indians. What are the stereotypes and untested assumptions that you bring with you into the classroom. How many negative attitudes towards Indians will you put before my child?

What values, class prejudices and moral principles do you take for granted as universal? Please remember that "different from" is not the same as "worse than" or "better than," and the yardstick you use to measure your own life satisfactorily may not be appropriate for their lives.

The term "culturally deprived" was invented by well-meaning middle-class whites to describe something they could not understand.

Too many teachers, unfortunately, seem to see their role as rescuer. My child does not need to be rescued; he does not consider being Indian a misfortune. He has a culture, probably older than yours; he has meaningful values and a rich and varied experiential background. However strange or incomprehensible it may seem to you, you have no right to do or say anything that implies to him that it is less than satisfactory.

Our children's experiences have been different from those of the "typical" white middle-class child for whom most school curricula seem to have been designed (I suspect that this "typical" child does not exist except in the minds of curriculum writers). Nonetheless, my child's experiences have been as intense and meaningful to him as any child's.

Like most Indian children his age, he is competent. He can dress himself, prepare a meal for himself, clean up afterwards, care for a younger child. He knows his Reserve, all of which is his home, like the back of his hand.

He is not accustomed to having to ask permission to do the ordinary things that are part of normal living. He is seldom forbidden to do anything; more usually the consequences of an action are explained to him and he is allowed to decide for himself whether or not to act. His entire existence since he has been old enough to see and hear has been an experiential learning situation, arranged to provide him with the opportunity to develop his skills and confidence in his own capacities. Didactic teaching will be an alien experience for him.

He is not self-conscious in the way many white children are. Nobody has ever told him his efforts towards independence are cute. He is a young human being energetically doing his job, which is to get on with the process of learning to function as an adult human being. He will respect you as a person, but he will expect you to do likewise to him.

He has been taught, by precept, that courtesy is an essential part of human conduct and rudeness is any action that makes another person feel stupid or foolish. Do not mistake his patient courtesy for indifference or passivity.

He doesn't speak standard English, but he is no way "linguistically handicapped." If you will take the time and courtesy to listen and observe carefully, you will see that he and the other Indian children communicate very well, both among themselves and with other Indians. They speak "functional English," very effectively augmented by their fluency in the silent language, the subtle, unspoken communication of facial expressions, gestures, body movement and the use of personal space.

You will be well advised to remember that our children are skillful interpreters of the silent language. They will know your feelings and attitudes with unerring precision, no matter how carefully you arrange your smile or modulate your voice. They will learn in your classroom, because children learn involuntarily. What they learn will depend on you.

Will you help my child to learn to read, or will you teach him that he has a reading problem? Will you help him develop problem solving skills, or will you teach him that school is where you try to guess what answer the teacher wants?

Will he learn that his sense of his own value and dignity is valid, or will he learn that he must forever be apologetic and "trying harder" because he isn't white? Can you help him acquire the intellectual skills he needs without at the same time imposing your values on top of those he already has?

Respect my child. He is a person. He has a right to be himself.

Yours very sincerely,

His Mother

SOURCE: "Respect My Child: He Has a Right to Be Himself." Wassaja, February 1976. Reprinted by permission of *The Indian Historian*.

opportunities, and enable all students to function comfortably and effectively in a pluralist democracy (Cortés, 1990; Nieto, 1992). Current theorists favor a social reconstructionist multicultural approach. Social reconstructionists work toward empowering students to actively engage their own life circumstances and alter them in the direction of social equity and justice. This point of view is rooted in the educational philosophy of critical pedagogy.

Critical pedagogy rejects what Paolo Freire (1970) has termed the "banking" concept of education, where teachers make deposits of knowledge into their students, a system which assumes that teachers are experts and students are not. In critical pedagogy, students are encouraged to pose their own questions and seek their own answers. Critical pedagogy assumes that students are inquisitive and creative and can use themselves and their environments as sources for both problems and their solutions.

Critical approaches underlie programs such as *Como Ellos Lo Ven* (Lessow-Hurley, 1977). In that project, students from migrant farmwork families in Longmont, Colorado, created a documentary of their lives, using their own photographs and narratives based on those images to produce a book that was then incorporated into the reading program in their class.

In another project based in critical pedagogy, Flor Ada engaged Spanish-speaking parents in the Pajaro Valley in California in developing their children's literacy skills (Flor Ada, 1988). Through presentations and small group discussions, parents were introduced to Spanish language children's literature and to ways of encouraging their children to read and write. As a result of their participation, parents came to understand the value of their home language, to see themselves as essential participants in their children's education, and to develop their own critical literacy skills as a key to understanding their world.

Multicultural education broadly conceived touches every aspect of school life, from the books and materials students use to the distribution of power within the school community. Nieto (1992) asserts that multicultural education is basic and pervasive. Cortés sums up his definition of multicultural education as "a continuous, integrated, multiethnic, multidisciplinary process for educating all American students about diversity, a curricular basic oriented toward preparing young people to live with pride and understanding in our multiethnic present and increasingly multiethnic future" (p. 3).

In its fullest sense, multicultural education is not a program that is implemented on Monday, or in January, but a total rethinking of the way we do schooling in a diverse society with a democratic civic framework.

WHAT IS THE CONNECTION BETWEEN BILINGUAL EDUCATION AND MULTICULTURAL EDUCATION?

In the professional arena, bilingual and multicultural education have developed separately, with separate journals, professional associations, and constituencies. Bilingual education is often erroneously construed as compensatory education for speakers of minority languages, while multicultural education is often mistakenly conceptualized as a program for African American students. We have seen that both bilingual and multicultural education admit to much more inclusive and useful definitions than those with a compensatory or deficit focus. What then is the connection between these two concepts?

Both multicultural and bilingual education subscribe to the fundamental idea that schooling should utilize students' knowledge of the world as a starting point and resource for learning. For all students, language is perhaps the single most important aspect of culture, since language is the primary means by which each of us is enculturated, that is, brought into our particular communities of behavior and belief. For language minority students, primary language is a deep resource that schooling should validate and enhance. Using the students' first language is empowering, since it validates students' culture. It is equitable to the extent that it provides equal access to the curriculum. And when it develops and maintains students' primary language alongside English, it enhances their preparation to function in an increasingly pluralist environment. In other words, bilingual education that values and promotes bilingualism and biliteracy is multicultural as well.

Bilingualism is an asset in an increasingly multicultural society and a global economy. English-only students benefit from an education that allows them to learn in more than one language and prepares them to function effectively in a world characterized by diversity. When we provide a bilingual education to all students we meet many of the goals embodied in broad definitions of multicultural education. In sum, while bilingual and multicultural education are not necessarily identical, all students can benefit from an education that is bilingual and multicultural.

Summary

The demography of the United States is changing significantly, due both to immigration and to differences among ethnic groups in average age and birth rates. Schools are particularly affected by these demographic changes, so that teachers are working increasingly with children from diverse linguistic and cultural backgrounds.

Culture is something we all have but often find difficult to perceive. Culture, like language, is dynamic, changing to meet the needs of the people it serves. All cultures have coherent, shared systems of action and belief that allow people to function and survive. Culture is manifested in our behaviors and beliefs about food, shelter, clothing, space, and time, as well as our value systems. We learn our cultures, and second language learning involves culture learning as well.

Bilingual and multicultural education are not identical, but many basic dispositions, concepts, and skills are common to both fields, and student empowerment is a key concept in both.

Questions to Think About and Discuss

1. How would you characterize your own culture? What values would you consider part of your cultural identity? What kinds of things do you do that you would consider cultural expression? (Remember, that's just about everything!) If you identify with a particular ethnic or religious group, what values do you hold as part of that identity and what behaviors do you engage in as a result of your identification with that group?

2. Often, people develop their understandings of cultural difference through travel. If you have traveled outside the United States, think about your experiences. Were there differences in everyday assumptions and transactions? Were there interactions where you were able to negotiate the differences? Were there occasions when differing assumptions caused you inconvenience or discomfort?

3. Think about the assumptions and behaviors that are commonplace in American schools. Imagine that you are an immigrant youngster entering an American school for the first time. What will you find perplexing? What would help you negotiate your new experience?

Activities

1. Look up demographics for your local school district(s). Your state department of education may have the data. School districts may also have the information. Local newspapers sometimes report on demographic changes. How has the population changed in the last ten years? How many English language learners are there in your area? What language groups are represented? Make an illustrative chart or map to share with your colleagues.

2. Teachers working with Navajo children need to be careful about field trips to the zoo and to certain museums. Navajo children should not see bears or snakes, nor should they be allowed to view human skeletal remain. In the event that they do, they must participate in cleansing ceremonies, which are lengthy and often costly. Study an ethnic or cultural group in your area. Use personal resources as well as the library. What values and assumptions does the group have that differ from your own? What can you learn that will help you provide relevant, motivating, and effective instruction for your students?

Suggestions for Further Reading

The study of culture includes the study of just about everything. From an academic standpoint, culture is studied by anthropologists, educators, linguists, psychologists, sociologists, and cyberneticists. It is impossible, therefore, to provide a comprehensive list of readings on the subject. In addition to books about the concept of culture in general, an abundance of scholarly literature describes particular cultures as well as cross-cultural communication and conflict.

We cannot, in addition, exclude the realm of fiction. The works of Isaac Bashevis Singer, Maxine Hong Kingston, Ernesto Galarza, Toni Morrison, Amy Tan, Jumpa Lahirí, and Ntozake Shange are a tiny sampling of the possibilities. Tony Hillerman's popular series of mystery novels set on the Navajo reservation provides fascinating insights into Navajo and Hopi cultures. The list below reviews books that highlight points in this chapter. It serves as a starting point for additional reading.

Arvizu, S. F., Snyder, W. A., & Espinosa, P. T. (1980). *Demystifying the concept of culture: Theoretical and conceptual tools.* Los Angeles: Evaluation, Dissemination, and Assessment Center, California State University, Los Angeles.
  An analysis of the nature of culture, with illustrative examples, this monograph contains clear, useful information for teachers in training.

Hall, E. T. (1959). *The silent language.* Garden City, NY: Doubleday.
  Hall defines culture as communication and analyzes modalities of communication, including language, space, and time, from a cross-cultural perspective.

Hall, E. T. (1966). *The hidden dimension.* Garden City, NY: Doubleday.

An examination of people's use of space in public and in private from an anthropological perspective, this classic book contains fascinating explanations and examples of concepts of proxemics.

Igoa, C. (1995). *The inner world of the immigrant child.* New York: St. Martin's Press.

This is a first-person account of the author's experiences as a teacher of immigrant children and an immigrant herself. Through her story and the stories of her students, she describes how she developed her philosophy and her methodology. Each chapter ends with a summary that provides concrete suggestions for teachers working with immigrant students.

Levine, R. (1997). *A geography of time: The temporal misadventures of a social psychologist, or how every culture keeps time just a little bit differently.* New York: Basic Books.

According to the author's research, Boston is America's fastest moving city. This might come as a surprise to New Yorkers, or even Angelenos, and if you find this kind of information interesting, this is the book for you.

Olsen, L. (1997). *Made in America: Immigrant students in our public schools.* New York: The New Press.

The author spent two and a half years at a large, ethnically diverse high school in northern California's Bay Area. The resulting ethnographic study describes the students, their aspirations, and the challenges that face them in a system that ultimately marginalizes and excludes them.

Philips, S. U. (1983). *The invisible culture: Communication in the classroom and the community on the Warm Springs Indian Reservation.* White Plains, NY: Longman.

In this fascinating work, the author studies communication patterns among adults in the Warm Springs Indian community and then analyzes the mismatch between the expectations Warm Springs Indian children have in communication settings and what they encounter in classrooms.

Saravia-Shore, M., & Arvizu, S. F. (1992). *Cross-cultural literacy: Ethnographies of communication in multiethnic classrooms.* New York: Garland.

This is a collection of studies that use microethnography to analyze multiethnic classrooms and schools in the context of their communities. The introduction provides an excellent overview of anthropological approaches to studying education. Articles included cover a broad scope of community and school settings as well as ethnicities.

Spradley, J. P. (Ed.). (1972). *Culture and cognition: Rules, maps, and plans.* San Francisco: Chandler.

The central theme of this book is the nature and structure of culture. Articles from the fields of anthropology, economics, linguistics, psychology, and sociology provide a wide variety of perspectives and examples.

Valdes, J. M. (1986). *Culture bound: Bridging the cultural gap in language teaching.* New York: Cambridge University Press.

Part 1 of this book presents a theoretical foundation about the relationship of culture, thought, and language. Part 2 describes cultural traits of several groups to alert language teachers to the characteristics of their students. Articles in Part 3 relate to classroom applications and present practical suggestions for working with non-native speakers of a language.

chapter 8

Culture and Schooling

— Culture and Academic Success

Differential achievement, or "the achievement gap," as it is commonly called, refers to the persistent differences between the achievement of students of color and white students, generally as measured on standardized achievement tests. The National Assessment of Educational progress, which calls itself "the nation's report card" (nationsreportcard.gov), tests a representative sample of students nationwide in grades 4, 8, and 12 in reading and mathematics. Results of its 2007 tests indicate that overall, scores are rising. The gap between African American students and white students has gotten somewhat smaller but is still large, and the gap between Latino students and white students persists without much change.

Analyses of the differences between cultures are often used to attempt to explain differences in educational performance among ethnic groups. Differential achievement has been viewed from a variety of perspectives. Some theorists have proposed that different groups have varying abilities that are genetically determined. Others have suggested that some cultures are inadequate or lacking in basic ingredients that are necessary for children to succeed in school.

A third viewpoint that has gained popularity is the cultural mismatch view. Mismatch theorists suggest that different groups have communication and learning styles that don't fit with mainstream styles usually found in classrooms. The mismatch model does not address the entire problem, but understanding communication and learning styles is essential for teachers.

It has been suggested that analysis of differential achievement among groups must go beyond analysis of teacher and student interaction in the classroom and has to be seen in the political and social context of the wider society. The contextual interaction model will be discussed here.

GENETIC INFERIORITY

The genetic inferiority model assumes that certain groups are inherently incapable of intellectual achievement. Rooted in nineteenth-century colonialism, genetic inferiority was a convenient way of justifying cultural domination and enslavement. In current thinking, it has similar convenience value: It blames the victim and eliminates the need for any transformation of our education systems—if heredity is at fault, there simply are no solutions.

The current debate on the relationship between heredity and academic ability was sparked by an article by A. R. Jensen published in the *Harvard Educational Review* in 1969. In that article, Jensen suggested that a person's intellectual ability is determined 80 percent by heredity and 20 percent by environment—hence, most differences in achievement between groups are based in genetic factors. Scholars have criticized Jensen's work extensively (Cortés, 1986; Feuerstein, 1978; Ogbu, 1978), and research generally disproves the notion that intellectual ability is genetically determined and inalterable. This unfortunate perspective has remarkable staying power, however. For example, in a 1988 survey of science teachers, 26 percent of the 200 respondents replied "definitely true" or "probably true" to an item that stated, "Some races of people are more intelligent than others" ("Study Reveals . . . ," 1988).

In *The Bell Curve,* Charles Murray and Richard J. Herrnstein (1994) reasserted the idea that white people are more intelligent than black people as a result of genetic factors. Despite widespread criticism (Beardsley, 1995; "Reacting to *The Bell Curve,*" 1995; Kamin, 1995) of Murray and Herrnstein's assumptions and methodology, the book captured the attention of a public frustrated by the perceived inefficacy of government programs and the failure of schooling to address the problem of underachievement among minority groups.

CULTURAL DEFICIT

The cultural deficit or deficiency model suggests that ethnic minorities fail in school because their cultures are inadequate in some way. The deficit view gained popularity in the 1960s, when it was suggested, for example, that black children suffered from language deprivation as a result of inadequate language development in their home backgrounds (Bereiter & Engelmann, 1966).

As we have seen, all cultures are rich and complex and, like languages, evolve to suit the needs of particular groups. African Americans, like other groups, have a coherent culture. Black American culture in particular includes a vibrant and dynamic tradition of oral language, as witnessed for example by the richness of the black preaching heritage. The notion that black children are deprived somehow of language experience is clearly a case of cultural tunnel vision.

The cultural deficit view blames the victims, but assumes that the deficit is correctable and offers the possibility of solutions through remediation. Critics, however, suggest that remediation efforts have proven ineffective and that, furthermore, the deficit view fails to account for the social and political context of schooling (Boykin, 1984).

CULTURAL MISMATCH

The cultural mismatch model suggests that members of minority groups do not succeed in school because the characteristics of their cultures are incongruent with those of the mainstream group and the school system. This view is supported by the work of researchers who have analyzed learning styles. Culture traits that are part of learning style and that may affect classroom dynamics include cognitive styles, communicative styles, and interaction styles—features that often overlap.

While differences in learning styles may not be the entire explanation for differential achievement among groups, they warrant a detailed look. Such traits are part of what might be called *invisible* or *deep* culture. Teachers need to understand and acknowledge aspects of culture beyond material manifestations.

Cognitive Style. Cognitive styles are ways of thinking or problem solving. For example, sometimes we acknowledge that a person is particularly good at understanding "the big picture." On the other hand, we might refer to a friend or a colleague as "detail oriented." In these examples, we are making reference to a person's cognitive style.

Similarly, it has been proposed that some people are field dependent or field sensitive, whereas others are field independent. Field sensitive students prefer to work cooperatively; field independent students prefer competitive learning situations. Field sensitive students are motivated by their relationship to their teacher; they seek social rewards. Field independent students are task-oriented and motivated by nonsocial rewards.

Ramírez and Castañeda (1974) suggested that Mexican American students tend to be more field dependent than their European American counterparts or European American teachers as a result of cultural values and socialization practices. Lack of congruence between the cognitive styles of Mexican American children and the expectations of the school environment was offered as an explanation for their failure to achieve in school. The children who succeeded had become bicultural—that is, bicognitive, or able to cope with the differing demands of more than one culture.

The notion of biculturalism as bicognitivism was thought-provoking and controversial. Critics, however, have suggested that the rate and manner of cognitive development are demonstrably the same for Mexican American children and European American children. Also, recent demographic analyses of U.S. Hispanics has spotlighted the complexity of Hispanic culture and demonstrated that many previous commonly held assumptions about how Hispanics live were false. Consequently, the cognitive style analysis has been seen as an oversimplification of issues affecting the achievement of Mexican American students.

Subsequent research into patterns of interaction and communication, however, demonstrates that there are discernible differences between parental and community socialized behaviors and expectations that minority children bring to school and the environment they encounter there.

Communication Style. The common assumption that all parties to a particular interaction are assigning similar meanings to the subject at hand often leads to miscommunication. Awareness of the possible pitfalls in cross-cultural communication has led to books and articles that analyze cultural differences for the benefit of business people involved in international negotiations (Pfeiffer, 1988). Handbooks in the popular press present do's and don'ts for travelers to avoid misunderstandings in foreign countries.

However, subtleties of communication style differences often go unnoticed in classroom situations, and they may cause misunderstandings that affect children's ability to achieve and succeed. One study (Gumperz, 1981) analyzed the difference between black and white children's reactions to a classroom task. Black children appeared slower to settle down, were more likely to ask for help, and said things like "I can't do this" or "I don't know" even after they had received instruction. Researchers noted that their comments repeatedly had an identifiable pattern of intonation.

Black adult judges were asked to analyze tape recordings of the black children's verbal responses. Their understanding of the children's comments was that the children were expressing a desire for company while they worked, rather than an actual inability to do the work itself. Failure on the part of a teacher to understand the intention of the children's remarks might lead to the assumption that the students were incapable of understanding or completing the assigned task, which was not the case.

Interaction Style. Patterns of classroom interaction determine who participates, how they participate, and when. For example, a teacher can interact with all students as a group. In that format, a teacher can address all the students, or address individuals while the rest look on. Students may be asked to respond as a group or individually. Sometimes students respond voluntarily; other times they are called on. In these kinds of situations, the teacher generally structures the interaction.

In other patterns, the class may be divided into small groups, with one group interacting with the teacher while others work independently. In some cases, all the students in a class may work independently, with the teacher functioning as a monitor or a resource. Students may also work in small groups, with selected individuals taking leadership roles. Variations of this format are gaining popularity as cooperative-learning-based curricula are developed. (See Chapter 5 for a discussion of cooperative learning.)

The way in which interaction is structured has an impact on student participation. It has been noted, for example, that Native American children seem to be unable or unwilling to participate verbally in classroom interactions. Analyses of classroom interaction styles indicate that patterns of classroom interaction are often incongruent with traditional Native American interaction patterns.

Susan Philips (1983) studied the interaction styles of school children from the Warm Springs Indian Reservation in Oregon. Philips also examined communication patterns among adult members of the community to determine their interaction styles. She found that Warm Springs children's patterns of discourse and interaction differ from the usual communication patterns found in their classrooms. The children have been socialized to interact in patterns appropriate for their community.

According to Philips, "Indian organization of interaction can be characterized as maximizing the control that an individual has over his or her own turn at talk, and as minimizing the control that a given individual has over the turns of others" (p. 115). Consequently, Native American children were much less likely than non–Native American children to respond in situations where they were called upon involuntarily, or where they were singled out. On the other hand, the Native American children in the study participated verbally in small group situations where students were allowed to control their own interactions.

In another study of Native American classrooms (Mohatt & Erickson, 1981), researchers analyzed the differences between a Native American and a non–Native American teacher in an Odawa school in Canada. The researchers noted differences in pacing, the directiveness of the teachers, and the structures used to stimulate participation. The Native American teacher's classroom was organized at a slower pace and seemed to be more responsive to the students' readiness to move to a particular activity. The Native American teacher paused longer to wait for responses and engaged in more face-to-face private interactions than the non–Native American teacher. The Native American teacher used small group work to a far greater extent than the non–Native American counterpart.

Interaction during reading instruction was analyzed in the Kamehameha Early Education Program (KEEP) in Honolulu (Au & Jordan, 1981). As a result of that research, KEEP has successfully developed reading skills with Hawaiian children by structuring lessons to make them similar to Hawaiian talk stories, a traditional form of didactic storytelling.

Studies of interaction style are of particular interest. In many cases the children involved are English speaking or even English monolingual, but still experience difficulties in classroom settings that are culturally inappropriate to their experience. This leads us to the conclusion that we must consider factors beyond language in dual language instructional settings.

Cultural Mismatch: Does It Answer the Question? The cultural mismatch perspective does not assign responsibility for school failure to anyone in particular. It does suggest that members of ethnic groups need to acculturate and become more "Americanized," while, at the same time, schools need to recognize and accommodate children's cultural differences.

Cultural mismatch is an attractive perspective in that it offers tangible solutions. Critics, however, suggest that this view is oversimplified. If differential achievement is a matter of miscommunication, why don't students and teachers negotiate solutions among themselves? People generally overcome obstacles to communication, even in complex situations, altering their communicative style and sometimes developing whole new languages to interact with others (McDermott & Gospodinoff, 1981).

Is it possible that minority children in school fail to negotiate miscommunications because they resist the notion of acculturation? Acculturation, after all, implies the superiority of a particular group (Sue & Padilla, 1986). Wolcott (1997), describing his experiences teaching Kwakiutl children in British Columbia, adopts the metaphor "teacher as an enemy." For the students, he observes, cooperating with the instructional program "may mean selling out, defecting, turning traitor, ignoring the succorance and values and pressures of one's peers, one's family, one's own people" (p. 89). Overall, the cultural mismatch view, while revealing in individual classroom situations, fails to take into account the larger social and political context of education (Cummins, 1984).

CONTEXTUAL INTERACTION

Cross-cultural miscommunication has attracted interest, for example, in the area of business, where it has been noted that failure on the part of U.S. citizens to understand differences in communication styles has been embarrassing and costly. In the area of education, dual language classrooms eliminate obvious language barriers to understanding and accomplishment. And, as previously discussed, microstudies of classroom interactions allow us to develop strategies to maximize opportunities for culturally diverse students to participate and succeed.

But interaction patterns within individual classrooms account only for the teacher–child relationship, which is but one small segment of the entire network of relationships that affect children in school. Critics of the cultural mismatch theory suggest that the mismatch view is too narrow and that it fails to explain why some groups of language minority children do well in school despite cultural difference and language barriers (Ogbu & Matute-Bianchi, 1986).

Koreans are a case in point. Korean students, descendants of forced laborers brought to Japan in the 1930s, do not do well in Japanese schools, where they are a minority. In the United States, on the other hand, Korean students, like many other Asian students, have a tendency to excel. This example is not unique—comparable patterns arise in many places around the world. Why, then, do some minorities do poorly in some settings and well in others?

The contextual interaction model recognizes that there are differences between ethnic minority cultures and mainstream values that may be prevalent in schools. Unlike the mismatch model, however, contextual interaction suggests that there is a dynamic power relationship between minority cultures and schooling that must be analyzed from a broad social and political perspective (Cortés, 1986).

JOHN OGBU'S TYPOLOGY

Some minorities do well in school; others do not. Some reasons for this inconsistency become apparent if we recognize that not all minorities have the same political and social status. John Ogbu (1978) has categorized minorities into three distinct groups which are described in the following sections. Success in school, according to Ogbu, is different for members of each of these groups, in keeping with the characteristics he has described.

Autonomous Minorities. Jews and Mormons are examples of autonomous minorities in the United States. While they are definitely minorities in the numerical sense, they are not perceived as second-class citizens. They maintain a distinct cultural identity, but are not socially or politically isolated.

Immigrant Minorities. Immigrants have moved to the United States for a variety of reasons, but to some extent it is possible to say that they have come here voluntarily. While they may be socially and politically subordinated and economically disadvantaged, they maintain a positive self-concept.

Some immigrants have come from societies where they were socialized as majority group members and have internalized a sense of their own power. They perceive the disadvantages in their new setting as temporary and alterable. Cubans who took refuge in the United States after the Cuban revolution, for example, were often highly educated professionals and business people who quickly entered the U.S. mainstream.

Many immigrants feel that despite the inconveniences of their new circumstances, their situation has improved in the United States. A woman living in a two-room shack with four children told me that her life is better in the United States than in her country of origin because "back home with all of us working we ate meat once a week. Here we can eat meat every day."

Suarez-Orozco and Suarez-Orozco (1993) used the Thematic Apperception Test to study the attitudes of immigrant high school students from Central America. They concluded that the students they worked with were motivated to work hard in school as a compensation for feelings of guilt, resulting from having left families behind, often to endure hardships so that they themselves might have better opportunities.

Castelike Minorities. Sometimes called *indigenous* or *traditional minorities*, castelike minorities "have become incorporated into a society more or less involuntarily and permanently through slavery, conquest, or colonization and then relegated to menial status" (Ogbu & Matute-Bianchi, 1986, p. 90). Castelike or indigenous minorities in the United States include African Americans, who were brought here as slaves, and Native Americans, who were subordinated by conquest. Mexican Americans were originally a conquered people, and newly arrived Mexican immigrants acquire subordinate status as they enter the preexisting infrastructure that makes Mexican Americans a castelike minority.

Secondary Cultural Differences. Ogbu (1994) points out that attempts to rectify inequality between minority and dominant culture groups are most often implemented at the instrumental level, that is, by attempting to provide equal access to educational and material resources. Such attempts, ineffective in and of themselves, also ignore relational differences between groups.

For example, minority groups develop a set of cultural characteristics that arise in contact with the dominant culture, which allow minority group members to function in social settings where they are subordinated (Ogbu, 1992).

In Ogbu's view, members of castelike groups may in fact engage in what he calls *cultural inversion,* or "the tendency . . . to regard certain forms of behavior, events, symbols, and meanings as inappropriate . . . because these are characteristic of White Americans" (Ogbu, 1992, p. 8). Among some black students, for example, succeeding in school is equated with "acting white" (Fordham, 1991). Richmond Community High School, founded in 1977 in Richmond, Virginia, recognizes the potential damage this attitude can do, and provides gifted African American students from low-income households "a safe and intellectually challenging place for disadvantaged kids to be smart" (Viadero, 1997, p. 33).

It should be noted that young women may avoid success in school because academic success contradicts the images they have internalized as feminine (Bell, 1991). In other words, being too successful might equate with "acting male." In early 1998, a Bay Area high school became the first in California to offer separate classes for boys and girls. The students in the special two-year pilot program enjoy coeducational lunch and class breaks, but attend separate classes for academic subjects during their first and second high school years. Supporters of this experiment maintain that separate classes will be particularly helpful in allowing girls to flourish academically and develop self-esteem (Aratani, 1998).

Foley (1994) notes that Ogbu's theory of oppositional culture is a negative characterization that fails to acknowledge the "positive, self-valorizing character of oppositional ethnic humor, dialect, musical, and street art forms" (p. 187). Referring to his own research in a South Texas high school, Foley notes that despite the historical and social context in that region, many Mexican American students have achieved success without relinquishing a sense of their own ethnicity. At least in the particular situation Foley studied, students whom Ogbu might characterize as involuntary or castelike minorities appeared to function in a manner more congruent with voluntary minorities. Foley encourages us to focus our research on why some involuntary minority students succeed, rather than why some fail.

STATUS, POWER, AND SCHOOL SUCCESS

People sometimes fail to realize the nature and amount of power that schools represent. Schooling in the United States is compulsory—all children must attend. For members of the economic and social mainstream, taking their children to the schoolhouse door is often emotional, but not necessarily intimidating or threatening. For people whose cultural, social, economic, or political perspectives differ from the mainstream, schools may represent a power structure that will indoctrinate their children away from the ways of living that their families value and cherish.

Choice in schooling is generally reserved for the more affluent members of our society, and awareness of options in schooling is most often the privilege of the educated. Most children attend the neighborhood public school; there is relatively little choice in the matter. Schools, therefore, become what Henry Giroux (1988) has called "contested sites"—arenas for political power struggles.

Such struggles take a number of forms. The debate, for example, regarding evolution versus creationism is a curriculum battle that has been waged furiously for over 70 years and continues unabated today. Other areas of tension are manifested in censorship battles, where texts or materials in the school library may be at issue; and home schooling conflicts, where parents or a group of parents may resist the notion of a majority-imposed curriculum (Arons, 1983).

Preservice teachers are often surprised by the disparity between the behavior of minority children at home, where they are required to carry out important responsibilities such as providing income and caring for younger siblings or elderly grandparents, and the behavior of the same children in school, where they may be irresponsible and even disruptive. The behavior of those children makes it clear that they do not respect or feel respected in the school environment.

The Role of Schools as Perceived by Minority Students. Members of autonomous and immigrant minority groups are more likely to succeed in school than members of castelike minority groups. Children are astute sociologists, quickly making accurate sense of the world around them. Children who are members of castelike minorities perceive that society has placed limitations on their aspirations and that schools serve as instruments for preserving the power status quo.

Ogbu and Matute-Bianchi suggest (1986) that the role of schools becomes part of folk culture, handed down from one generation to the next. Among castelike minority groups, school is not seen as a way of getting ahead. The motion picture *Stand and Deliver* (Menendez, Musca, & Olmos, 1988) tells the true story of Jaime Escalante, a Bolivian-born school teacher, and his first year in an urban high school in Los Angeles. Escalante's entire math class, with many students who could not manage basic mathematics at the outset, passed the Advanced Placement calculus test.

In one striking scene, a student asks Escalante for an extra book to keep at home so his friends won't see him looking studious. He is not yet ready to give up his identity in a social setting that assures him success, to take on the identity of a student, in a world he mistrusts and may not be able to master. The students who did pass the Advanced Placement test were accused of cheating and were required to take the test again. The students were subsequently vindicated, but the accusation corroborates the contextual interaction model and speaks to the accurate awareness minority students may have that they are not welcomed by the system.

Contextual Interaction as a Solution to Differential Achievement. Contextual interaction, unlike the genetic inferiority or cultural deficit views, does not blame the victim. And while it incorporates the notion of cultural mismatch as part of the explanation for differential achievement, it suggests that we have to seek solutions beyond the classroom door. Contextual interaction requires that we consider the complex network of factors that schooling involves.

McDermott (1997) suggests that failure is a social construction. He asks us to reframe our essential question:

> Instead of asking why half the individuals in a culture do less well than the others, we can ask why a culture would acquire so many individuals in failing positions. Instead of asking why so many individuals do not learn what they need to get around in the culture, we can ask why a culture would organize opportunities for individuals to learn to behave in ways that would make them look like failures. (p. 121)

Summary

Educators have devised several theoretical frameworks to explain differential achievement among diverse ethnic groups. The genetic inferiority model suggests that ability is innate and consequently inalterable. The cultural deficit model posits that some cultures are inadequate.

The cultural mismatch model proposes that children come to school with values and behaviors that don't fit the school environment. Cultural mismatch theorists have provided some significant insights into culture differences in communication, but the model does not account for the fact that some children succeed in spite of language and culture differences. The contextual interaction model suggests that the failure of some children to achieve in school can be explained only by taking political and social factors into account.

Questions to Think About and Discuss

1. Was there ever a time when a teacher or somebody important to you made you feel that you were not a capable person? How did you react to that? Is there anything in our present system of schooling that might suggest to some students that they are not capable of success?

2. In 1989, Peggy McIntosh published a ground-breaking article that contained the now famous "White Privilege Checklist." The checklist is widely available on the web. Working with a group of colleagues, read the checklist and use the issues to interrogate the questions of race and color in the United States. What other kinds of privilege can you identify? Do you feel privileged in some way? How do hidden assumptions of privilege affect schools?

Activities

1. Look up recent citations under *academic achievement, achievement gap,* and *minority achievement* in the publications prepared under the U.S. Office of Education by the Educational Resources Information Center (ERIC). Survey titles and abstracts to see which approaches researchers are using to analyze minority student achievement.
2. How is academic achievement reported in your state/district? What tests are used? How are scores grouped? What patterns can you discern? Testing information may be available from your state department of education or from local district offices. Test results are sometimes reported in local newspapers.
3. Investigate placement procedures for special education in your local district. How is cultural diversity accommodated in the process?

Suggestions for Further Reading

California State Department of Education (Ed.). (1986). *Beyond language: Social and cultural factors in schooling language minority students.* Los Angeles: Evaluation, Dissemination, and Assessment Center, California State University, Los Angeles.

This book was constructed as a companion piece for "Schooling and language minority students: A theoretical framework" and "Studies on immersion education: A collection for United States educators," edited by the California State Department of Education (see Chapters 1 and 6). "Framework" and "Immersion" address educational issues of first and second language. Beyond Language *considers social and cultural factors that have an impact on the education of language minority students. The book provides theoretical analyses and data that support the contextual interaction model. This book is basic reading for those concerned with the relationship of sociocultural factors and schooling.*

Ogbu, J. U. (1978). *Minority education and caste: The American system in cross-cultural perspective.* New York: Academic Press.

Ogbu presents a structural argument for the underachievement of minority children in school. The contextual interaction model owes much to his analysis of schooling for minority children in cross-cultural settings. Articles by this author are included in Beyond Language *and* Language, Literacy and Culture.

Trueba, H. T., Guthrie, G. P., & Au, K. H. (Eds.). (1981). *Culture and the bilingual classroom: Studies in classroom ethnography.* Rowley, MA: Newbury House.
The studies in this volume use microethnography to focus on patterns of interaction between teachers and ethnically diverse students in schools and classrooms. Included are a study of teaching styles in an Odawa school (Gerald Mohatt and Frederick Erickson) and a discussion of the KEEP reading program for Hawaiian students (Kathryn Hu-Pei Au and Cathie Jordan), both of which are often mentioned in analyses of teaching and interaction styles in cross-cultural settings. A section on theoretical and methodological issues is useful to the beginning student of ethnography.

Legal Foundations of Dual Language Instruction

As we saw earlier, dual language instruction was widely available in the United States in the nineteenth century but became unpopular in reaction to large-scale European immigration. Anti-German feeling was particularly powerful, peaking with the advent of World War I. Because of the strong anti-foreign feelings the war engendered, there was little support for instruction in languages other than English in the period between World War I and World War II.

World War II marked the beginning of the American civil rights movement, initially among African Americans. The civil rights movement came to have significant impact on education in general and bilingual education in particular. This chapter will review the events that laid the groundwork for the legal foundations of dual language instruction.

The educational rights of limited English proficient children are protected by law in the form of legislation, court decisions, and administrative implementation and enforcement regulations. There is no single piece of legislation or court decision that requires dual language instruction for *all* limited English proficient children. Instead, there is a complex mesh of statutes and case law that defines the educational entitlements of limited English proficient students and affects the ways programs are funded for them. This chapter will review federal and state legislation and case law regarding dual language instruction and describe their impact on policy and program implementation.

The Historical Context for Dual Language Instruction: World War II and Beyond

WORLD WAR II AND FOREIGN LANGUAGE INSTRUCTION

Fueled by reactions to large waves of immigration and the imminence of World War I, the popularity of dual language instruction in the nineteenth century dwindled rapidly as antiforeign and anti-German sentiments reached a fever pitch. Nor did the Armistice end the disfavor into which dual language instruction had fallen. Following World War I, dual language instruction in general fell into disfavor, and even traditional foreign language instruction was viewed with distaste. The state of Nebraska went so far as to outlaw the teaching of foreign languages altogether, but that effort was deterred by a United States Supreme Court decision (*Meyer v. Nebraska*, 1923) that held the prohibition unconstitutional, making a case that is based on the Fourteenth Amendment.

The court case did little to inspire an increase in dual language and foreign language instruction, which remained in public disfavor and suffered from disinterest until World War II. With the onset of that war, a renewed interest in foreign language instruction was triggered by the immediate need for expertise in a variety of languages in order to communicate with our allies and maintain effective intelligence efforts.

The value of bilingualism to the war effort was demonstrated dramatically when the U.S. Marine Corps began using the Navajo language for radio communications. After the Japanese had deciphered all military codes, 400 Navajo marines volunteered to transmit top secret information in their first language. Ironically, the "code talkers" had been forbidden to speak their language in many places at home. Carl Gorman, the oldest of the group, who died at the age of 90 in 1998, "recalled that as a student at a mission school he had once been chained to an iron pipe for a week because he insisted on speaking his native tongue" (Thomas, 1998). The Japanese were never able to break the "code," and the Navajo effort made a significant contribution to U.S. military success in the Pacific. Many American lives were saved as a result of the contributions of the Navajo code talkers.

U.S. servicemen who were fluent in German, Italian, and Japanese were considered extremely valuable. To increase the number of military personnel who could be useful for intelligence gathering, the U.S. Army took a leadership role in developing methodologies for fast and effective foreign language instruction, as discussed in Chapter 6. After World War II, the federal government passed the National Defense Education Act (1958), which included support for foreign language instruction. The experiences of World War II taught the United States that the nation needed expertise in foreign languages as part of our national defense.

WORLD WAR II AND CIVIL RIGHTS

In addition to an awareness of the need for expertise in foreign languages, World War II affected many Americans' consciousness about their own status and rights. For indigenous minorities, as well as the children of immigrants, serving in World War II bolstered a self-concept of "Americanness." Having proved their commitment to the United States by offering their lives for their country, members of minorities were no longer willing to be regarded as outsiders or second-class citizens.

For many, military service provided the first opportunity to travel outside the United States (or even outside their home towns) and to experience cultures and lifestyles different from their own. Many Americans returned from Europe and Asia, where cultural diversity and multilingualism were the norm, with a more sophisticated view of themselves and American society.

The awareness gained through exposure to different cultures and viewpoints extended beyond acceptance of cultural and linguistic diversity. U.S. military personnel were viewed as liberators, and their presence was greeted with great excitement and gratitude. People literally crawled out of concentration camps in Europe to kiss the feet of American G.I.s. It mattered not at all to the Nazis' victims whether the feet and the people they belonged to were black or white or brown.

It is difficult to imagine how U.S. war veterans felt, having served their country and hailed as liberators, only to suffer the indignities of legalized segregation and discrimination on returning home. In 1948, when local authorities in Three Rivers, Texas, refused to bury a Mexican American war hero in the local veterans' cemetery, World War II veterans in Corpus Christi, Texas, founded the American G.I. Forum. The American G.I. Forum became an organization devoted to fighting discrimination in all areas. The incident in Texas was not the first or only demonstration of racism in our history, and the American G.I. Forum is not the first or only organization devoted to antidiscrimination, but the event shows how World War II had raised the consciousness of minority groups in the United States.

BROWN V. THE BOARD OF EDUCATION (1954)

This changing American consciousness provided the backdrop for the civil rights movement, which reached its most important legal expression in the U.S. Supreme Court decision in *Brown v. the Board of Education* of Topeka in 1954. The *Brown* decision established the principle that separate facilities that were the product of intentional segregation were inherently unequal, reversing a decision by the Court 58 years earlier that separate but equal facilities, or segregation, constituted equality (*Plessy v. Ferguson*, 1896).

The *Brown* decision was a landmark in U.S. history and had a significant impact on all forms of segregation. For example, it was used to break down segregation on buses, trains, restaurants, and (eventually) housing. But the immediate concern of *Brown* was schooling, and to this day schooling remains an arena in which the impact of *Brown* is continually felt.

Judicial efforts to desegregate the schools have been slowed and often stalled due to the resistance of state and local governments. De facto segregation continues to plague public schools today. Efforts to speed school desegregation included the Civil Rights Act of 1964, which contained provisions strengthening the federal government's ability to enforce desegregation and integration. Title VI of the Civil Rights Act plays a key role in the establishment of the rights of language minority children, as we will discuss later in this chapter.

THE CIVIL RIGHTS MOVEMENT AND DUAL LANGUAGE INSTRUCTION

Overall, the climate of the times in the late 1950s and early 1960s favored the establishment of dual language programs. As described in Chapter 1, the influx of Cuban refugees and the establishment of bilingual programs for Spanish-speaking children in Florida catalyzed the demand for programs for other non-English-speaking children. The success of the program in Florida, combined with increased ethnic self-awareness among minority groups and the philosophical impetus of the civil rights movement, led to legislation and litigation that established the educational rights of language minority children.

Who Governs Education?

The rights of language minority children are protected by legislation, case law, and other governmental actions. Because much of what we shall discuss is rooted in federal law, it is important to understand the avenues by which the federal government acquires jurisdiction over schooling.

The U.S. Constitution gives the federal government, among other things, the power to coin money, to declare war, and to regulate patents and copyrights, and prohibits individual states from acting in those areas without the consent of Congress. The functions not allotted to Congress or prohibited to the states are reserved to the states.

Under this constitutional arrangement, education, which is neither specifically assigned to the federal government nor prohibited to the states, is a state government function. The result is variety in education systems across the states.

For example, organization of school governance varies. Hawaii has one school district; California has over a thousand, some consisting of only one school and some consisting of many. Curriculum and funding mechanisms differ from state to state. If you are a certified teacher who has moved from one state to another, you have encountered the lack of uniformity in educational systems and have discovered that each state has its own certification requirements.

FEDERAL INVOLVEMENT IN EDUCATION

Despite the fact that education is theoretically reserved to the states, the federal government exerts powerful influence on schooling through funding, legislation, and judicial action. The federal government apportions funds for education at all levels and supports services that could not be sustained by state budgets. In 1998, PL 105-78 provided $29.4 billion in discretionary funds for the Department of Education. The bill allotted nearly $200 million dollars for instructional services to LEP students, $150 million for instructional services for immigrant children, funds for financial assistance for college students and after school programs, as well as support for school reform and technological innovation in schools.

In addition, federal agencies such as the National Science Foundation, the Department of Agriculture, the U.S. Information Agency, and others spend substantial sums for educational programs. Federal spending is accompanied by federal regulation. Federal dollars imply federal influence in the area of education.

The influence of federal spending on education is doubly felt because Title VI of the Civil Rights Act of 1964 prohibits institutions that receive federal assistance from discriminating on the basis of race, color, or national origin. Any institution failing to comply with the Civil Rights Act may lose all its federal funding. Most institutions receive federal funding and must therefore support the government's agenda of protecting minorities.

As we have already seen, the federal government also influences education through judicial action. It might be said, in fact, that the U.S. Supreme Court is the government's most powerful educational decision maker. Almost every analysis of law or policy in education must include consideration of the high court's decisions, which have had a strong impact on areas such as desegregation, religion in schools, student discipline, rights of handicapped and gifted students, and private schooling, to name just a few.

We have considered the impact of the federal government on education in some detail because it has bearing on the education of limited English proficient students through all three areas of influence. Funding, Title VI of the Civil Rights Act, and the U.S. Supreme Court, along with other federal legislation, case law, and regulation, provide a firm foundation for the rights of students who don't speak English.

The Bilingual Education Act (Title VII)

In 1968 Congress passed Title VII of the Elementary and Secondary Education Act, or the Bilingual Education Act, and in 1969 appropriated $7.5 million dollars to support its programs. Title VII was directed at children from environments where the dominant language was not English and at those whose families had incomes of less than $3,000 per year. Seventy-six projects were funded during the first year of appropriations, serving 27,000 children (Castellanos, 1983).

The 1974 reauthorization of the act broadened the definition of the children served to include those of limited English-speaking ability and eliminated the income requirements. In 1978 the population to be served was again redefined to include children of limited English proficiency (1978). This is important because proficiency is broader than speaking ability and implies that children should not be exited from programs based on speaking ability alone. The 1984 reauthorization included provisions for family English literacy programs for families of children served and for developmental (two-way) bilingual programs.

Over the course of 25 years, expansions of Title VII provided funding for a wide range of activities associated with dual language instruction. Basic services to children, preservice and in-service training for teachers and trainers of teachers, research activities, program evaluation, and nationwide dissemination of information on bilingual education were all funded through Title VII.

DISCRETIONARY FUNDING

Some forms of government funding are available to individuals who are members of a defined class. For example, Chapter 1 support for academic assistance is available from the government for any child who meets the established academic and income criteria. Other forms of government funding are not automatically available to defined classes of people, but are awarded on a competitive basis. Title VII did not require dual language instruction for every student who is limited English proficient, nor did it provide monetary assistance for every individual who qualified.

Instead, local school districts, universities, or state agencies applied for Title VII funds by submitting a grant application to the federal government. Applicants were required to describe the proposed program, indicate the need for it, describe the qualifications of the personnel involved, and provide an evaluation plan.

The funding process was competitive; thus, not all applicants received funding. Title VII was intended to help educational agencies to establish mechanisms for delivering services for limited English proficient students that would then become part of the agency's regularly funded and supported activities.

TITLE VII AND POLICY

Title VII did not mandate dual language instruction for all students or any students. Such a mandate would be out of keeping with the federal role in education. Title VII did, however, set national policy regarding services for limited English proficient children. It did so in two ways.

The first was through legislative language. The act acknowledged that there were large numbers of children who would benefit from instruction in their primary language using bilingual educational methods and techniques and went on to say:

> Congress declares it to be the policy of the United States, in order to establish equal educational opportunity for all children, to encourage the establishment and operation, where appropriate, of educational programs using bilingual educational practices, techniques, and methods. . . .

The second way Title VII influenced policy was through infrastructure. Title VII funding provided for the establishment of basic programs and also supported training for school personnel in the area of dual language instruction. In addition, money provided for basic research and program evaluation allowed educators to develop the theory and methodology necessary to properly serve children in dual language programs. National networking disseminated information, making it possible for educational agencies to benefit from each other's experiments and expertise. To the extent that funding permitted, programs, training, and research resulted in a knowledge and advocacy base that created infrastructure for dual language education.

Lau v. Nichols (1974)

As mentioned earlier, the U.S. Supreme Court has played a decisive role in many areas of education, and dual language instruction is no exception. In 1969, plaintiffs representing 1,800 language minority children in the San Francisco Unified School District sued the district, claiming that limited English proficient children were being denied equal educational opportunity in English-only classrooms.

Overturning the decision of a lower court, the Supreme Court decided in favor of the plaintiffs under Title VI of the Civil Rights Act. The language in the decision was strong. Justice William O. Douglas wrote:

> There is no equality of treatment merely by providing students with the same facilities, textbooks, teachers, and curriculum; for students who do not understand English are effectively foreclosed from any meaningful education. Basic skills are at the very core of what these public schools teach. Imposition of a requirement that before a child can effectively participate in the educational program he must already have acquired those basic skills is to make a mockery of public education. We know that those who do not understand English are certain to find their classroom experiences wholly incomprehensible and in no way meaningful.

INTERPRETATION OF *LAU*

The Court held for the plaintiffs in the *Lau* decision, and the case undoubtedly represents a victory for the rights of language minority children. There are several points, however, that should be borne in mind when considering *Lau* and its effects.

The *Lau* decision was an interpretation of the Civil Rights Act. At the time the Supreme Court agreed to review *Lau*, they refused to review *Serna v. Portales* (1974), a similar case that was argued on the basis of the equal protection clause of the Constitution. In deciding *Lau*, the Court avoided the constitutional issue. A decision on constitutional grounds would have been stronger than the decision rendered on the basis of a statute. This is true because Congress could make *Lau* irrelevant by simply passing a different law. In contrast, a constitutional amendment would be necessary to overturn a Supreme Court decision interpreting the Constitution.

Another issue that was raised by the case was numbers. In his concurring opinion in the *Lau* case, Justice Harry A. Blackmun observed that for him numbers were "at the heart of this case," suggesting that he might have viewed the situation differently if smaller numbers of children had been involved.

Finally, it should be noted that in deciding *Lau* the Court did not specify any particular remedy. The Court held that districts failing to provide services for children who could not function in English were violating the civil rights of those children. And it did require that the San Francisco Unified School District take affirmative steps to eliminate the inequities suffered by limited English proficient children as a result of its policies. But there is no requirement in *Lau* that districts must establish bilingual programs.

EFFECTS OF *LAU*

The *Lau* decision had several dramatic and immediate effects. In 1975 the Department of Health, Education, and Welfare (HEW) and the Office of Civil Rights (OCR) of the federal government developed a document to provide districts with guidance for implementing programs in compliance with Title VI of the Civil Rights Act as interpreted in *Lau*. The document, known as the "*Lau* Remedies," established standards for identifying limited English speaking children, assessing their language ability, and meeting their needs. The *Lau* Remedies were never formally accorded regulatory status, but did serve as the basis for compliance reviews by the Office of Civil Rights, which meant that districts generally attempted to abide by the requirements in the document.

Lau had an impact on other court cases that were pending at the time. In New York, for example, Aspira, a Puerto Rican community group, had filed suit against the New York City Board of Education on behalf of the system's approximately 182,000 Spanish-speaking students (*Aspira of New York, Inc. v. Board of Education*, 1972). Shortly after *Lau* was decided, the parties to the suit entered into a consent decree in which the New York City Board of Education agreed to provide substantial bilingual services to children of limited English ability.

Also, soon after *Lau* a number of states, including California and Texas, passed laws mandating some form of bilingual education (McFadden, 1983).

While *Lau* did not require any specific remedy or form of program, it favored the establishment of bilingual programs as a way of avoiding civil rights violations.

Advocates for the rights of language minority children now rely less on *Lau* and instead base their arguments on the Equal Educational Opportunities Act of 1974.

Equal Educational Opportunities Act of 1974

Section 1703(f) of the Equal Educational Opportunities Act (EEOA) states:

> No state shall deny equal educational opportunity to an individual on account of his or her race, color, sex, or national origin by . . . (f) the failure by an educational agency to take appropriate action to overcome language barriers that impede equal participation by its students in its instructional programs.

Section 1703(f) of EEOA restates the underlying principle of the *Lau* decision in statutory form. There is a growing body of federal case law that interprets the statute (*Castañeda v. Pickard*, 1981; *Gomez v. Illinois*, 1987; *Idaho Migrant Council v. Board*, 1981; *Keyes v. School District No. 1*, 1983). The cases do not require bilingual education but they do require equal access to the curriculum. In other words, children may not sit in classrooms where they cannot understand what is going on. Affirmative steps must be taken to ensure that all children have a meaningful educational experience. As articulated in the case law, in order to properly serve students who are limited English proficient, districts must:

- Develop a program based on a sound theoretical rationale.
- Provide trained teachers and sufficient material resources to implement the program.
- Develop an evaluation system for the program and refine the program in accordance with information from the evaluation.

Federal law protecting the rights of language minority children is of particular importance in areas where states have weakened or eliminated their own requirements regarding bilingual education. Under federal law, children who lack sufficient English skills to succeed in English-only classrooms are entitled to an educational opportunity equal to that of their English-speaking peers.

No Child Left Behind

In January, 2002, President George Bush signed into law the current reauthorization of the Elementary and Secondary Education Act, the No Child Left

Immigrant Students' Rights to Attend Public Schools

Educators sometimes question whether undocumented immigrant children have the right to attend public schools. Educators should be aware that, as a result of the United States Supreme Court decision in *Plyler v. Doe*, [457 U.S. 202 (1982)], all children who reside in the United States have the right to attend public schools, regardless of their immigration status.

Under *Plyler*, public schools may not:

- Deny a student admission based on immigration status.
- Make inquiries of students or parents that would expose their status.
- Require students or parents to document their status.
- Require social security numbers of students.

The National Coalition of Advocates for Students (NCAS), a national nonprofit advocacy organization, has an annual campaign to alert educators, parents, and students to students' rights as a result of *Plyler*. According to NCAS, recent changes in the Student Visa Program do not change the *Plyler* rights of undocumented children. Furthermore, the Family Education Rights and Privacy Act (FERPA) prohibits schools from providing any outside agency with information from a child's school file that would expose the student's undocumented status without first getting parental permission, unless the agency has a court order.

Educators can look for updated information on the NCAS website at www.ncasboston.org. The School Opening Alert is published on the site in several languages and can be downloaded and used to inform parents of their rights.

Behind Act of 2001 (NCLB). Title III of the NCLB, the English Language Acquisition, Language Enhancement and Academic Achievement Act consolidates programs previously funded under the Bilingual Education Act (BEA) and the Emergency Immigrant Education Act (1984), an impact aid program designed to help states cope with newly arrived immigrant students.

The NCLB signals a shift in emphasis and support from the BEA, which funded programs that supported students' first languages, to programs that focus exclusively on English development. Unlike the BEA, the NCLB makes no reference to bilingualism. For example, the Act continues funding for an informational clearinghouse, but renames the National Clearinghouse for Bilingual Education (NCBE) as the National Clearinghouse for English Language Acquisition (NCELA).

NCLB FUNDING

Unlike the BEA, the NCLB is a formula grant program with a funding level trigger. Under NCLB, as long as Congress appropriates at least $650 million, the program is funded as a state formula grant, that is, categorical rather than discretionary funding. This will benefit states that have seen a sudden increase in the number of English language learners in their schools. Under the BEA, states like New York and California, with large numbers of English language learners and significant experience in offering bilingual programs, had the advantage in competing for Title VII funds. Now states where demographics are changing may be eligible for federal funds without having to compete with traditionally successful grant makers.

The federal government is likely to keep funding to serve English language learners at a reasonably high level, but the funding will provide a strong policy push toward English-only in the schools. Also, while overall funding levels may appear higher than previous appropriations under the BEA, the money will be spread more thinly, resulting in less money per child.

What the NCLB Requires.   The NCLB requires states to develop annual achievement objectives for English language learners and to include all LEP students in statewide assessments in the areas of reading/language arts and mathematics. In addition, science is added to the mandatory assessments in 2007–2008. Schools are to be held accountable for meeting annual achievement objectives and for ensuring that LEP students make adequate progress in all areas.

English language learners are not required to take the reading and language arts assessments during their first year in U.S. schools, but must take an English language proficiency test and a math assessment. States may make some accommodations for second language learners. English language learners may be assessed in their first language for several years if such assessments can be made available. Assessments in languages other than English must align with state standards. Other accommodations such as simplified or native language instructions are permitted under the law, but English language learners must take the reading and English language arts tests after they have attended schools in the United States for three consecutive years.

NCLB provides funds for English instruction, curriculum development, professional development for teachers, tutoring, teacher aides, and technology. Native language instruction is permissible under the act. However, the act requires that states implement language instruction based on scientifically based research on teaching limited English proficient students. Research on the effectiveness of bilingual education (or any other kind of educational program) is likely to be inconclusive, for good reasons. Program evaluation studies are difficult to design. Random assignment of students to programs is unethical. Furthermore, it's hard to determine the effectiveness of programs through comparisons because programs are generally not truly comparable: Communities and schools vary in myriad ways.

Finally, research about schooling is generally politically informed. Given the particularly acrimonious debate about bilingual education, the term "scientifically based research" has excited controversy across the educational community.

NCLB PROS AND CONS

Advocates for English language learners are not unified in their response to NCLB. Some analysts see potential benefit for second language learners in the requirements of the NCLB. According to the nonprofit advocacy organization Education Trust, "The accountability provisions require states to set clear time-lines for improving student achievement, with particular emphasis on closing achievement gaps between low-income and minority students and their peers (2003, p. 2)." Mayer (2002) points out that NCLB requires states to implement a statewide accountability system for all students, and to measure the academic progress of LEPs along with all other students on an annual basis. A policy brief published by the Urban Institute concurs, suggesting that NCLB puts "English language learners on the map" (Consentino de Cohen & Chu Clewell, 2007, p. 1). This is viewed as a good thing; in other words, states have to keep track of what's happening academically to English language learners along with everyone else.

One positive outcome of the emphasis on accountability is the move to statewide uniform language proficiency testing. The standardized use of tests across entire states will provide teachers with language proficiency informa-tion that is comparable from child to child. California, for example, has devel-oped and implemented the California English Language Development Test (CELDT), and CELDT scores are reported along with student scores on other state-mandated standardized achievement tests.

English language learners may well be getting increased attention. And it is inarguable that assessment of student progress can inform instruction and support student success. However, for accountability to be meaningful, resources have to be equitably distributed. As both the Education Trust and the Urban Institute have documented, the students with the highest needs gener-ally receive instruction from the least-qualified teachers in settings with the least resources (Peske & Haycock, 2006; Weiner & Pristoop, 2006; Consentino de Cohen & Chu Clewell, 2006).

Furthermore, implementation of NCLB has narrowed the focus of instruc-tion, A recent report published by the Center on Education Policy (McMurrer, 2007) notes that emphasis on reading and mathematics has increased, and there has been a decrease in the time spent on social studies, science, music, and art. It can be argued that students with the least economic and social privi-leges at home need the most enriched experiences in school since their parents are unlikely to have the resources to support extra activities.

James Crawford, a well-regarded advocate for second language learners, strongly agrees that NCLB has diminished the quality of education for under-served students. Crawford notes concerns that have been seconded by many classroom teachers regarding "excessive class time devoted to test preparation, a curriculum narrowed to the two tested subjects, neglect of critical thinking in favor of basic skills, pressure to reduce or eliminate native-language instruction, demoralization of teachers whose students fall short of unrealistic cut scores, demoralization of children who are forced to take tests they can't understand, and, perhaps worst of all, practices that encourage low-scoring students to drop out before test day" (Crawford, 2007).

State Laws Regarding Bilingual Education

Prior to *Lau*, the only state-mandated dual language program in the United States was in Massachusetts. Massachusetts's vanguard bilingual education law required a transitional program if 20 or more children in a school district on the same grade level were limited English proficient and had the same primary language. Many other states, to the contrary, required by law that instruction be delivered in English. The passage of the federal Bilingual Education Act in 1968 had a positive effect on the political climate regarding dual language instruction, but funded only a relative handful of programs to meet the needs of children with limited English abilities.

By the mid-1980s, 20 states had bilingual education requirements. The majority of those laws, however, required programs that were transitional and compensatory in nature. This was unfortunate, because compensatory programs are perceived by the general public as peripheral. Without wide popular support, dual language programs are at risk, especially since the population they attempt to serve is often disenfranchised by its lack of English proficiency. Two-way programs offering second language skills to all students are more likely to build a broader political base, but such programs are relatively rare.

The future of state-mandated bilingual education is insecure at the present time. Illinois repealed its statute in 1980 but reinstated it under community pressure. California, with a school enrollment of nearly a million and a half limited English proficient children, allowed its legislation to lapse in 1987, and in 1998 passed an initiative that outlaws nearly all primary language instruction. Arizona followed suit, passing similar legislation in 2000, as did Massachusetts in 2002.

It is worth noting that despite policy shifts in federal legislation, federal judicial protections of the rights of limited English proficient students are still in effect. In the face of increasing needs, communities will undoubtedly need to use them to support dual language instructional programming.

Summary

Legislative and judicial support for publicly funded dual language instructional programs is rooted historically in the civil rights movement. Support at the federal level resides in legislation that provides funding for bilingual programs, civil rights legislation, and case law that requires that limited English proficient students be served. Some states have laws requiring some form of dual language instruction for students who need it, but several key states have all but eliminated primary language instruction for second language learners. Two-way programming rarely receives legislative support. The future of requirements for bilingual education at the state level is more uncertain at the present time than it has been in recent decades.

Questions to Think About and Discuss

1. Should the United States have one set of educational standards and assessments for all public schools? Why or why not?
2. If you are of the opinion that all the public schools in the United States should have one set of standards and assessments, who should determine what those standards and assessments would be?

Activities

1. Speak to the person in your local school district who is in charge of federally funded projects. How much federal money does the district receive annually? What kinds of activities are funded by federal dollars?
2. Does your state have a bilingual education statute? What kinds of programs are mandated? How are they implemented?

Suggestions for Further Reading

Readings on the legal foundations of bilingual education are difficult to identify, since statutes, court cases, and their interpretations are generally available in formats appropriate for legal professionals, while failing to meet the needs of lay readers. In today's world, readers who wish to stay abreast of law and public policy will find the most up-to-date information on the web. National organizations such as the National Association of Other Languages, www.nabe.org, and Teachers of English to Speakers of Other Languages, www.tesol.org, address legislation and policy on their websites and are excellent sources of current information.

chapter 10

Language Policy and Planning

$\mathcal{I}$n preceding chapters we have considered language and culture and have also built an educational rationale to support primary language instruction for limited English proficient students and second language enrichment for monolingual English speakers. While we have generally emphasized the benefits of dual language instruction for individual students, schooling exists within a larger social and political framework. Teachers don't generally think of themselves as government agents. But when we make decisions about language use in public school classrooms, we are also implementing government-sponsored language policy.

Shirley Brice Heath (1983), a prominent sociolinguist, defines language policies as "what the government says and does through its laws, legislative statues, regulations and bureaucratic practices that affect the choices and uses of one or more languages used by the people it represents" (p. 156). Sometimes a nation's policy is stated in the form of recognition of official languages, either through legislation or in a national constitution. At other times, language policy is established by legislation and regulation of language use in courts, schools, and other government agencies, or through a government body such as a language academy.

This chapter will discuss how governments can promote or suppress languages. In other words, we will look at aspects of language policy and language planning.

Language Support

Language support includes graphization, the creation of a writing system; standardization, the creation of an orthography and grammar; modernization, expansion of the vocabulary; and dissemination, usually through teacher training and support in the schools.

The University of Hawaii, for example, with the support of the government of the Trust Territory of the Pacific Islands, has provided support for the languages of the Trust Territories (now the independent countries of the Federated States of Micronesia, the Republic of Belau, the Commonwealth of the Marianas, and the Marshall Islands). The university's support for local languages has included the development of orthographies, the publication of dictionaries and grammars, and teacher preparation to support dissemination of orthographies and to encourage primary language literacy in schools.

Language planning strategies are easy to formulate on paper. In practice, however, they are complicated by historical and social factors. In the case of the Trust Territories, for example, new orthographies are difficult to establish. Except for the Bible, published in vernaculars by missionaries, there was little printed matter in local languages prior to World War II. Old habits die hard, and the old-fashioned printing methods still in use in these remote areas are cumbersome to retool for new writing systems.

New writing systems are difficult to disseminate for other reasons. After a century of colonial domination by a series of foreign powers, teachers in the Pacific Islands have internalized the idea that primary languages should not be used for instruction, and they associate modernization and economic success with the use of English. And while some teachers have become convinced that primary language instruction is valuable, materials in local languages are limited. Basic instructional materials have been created in local languages, but the development of primary language literacy skills has been hampered by the fact that local languages generally have oral traditions. There is, for example, no backlog of written children's literature as we know it in English, and teachers cannot easily find children's books to supplement skills development.

Language Suppression

It is possible for a government to suppress a minority language in a number of ways. Governments can ban the use of minority languages in the media and in public life. Basque, for example, was vehemently suppressed during the Franco regime in Spain but has been restored to the status of an official provincial language under the current liberal monarchy (Grosjean, 1982).

Another way to suppress a minority language is to promote the idea that it is a substandard dialect of a majority language. Catalan, the language of Catalonia in northeastern Spain, is similar to Spanish in several ways, but linguists and speakers alike agree that Spanish and Catalan are different languages. Catalonia resisted the Franco regime, and in an attempt to silence Catalonian resistance, Franco's government deemed Catalan a dialect and made attempts to eradicate it.

Catalan was restored to the status of an official language after Franco's death, and a provincial government agency was established to stimulate its reinstitution (Woolard, 1985). The program to normalize Catalan, as it was called (Miller & Miller, 1996), has been fairly successful, but has had its challenges. Initial attempts to impose Catalan as the only language of instruction in the schools as an attempt to undo the previous damage under Franco's rule met with resistance from some Spanish-speaking parents of school children, who went to court to block the government's implementation of it (Battle in Spain, 1993). Also, as a result of years of language suppression, it was difficult to find qualified bilingual and biliterate teachers (Siguan, 1991).

Currently, students attend school in both languages in a variety of models and settings. While Catalan appears strong at the present time, in an increasingly globalized marketplace the value of Spanish as a world language may yet take its toll.

LANGUAGE SUPPRESSION AND THE MEDIA

Lippi-Green (1997) points out that the media have a role in what she calls the "language subordination process" (pp. 67–69). Her analysis of 371 characters in 24 animated feature films produced by the Disney Corporation indicates that characters with foreign accents are more likely to be "bad guys" than characters who speak either British or American English (Lippi-Green, 1997). Lippi-Green proposes that socialization through the media and the schools teaches children to adopt deprecatory attitudes toward English speakers with foreign accents.

At a macro level, the overwhelming presence of English in the media has a tendency to overpower other languages and even eliminate smaller, less powerful ones. A quick Google search of "English Dominance + Web" turns up multiple "hits" that indicate concern over the fact that English does, in fact, dominate in cyberspace.

ENDANGERED LANGUAGES

The ultimate outcome of language suppression is the disappearance of languages. According to Krauss (1992), an expert on indigenous languages at the Alaska Native Language Center, 40 percent of the world's languages are endangered, and another 50 percent are moribund, literally at death's door, because they are spoken only by adults who are not transmitting them to children. "Languages no longer being learned as mother-tongue by children are beyond mere endangerment, for, unless the course is somehow dramatically reversed, they are already doomed to extinction, like species lacking reproductive capability" (p. 4). Speaking at the turn of the twenty-first century, Krauss highlighted the gravity and immediacy of language death, reflecting, "I consider it a plausible calculation that—at the rate things are going—the coming century will see either the death or doom of 90 percent of mankind's languages" (p. 7). Nothing in the literature to date would indicate that his alarming prediction was wrong.

DOES LANGUAGE LOSS MATTER?

Whether through active suppression or the unintended consequences of mass communication, the world's languages are disappearing at an alarming rate. The world's leading language scholars insist that we should all be deeply concerned about language loss. Crystal (2000) reminds us that diversity is essential to human experience and that "language lies at the heart of what it means to be human" (pp. 33–34).

Some scholars propose that language, culture, and the biosphere may be inextricably linked (Skutnabb-Kangas, 1998). This idea is based on the theory that languages are not simply sets of labels superimposed on the material world, but rather "every language reflects a unique world-view and culture complex mirroring the manner in which a speech community has resolved its problems in dealing with the world, and has formulated its thinking, its philosophy and understanding of the world around it" (Wurm, 1996, p.1).

In other words, languages encode complex relationships with and understandings of the world we inhabit. Each culture relates to the environment in a different way and forms part of the world's ecological whole. Homogenizing the world's languages, and by extension, its cultures, limits the ways that we interact with our environments, and ultimately disturbs the balance that biological, cultural, and linguistic diversity create.

Along with the idea that losing a language costs us the knowledge embedded in a particular code and the way of seeing and expressing the world that the code embodies, we should also be concerned about the loss of the ultimate dynamic richness of language in general (Dalby, 2003). All languages are rich and full, and each language gains from its contact with others. Crystal reminds us that "languages are interesting in themselves" (2000, p. 54). And as Dalby eloquently states, the price we pay when we lose a language is that the "creativity and flexibility that our descendants will need in their language, if they are to survive and prosper, will in due course wither away" (2003, p. 287).

Language Policy and Schooling

It has long been recognized that one potent way to suppress a particular language is to establish laws or policies forbidding its use in schools. Examples of this practice are numerous. During the Spanish colonial period in Latin America, missionaries were directed to provide instruction for Indians in Castilian in an attempt to replace indigenous languages (Weinberg, 1977). During the Japanese colonial period in the Pacific Islands between World Wars I and II, schooling was compulsory and all instruction was delivered in Japanese.

United States colonial policies have included attempts to use schools as a tool for replacing local languages with English in Hawaii, the Philippines, and Puerto Rico. Replacement of Native American languages through forced schooling played a significant role in debilitating Native American societies and destroying indigenous North American cultures.

The use of Spanish in the United States has traditionally provoked repressive reactions. Spanish is indigenous to the Southwest, and its continued use there is supported by substantial and continuing immigration by Spanish speakers. Our proximity to Mexico and a thousand miles of border make Spanish a viable southwestern language. On the East Coast, there are large numbers of Puerto Ricans who are citizens by birth and native Spanish speakers. The United States is the logical destination for Spanish-speaking refugees and immigrants from all of Latin America and the Caribbean. As a result, Spanish is widely spoken in the United States and seems to have staying power. There have historically been rigorous and ongoing attempts to suppress the use of Spanish in schools, including ridiculing, punishing, and expelling children for speaking it, even in play (Carter, 1970).

Ode to Sequoyah

The names of Waitie and Boudinot—
    The valiant warrior and gifted sage—
And other Cherokees, may be forgot,
    But thy name shall descend to every age;
The mysteries enshrouding Cadmus' name
Cannot obscure thy claim to fame.

The people's language cannot perish—nay,
    When from the face of this great continent
Inevitable doom hath swept away
    The last memorial—the last fragment
Of tribes,—some scholar learned shall pore
Upon thy letters, seeking ancient lore.

Some bard shall lift a voice in praise of thee,
    In moving numbers tell the world how men
Scoffed thee, hissed thee, charted with lunacy!
    And who could not give 'nough honor when
At length, in spite of jeers, of want and need,
Thy genius shaped a dream into a deed.

By cloud-capped summits in the boundless wet,
    or mightly river rolling to the sea,
Where'er thy footsteps led thee on that quest,
    Unknown, rest thee, illustrious Cherokee!

SOURCE: Sequoyah invented the Cherokee writing system. This poem in his memory was written by Alexander Lawrence Posey, a nineteenth-century Creek Indian poet. Used with permission of the Five Civilized Tribes Museum, Muskogee, OK 74401.

Schools have also been viewed as an avenue for language revitalization. One example is the successful revitalization of Hebrew in Israel. In a period of about 50 years, Hebrew, a language that had been used largely for liturgical purposes, was completely revitalized and established as the official language of a modern state. According to Spolsky, Hebrew was "vital in that it was passed on to children at home, vernacularized in that it was used as the daily spoken language of all classes, standardized in that it had not just dictionaries and grammars and an academy but a school system ranging from kindergarten to postgraduate university levels, and modernized in that it could be used to talk about sport or physics or politics or any topic" (2004, p. 192).

Spolsky notes that Israel is multilingual and that English is taught and widely spoken. This is as might be expected given that Hebrew is not a language of wider communication and that Israel has strong social, economic, and strategic ties to the United States. But from a language planning and policy perspective, the expansion of Hebrew from a language with limited uses to a language of everyday life is remarkable among efforts to revitalize minority languages. Unfortunately, as Dalby suggests, in many cases teachers are "powerful enough to kill the indigenous languages: they are not powerful enough to bring them back to life" (2003, p. 163). Ireland is a case in point. In 1922, with the establishment of the Republic of Ireland, the Irish language was recognized as the official national language (O'Riagain, 1997). The new government took a variety of measures to revitalize the language. All teachers were required to be proficient in Irish, and Irish instruction was required in the schools.

Revitalization efforts in Ireland have extended the social and geographic reach of the language (O'Riagain, 1997). Nevertheless, Irish has never achieved the status that was hoped for, and English is currently the prevailing medium

ℒanguage Suppression in Schools

The *Genius of Language* is a collection of essays written in English by writers for whom it is their second language. In his essay "Recovering the Original," Ngugi wa Thiong'o, the internationally known Kenyan writer, describes his experience as an elementary school student in Kenya in the 1950s, at a time when schools were directed to eradicate indigenous African languages:

He lay on his tummy on a high table in the assembly hall with all the students and the staff present. Two teachers held his head and legs and pinned him to the table and called him monkey, as the third whip lashed his buttocks. No matter how horribly he screamed and wriggled with pain, they would not let him go. . . . Eventually the shorts split and blood spluttered out, some of it on the shirts of those who held him down, and only then did they let him go. . . . His fault? He had been caught in the act of speaking Gikuyu in the environs of the school.

SOURCE: Thiong'o, N. (2004). Recovering the original. In Lesser, W. (Ed.), *The genius of language* (pp. 102–110). New York: Pantheon.

of communication in Ireland (Dalby, 2003). Given the growth and globalization of the Irish economy in the context of the European Union, Irish, a minority language at the outset of the Republic (O'Riagain, 2001), is likely to remain so.

Tollefson (2002) asserts the importance of a critical view of language planning that "explores the links between language policies and inequalities of class, region, and ethnicity/nationality" (p. 5). From that perspective, language policy in education must be seen as a factor in minority groups' struggle for social and economic empowerment. It is worthy of note then, that in the current political climate in the United States, there are few opportunities in public school settings to sustain or develop minority languages for speakers of languages other than English.

Therefore, most teachers in the present circumstances, whether they like it or not, are engaged in the development of students' English language skills to the ultimate detriment of students' home languages. There may be little any individual teacher can do to turn the tide of thinking about language in American educational policy. Nevertheless, understanding the dynamics of language planning and policy is key for teachers who work with second language learners.

Summary

Governments have language policies, or ways of promoting the use of particular languages for particular purposes. Governments can promote languages through standardization and dissemination or suppress them by prohibiting their use in public life. Language suppression leads to language loss, and language loss may have serious consequences for all people. Even though teachers do not see themselves as implementing language policy, schools are central institutions in the public sphere, and teachers have an important role in language planning.

Questions to Think About and Discuss

1. Should public schools support minority languages? Why or why not?
2. Should languages other than English be allowed for use in the workplace? In courts? In hospitals? Why or why not?

Activities

1. Interview a colleague, friend, or family member who has children and whose first language is a language other than English. Do this person's children speak their parents' language? How do parents (and children) feel about their language abilities?

Suggestions for Further Reading

Crystal, D. (2000). *Language death.* Cambridge, UK: Cambridge University Press.

Crystal describes the dynamics of language loss, communicates the urgency to address the issue, and turns our attention to strategies for revitalizing languages. The last chapter introduces the role of schooling and identifies the tensions that can arise when schools intervene in language policy.

Dalby, A. (2003). *Language in danger: The loss of linguistic diversity and the threat to our future.* New York: Columbia University Press.

This book will start you thinking about the consequences of language loss for us all. Written in a lively and conversational manner and full of interesting examples from a variety of languages, it's an excellent starting point for anyone interested in language policy and planning.

Fishman, J. A. (Ed.). (2001). *Can threatened languages be saved? Reversing language shift revisited: A 21st century perspective.* Clevedon, UK: Multilingual Matters.

According to the articles in this collection, the answer to the question posed in the title is a qualified "yes." Language shift can, in some cases, be reversed, but it's clearly an uphill battle. Chapters discuss French in Quebec, Quechua in South America, and Basque and Catalan in Spain, among others.

Haugen, E. (1987). *Blessings of Babel: Bilingualism and language planning.* Berlin: Mouton de Gruyter.

Not intended for the layperson or the beginner, this discussion of bilingualism in individuals and societies is nevertheless recommended as a synthesis of up-to-date thinking in the area of sociolinguistics. The author's personal observations as a bilingual person add a note of warmth and familiarity to abstract concepts of language contact, language shift, and language planning.

Robins, R. H., & Uhlenbeck, E. M. (Eds.). (1991). *Endangered languages.* Oxford, UK: Berg.

The first article in this collection, by Stephen A. Wurm, details the circumstances under which languages die or disappear. Following articles describe the condition of various languages around the world. Languages are dying at an incredible rate, and these scholarly analyses will fascinate and upset the reader who cherishes language and linguistic diversity.

Wurm, S. A. (Ed.). (1996). *Atlas of the world's languages in danger of disappearing.* Paris/Canberra: UNESCO Publishing/Pacific Linguistics.

This short volume will unsettle anyone concerned about the preservation of linguistic and cultural diversity. Wurm describes the ways that languages become endangered or moribund and catalogues some of the world's endangered languages. Maps by Theo Baumann offer disturbing images that highlight the extent of the problem. The editor comments, "The impression created [by this book] will be augmented and enhanced when the reader realizes that he or she is only looking at a sample and selection of the problem, and that the full truth is very much grimmer" (p. 17).

chapter 11

National Unity and Diversity

The United States in the Twenty-First Century

*O*ur national motto is "E Pluribus Unum"—one out of many. Much of our political heritage has evolved from the tension implicit in the complex philosophy underlying those three words. While we hope to forge one nation from our many peoples and cultures, the nation we intend to create is one that protects our individual right to maintain our differences. As the nation progresses and grows, we try to make sense out of U.S. society. It is difficult to decide who we are, because U.S. identity is complex and constantly changing, and sometimes the debate, which ought to involve thoughtful negotiation, turns angry and acrimonious.

Current immigration trends have once again brought tension about culture and language difference to the forefront of debate at every level, from the United States Congress to the local coffee shop. This chapter will explore questions about cultural and linguistic assimilation in the American context and revisit the way these issues, especially those related to language, play out in public schools.

Immigration

According to a working paper published by the U.S. Census Bureau, "The estimated size of the foreign-born population of the United States in 2002 was 32.5 million. . . . In absolute terms, this estimate represented an increase of 64.2 percent or 12.7 million over the estimated 19.8 million in the 1990 census, the largest foreign-born population living in the United States since record-keeping began in 1850" (Schmidley & Robinson, 2003, p. 1). Suarez-Orozco notes (2005) that the current wave of immigrants differs from previous immigrants in its intensity and diversity. "Until 1950, nearly 90 percent of all immigrants were Europeans or Canadians. Today, more than 50 percent of all immigrants are Latin American, and more than 25 percent are Asian" (p. 13).

Furthermore, newly arrived immigrants come from incredibly diverse backgrounds, from the highly skilled Asian Indians who find work in Silicon Valley to the uneducated and unskilled workers, many undocumented, who do farmwork, child care, housecleaning, and fly under the radar in any number of low-paid jobs (Portes and Rumbaut, 2006).

It's interesting to note that immigration to the United States is increasing, but the states that traditionally have been the destinations for new Americans (California, New York, Texas, Florida, New Jersey, Illinois) have seen a decline in the growth rates of their immigrant populations, while North Carolina, Georgia, Nevada, and Arkansas saw high growth entering the new millennium (Capps et al., 2002). The new diversity of immigrants, and their presence across the United States and especially in areas that have traditionally been homogenous, may well contribute to the current anxiety about immigration playing out in the political arena.

A HISTORICAL PERSPECTIVE

Suarez-Orozco comments that the United States is "arguably the only postindustrial democracy in the world where immigration is at once history and destiny" (2005, p. 70). Immigration is indisputably a constant in American history; equally constant is that immigration invariably provokes reactionary movements designed to limit the arrival of newcomers.

Many newcomers headed for American shores throughout the nineteenth century. As we saw in Chapter 1, the Irish, fleeing starvation and oppression, were one of the most significant groups seeking refuge in the United States, where they were greeted with open hostility. Their inability to speak English and their Catholicism were focal points for nativist attacks and gave rise midcentury to the Know Nothing party that sought to restrict immigration.

On the West Coast, nineteenth-century nativism focused on Chinese immigrants who came during the California Gold Rush and stayed to build the railroads and work in agriculture. The Naturalization Act of 1870 barred Asians from citizenship, and the Chinese Exclusion Act of 1882 denied citizenship to Chinese workers already in the United States while barring further entries.

In the early part of the twentieth century the country saw an enormous wave of European immigrants fleeing political unrest and persecution and seeking economic opportunity in the United States. Italians and Jews, along with many others, arrived at Ellis Island, Galveston, Baltimore, and other ports of entry, where they were received with the distrust and distaste that seems to greet all newcomers to our shores.

Mexicans, displaced by the Mexican Revolution in 1910, headed north in unprecedented numbers. Following the stock market crash of 1929 and the onset of the Great Depression, President Herbert Hoover, scapegoating Mexicans immigrants, initiated a repatriation movement. Concentrating on southern California and Texas, immigration officers conducted massive raids in parks, social halls, and workplaces and unceremoniously loaded literally thousands of people, irrespective of their status, onto trains headed for Mexico. Many deported in that fashion were American born and had never stepped foot on Mexican soil. Children were separated from their parents, husbands from their wives, people lost their livelihoods and their homes, and lives were irreversibly shattered in one of the most ignominious chapters in American history (Boisson, 2006).

Over the course of the twentieth century, various kinds of legislation limited immigration. In some cases, limitations were based on place of origin (McCarran-Walter Immigration Act, 1952) or political affiliation (Internal Security Act, 1950). Policy in the latter half of the twentieth century, however, keeping pace with changing public attitudes and economic conditions, took a new and somewhat less reactionary direction. The Immigration and Nationality Act (1965), which dramatically altered the shape of U.S. immigration policy, eliminated the national origin quota system and opened our doors to unprecedented diversity. Other kinds of legislation offer exceptions for refugees (Refugee Act, 1980). In 1986, the Immigration Reform and Control Act created an amnesty and offered an opportunity for undocumented residents to become citizens. The number of immigrants allowed into the United States annually was increased by the Immigration Act of 1990.

Current immigration reform efforts focus on undocumented immigrants. The estimated number of undocumented people in the United States and the impact of their presence on the economy, which is often the flashpoint for debate, vary dramatically, depending on who is counting and for what purpose. Generally, supporters of anti-immigration legislation target Mexicans, on the assumption that they comprise the largest number of undocumented entries to the United States. At this writing, the federal government has stalled in efforts to address the question of undocumented immigration through legislative reform. This failure has opened the door to any number of local initiatives, many of which trade on xenophobia and resemble the misguided nativist efforts of our past (Kotlowitz, 2007).

ASSIMILATION VERSUS PLURALISM

In the eighteenth and nineteenth centuries, political emphasis was placed on the concept of *unum*, crystallized at the beginning of the twentieth century as the "melting pot" (Gleason, 1984). The melting pot was envisioned as a process of ethnic and racial fusion, but it can also be seen as a call for Anglo-conformity. In the melting pot, a person was expected to "Americanize"—to emerge looking, sounding, and acting like a white person of northern European background. "Melting" was a misnomer in this context, because it did not involve a synthesis of all the elements involved.

As the various ethnic groups comprising the population of the United States have established themselves socially and politically, they have begun to view their ethnic heritages positively. Emphasis has moved to *pluribus;* a cultural pluralist view of American society has emerged, suggesting that it is possible to be unified while still maintaining diversity. The most common analogy for the cultural pluralist view is the salad bowl. All the ingredients in a salad bowl make contributions to the whole, but each one maintains its own distinguishable identity.

The salad bowl image is still a useful way to think about ourselves, but the question of American identity is further complicated by the emergence of new technologies. Unlike immigrants in earlier times, new Americans do not have to sever ties with their original homelands. The availability and low cost of email and other telecommunications make it possible to stay in touch across enormous distances. Transcontinental travel, once available only to the wealthy, is relatively inexpensive, and barring political barriers, people can, and often do, return regularly to their places of origin.

It's worth noting, as Suarez-Orozco points out (2005) that technological changes in communication and transportation create two-way streets. As American culture is changed by the arrival of newcomers, root cultures in today's world are changed by their exposure to American values, images, artifacts, and lifestyles. Often the conduit for that change is the immigrants themselves, who transmit resources, ideas, and political influence from the United States with every phone call or visit.

In any event, we are increasingly a nation of minorities and our identities play out across a spectrum of multiple hues and shades. At one end, American Amish live in separate enclaves, maintaining their own distinctive social organization and language. At the other end, many Americans function almost exclusively in the cultural mainstream, affirming their ethnicity only on special occasions, if at all, with traditional food, dress or rituals. Many of us are multicultural and don't readily fall into easily defined categories. In other words, ethnicity itself has been altered by the American experience.

—Unity, Diversity, and Language

You've probably recently heard somebody complain that they can't understand customer service personnel who speak English as a second language. Or maybe you've heard somebody ask, "Why should I press 'one' for English?!" Nativist reactions to immigration invariably include language resistance.

Language resistance includes language parochialism, the attitude that multilingualism is not useful and may even be harmful, and language elitism, the attitude that bilingualism is desirable for individuals of elevated status but unacceptable for members of ethnic minority groups. Parochialism and elitism are costly—both economically and politically—and they set the stage for restrictionism. Language restrictionism is the attempt to formally promulgate a language policy that imposes restrictions on language use.

LANGUAGE PAROCHIALISM

Language parochialism might be characterized as an attitude about language that holds multlingualism in low regard and fails to acknowledge the benefits of language sophistication. Over 25 years ago, Paul Simon, at that time a congressman from Illinois, wrote a book titled *The Tongue-Tied American* (1980), which details the effects of language parochialism. Simon was ahead of his time in his insistence that American resistance to language learning and negative attitudes about bilingualism are costly to our nation. In the twenty-first century, the ability to speak languages other than English is critical both politically and economically.

International Trade. It is common wisdom that you can buy in any language but you should sell in the language of your customer. Around the world, salespeople are expected to be multilingual. U.S. business people, however, generally expect to conduct business in English, and our monolingualism and lack of cultural sensitivity has damaged our viability in the international marketplace. Simon (1980) has cataloged some of our more embarrassing attempts to advertise in foreign markets:

> "Body by Fisher," describing a General Motors product, came out "Corpse by Fisher" in Flemish. . . . Schweppes Tonic was advertised in Italy as "bathroom water." . . . "Come Alive With Pepsi" almost appeared in the Chinese version of the *Reader's Digest* as "Pepsi brings your ancestors back from the grave." (p. 32)

Translation errors are amusing, but the economic outcomes of our parochialism are not. A recent study evaluating the Fulbright-Hays programs that support research on language acquisition and language training is emphatic: "Growth in the language services sector has been explosive in recent years, reflecting similar growth in private-sector demand for language expertise. Large sectors of the economy—such as software, telecommunications, and financial services—are unable to penetrate foreign markets or . . . to develop products and services in the languages of their prospective customers, because of a shortage of language expertise" (Brecht & Rivers, 2000, p. xi).

National Security. During World War II, the military recognized the need for personnel with skills in foreign languages as essential to our national defense. As we discussed in Chapter 6, the U.S. Army took a leadership role in developing innovative language teaching strategies. After the war, the National Defense Education Act (1958) provided financial assistance to stimulate foreign language study. Funding for the act continued for a decade, and during that period of support, enrollment in high school foreign language courses in the United States increased from 16.5 to 27.7 percent (Benderson, 1983).

Unfortunately, in the decades following the act, national interest in the study of foreign languages declined, and monolingualism hampered our national security efforts.

For example, during the revolution in Iran in 1978 only 6 of the 60 U.S. Foreign Service officers assigned there were Farsi speakers (Kondracke, 1979). As you may remember, anti-U.S. feeling in Iran escalated to monumental proportions that year, culminating in a situation where 53 U.S. embassy personnel were held hostage for nearly a year. According to Simon (1980), only one of the 120 journalists assigned to Iran during the hostage crisis spoke Farsi.

More recently, the demand has surged for speakers of Arabic and other Middle Eastern languages (Dillon, 2003). In a government report (U.S. General Accounting Office, 2002) highlighting the issue, the GAO reviewed four federal agencies, including the U.S. Army, the U.S. Department of State, the Foreign Commercial Service, and the FBI and found shortages of speakers of foreign languages. The report also found deficiencies in the skills of people who hold positions that require abilities in foreign languages. For example, the U.S. Army reported in 2001 that they had only filled 42 of 84 positions authorized for Arabic interpreters and translators (p. 7). And even five years after the events of September 11, 2001, citing the agency's own statistics, the *Washington Post* reported that "only 33 FBI agents have even a limited proficiency in Arabic, and none of them work in sections of the bureau that coordinate investigations of international terrorism" (Eggen, 2006). The FBI has, however, begun an aggressive campaign designed to identify and fast-track recruits who have proficiency in languages essential to national defense (Temple-Raston, 2007).

Americans often assume that everyone speaks English. English is widely used as the language of science and commerce and is the language most used as a second language around the world (Ferguson, 1978). Widespread use of English may facilitate your shopping on a pleasure trip. It is unlikely, however, that you would be able to take the measure of a sensitive political situation in a foreign country using only English.

English speakers in non-English-speaking countries are likely to be members of a country's educated elite and may therefore be incapable of properly assessing the total political climate in which they live. Also, intelligence gathered in English or translated may be inaccurate, lacking in significant cultural and social nuances. The Iranian situation is but one instance where lack of language resources has placed us in a politically dangerous situation.

Recently, there has been renewed interest in foreign language instruction at the elementary level. According to Glod (2006), a significant number of elementary schools in the Washington, DC, area, responding to calls of business and government leaders, have initiated programs in Spanish, French, Arabic, and Mandarin, among other languages. In addition, enrollments in foreign language classes at the university level are increasing. A survey by the Modern Language Association (Welles, 2004) indicates that between 1998 and 2002, the number of college students studying a language increased 17.9 percent, to 1.4 million. After Spanish, French, and German, students favored Italian,

American Sign Language, Japanese, Chinese, Latin, Russian, ancient Greek, biblical Hebrew, Arabic, modern Hebrew, Portuguese, and Korean. In addition, there has been a noticeable growth in student enrollment in languages that the Association identifies as "less commonly taught," including Vietnamese, Hindi, Aramaic, and Swahili.

Finally, early in 2006, the Bush administration launched the National Security Language Initiative (NSLI) to address the need to strengthen national security through foreign language study (U.S. Department of State, January 5, 2006). Although the initiative designated significant funds to support foreign language instruction at every level of education, it was never fully funded (Zehr, 2007). As other countries have known for some time (Pufahl et al., 2000), foreign language instruction takes time and requires a supportive policy infrastructure. NSLI has made modest inroads. With time and full funding, it might enable us to overcome our parochialism and use our language resources effectively for diplomacy and national defense.

LANGUAGE ELITISM

In the United States, bilingualism has often been viewed with disfavor. This is particularly wasteful given that we have large numbers of people within our borders who speak languages other than English and who could serve as language resources to our entire nation.

Yet our attitudes toward bilingualism are ambivalent. We consider it a worthwhile accomplishment for a college graduate from an English-speaking background to master a second language. But we insist that the children of immigrant families relinquish their first languages as part of their "Americanization." Kjolseth (1983) has suggested that we tend to admire individual bilinguals, such as celebrities, scholars, and diplomats, and to disparage group bilinguals, or members of ethnic groups. In the popular view, individual bilingualism is often associated with elevated socioeconomic status; group bilingualism is generally associated with poverty and lack of education. Individual bilinguals acquire their second language through effort and scholarship; group bilinguals acquire their second language at home.

An eighth-grade student from a family of migrant farmworkers in Colorado told me, "I like school better here than in Texas. In Texas they punished me for speaking Spanish in school. The white kids were learning Spanish and tried to practice with us, but when we answered them we got punished." We fail to recognize that bilingualism is valuable regardless of its source.

Hunger of Memory (Rodriguez, 1982), the autobiography of a Mexican American writer and scholar, received much attention when it was published, because the author suggested that giving up Spanish was a first and essential step on his road to "Americanization." Opponents of dual language instruction hailed the book and pointed to the author's experiences as proof positive that English monolingualism leads to successful assimilation. But a persistently apologetic and yearning tone underlies Rodriguez's autobiography, leading the reader to question his assertion that giving up Spanish was necessary and positive in establishing his identity as a North American.

Einar Haugen (1987), a bilingual Norwegian American sociolinguist, observed:

> The loss of the mother tongue in home and church could be a bitter experience. It is well known that a second language learned in later life often fails to convey the cultural, emotional, or religious power of the first language, the mother tongue. Even with my entire schooling in English, my Norwegian background somehow makes a Norwegian poem or quotation warmer and more deeply moving than its English equivalent. (p. 24)

American attitudes toward language study are not shared around the world. Following the European Year of Languages in 2001, in 2003 the European Commission, the executive branch of the European Union, adopted an action plan that promotes language learning and language diversity. The introduction to the action plan states quite simply that "the ability to understand and communicate in other languages is a basic skill for all European citizens" (Commission of the European Communities, 2003, p. 1). And an informal survey in my own classrooms each semester reveals that, unlike students educated in the United States, students educated in Asia, Latin America, and the Middle East almost always were required to study at least one foreign language as a matter of course. (See Chapter 1 for a discussion of dual language instruction in other countries.)

Elitist attitudes about bilingualism cause us to squander our linguistic resources. One can only wonder how many children enter schools in the United States where the use of their first language is discouraged or even punished, only to enroll in high school foreign language classes to try to recapture some of their lost language wealth. Entrenched in English monolingualism, we fail to acknowledge our multilingualism as a national resource, limit our ability to trade on world markets, and endanger our security as a nation.

LANGUAGE RESTRICTIONISM

Language restrictionism is not new in the United States, but it is currently enjoying a renaissance and may have devastating effects both on our education systems and on our political and economic success as a nation. The most visible face of language restrictionism is U.S. English. Founded in 1983 by then Senator S. I. Hayakawa, U.S. English claims 1.8 million members (U.S. English, 2007). Its efforts are directed primarily at making English the official language of the United States. While U.S. English has not been successful at the federal level, it has contributed to the success of official English legislation in 28 states. English First, which claims 150,000 members, intends to "make English America's official language, give every child the chance to learn English, and eliminate costly and ineffective multilingual policies" (English First, 2007).

Language and Loyalty

Periods of intense immigration often provoke U.S. nativism and with it, language restrictionism. People who want to restrict language often tie language to political loyalty, even though history bears witness that demeaning or restricting people's use of a particular language is usually a veiled way of demeaning the people themselves. Some prominent U.S. political figures have made the mistake of confusing language and loyalty. In 1751, referring to German immigrants, who were numerous at the time, Benjamin Franklin complained:

Why should the Palatine Boors be suffered to swarm into our settlements and by herding together, establish their language to the exclusion of ours? Why should Pennsylvania, founded by the English, become a colony of aliens, who will shortly be so numerous as to Germanize us instead of our Anglifying them? (Conklin & Lourie, 1983, p. 69)

In 1753, in a letter to a member of the British parliament, Franklin commented:

Those [Germans] who come hither are generally the most ignorant Stupid Sort of their own Nation, and as Ignorance is often attended with Credulity when Knavery would mislead it, and with Suspicion when Honesty would set it right; and as few of the English understand the German Language, and so cannot address them either from the Press or Pulpit, 'tis almost impossible to remove any prejudices they once entertain. (Crawford, 1992b, p. 19)

Two hundred and fifty years later, Newt Gingrich, then Speaker of the House, commented in his book, *To Renew America* (1995, p. 176–78):

if people had wanted to remain immersed in their old culture, they could have done so without coming to America. . . . Bilingualism keeps people actively tied to their old language and habits and maximizes the cost of the transition of becoming an American. . . . America can absorb an amazing number of people from an astonishing range of backgrounds if our goal is assimilation. If people are being encouraged to resist assimilation, the very fabric of American society will eventually break down. . . . The only viable alternative for the American underclass is American civilization. Without English as a common language, there is no such civilization.

Thumbs up to the United States Supreme Court, which declared in 1923 in *Meyer v. Nebraska* (62 U.S. 390, [1923]) that:

the individual has certain fundamental rights that must be respected. The protection of the Constitution extends to all, to those who speak other languages as well as to those born with English on the tongue. Perhaps it would be highly advantageous if all had ready understanding of our ordinary speech, but this cannot be coerced with methods which conflict with the Constitution. . . . No emergency has arisen which renders knowledge by a child of some language other than English so clearly harmful as to justify its inhibition with the consequent infringement of rights long freely enjoyed.

And to the New Mexico State Legislature that declared in 1989 in an English Plus Resolution (Crawford, 1992b, p. 154):

Proficiency on the part of our citizens in more than one language is to the economic and cultural benefit of our state and the nation.

English First is currently targeting Executive Order 13166, Improving Access to Services for Persons with Limited English Proficiency. According to a Department of Justice publication, the Order, signed by President Bill Clinton in 2000, requires "federal agencies to take reasonable steps to provide meaningful access for LEP people to federally conducted programs and activities" (2004, p. iii), meaning essentially everything the federal government does. The order also requires the federal government to assist nonfederal agencies that receive federal funds to come into compliance.

Support for the English-only movement is far from unanimous, and language restrictionist laws have not gone unchallenged. Arizona, for example, amended its state constitution in 1988, making English the language of all government actions. In 1994, however, the U.S. Court of Appeals for the Ninth Circuit upheld a federal district court ruling that held the Arizona English-only law in violation of constitutional First Amendment protection of free speech (Contín, 1995). In 1998, Alaska passed an English-only initiative, but in 2002 a Superior Court judge ruled that the initiative violated the free speech provisions of the Alaska Constitution. Figure 11.1 is an amusing but pointed reflection on language restrictionism in the United States.

Chen (1995) has suggested that English-only laws can be challenged on two bases. First, to the extent that language restrictionist laws limit a person's access to government services or ability to communicate with the government, those laws may violate a constitutional right to equal protection under the law. This potential violation is enhanced by the fact that language and national origin tend to overlap, and denial of services based on national origin is clearly illegal. Secondly, English-only laws may restrict government employees from serving the public in languages other than English, which can be seen as a violation of their civil right to free speech.

Voting. Voting is a fundamental right. In 1975 Congress amended the Voting Rights Act to prohibit English-only elections and to require bilingual ballots in jurisdictions where the language minority population exceeds 5 percent and illiteracy rates exceed national norms. English-only advocates have targeted bilingual ballots and voting materials. In 1984, for example, California voters passed an initiative instructing the governor to inform Congress that California wanted to eliminate ballots in languages other than English. Supporters of the proposition no doubt felt that they were voting for assimilation. As legal scholar Kenneth Karst (1986) has observed, however: "Voting is not just an expression of political preferences; it is an assertion of belonging to a political community" (p. 347).

Encouraging people to vote, regardless of their English proficiency, encourages the assimilation process. Where bilingual ballots are used, ethnic minorities' participation in the political system has increased. New Mexico has had bilingual voting since it became a state in 1912, and it is the only state

● FIGURE *11.1* Language Restrictionism

SOURCE: "Language Police," David Fitzsimmons © *The Arizona Daily Star.* 1988. Reprinted with permission.

where the number of Hispanics in the state legislature is in proportion to their representation in the general population (Trasvina, 1981).

IMPLICATIONS FOR SCHOOLING

As part of their agenda, English-only proponents want to limit the time children spend in bilingual education programs. Del Valle points out (2003, p. 56) that "deciding in which language to educate students is a distinctly different inquiry than whether the parents of these children should be able to vote in a language they can understand. Supporters of English-only, however, can garner greater support by conflating the two issues, especially when there is such national anxiety over bilingual education in particular."

English for the Children, a language restrictionist organization that targets bilingual education, has leveraged the general public's anxiety to great advantage. Formed in 1997 by Ron Unz, a California businessman, the organization promoted laws against bilingual education that were successful in California, Arizona, and Colorado. "English for the children" is misleading, given that bilingual programs for English language learners are meant to facilitate English acquisition. But as we have seen, the rationale for primary language instruction for second language learners is complex and requires an understanding of language, linguistics, and pedagogy. The "English for the Children" message is simple and saleable and does well in referendum votes.

As we saw in Chapters 2 and 5, bilingual programs for limited English proficient children focus largely on English language acquisition, and research shows that primary language instruction is a useful instructional bridge to English. Furthermore, full development of two languages is beneficial to the education of any child. It's difficult to imagine subjecting any other form of pedagogy to a referendum vote, but educational success for second language learners is not the real center of the debate for opponents of bilingual education. Rather bilingual education is one battlefield in a larger political war about American identity.

Dual language instruction will be the subject of ongoing controversy, persisting at best in a transitional and compensatory mode, until the U.S. public begins to understand what privileged classes around the world have always known—that bilingualism is socially, politically, and economically desirable. In discussing U.S. language policy, the sociolinguist Joshua A. Fishman (1981) observed:

> Language policy involves a vision of America. A multilingual enrichment policy envisages a multilingual America as being in the public good. We support a multiparty system. . . . Our anti-trust laws aim to diversify the economic market place. We can similarly diversify the cultural market place. . . . There is a vision of American magnanimity involved, but more than that, a vision of American possibilities, opportunities, appreciations, sensitivities, that we all should savour. (pp. 525–526)

Outcomes. The fears of those who oppose the English-only movement have not been fully realized. In most areas, practical considerations require provisions for non-English speakers in schools, courts, hospitals, and social services. In the private sector, the profit motive promotes multilingual accommodation in businesses, and in many communities advertising and marketing in several languages is the norm. Several major metropolitan areas, for example, support classified telephone directories in languages other than English. Nevertheless, English-only legislation opens the door to restrictions on public service assistance and free speech.

A friend of mine, a physician, voted in favor of an amendment to the California Constitution declaring English as the official language. He explained, "People come into my office every day, and they can't speak a word of English." His reasoning is flawed, because people cannot be legislated into English proficiency.

Language restrictionist legislation often ignores the need for widescale programs to assist newcomers in learning English. It would be far more useful to expand underfunded adult education programs, where waiting lists for English classes are common. In general, limitations on language use threaten to exclude large sectors of our population from the mainstream instead of providing the education and services necessary to enfranchise them.

Summary

In the United States we tend to be linguistically unsophisticated, and our parochial attitudes about multilingualism have hurt us in international trade, national security, and diplomacy. The narrow view we often have about multilingualism, combined with reactions to increased immigration and population changes, provides a growth medium for language restrictionists. Language restrictionism is not new in the United States. Immigration is a constant in American history and has always provoked nativist responses. Currently, increased immigration has turned up the heat on debates about American identity, immigration reform, and language policy. The current movement, like its predecessors, is attempting to limit the use of languages other than English in a variety of areas. The melting pot and salad bowl models may be inadequate in the twenty-first century, with the increased availability of communication and transportation. Language restrictionism is not new in the United States, but the current restrictionist movement has had some success in the arena of public education.

It is difficult to characterize American identity. While assimilationism and pluralism seem to represent polar opposites, in fact "Americanization" is a process that includes both. National language policy is unclear, but multiple languages are part of our American identity and are also socially, politically, and economically valuable. Schools can assist in promoting positive bilingualism for all children, but that will require rethinking our national position on dual language instruction.

Questions to Think About and Discuss

1. Should the United States restrict immigration? Why or why not? If you think immigration should be restricted, what restrictions would you favor?
2. Should the United States have an official language? Why or why not?
3. Is there anything that your school or district does that promotes or represses the use of languages other than English?

Activities

1. Survey colleagues or classmates who have been educated outside the United States. Find out what the requirements were for foreign language learning in their native schools.
2. Survey high schools and colleges in your area. What, if any, are the foreign language requirements for graduation? What languages are offered? Which ones have the highest enrollments?
3. Survey friends, relatives, and colleagues. Ask how many of them would like to know another language. How many would favor foreign or modern language instruction in the schools? How many of them consider bilingual education desirable for limited English proficient children?
4. Is there a local ordinance, a statewide law, or language in the state constitution amendment that makes English the official language in your area? Is such legislation under consideration? What are the potential impacts of such legislation?
5. Create an ethnic profile of the students in your class. How many different backgrounds are represented? To what extent do those having foreign backgrounds feel they have maintained ties with their ethnic heritage(s)? With their language(s)? How do they feel about their relationship to their ethnic and linguistic heritage(s)?

Suggestions for Further Reading

Adams, K. L., and Brink, D. T. (Eds.). (1990). *Perspectives on official English: The campaign for English as the official language of the USA.* Berlin: Mouton de Gruyter.

This book contains an overview of the general issue of language policy and analyses of language policy around the world. The book then zeroes in on language policy in the United

States with a detailed discussion of California's English-only proposition, as well as discussions of language use and legislation in Florida, New York, and parts of the Southwest. One whole section is devoted to language legislation from the perspective of constitutional law. An appendix contains language legislation from several states, as of 1990.

Baron, D. (1990). *The English-only question: An official language for Americans?* New Haven, CT: Yale University Press.
This book is a detailed history of language policy in the United States. An appendix contains a map overviewing state legislation on English-only as of mid-1990.

Crawford, J. (1992a). *Hold your tongue: Bilingualism and the politics of "English Only."* Reading, MA: Addison-Wesley.
This book is a comprehensive discussion of American reactions to language diversity and an analysis of the English-only movement in the United States.

Crawford, J. (Ed.). (1992b). *Language loyalties: A source book on the official English controversy.* Chicago: The University of Chicago Press.
A collection of articles and legal documents that reflect on language issues in every area of public life, this is an invaluable collection for a serious student of American language policy.

Dicker, S. J. (1996). *Languages in America: A pluralist view.* Clevedon, UK: Multilingual Matters.
At a time when language policy is the subject of constant, and often vituperative, debate, this book makes the case for linguistic diversity, drawing on linguistics, history, sociology, and law.

Kloss, H. (1977). *The American bilingual tradition.* Rowley, MA: Newbury House.
Already recommended in Chapter 1, this book bears another mention as a classic analysis of U.S. language policy.

McCarty, T. L., & Zepeda, O. (1995, Winter). Indigenous Language Education and Literacy. *Bilingual Research Journal, 19*(1).
This special issue of the Bilingual Research Journal *examines the goals and outcomes of bilingual programs in indigenous communities in North America. It merits the attention of those interested in Native American languages and education and contains an article by James Crawford on language endangerment.*

Perea, J. F. (Ed.). (1997). *Immigrants out! The new nativism and the anti-immigrant impulse in the United States.* New York: New York University Press.
This collection of articles reflects on nativism in the United States from both historical and contemporary perspectives. The relationships between newcomers and native-born Americans are analyzed historically, politically, and economically.

Piatt, B. (1990). *¿Only English? Law and language policy in the United States.* Albuquerque: University of New Mexico Press.
A historical and legal analysis of U.S. language policy, this book calls for a balanced formulation of language policy that can meet our political and personal needs in a multicultural and multilingual society.

Simon, P. (1980). *The tongue-tied American.* New York: Continuum.
While not a new publication, this collection of data, anecdotes, and information is still noteworthy. Simon's examples of the outcomes of our national monolingualism in the areas of international trade, national security, and diplomacy call our attention to issues and problems that still exist today.

Skutnabb-Kangas, T., & Phillipson, R. (Eds.). (1994). *Linguistic human rights: Overcoming linguistic discrimination*. Berlin: Mouton de Gruyter.
The editors of this volume are language scholars and well-known proponents of the rights of language minority students. The papers in this book support the idea that "linguistic rights should be considered basic human rights" (p. 1), through an exploration of the issues of language policy in general, and specifically in a number of places around the world.

Tse, L. (2001). *Why don't they learn English? Separating fact from fallacy in the U.S. language debate*. New York: Teachers College Press.
English-only advocates, equating English with political loyalty and personal allegiance, often claim that immigrants don't want to learn English. Tse refutes their arguments and points out that "myths about immigrant language learning skew the public mindset on language-related issues, causing a misdirection of energy . . . toward solving phantom problems while ignoring true crises" (p. 72).

chapter 12

Meeting State Objectives and Standards: Making Good Choices

THEORY TO APPLICATION: GUIDELINES FOR PRACTICE

- Maintain a high level of cognitive challenge by selecting content material for ELLs based on depth, not breadth.

- Make content material meaningful, interesting, and relevant to maintain a high level of cognitive challenge and to expand students' areas of potential learning.

- Provide opportunities for students to experience success in the classroom: Success in learning promotes more success by increasing learner motivation, interest, and self-confidence.

State academic standards serve as rigorous goals for teaching and learning. They specify what students should know and be able to do in designated core areas of instruction as a result of their K–12 schooling. Standards align classroom instruction and establish a content base for statewide assessment.

State standards are not drawn arbitrarily. They are derived from a detailed web of topics, concepts, and skills essential for each grade level that professional organizations in each of the major content areas have created. States have used this information to develop their own sets of state standards and grade-level curricula. Classroom content teachers know these standards well—better, perhaps, than those that relate to the ELLs in their classrooms.

Standards for English Language Learners

In 1997, the organization Teachers of English to Speakers of Other Languages (TESOL) created a set of English as a Second Language (ESL) standards designed to complement the content area standards created by other professional associations. In 2006, TESOL extended and refocused those standards in a new document, *PreK–12 English Language Proficiency (ELP) Standards*, which reflects a number of trends relating to standards, content-based instruction, ELLs, and the provisions of the No Child Left Behind (NCLB) Act of 2001. The new standards set high expectations for achievement in the realms of English language and general academics.

The five ELP standards (see Figure 12.1) acknowledge the central role of language in the achievement of content. They form the bridge between language learning and national standards in the core curriculum areas of English language arts, mathematics, science, and social studies.

The standards are organized in a matrix that delineates expectations by grade level cluster, language proficiency level, and language domain (see Figure 12.2) for specific topics in the core academic content areas. By aligning academic content standards with language domain and proficiency levels, TESOL has produced a framework that can serve teachers, schools, and districts in establishing realistic expectations and meaningful instruction for their ELL student populations. The clear standards and model performance indicators define concrete goals for student achievement at each level of language proficiency. They serve to ensure that all students reach their full potential for academic success.

● FIGURE *12.1* TELSOL's 2006 PreK–12 English Language Proficiency Standards

Standard 1: ELLs communicate for social, intercultural, and instructional purposes within the school setting.

Standard 2: ELLs communicate information, ideas, and concepts necessary for academic success in the area of English language arts.

Standard 3: ELLs communicate information, ideas, and concepts necessary for academic success in the area of mathematics.

Standard 4: ELLs communicate information, ideas, and concepts necessary for academic success in the area of science.

Standard 5: ELLs communicate information, ideas, and concepts necessary for academic success in the area of social studies.

• FIGURE *12.2* Differentiated Areas of TESOL's 2006 PreK–12 English Language Proficiency Standards

Grade Level Clusters	Language Domains	Language Proficiency Levels
PreK–K: The Early Years	Listening	Level 1: Starting Up
Grades 1–3: Primary Years	Speaking	Level 2: Beginning
Grades 4–5: Middle Elementary	Reading	Level 3: Developing
Grades 6–8: Middle School	Writing	Level 4: Expanding
Grades 9–12: High School		Level 5: Bridging Over

The Dilemma of Standards

Academic standards, whether discipline specific or ELP, specify what students should know and be able to do at each grade level and in each of the core content areas. They establish common yardsticks of instruction and curriculum. The dilemma they present to classroom teachers is one of curricular depth versus breadth: Should students spend a longer time on fewer topics or a shorter time on more topics?

Teachers have long felt torn between conflicting beliefs. On one hand, covering fewer curricular objectives and topics in greater depth allows opportunities to approach subject material in creative ways that can increase students' interest and motivation. On the other hand, teachers also believe that they have a responsibility to expose their students to all objectives and topics in the curriculum to prepare them, at least minimally, for future learning.

The issue of depth versus breadth has become even more serious for teachers in light of high-stakes testing. Because state accountability tests are directly linked to the standards, teachers feel themselves under intense pressure to cover these standards in the course of a school year. If this is a challenge with the *native* English-speaking students in their classes, can teachers possibly meet those standards with their ELLs? And if not, then what?

SELECTING STANDARDS, TOPICS, AND OBJECTIVES

The Objective: Analyze Standards, Topics, and Objectives to Make Sound Choices.

The Rationale
The preceding questions must be addressed realistically. ELLs, simply because they are in the process of learning English, may not be able to master the complete curriculum, but they will be able to learn a great deal of it. While the 2006 ELP Standards serve as a valuable guide, it is ultimately teachers' responsibility to select the standards, concepts, topics, and skills they believe are most essential for their ELLs. Those chosen should be core concepts that are individually interesting and cognitively challenging.

STRATEGY 1 SELECT CORE CONCEPTS

IN CONCEPT

Core concepts are those that most benefit students' future learning. Take a close look at the standards, objectives, unit topics, and subtopics in your curriculum. It will be obvious that all have not been created equal. Some standards encompass high-level thinking skills and broad concepts; others are more narrowly based on separate, discrete skills and information. Topics, as well, can be viewed in a similar manner. Certain topics in your curriculum contain *core* concepts, those that recur and are conceptually extended in each successive year of schooling. Concepts such as those shown in Figure 12.3 form the foundation of knowledge upon which the understanding of more advanced and complex information, ideas, and relationships will depend and, as such, should be given higher priority.

IN PRACTICE

You can best help the ELLs in your classroom today by selecting and concentrating *first* on the core topics, skills, and standards that they will be expected to know and do in the academic years that follow. Start by examining the content standards and benchmarks—the topics, concepts, and skills—for your grade or grade grouping, and then compare them to those at the next higher level.

The Sunshine (Florida) State Science Standards, for example, are delineated by strands and by grade level groupings. Figure 12.4 shows the standards and benchmarks of the Earth and Space strand for Grades 6–8 and 9–12. A middle school science teacher, after examining the corresponding high school standards, will recognize that the single benchmark in Standard 2 for Grades 6–8 is more critical than it might seem at first glance. It forms the core of understanding for the seven benchmarks at the next level. Its importance as a key to understanding future benchmarks makes it a core topic.

Keep in mind that ELLs are learning a new language at the same time they are trying to learn content. Focusing on core concepts for your ELLs does not lower your expectations—it simply repositions them at a more realistic level.

● FIGURE *12.3* Some Core Topics in Math, Science, and Social Studies

Math	Science	Social Studies
equality	adaptation	culture
operations	energy	liberty
equivalence	force	change
symmetry	matter	exploration
number systems	properties	rights/responsibilities

● FIGURE *12.4* Sunshine State Science Standards: Earth and Space Strands for Grades 6–8 and Grades 9–12

Grades 6–8 Earth and Space
Standard 1: The student understands the interaction and organization of the Solar System and the universe and how this affects life on Earth.

1. understands the vast size of our Solar System and the relationship of the planets and their satellites.
2. knows that available data from various satellite probes show the similarities and differences among planets and their moons in the Solar System.
3. understands that our sun is one of many stars in our galaxy.
4. knows that stars appear to be made of similar chemical elements, although they differ in age, size, temperature, and distance.

Standard 2: The student recognizes the vastness of the universe and the Earth's place in it.

1. knows that thousands of other galaxies appear to have the same elements, forces, and forms of energy found in our Solar System.

Grades 9–12 Earth and Space
Standard 1: The student understands the interaction and organization of the Solar System and the universe and how this affects life on Earth.

1. understands the relationships between events on Earth and the movements of the Earth, its moon, the other planets, and the sun.
2. knows how the characteristics of other planets and satellites are similar to and different from those of the Earth.
3. knows the various reasons that Earth is the only planet in our solar system that appears to be capable of supporting life as we know it.

Standard 2: The student recognizes the vastness of the universe and the Earth's place in it.

1. knows that the stages in the development of three categories of stars are based on mass: stars that have the approximate mass of our sun, stars that are two-to-three stellar masses and develop into neutron stars, and stars that are five-to-six stellar masses and develop into black holes.
2. identifies the arrangement of bodies found within and outside our galaxy.
3. knows astronomical distance and time.
4. understands stellar equilibrium.
5. knows various scientific theories on how the universe was formed.
6. knows the various ways in which scientists collect and generate data about our universe (e.g., X-ray telescopes, computer simulations of gravitational systems, nuclear reactions, space probes, and supercollider simulations).
7. knows that mathematical models and computer simulations are used in studying evidence from many sources to form a scientific account of the universe.

Florida Department of Education. (2005). *Sunshine State Standards for Science, Grades 6–8.* Retrieved April 26, 2006, from *http://www.firn. edu/doe/curric/prek12/pdf/science6.pdf.*

Florida Department of Education. (2005). *Sunshine State Standards for Science, Grades 9–12.* Retrieved April 26, 2006, from *http://www.firn. edu/doe/curric/prek12/pdf/science9.pdf.*

STRATEGY 2 SELECT INTERESTING TOPICS

IN CONCEPT

Inherent interest in a topic is a natural motivator to learning. Students learn better—more quickly and in greater depth—when they are motivated. Developing a great deal of knowledge about a single topic, rather than a little bit of knowledge about a lot of topics, also promotes long-term retention of learning.

In general, students are interested in topics that relate to previous personal experiences, to prior learning, and/or to real-world connections. Linking standards, topics, and skills to the individual interests of students makes learning meaningful to them, and meaningful content is understood more easily and retained longer.

IN PRACTICE

There is no doubt that you will have to make some content choices for the ELLs in your classrooms. You can facilitate their learning by offering them a degree of choice in selecting topics that appeal to them.

The four benchmarks in Grades 6–8 Standard 1 (see Figure 12.4) cover a range of interesting topics: the planets, their moons, satellite probes, the sun, the stars. ELLs may discover a particular fascination with one of these topics. Encourage them to select that topic for in-depth study. Their motivation and personal interest may lead them toward expanding their knowledge of science and, in the process, building their English language skills as well.

STRATEGY 3 SELECT CHALLENGING TOPICS

IN CONCEPT

Any topic selected for study by teacher or student must maintain a high level of academic challenge. ELLs will not benefit in the long or short run from a watered-down curriculum or from lowered expectations. Thoughtful selection of content involves combining cognitively demanding topics and concepts with activities that require the use of higher level thinking skills.

IN PRACTICE

To achieve this, allow your ELLs to focus on content *depth* rather than *breadth*. Turn your ELLs into class specialists by having them concentrate their attention on a narrow section of content instead of trying to cover all the information that the other students will be learning. Figures 12.5 and 12.6 offer samples of subtopics for your ELL specialists to study. Table 12.1 includes suggested assignments.

● FIGURE *12.5* Topics for Class Specialists in Earth Science

Unit	Expert Focus
Freshwater resources	Water pollution
Ocean motions	Currents
Weather factors	Precipitation
Energy resources	Fossil fuels

● FIGURE *12.6* Topics for Class Specialists in Life Science

Unit	Expert Focus
Human anatomy	Skeletal system
Human physiology systems	Circulatory system
The sense organs	The sense of sight
Mammals	Mammal habitats

● TABLE *12.1* Topics for Class Specialists in American History

Unit	Expert Focus	Assignment Type
The Constitution	Amendments	Timeline
	The 7 Articles	Graphic representation
	Separation of powers	Graphic representation
	U.S. government vs. system of government in ELLs' native countries	Venn diagram
The Civil War	Life in the North vs. life in the South	Venn diagram
	One battle: Antietam	Map, outcome graphic
	One general: Lee or Grant	Timeline
	The two generals compared	Venn diagram
Growth of the West	Railroads	Timeline, map
	Mining	Map, products
	Effects on Native American tribes	Graphic representation
The Progressive Era	The rise of unions	Timeline
	Reforms for women	Timeline
The Great Depression	Causes of the Depression	Graphic representation
	New Deal program summary	Graphic representation

Offering ELLs a choice of areas to develop as their field of expertise will feel empowering and motivating to them. ELLs can be working on their expert topics at their own pace independently, in pairs, or in small groups, producing an example such as the graphic shown in Figure 12.7, while you continue your lessons with the class.

When ELLs complete their individual assignments, they present their areas of expertise to others in a group information exchange. This pattern of assignment allows all aspects of a topic to be covered—the five senses, for example—but with each student assuming a reasonable language/academic challenge. Through this type of cooperative or shared activity, ELLs learn a great deal about content, concept, and language. It also creates the opportunity to show your ELLs in a positive light when you "call on the experts" to share knowledge as their topics arise during class discussion.

Inviting ELL students to become specialists in a narrow field of study is a pedagogically sound approach to learning. Long-term retention of knowledge is dramatically increased when learning is focused on the principle of *learn more about less*. Students who merely learn facts for the test often retain the informa-

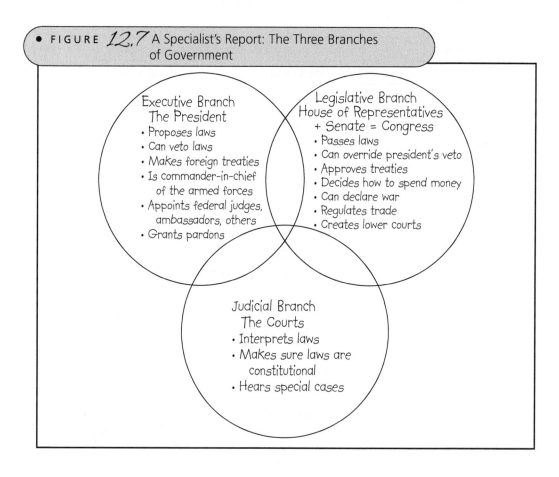

● F I G U R E *12.7* A Specialist's Report: The Three Branches of Government

Executive Branch
The President
• Proposes laws
• Can veto laws
• Makes foreign treaties
• Is commander-in-chief of the armed forces
• Appoints federal judges, ambassadors, others
• Grants pardons

Legislative Branch
House of Representatives + Senate = Congress
• Passes laws
• Can override president's veto
• Approves treaties
• Decides how to spend money
• Can declare war
• Regulates trade
• Creates lower courts

Judicial Branch
The Courts
• Interprets laws
• Makes sure laws are constitutional
• Hears special cases

tion only until the test is over. Memorized lists are quickly forgotten, while information that has been thoroughly researched is often long remembered.

Combining depth of study with choice based on interest will give your ELLs a solid chance to learn challenging material. You will have offered them the best possible means of becoming actively and effectively involved in their own learning.

STRATEGY 4   SELECT PRACTICAL TOPICS

IN CONCEPT

Standards, objectives, topics, and concepts may vary in terms of practicality. A practical approach involves selecting topics that are easier to make comprehensible to ELLs because they are more concrete and demonstrable in content and process. These will be linguistically easier for ELLs to understand because they lend themselves to graphic representation and perhaps even direct inquiry learning.

IN PRACTICE

If you are deliberating among several topics that appear to offer equal challenge and long-term importance such as those in the Grades 6–8 benchmarks of Standard 1 (Figure 12.4), use practicality as a criterion of selection. The first benchmark about the solar system and the relationship of the planets and their satellites contains content that is practical because it can be broken into small, concrete chunks of information and then slowly built into the whole through demonstration, discovery learning, and multimedia graphics. Practical content offers you more ready access to the variety of strategies that scaffold instruction.

——In Summary: Selecting Standards, Topics, and Objectives

State standards are, at their best, a means to raise expectations for *all* students by improving the quality of learning in classrooms. At their worst, when too closely tied to high-stakes tests, state standards narrow curricula into little more than test preparation. Realistically, in the broad middle range, state standards maintain content integrity and use assessment to inform instruction. For better or worse, however, state standards are something all teachers have to work with for all their students.

It would be wonderful if all students could meet all the standards and learn everything in your curriculum. In an ideal world they could, but in the real world in which you teach, some of your students will do it all and some will not. Many ELLs, because they are learning the language while they are learning the content, will be in the group that will not. The medium of instruction is, for them, as challenging as the instruction itself.

The reality is that you must make curricular choices. Your most sincere attempts to cover the entire range and breadth of requirements with your ELLs—to meet all the standards—may well result in little real learning and a great deal of confusion and frustration. You can help ELLs so much more by maintaining high expectations that focus on topics, concepts, and standards that are important, foundational, cognitively challenging, interesting, and practical. You will be giving them the gift of academic success.

Questions for Discussion

1. How do the strategies for selecting content reflect the *Guidelines for Practice* presented at the beginning of this chapter?

2. Research the state standards for the grade(s) and content area(s) you are now teaching or will soon teach. Then research the state standards for ELLs. To what degree are the two sets of standards related to each other? If they are less than fully interrelated, propose a plan or outline for improvement.

3. What is the relationship between your state's standards and its accountability system? What advantages and disadvantages do you see in this arrangement? If you are not yet teaching, interview a teacher in your field about this and report the results.

4. Investigate the accommodations made for ELLs in your state accountability systems. Do they reflect the guidelines for practice at the beginning of the chapter? In what ways do you believe they should be modified?

References and Resources

Echevarria, J., & Graves, A. (2005). Curriculum adaptations. In P. Richard-Amato & M. A. Snow (Eds.), *Academic success for English language learners: Strategies for K–12 mainstream teachers* (pp. 224–247). White Plains, NY: Pearson Education.

Echevarria, J., Short, D., & Powers, K. (2003). *School reform and standards-based education: How do teachers help English language learners?* (Technical report). Santa Cruz, CA: Center for Research on Education, Diversity, and Excellence.

Falk, B. (2005). Possibilities and problems of a standards-based approach: The good, the bad, and the ugly. In P. Richard-Amato & M. Snow (Eds.), *Academic success for English language learners: Strategies for K–12 mainstream teachers* (pp. 342–362). White Plains, NY: Pearson Education.

Freeman, Y. S., Freeman, D. E., & Mercuri, S. (2002). *Closing the achievement gap: How to reach limited-formal schooling and long-term English learners*. Portsmouth, NH: Heineman.

Lachat, M. (2004). *Standards-based instruction and assessment for English language learners.* Thousand Oaks, CA: Corwin Press.

Teachers of English to Speakers of Other Languages (TESOL), Inc. (2006). *PreK–12 English language proficiency standards.* Alexandria, VA: TESOL, Inc.

The TechConnection

www.inspiration.com
   Find activities and learning tools matched to individual state standards.

Professional Organizations

The following professional organization Web sites contain a wealth of information on standards and topics that students should know at each grade level. Those relating to ELLs are listed first, followed by the national organizations for the major content areas.

California Association for Bilingual Education (CABE), *www.bilingualeducation.org*

National Association for Bilingual Education (NABE), *www.nabe.org*

TESOL, Inc. (Teachers of English to Speakers of Other Languages), *www.tesol.org*

National Council of Teachers of English, *www.ncte.org*

National Council of Teachers of Mathematics, *www.nctm.org*

National Science Teachers Association, *www.nsta.org*

National Council for the Social Studies, *www.socialstudies.org*

Information and Research Centers

These Web sites make available extensive information relating to the education of ELLs, including answers to questions, research findings, databases of education literature, and links to additional Internet resources.

Education Resources Information Center (ERIC), *www.eric.ed.gov*

Center for Applied Linguistics (CAL), *www.cal.org*

National Clearinghouse for English Language Acquisition (NCELA) and Language Instruction Educational Programs, *www.ncela.gwu.edu*

Center for Research on Education, Diversity, and Excellence (CREDE), *www.crede.org*

chapter 13

Learning Strategies for English Language Learners

THEORY TO APPLICATION: GUIDELINES FOR PRACTICE

- Actively teach learning strategies to give students a "menu" of ways to process and learn new information.

- Use scaffolding strategies to challenge ELLs to advance beyond their present state of independent activity, into their areas of potential learning in which content is learnable with the assistance of teachers and peers.

- Provide opportunities for students to experience success in the classroom: Success in learning promotes more success by increasing learner motivation, interest, and self-confidence.

The Importance of Learning Strategies

Learning strategies are the keys to academic success for all students. Effective learners in all subject areas are those who have discovered and developed techniques of learning that work best for them. They have available to them a repertoire of learning strategies and know which to select to meet their immediate learning needs. They have acquired the tools for successful academic learning.

All students need to use learning strategies, but not all students develop them intuitively. It is surprising that many students believe that those who achieve high grades do so because they are "smart," not because they work hard and study effectively.

All students benefit from direct instruction in choosing and using learning strategies. ELLs, even more so, need this guidance to overcome the challenge of learning a new language while trying to use that language as the means to learn content.

LEARNING STRATEGIES DEFINED

Learning strategies are techniques that facilitate the process of understanding, retaining, and applying knowledge. They are the "specific actions taken by the learner to make learning easier, faster, more enjoyable, more self-directed, and more transferable to new situations" (Oxford, 1990, p. 8). These "tricks of the learning trade" come in many varieties, but not all strategies work equally well for all learners, nor do they work equally well in all learning situations. Exposure to different types allows students to develop their own personal menu of strategies—a repertoire of techniques that work well for them. Students choose appropriate strategies in combination with their personal learning styles to fit the type of knowledge they need to learn. For ELLs in content classrooms, these tricks of the learning trade take on extra importance and value.

LEARNING STRATEGIES AND TEACHING STRATEGIES: SAME OR DIFFERENT?

Learning strategies and teaching strategies are often thought of interchangeably, but they are definitely *not* the same. Learning strategies are used *by the student* to understand, retain, and apply new knowledge. They are not readily visible or immediately identifiable.

Teaching strategies are used *by the teacher* to facilitate understanding for students and to make content more accessible to students. These are the techniques, approaches, activities, and assignments that teachers use to help students process new information and apply prior learning. Teaching strategies are immediately visible and identifiable: Indeed, they are what administrators evaluate when they do classroom observations. The subset of teaching strategies used for ELLs is part of *scaffolded instruction*. Teaching strategies are concerned with how teachers *send* the message; learning strategies deal with how the message is *received*, and that is the focus of this chapter.

LEARNING STRATEGIES AND LEARNING STYLES: SAME OR DIFFERENT?

Again, learning strategies and learning styles are *not* the same thing. Learning styles involve preferences of particular work patterns *within* an individual.

Learning styles are personal, enduring, and often unconscious choices of ways to learn, such as individual or group work, auditory or visual input, a quiet environment or background noise, and single-task or multitask focus. Learning strategies, in contrast, are learned, changeable from task to task, and often consciously chosen.

Although learning styles are individual, teachers should be aware that education systems around the world value and reward different learning styles. As discussed earlier, ELLs may prefer styles of learning that have been shaped by their cultures.

The Types of Learning Strategies

Having now sorted out any confusions about what learning strategies are and are not, it is time to focus on ways of classifying them. Much has been written about how students learn and the strategies they use in the process. The classification of strategy types used in this text is built largely upon the research and writings of O'Malley & Chamot (1990) and Oxford (1990).

Learning strategies for ELLs fall into four broad types—metacognitive, cognitive, social, and compensation—with a subtype within the cognitive category, memory strategies. It is important to understand how each of these strategy types helps students learn.

METACOGNITIVE STRATEGIES

Metacognitive strategies are those that involve *thinking* about learning. These can be divided into two subtypes of techniques: those that deal with *organizing* and *planning* for learning, and those that deal with *self-monitoring* and *self-evaluating* learning.

Examples of Metacognitive Strategies Dealing with Organizing and Planning for Learning

- Using a homework notebook to write down all assignments.
- Keeping a calendar/organizer to write down long-term assignments.
- Dividing long-term assignments into shorter segments and tasks.
- Setting deadlines for completion of each segment or task.
- Determining the most appropriate and efficient strategies to learn specific content.
- Planning *how* to study for a test

Examples of Metacognitive Strategies Dealing with Self-Monitoring and Self-Evaluation of Learning

- Recognizing your own knowledge gaps or weaknesses
- Discovering strategies that work best for you (and those that don't)

- Training yourself to monitor your own progress in learning—to awaken the little voice in your head that asks, "How am I doing?" and "Am I understanding this?"
- Checking your progress frequently by responding to that little voice
- Recognizing the need to find a new strategy if the one you're using isn't working

COGNITIVE STRATEGIES

Cognitive strategies are those that involve any type of *practice* activity. These are techniques that promote deeper understanding, better retention, and/or increased ability to apply new knowledge. The techniques that fall into this category are familiar to successful learners and are used on a regular basis.

Examples of Cognitive Strategies
- Making specific connections between new and old learning
- Making specific connections between English and the student's native language
- Highlighting important information while reading
- Dividing a large body of information into smaller units
- Note taking (even in student's native language)
- Condensing notes to study for a test
- Making and using flash cards to test yourself
- Making visual associations to aid in retention
- Creating graphic organizers, maps, charts, diagrams, timelines, and flow-charts to organize information
- Making categories and classifications

Cognitive strategies form the core of learning techniques. They fall into the general category that students call *studying*. Cognitive strategies that are creative, interesting, even gamelike in nature, put a positive spin on studying, making it more motivating and productive to all students.

MEMORY STRATEGIES

Memory strategies consist of any technique that aids *rote recitation* of learned material. Memory strategies are devised simply to recall elements without any attempt to understand the material more completely. They are a subtype of cognitive strategies because their purpose is to trigger the recall of specific groups of items, concepts, or ideas that have been learned through other cognitive techniques.

A simple example of a memory strategy is the *Alphabet Song* learned by young children often long before they have any concept of letters. It is strictly a rote memory device—a *mnemonic*—and indeed, a very effective one. Later, as children learn to recognize and write their letters, they use the *Alphabet Song* to remind themselves of alphabetic order.

Mnemonics in academia are created, often by individual students, to help remember rules, key words, lists, and categories. Memory strategies such as poems, songs, acronyms, sentences (the first letter of each word in the sentence is the same as an item in an ordered list), and word patterns are very effective in triggering the recall of much larger bodies of information that have been learned through other cognitive approaches. ELLs can even use their native languages to create their own memory devices.

Examples of Familiar Mnemonics

- The "I before E" poem to recall spelling rules
- The poem and the "knuckle technique" for remembering which months of the year have less than 30 days (see Figure 13.1)

● FIGURE *13.1* Two Mnemonics to Remember the Number of Days in the Months

You May Know This Poem:

> Thirty days hath September
> April, June, and November
> All the rest have thirty-one
> Excepting February alone
> It has twenty-eight days time
> And each leap year twenty-nine

But Do You Know The Knuckle Technique?

Hold your hand forward, palm down, and make a fist.

Starting with the knuckle above the index finger, count off the months, naming a month as you touch *each knuckle and the spaces* between.

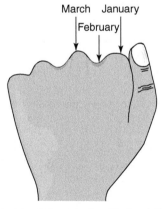

When you get to July at the pinky knuckle, touch that knuckle again for August and reverse direction.

Have you noticed that all the months that fall into the spaces have fewer than thirty-one days?

- The made-up word to remember the color spectrum in which the letters recall the colors in their correct order (see Figure 13.2)
- The silly sentence to remember the notes on a treble staff (see Figure 13.2)
- The "tricks" of the multiplication table (see Figure 13.3)

● FIGURE *13.2* More Mnemonics

For the Color Spectrum

"Roy-G-Biv" = red, orange, yellow, green, blue, indigo, violet

For the Notes on a Treble Staff

E, G, B, D, F = Every good boy does fine.
Every good boy deserves fudge.

● FIGURE *13.3* Multiplication Mnemonics

The 9 Times Trick

Hold both hands in front of you with your fingers spread out.
For 9 × 3, bend your third finger on your left hand down.
    (9 × 4 would be the fourth finger, and so on.)
You have 2 fingers in front of the bent finger and 7 after the bent finger. And there's the answer: 27.
This technique works for the 9 times tables up to 10.

The 4 Times Trick

For this one, you only need to know how to double a number. Simply, double a number and then double it again!

The 11 Times Trick

To multiply 11 by any two-digit numbers:

Example 1

Multiply 11 by 18. Jot down 1 and 8 with a space between:
    1   8
Add the 1 and the 8 and put that number in the middle: 198.
    11 × 18 = 198

Example 2

When the digits of the multiplier add up to 10 or more, do it this way:
Multiply 11 by 39. Jot down 3 and 9 with a space between:
    3   9
Add the 3 and the 9 to get 12.
Put the 2 in the middle between the 3 and the 9, then add the 1 to the 3:
    4
    3   2 9   11 × 39 = 429

> • FIGURE *13.4* Assign a Mnemonic for Homework: It's
> Challenging, Fun, and Effective
>
> Ask students to create a mnemonic designed to recall the elements in a set
> of information. The mnemonic can be an acronym that sounds good or a silly
> sentence that works.
>   Students will have to process the content under study to
> complete this assignment, but they'll hardly know they're doing it!

As students recognize the efficiency of mnemonics as a recall tool and feel comfortable using them, you can assign the creation of a mnemonic as a creative homework assignment, as described in Figure 13.4.

SOCIAL STRATEGIES

Social strategies are of two types. In the first type, language learners attempt to learn English by interacting with the environment. They expand their vocabularies by listening as English is being spoken and by attending to written English as it appears around them.

The second type of social strategy is more closely related to the classroom. Here language learners work with one or more other students to learn information or to complete a task. Group work and cooperative learning are social learning strategies. Because social strategies are, as the name states, social, they often feel less like practice and occasionally even like fun.

Examples of Social Strategies

- Working in class in pairs or small groups to clarify content, solve problems, and complete projects
- Playing teacher-made or professionally designed games to sharpen skills
- Doing homework with a friend
- Studying with a partner for a test
- Watching select television programs
- Observing peers to learn more about culture and language
- Asking questions and making requests (see Figure 13.5)

COMPENSATION STRATEGIES

Compensation strategies are techniques used to make up for something that is either unknown or not immediately accessible from memory. Proficient speakers of English regularly use this type of strategy in conversations when they use words or phrases such as *whatchamacallit*, the *thingamajiggy*, or just plain *that thing—you know what I mean* to replace the language they are searching for but cannot find at the moment.

> ● FIGURE *13.5* Questions and Requests: A Social Strategy
> for English Language Learners
>
> Please say that again.
> Would you write that word on the board, please?
> Could you speak more slowly, please?
> Can you give more examples, please?
> Would you please explain what _____ means?
> Can you say the directions again, please?

Examples of Compensation Strategies

- Stalling for time while we think of an appropriate response
- Making an educated guess that extends and generalizes what we know to what we don't know
- Using a circumlocution, a substitute phrase that "talks around" the word we don't know or "writes around" the word we can't spell

Figure 13.6 gives examples of specific usages of each of these compensation strategies. Explaining the concept of compensation strategies to your ELLs and encouraging them to use them may go a long way toward making ELLs feel more willing to participate in class.

> ● FIGURE *13.6* Examples of Compensation Strategies
>
> **Stalling for Time**
>
> - Repeating the question or statement
> - Using fillers like *Well. . .* or *Hmmm. . . .*
> - Using expressions such as *"That's a tough question"* or *"That's a complicated issue"*
> - Coughing or clearing your throat
> - Any combination of the above
>
> **Making Educated Guesses**
>
> - Using *airplane driver* as an extension of known expressions, such as *truck driver* and *taxi driver*, when the word *pilot* is not known
>
> **Using Circumlocutions**
>
> - Using the descriptive phrase *the man who drives the airplane* instead of the unknown word *pilot*
> - Using the phrase *the machine that cooks the bread dark* in place of the unknown word *toaster*

WORKING WITH LEARNING STRATEGIES

The Objective: Combine Strategies and Strategy Types.

The Rationale
While all students need to use a variety of strategy types, ELLs, in particular, will benefit from using strategies in combination. Using two or more cognitive strategies in tandem or sequentially, or grouping one or several cognitive strategies with social strategies, offers ELLs more opportunities to hear the language structures and vocabulary that support the conceptual ideas.

STRATEGY 5 USE TWO OR MORE COGNITIVE STRATEGIES TOGETHER

IN CONCEPT

Trying to learn by repeating one cognitive strategic technique over and over is often not the most productive approach to learning. Using several techniques in combination strengthens the effectiveness of each and reinforces student learning.

IN PRACTICE

Show students how powerful learning strategies can be when they are combined sequentially. A guided whole-class activity that takes students through a series of cognitive learning strategies to learn information and concepts presented in a reading passage can demonstrate the value of combining strategies. Using a photocopied reading passage, guide students as they read and highlight important information and concepts for them. As the next step, have students write up a set of notes based on the highlighted sections. Then have them condense their notes and make flash cards to study in preparation for a quiz. The grades on the quiz should speak well for this combined strategic approach.

You also may want to underscore the effectiveness of combining strategies by doing a guided whole-class activity, either prior to or following this activity, in which your students use only one cognitive strategy to learn the elements of a similar reading passage. Comparing the two approaches to learning should bring about a lively class discussion.

STRATEGY 6 USE SOCIAL AND COGNITIVE STRATEGIES TOGETHER

IN CONCEPT

ELLs increase their opportunities for academic success when they work in collaboration with their native English-speaking peers, using interaction to negotiate meaning of both language and content. Working in pairs and small groups serves to widen the language learner's zone of proximal development.

IN PRACTICE

Students have, for many decades, spontaneously created their own strategy combinations. You may remember making flash cards to help you learn large sets of information. Then you used them to check yourself to see how much you really knew. Finally, you and a friend or classmate quizzed each other. You were combining a cognitive technique with a social one, which is an excellent way to learn.

To see the benefit of combining strategy types, look at the scenario described in Figure 13.7. Math word problems are almost always a challenge for ELLs. ELLs need a plan to help them separate the actual math knowledge required to solve the problem from the English language knowledge that is impeding them. The multistep approach called *streamlining*, a structured combination of cognitive and social learning strategies shown in Figure 13.8, offers this kind of support.

WORKING WITH LEARNING STRATEGIES

The Objective: Actively Teach Learning Strategies

The Rationale
You may already be aware that strategy training should not be subtle. It needs to be taught explicitly and overtly. For students to recognize the usefulness of learning strategies in general, specific strategies must be directly tied to learning specific content as they are taught.

STRATEGY 7   USE THE FIVE-STEP APPROACH TO TEACH
LEARNING STRATEGIES

IN CONCEPT

Strategy teaching is a five-step process. First, introduce the strategy to your students and *label* it as a new learning strategy. Next, *identify* it with a name and explain how it is used. Then, *demonstrate* how to use it by applying it directly to specific content. Next, give students the time and opportunity to *practice* using it with that content. Finally, *discuss* with your students how effective they found this strategy to be for them and ask them for which other types of tasks this new strategy might be good. These steps are summarized in Figure 13.9.

● FIGURE *13.7* Is This Math Class or English Class?

Wei looks at the assigned word problems in his math book and knows that there is no way he can possibly figure out any of the answers. It's not that Wei's math skills are weak—in fact, he knows he's really pretty good at computation. He also knows that, once again, it's all those words in the problem that will bar his way to success. Wei is an English language learner.

● FIGURE *13.8* Streamlining: A Multistep Approach for Math Word Problems

Step 1: Make language substitutions.

In pairs or small groups, students look for words or phrases that can be eliminated or replaced with more simple language. They use a bilingual dictionary or a student dictionary as needed.

Step 2: Determine the information presented.

Students, still in pairs or groups, reread the now-simplified wording of the problem. They search out and write down all information given in the problem.

Step 3: Determine the information needed for solution.

Students now look for words that offer clues to the information needed in the solution. They first eliminate extraneous words and information, and then write out the words and phrases that tell how to process the information in the problem.

Step 4: Determine the process needed for solution.

Using the words or phrases from Step 3, students figure out the process needed to find the solution.

Step 5: Solve the problem.

Students perform the necessary computations and compare results.

● FIGURE *13.9* Strategy Teaching in Five Steps

1. *Introduce* it and label it as a new strategy.
2. *Identify* it by name and explain its use.
3. *Demonstrate* how to use it.
4. Give students time and opportunity for *practice*.
5. *Discuss* effectiveness and application to other tasks.

IN PRACTICE

The clearest way to understand the five-step approach is to examine in detail an actual example of a strategy lesson. The teacher in this example has observed when he teaches that few of the students are able to distinguish the important concepts and ideas from the less important details. The lesson he planned will give students a strategy for listening for key pieces of information during class lessons and discussions.

For Step 1—*Introduce it and label it as a new strategy*—he opens the lesson with a question: "Do you have trouble knowing what's *really* important when I teach? Today we're going to learn a new strategy that will help you with this."

Moving immediately to Step 2—*Identify it by name and explain its use*—he says, "We're going to call this strategy *Listening for Key Words* *. (The asterisk symbolizes words that the teacher writes on the board as she or he speaks them.) Here's how it works."

LISTENING FOR KEY WORDS

"When I teach, I often use phrases like 'This is really important *,' and 'Here's the important part *,' and 'This is a key point *.' Have you ever heard me say any of those? Or have you heard me *repeat words or phrases* * or say something several times? I do that because I want you to know it's really important."

LISTENING FOR KEY WORDS
"This is really important."
"Here's the important part."
"This is a key point."
REPEAT words or phrases.

"So look at what I've written on the board. Let's call these *listening cues* *. They're like flags that wave at you to tell you to listen and remember."

LISTENING FOR KEY WORDS

"This is the important part."
"Here's the important part."   **LISTENING CUES**
"This is a key point."
REPEAT words or phrases.

The teacher continues to Step 3—*Demonstrate how to use it*—by saying, "OK, let's try it. For the next five minutes, while I teach, I want you to raise your hand every time you hear me say one of these phrases (Teacher points to and repeats phrases on board). Then we'll talk about how they tell you that something important is coming up next."

After the five-minute segment, he moves to step 4—*Give students time and opportunity for practice*—explaining to the students that they are to listen carefully for these phrases for the rest of the instructional period. Any time they hear one, they are to write down the information that comes immediately after the phrase.

In Step 5—*Discuss its effectiveness and application to other tasks*—the students share the information they have written down. The strategy session concludes with a discussion about whether they found the strategy helpful as a means of recognizing important facts and concepts during oral instruction, as well as where else they think this strategy might be useful.

The students have learned a specific strategy for recognizing important pieces of information. To reinforce this learning, this teacher will remind students to use this strategy at the opening of subsequent lessons and class discussions.

STRATEGY 8   USE THINK-ALOUDS AND MODELING

IN CONCEPT

Think-alouds and modeling demonstrate the step-by-step process involved in completing many types of activities. In think-alouds, you, the teacher, explain how your brain is working at each step on the way to the solution of a problem. Modeling does the same but with actual samples and examples of steps along the way. The two techniques are nonexclusive; indeed, they work most effectively when used together.

IN PRACTICE
Technique I
When students are faced with a complicated learning task, you might say something like "If I had to learn this, I would probably . . . ," giving a detailed,

step-by-step description of the *process* you would use. You are, in effect, modeling the how-to of learning.

Technique II

Students themselves can be a good source for think-aloud strategy training. Guided questions such as those in Figure 13.10 about how they knew or learned specific information will allow ELLs (and others, of course) to see how their peers approach a task and to learn directly from them.

If one of the students describes a way of learning that is new to the class, you can label that strategy with the name of the student who contributed it. Imagine how empowering it is to have a strategy named for you!

STRATEGY 9 BRAINSTORM LEARNING STRATEGIES

IN CONCEPT

While some students may easily organize their plans for learning, for others it is a daunting task. Brainstorming ideas for learning in a class discussion can be a productive strategy.

IN PRACTICE

When students are facing a difficult learning task—memorizing the table of periodic elements in chemistry, for example—you can conduct an open-ended discussion about which learning strategies they think they could use to accomplish this feat. Discuss with them any specific strategies they've used in the past that they think might help them to learn the type of content they're facing now. It is of equal value to include in the discussion approaches to learning that probably will *not* be particularly helpful.

● FIGURE *13.10* Think-Aloud Applications for Strategy Training

> **Your student correctly infers information from the text.**
> ASK: *Where did you find the information that helped you with that answer?*
>
> **Your student solves a complex problem.**
> ASK: *How did you arrive at that answer?*
>
> **Your student presents an informed opinion on a topic.**
> ASK: *What information led you to this opinion?*
>
> **Your student gets a good grade on a test.**
> ASK: *How exactly did you study for this test?*

STRATEGY 10 IDENTIFY STUDENTS' PERSONAL PREFERRED STRATEGIES

IN CONCEPT

Because not all learning strategies work for all students in all situations, it is important that students understand that strategy usage is personal and individual.

IN PRACTICE

Teachers can help students identify their own current learning strategies through survey questions and discussion. To keep learning strategies at the forefront of students' thinking, use a bulletin board or wall space to make a display naming the strategies and showing how they are used. As each new strategy is taught, add it to the wall poster or bulletin board. Students can keep their own learning strategy logs or journals. In either case, students will have a ready reference—a menu or guide—from which to draw.

STRATEGY 11 INTEGRATE LEARNING STRATEGY TRAINING INTO DAILY INSTRUCTION

IN CONCEPT

The more seamlessly you integrate learning strategy training into your instruction, the more students will incorporate learning strategies into their thinking about learning. Making conscious decisions about which learning strategies to use for which tasks will become a deeply ingrained pattern for learning.

IN PRACTICE

Technique I
Give students frequent tips—strategies to help them manage their time, take notes, classify and categorize information, and study for tests. Before students begin a class or homework assignment, ask them which learning strategies they think might be most appropriate, effective, and efficient to achieve a successful outcome. Make sure the students remember to refer to the wall display as a resource.

Technique II
Students of every age love to hear about the lives of their teachers. They will listen in rapt attention when you talk about your own personal learning experiences. Tell them about the successful and not-so-successful strategies you used to learn things. Talk about how you learn now. Take advantage of every possible opportunity to bring learning strategies into class lessons and discussion.

In Summary: Working with Learning Strategies

Teachers who recognize the value of learning strategies and the potential of each strategy type, alone and in combination, understand the importance of making strategy training an ongoing part of their classroom instruction. Their students will develop a repertoire of effective learning strategies and know how to make task-appropriate choices. Actively teaching learning strategies offers students the best chance to meet with academic success.

Questions for Discussion

1. How do the strategies for teaching learning strategies reflect the *Guidelines for Practice* presented at the beginning of this chapter?

2. Label each of the following examples of learning strategies by type—metacognitive, cognitive, memory, social, or compensation:

   a. Helping friends with homework
   b. Making flash cards and using them to study
   c. Substituting a synonym for a word you can't pronounce or spell
   d. Breaking an assignment into its component parts, ordering the parts, and setting timelines for completion
   e. Taking notes from highlighted text sections
   f. Reading the questions at the end of the passage before actually reading the text
   g. Using "the next day" instead of "tomorrow" in writing
   h. Testing your understanding by making up your own quizzes
   i. Actively reading and interpreting street signs and billboards
   j. Asking another student or a sibling to quiz you
   k. Guessing at new words
   l. Keeping a vocabulary journal

3. Classify by learning strategy type each step in streamlining, shown in Figure 13.8.

4. Think about the learning strategies you used as a learner. Which ones were successful for you? How did you learn them? Did you have any learning strategies that you discarded because you realized they weren't working well for you?

5. Analyze the learning strategies that you now use most frequently. Do you use different strategies for different types of tasks?

6. Prepare a think-aloud demonstration (Strategy 8) to present in class. Your colleagues will offer verbal feedback or a written critique.

References and Resources

Chamot, A. U., Barnhardt, S., El-Dinary, P. B., & Robbins, J. (1999). *The learning strategies handbook.* White Plains, NY: Pearson Education.

O'Malley, J. M., & Chamot, A. U. (1990). *Learning strategies in second language acquisition.* New York: Cambridge University Press.

Oxford, R. (1990). *Language learning strategies: What every teacher should know.* New York: Newbury House.

Reid, J. (Ed.). (1998). *Understanding learning styles in the second language classroom.* Upper Saddle River, NJ: Prentice Hall Regents.

A Solid Start: Building and Activating Background Knowledge

THEORY TO APPLICATION: GUIDELINES FOR PRACTICE

- Activate and develop background knowledge to make new content meaningful and to form a foundation upon which new learning can be built.

- Make content material meaningful, interesting, and relevant to maintain a high level of cognitive challenge and to expand students' areas of potential learning.

- Lower learner anxiety in the classroom to create students who are more willing to participate in class, to become risk takers in the learning process, and ultimately to become more successful learners.

- Provide opportunities for students to experience success in the classroom: Success in learning promotes more success by increasing learner motivation, interest, and self-confidence.

Background Knowledge and Learning

What makes something easier or harder to learn? Most answers to this question would include two factors among possible others: motivation and preexisting knowledge.

Motivation

People learn what they want or need to learn. They learn because it is important to some aspect of their lives, perhaps even to their very survival. How fast they learn depends on how valuable, interesting, or necessary they perceive the new learning is to them. The greater the felt need or desire to learn, the easier and faster the learning will be. Motivation is a powerful influence on the learning process.

Preexisting Knowledge

The other factor influencing the learning process is the amount that is already known about the topic (Leinhardt, 1992). People learn most readily by adding new data to preexisting information. It is a far greater challenge to learn something entirely new.

Learning something completely new is like gathering individual grains of sand. Imagine each new fact as a single grain of moist sand. At the start, it is hard to form a whole from the tiny disparate grains because each grain can stick to so few others. Eventually enough sand accumulates to form a small mass. Then, new grains have an easier time finding a spot to fit in.

So too it is with facts: Like sand, each new fact about an unknown topic is unrelated to any other and must be processed individually. Eventually, enough facts accumulate to form a small mass of knowledge. As the mass of facts grows, new facts begin to relate more easily to what has already been learned, and this is where background knowledge enters the picture. Background knowledge is the mass that makes new facts meaningful. The larger the mass of background knowledge and the more it can be actively recalled, the easier it will be for new knowledge to find a place to fit in.

All Students Need Background Knowledge

The student's own background knowledge forms the building blocks upon which new learning is built. Why, then, is this a special issue for ELLs?

A school curriculum is planned around a set of basic assumptions about common academic background and life experience of students at each grade level. Students entering U.S. schools from other countries, however, have generally had differing sets of personal, cultural, and academic experiences. Teachers with ELLs in their classrooms must first determine that these students actually *have* prior learning or experience that is relevant to their success in learning new content. The second step is then to *build* background knowledge where it is lacking before presenting the new material.

WORKING WITH BACKGROUND KNOWLEDGE

The Objective: Use Varied Techniques to Activate and Build Background Knowledge.

The Rationale

All students, not only language learners, learn more effectively and efficiently when teachers make explicit connections between past and present learning and take time to build up weak foundational backgrounds. Indeed, a strong indicator of how well a student will learn new content is the amount of relevant background knowledge or experience he or she already has. That is why activating students' prior knowledge is an essential teaching strategy.

Activating background knowledge not only makes learning easier; it also makes learning meaningful, awakens interest in the topic, and increases motivation. Students who can see the relevance of a topic to their own lives will be interested in learning about it. Teachers who understand the importance of background knowledge and motivation can facilitate learning for their students. Finding the right connection pulls students directly into the material.

Strategies to build background knowledge aim to connect what students already know with what they will be learning and to develop a strong foundation of background for new learning. The strategies presented in this section simultaneously activate prior knowledge for students who have it and build new knowledge for those who need it.

STRATEGY 12 BEGIN WITH BRAINSTORMING

IN CONCEPT

Brainstorming is the strategy of asking students to think about and tell what they already know (or think they know) about a new topic before it is actually introduced. It activates existing background knowledge in those students who have it, fills gaps for those students who lack it, and engages student interest for all.

For ELLs, brainstorming may be a first exposure to new vocabulary as they hear the pronunciation of a word and see it written at the same time. Teachers benefit, too, by being able to immediately assess whether or not students have enough background knowledge to move ahead.

IN PRACTICE

Technique I

To begin brainstorming, write a topic word on the board or on an overhead transparency. Accompany it with the open-ended question *"What do you think of when I say the word _____?"*

As students respond, write their words and phrases around the topic word to form a graphic display. Accept all answers, right or wrong. When you feel ready to move on with the lesson, tell students that you will return later to reexamine these ideas by saying something like *"Let's save these answers. We'll come back to them later to see what we found out about them."*

● FIGURE *14.1* Carousel Brainstorming

> Tape sheets of chart paper on the walls at various locations around your classroom. At the top of each sheet, write a word or phrase pertaining to the new topic to be studied. For large groups and to save time, have several sets of the same words or phrases.
>
> Following your signals, students walk around the room in small groups writing their associations to the word at the top of the paper. Allow no more than two minutes before signaling time to move to the next location.

Technique II

A variation of this strategy is called *carousel brainstorming* (see Figure 14.1). This technique offers the additional benefits of getting students up and physically moving, involving all students simultaneously. It is exciting to watch students' faces as they think of new ideas triggered by reading what other students have written. At the end of the activity, groups can read out items from each sheet of chart paper as you create a single brainstorming graphic based on all the information written.

Technique III

Use the brainstorming graphic at the end of the lesson as the lesson summary and review. Ask, as you point to each item, *"Did we talk about this?"* Students can review what they learned in the lesson. They can add new words and phrases and correct misconceptions. You can make connections to subtopics to be covered in later lessons.

Technique IV

Write the initial brainstorming graphic on an overhead transparency or chart paper and save it to start the next day's lesson. Students can add newly learned information as they review previous learning.

STRATEGY 13   USE THINK–WRITE–PAIR–SHARE

IN CONCEPT

Think–Write–Pair–Share is a technique that encourages participation at the same time that it activates students' prior knowledge. It is a way of getting students actively and immediately involved in learning new concepts and topics.

IN PRACTICE

Start with the same open-ended question as in the brainstorming activity, but this time, instead of asking the class for an immediate oral response, give students a short time—no more than two minutes—to *think* about and *write* down any relevant words or phrases they can come up with. For the next minute or two, *pair* each student with a partner to discuss and expand each individual's list. Finally, invite students to *share* their ideas with the rest of the class. A great way to do this is to ask students to tell you an idea they either *had* or *heard*.

STRATEGY 14   USE K–W–L CHARTS

IN CONCEPT

A graphic organizer that complements the think-write-pair-share activity is the K–W–L chart (see Figure 14.2). This is a strategy that is best completed in a small group environment. Talking about the topic helps students generate the ideas and vocabulary needed to complete the columns.

IN PRACTICE

Technique 1

Students are asked to write what they already **know** (or think they know) about a topic in the **K** column. Then, with a partner or in a small group, they discuss what they **want** to know to complete the **W** column. The **L** column gets completed at the end of the lesson with students, again in pairs or small groups, listing what they **learned**. K–W–L charts, used to open a lesson on a new topic, may help bolster confidence and motivation as students begin to realize that they already know something about the forthcoming material.

As topical information builds, making daily entries in each column provides an ongoing means of activating students' prior knowledge and stimulating critical thinking. The completed K–W–L chart at the end of a unit serves as an excellent source of summary information from which to study for tests.

● FIGURE *14.2* K–W–L Chart

What do I **know**?	What do I **want** to know?	What have I **learned**?

Technique II

You may want to include two additional columns on your K–W–L charts. The first (see Figure 14.3) adds an **H** column for students to write **h**ow they learned the information in the **L** section. Including an **H** column is an effective way of focusing awareness on learning strategies.

The second variation is to add a **Q** column, "What **q**uestions do I still have?" (see Figure 14.4). The **Q** section may seem, at first, repetitive of the **W** section, but it is not. The **W** column, "What do I want to know?" is anticipatory—it is designed to get students thinking about the topic. The **Q** column, on the other hand, deals with questions students may have about information they just learned and added to the **L** column. These questions can cover anything students are not completely sure about: concepts, vocabulary, even how to go about learning the material. Student-generated items in the **L** and **Q** sections are a good way to open the next day's lesson: They activate background knowledge and serve as an immediate connection between past and present learning.

● FIGURE *14.3* K–W–L–H Chart

What do I know?	What do I want to know?	What have I learned?	How did I learn it?

● FIGURE *14.4* K–W–L–Q Chart

What do I know?	What do I want to know?	What have I learned?	What question do I still have?

STRATEGY 15   PERSONALIZE THE LESSON

IN CONCEPT

Students enjoy sharing their own and hearing about others' life experiences. They also are universally fascinated with stories about their teachers' experiences. Personalizing a lesson is an attention-getting way to begin a new topic.

Students, especially those who have lived in other countries and cultures, may have had personal experiences that relate to some aspect of the content being introduced. Asking students to talk about these experiences is an excellent way to activate and build background knowledge for all students. It increases motivation by stimulating student interest in and curiosity about the topic and demonstrating its relatedness to the real world.

IN PRACTICE

ELLs may be able to contribute interesting and uncommon items of topical knowledge and life experience. An introduction to a unit on the Civil War, for example, often includes a discussion of how differences among individuals and groups can lead to conflict. Students who have lived outside the United States may lack background knowledge about the U.S. Civil War, but they may have firsthand knowledge of conflicts based on political, ethnic, or religious differences in their native countries. On a more personal level, some students, including the native English speakers, may want to share stories about family feuds.

For another example, ELLs may know little about the American Revolution, but they may have lived in an area that had its own revolution from a colonial power in the much more recent past. Students may have heard family stories about life in times of war or conflict. They even may be willing to share with the class their own firsthand experiences of difficult times.

In science, some students may have firsthand knowledge of terrain or weather uncommon to your area. Can any of your students talk about living in or near rainforests, mountains, deserts, oceans or rivers, or experiencing a tornado, hurricane, or earthquake? Some may have lived in or near areas with visible air or water pollution. Sharing this type of knowledge awakens immediate personal interest and allows you to draw comparisons and make generalizations.

In math, ELLs often come from educational systems that introduce concepts and processes earlier in the curriculum than is common in the United States. Those students can show others the particular algorithms or explain real-life applications. They can serve as peer tutors for their classmates in an unusual role reversal that will raise their peers' respect and bolster their own self-confidence.

STRATEGY 16   SPARK INTEREST

IN CONCEPT

Interest in a topic is a natural motivator to learning. Activities that create an element of excitement or curiosity will raise students' interest levels at the same time that they activate background knowledge.

IN PRACTICE

Technique I

Try something graphic and visual to catch your students' interest in a new topic. Obvious choices are photos, videos, or short films relating to the topic.

Magazines and newspapers, not necessarily current, are other good sources of material appropriate for building motivation and interest. Or start with an exciting science demonstration to capture student interest and imagination. Try to recapture that "Wow!" sensation for your students, like the first time you witnessed the effect of dry ice in water. Interest acts as a motivator that facilitates learning for students.

Technique II

Another means of jump-starting student interest is to engage students in a short activity that might be named *Start Your Brain Engines!* or *Think About It!* There are many variations of this type of activity, several of which are shown in Figure 14.5 through 14.8.

● FIGURE *14.5* What Do You Know About Speed?

Rank these forms of transportation in order from slowest to fastest. Write number 1 next to the one you think is the slowest, up to number 10 next to the one you think is the fastest. When you finish numbering, write down a speed for each one.

_____ Motorcycle

_____ Train

_____ Skateboard

_____ Race car

_____ Tractor

_____ Bicycle

_____ Inline skates

_____ Rowboat

_____ Jet plane

_____ Ship

● FIGURE *14.6* Wake Up Your Thinking About Prehistoric Times

Directions: Number these events in the order you think they occurred. Write the number 1 next to the first (or earliest) through number 7 for the last. Can you "smart-guess" how long ago each of these happened?

Number   **How long ago?**

_____ Humans acquire language.   _____
_____ Humans learn to grow crops.   _____
_____ Humans invent the wheel.   _____
_____ Humans make the first tools.   _____
_____ Humans invent writing.   _____
_____ Humans make tools from metals.   _____
_____ Humans discover fire.   _____

● FIGURE *14.7* What Do You Know about Matter, Mass, and Molecules?

Look at the pictures below. Read what is in each cup. Working with your partner, decide which cup is the lightest. Mark it number 1. Which cup is the heaviest? Mark it number 6. Mark the other four cups in order of their weight.

#_____   1 cup of water

#_____   1 cup of glass marbles

#_____   1 cup of cotton balls

#_____   1 cup of sand

#_____   1 cup of cooked rice

#_____   1 cup of flour

From *Earth and Physical Science: Content and Learning Strategies* by Mary Ann Christison and Sharron Bassano © 1992 by Pearson Education, Inc., publishing as Addison-Wesley (p. 67.) Used by permission.

• FIGURE *14.8* Fact or Fiction?

Is what you "know" really true? For each of the following statements, decide whether or not it is true. If it is true, write FACT, and if it not true, write FICTION.

_____ Sound travels in waves.
_____ Sound is caused by vibrations.
_____ Sound travels through the air.
_____ Sound travels through water.
_____ Sound travels through steel.
_____ Sound always travels at the same speed.
_____ Sound travels faster than light.
_____ Sound is measured in amperes.
_____ Technically, there is no real difference between music and noise.
_____ When people have excellent hearing, they can hear every sound that is made.
_____ Sound can be unhealthy for people.

Regardless of its form, this activity serves as an ungraded pretest, designed to get students thinking of the new topic in advance. It is inherently motivating: Students like to see how close they came to the right answers. Those who did better than they expected may be more motivated to learn when they discover that they already know more than they think about a topic.

Anticipation activities, first introduced by Readence, Bean, and Baldwin (1981), can be done individually, but they will be completed more productively in pairs or small groups. Class discussion when students' answers are checked and compared serves as an introduction that forms a natural bridge to new learning.

STRATEGY 17   LINK LESSONS

IN CONCEPT

Every lesson benefits from linking students' past learning and experiences to new concepts about to be presented. Making explicit connections among concepts serves as a form of reinforcement and review. Explicit linking also helps students understand the interrelatedness of information as it exists in the real world. The more frequently you revisit conceptually important pieces of information, the more opportunity students have for learning. By regularly stimulating background knowledge, you facilitate students' continuing conceptual development and increase the potential for new learning and enhanced retention.

> • FIGURE *14.9* How Much Do You Remember About CLOUDS?
>
> Before we learn more about meteorology, check yourself to see what you remember about clouds. Next to each statement, put a T for TRUE or an F for FALSE. If you think the statement is false, rewrite it to make it true.
>
> _____ Clouds are masses of water droplets and ice crystals.
> _____ Clouds change shape because of wind and sunlight.
> _____ Clouds are grouped into classes according to their size.
> _____ Certain clouds are formed entirely of ice crystals.
> _____ High, thin clouds cause thunderstorms.
> _____ Clouds cause tornadoes and hurricanes.
> _____ Clouds at night lower ground temperature.

IN PRACTICE

Technique I

Simple questions form effective links to prior knowledge. Start your daily instruction by activating previous learning with questions like these:

What did we talk about yesterday when we were discussing the _____?

Who remembers the reasons for _____?

What did we learn about _____?

Who remembers some examples of _____?

What were some new words we used yesterday when we discussed _____?

Technique II

Another type of linking attempts to reactivate previously taught concepts that may serve as background knowledge for new learning. Review questions at the ends of chapters make excellent material to create this type of linking activity, an example of which is shown in Figure 14.9 You can also reintroduce topics using questionnaires similar to those illustrated in Figures 14.5 through 14.8.

STRATEGY 18   PREVIEW THE LESSON

IN CONCEPT

Previews create a framework for understanding a challenging reading on a new topic at the same time that they supply critical pieces of background information. Previewing information makes a new undertaking appear more learnable and facilitates students' comprehension.

IN PRACTICE

When you recognize that a reading passage may present difficulties for students, give them a written introduction that outlines important information they will need for comprehension. Include such items as definitions of new vocabulary and explanations of complex concepts. Add supporting visuals (graphics, maps, tables, charts, photos) as an extra aid to understanding. Think of previewing as the *Cliff Notes* of background knowledge.

For example, previewing is an excellent strategy to use at the start of a long and detailed work of fiction. Students might receive a preview with a list of the major characters, including some details about their personalities and their relationships to others in the book, brief notes about historical events and cultural understandings that are important to the plot, and maps showing routes of journeys or places of significance to the story line. Previews are useful initially in providing requisite background knowledge, and then continue to guide students as they read.

STRATEGY 19   MAKE NEW LEARNING FEEL LEARNABLE

IN CONCEPT

Many ELLs feel intimidated by the amount of learning they are expected to undertake and complete. A new topic can feel overwhelming in its breadth and scope. Strategies that make new learning feel learnable help students build confidence in themselves as learners. They are an important tool to success. The previewing strategy previously described builds students' self-confidence in their abilities to learn at the same time that it builds background knowledge.

IN PRACTICE

Technique I

For some students, the thought of a new topic is daunting. The vast amount of information to be learned feels much like starting a 1,000-piece jigsaw puzzle—just too many little, indistinct pieces. When introducing a new topic to students, use *Spiraling* to actively tie new information to concepts that have been learned in the past; this has the dual purpose of building self-confidence as it builds background knowledge.

Spiraling strategies reactivate known concepts that are related to a new topic. Showing students that they already have some pieces of the puzzle in place gives them a more positive attitude with which to approach the new topic.

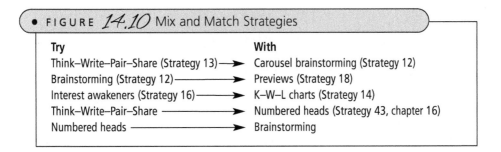

● FIGURE *14.10* Mix and Match Strategies

Try	With
Think–Write–Pair–Share (Strategy 13) ➔	Carousel brainstorming (Strategy 12)
Brainstorming (Strategy 12) ➔	Previews (Strategy 18)
Interest awakeners (Strategy 16) ➔	K–W–L charts (Strategy 14)
Think–Write–Pair–Share ➔	Numbered heads (Strategy 43, chapter 16)
Numbered heads ➔	Brainstorming

Technique II

When you announce that students will be learning a completely new topic, start by acknowledging that it is complex. Then explain that *all* new topics appear complex before you learn them. Help them recall other topics they learned that seemed so difficult at the beginning but were, after all, quite learnable. Assure them that this new topic is no different. A positive mind-set motivates learning.

STRATEGY 20   COMBINE STRATEGIES TO INCREASE EFFECTIVENESS

IN CONCEPT

All the individual strategies in this section are effective in building and activating background knowledge for your students. However, pairing individual strategies often produces even better results. The more background knowledge students develop, the more easily they will process, retain, and apply new information.

IN PRACTICE

Using the Think–Write–Pair–Share strategy (Strategy 13) in combination with carousel brainstorming (Strategy 12), for example, offers an extra opportunity to hear ideas related to the new topic. Interest awakeners (Strategy 16) also lend themselves well to pairing with other background knowledge strategies. Figure 14.10 lists these and other suggested pairings for mixing and matching strategies. Combinations are limited only by your own creativity and imagination.

In Summary: Working with Background Knowledge

It is worth repeating: How well a student learns new content is directly related to the amount of relevant background knowledge and/or experience he or she already has. The minutes—even hours—you spend in class activating and building background knowledge will pay you and your students back many times over by facilitating their learning and maximizing their possibilities for academic success.

Questions for Discussion

1. How do the strategies dealing with activating and building background knowledge reflect the *Guidelines for Practice* presented at the beginning of this chapter?

2. Think back to something you learned from scratch. How did you feel as you were starting? Did you feel like you were looking up from the bottom of a tall mountain and feeling very small? Can you think of anything that would have made you feel better about starting on the new topic? At what point did you realize that you were finally "getting it?" Did your ability to learn and/or your feeling about learning change after that? If so, how?

3. *If you are currently teaching:* Select a lesson you taught that began with a particularly effective introduction to build and activate background knowledge. Describe the strategies you used and why you believe they were effective.

   If you are not currently teaching: Work with a partner or a small group to plan interesting ways to build and activate background knowledge as an introduction to the following topics:

   Violent weather: Thunderstorms, tornadoes, earthquakes, and hurricanes
   The rise of labor unions
   Human anatomy: Skin, muscles, and bones of the human body

References and Resources

Chamot, A. U., & O'Malley, J. M. (1994). *The CALLA handbook: Implementing the cognitive academic language learning approach.* (pp. 84–86, 199–200, 263–264, 283–284, 293–294). Reading, MA: Addison-Wesley.

Echevarria, J., & Graves, A. (2005). Curriculum adaptations. In P. A. Richard-Amato & M. A. Snow (Eds.), *Academic success for English language learners: Strategies for K–12 mainstream teachers* (pp. 224–247). White Plains, NY: Pearson Education.

Leinhardt, G. (1992). What research on learning tells us about teaching. *Educational Leadership*, 49 (7), 20–25.

Readence, J. E., Bean, T. W., & Baldwin, R. S. (1981). *Content area reading: An integrated approach* (2nd ed.). Dubuque, IA: Kendall/Hunt.

The TechConnection

http://www.state.ia.us/educate/ecese/tqt/tc/prodev/reading_activating.html

Summaries of research studies about activating background knowledge with compilations of grade-leveled strategies and links to more information.

chapter 15

Presenting New Material: Teaching the Lesson

THEORY TO APPLICATION: GUIDELINES FOR PRACTICE

- Use scaffolding strategies with ELLs to facilitate comprehension of the specialized academic language of content classrooms.
- Use scaffolding strategies to challenge ELLs to advance beyond their present state of independent activity, into the areas of potential learning in which content is learnable with the assistance of teachers and peers.
- Use scaffolding strategies that embed the oral and written language of content material in a context-rich environment to facilitate learning for ELLs.
- Use scaffolding strategies that maintain a high level of cognitive challenge, but lower the language demand by embedding it in context.
- Lower learner anxiety in the classroom to create students who are more willing to participate in class, to become risk takers in the learning process, and ultimately to become more successful learners.
- Provide opportunities for students to experience success in the classroom: Success in learning promotes more success by increasing learner motivation, interest, and self-confidence.

*Y*ou've introduced the new topic to your students and sparked their interest. You've activated your students' prior knowledge and built a foundational background for those who needed it. You've motivated your students by demonstrating the usefulness to real-life applications. Your students now seem ready to learn the material that you've planned to teach. The strategies in this chapter will help you present information in ways that will make it easier for the ELLs in your class to understand it.

Oral Academic Language

Have you ever had the experience of trying to talk to someone in a foreign language? You may have had an opportunity to visit a country whose people speak a language you studied in school. Perhaps you tried to learn a few useful phrases in preparation for a trip.

You managed to ask *Où est la gare?* or *¿Dónde está la playa?* You felt delighted to be understood. Then you got the answer—and poof! the bubble of satisfaction burst. You didn't have the faintest idea where the train station or the beach really was. The words seemed to be coming at you so fast that you couldn't make sense of them at all.

Why do speakers of foreign languages seem to be speaking so fast? It's actually not because of the rate of speech but rather the rate of listening: nonnative speakers are *slow listeners*. They need extra time to bring meaning to what they're hearing, to actively process the incoming language. That is not easy to do, especially while trying to pay attention to the flow of new words that continue to be spoken.

Imagine now that these foreign words are not about something as simple as the price of a souvenir or the directions to the restroom. Imagine instead that they deal with complex academic concepts in math, science, and social studies. That is the challenge faced by ELLs in content classes.

THE DIFFICULTIES OF ORAL ACADEMIC LANGUAGE

The spoken language of academic instruction is difficult for language learners for several reasons. First, oral language is ephemeral in nature. Words, once spoken, are gone. You cannot rehear them for review.

Second, the nonnative listener takes more time to process the incoming words than the speaker takes to deliver them. Concentrating on the meaning of one spoken sentence interferes with the ability to listen to the next one. Listening is such a complex task that even native speakers have occasional difficulty processing spoken language in some circumstances, such as listening to TV news or radio traffic reports.

Third, English, the language students are trying to learn, is the *medium* through which academic content is delivered. For ELLs, the language itself adds an additional burden of complexity to understanding the content. Understanding academic concepts depends not just on *what* the teacher says but also on *how* the teacher says it. For ELLs, the *how* can help bring meaning to the *what*.

TEACHER TALK

The Objective: Pace Your Speech.

The Rationale

Oral instruction becomes more comprehensible for ELLs when the speaker focuses on *how* the words of instruction are delivered. Although most teachers speak clearly enough for native English-speaking students, ELLs benefit when those teachers use strategies to enhance the clarity and reduce the complexity of the language they use when presenting new information. Language-sensitive instruction facilitates the challenge of academic listening for ELLs.

STRATEGY 21 SLOW DOWN!

IN CONCEPT

The simplest and most helpful strategy to modify the way you speak is to slow down. The goal is to speak at a slightly slower pace—but not so slowly that it feels or sounds unnatural. A good way to slow down speech is to pause for an extra beat or two at natural breaks between phrases or sentences.

IN PRACTICE

Examine in Figure 15.1 the pausing the teacher uses in her delivery of this overview of the eighth-grade American history curriculum on the first day of school. The dots between phrases represent pause time, two dots for shorter pauses and four dots for longer ones. Each pause offers ELLs valuable extra time to process the language of the incoming content.

STRATEGY 22 ENHANCE THE INTONATION OF YOUR WORDS

IN CONCEPT

Enhanced pronunciation helps you to enunciate the words you speak. Highlight important words by raising or lowering your voice level and your pitch. Giving special intonation when speaking key content words is the

● FIGURE *15.1* Pausing Slows Down Speech

What are we going to study this year? . . . . This year . . we'll be studying the significant . . historical . . events . . . . that led to the development . . of our nation's traditions . . . . We'll survey American history . . . . with a special emphasis . . on the nineteenth century . . . . First, . . we'll examine in detail . . the Declaration of Independence . . . . and the Constitution . . . . because they're fundamental . . to the history of the United States . . . . Then . . we'll study topics such as slavery, ... the Civil War, ... reconstruction, ... industrialization, ... and the United States as a world power.

equivalent to underlining, bolding, or italicizing words in writing. Clearly enunciated, well-paced speech with interesting patterns of tonal variation is much more enjoyable to listen to and easier to understand than speech that is rapid or monotonal or—even worse—both.

IN PRACTICE

Return now to the social studies course overview in Figure 15.1. Even with the pausing, it is a heavy dose of language for ELLs. Using rising and falling intonation to emphasize important content words signifies to ELLs which words to focus on at the same time that it slows the pacing of speech even further. Read aloud the overview in Figure 15.2, this time giving special emphasis to the boldfaced words. You should be able to hear the difference pauses and intonation can make for your ELLs.

To demonstrate how effective this strategy is, look at the list of words in Figure 15.3. These are the boldfaced words designated for enhanced intonation that appear in Figure 15.2. Reading through the list of just those words alone gives you a pretty good idea of the message the passage will convey. You can make your oral instruction easier to understand for your ELLs by speaking more clearly through pausing and intonation.

TEACHER TALK

The Objective: Simplify Your Speech.

The Rationale

Native speakers use speech patterns that differ greatly from patterns used in writing. Simply put, we speak differently than we write, and it is all perfectly normal and correct. Speakers tend to use familiar or informal words in short, simple sentences. Often they use phrases instead of complete sentences. Speakers lose their place and backtrack, or they repeat themselves, or they correct themselves. They make false starts and use extraneous words as fillers

> **FIGURE *15.2*** Enhanced Intonation Slows Speech Even More
>
> What are we going to study this year? . . . . This year . . we'll be studying the significant . . **historical** . . **events** . . . . that led to the development . . of our **nation's traditions**. . . . . We'll survey **American history** . . . . with a special emphasis . . on the **nineteenth century** . . . . **First,** . . we'll examine in detail . . the **Declaration of Independence** . . . . and the **Constitution** . . . . because they're **fundamental** . . to the history of the United States. . . . . **Then** . . we'll study topics such as **slavery,** . . . . **the Civil War,** . . . . **reconstruction,** . . . . **industrialization,** . . . . and the United States as a **world power.**

or spacers. They regularly use contractions and merge words together. Teachers can facilitate comprehension of spoken academic language by making minor adaptations to their normal speech patterns.

STRATEGY 23 LIMIT USE OF CONTRACTIONS

IN CONCEPT

All fluent English speakers contract words when speaking. It is one of the normal differences between spoken and written English, as well as a salient difference between language learners and native speakers.

For ELLs, contractions are a source of misunderstanding. Words like *they're* and *it's* are easily confused with their other forms: *there/their* and *its*.

> **FIGURE *15.3*** Getting the Message from Only the Boldfaced Words
>
> historical events
> nation's traditions
> American history
> nineteenth century
> First
> Declaration of Independence
> Constitution
> fundamental
> Then
> slavery
> the Civil War
> reconstruction
> industrialization
> world power

Another issue is the two ways of contracting the phrase *it is not*. Do *it isn't* and *it's not* really mean the same thing? Many ELLs do not connect the spoken *should've*, which sounds like *should of*, with its written form, *should have*. And almost every listener has experienced the difficulty of hearing the difference between *can* and *can't*.

IN PRACTICE

You can help your ELLs by using the full form of these and other contracted words—such as *they are, it is, it is not*, and *cannot*—as often as you can. The uncontracted forms help ELLs not only by making the meaning more apparent but also by slowing down your rate of speech.

STRATEGY 24 USE FEWER PRONOUNS

IN CONCEPT

ELLs can bring meaning to spoken language more readily when they hear more nouns and fewer pronouns. Pronouns involve some extra language processing and can slow down comprehension.

IN PRACTICE

Although it may sound a bit strange or stilted to you, try to repeat names and other nouns more frequently than you might normally. Look at the nouns in the following sentence:

> **The colonists who participated in the Boston Tea Party were willing to risk depri-vation, even their lives, for the principle of *no taxation without representation*.**

For ELLs, any pronoun that might follow in the next sentence will require a great deal of grammatical processing to determine its antecedent noun. Instead of *they*, repeat *the colonists*; instead of *it*, repeat *the Boston Tea Party* or *no taxation without representation*. Even native speakers occasionally become confused when pronouns like *it* or *they* are used too many times.

STRATEGY 25 SIMPLIFY YOUR SENTENCE STRUCTURE

IN CONCEPT

Teachers often bring to class articles or books to supplement information in their lessons or in students' textbooks. They read aloud passages that were meant to be read silently and processed slowly. The long, complex sentences of written text make them difficult to process orally.

IN PRACTICE

Modify the text materials you read aloud during oral instruction by shortening the sentences and simplifying the structure. Consider the following textbook sentence:

> **The Civil War, which took more American lives than any other war in our history, divided the people of the United States, so that in many families, brother fought against brother.**

You could facilitate the listening comprehension of this passage for your ELLs by subdividing the sentences and paraphrasing the wording to this:

> **The Civil War divided the people of the United States. It even divided families. In many families, brother fought against brother. More Americans died in the Civil War than in any other war in American history.**

STRATEGY 26 USE FAMILIAR WORDS AND BE CONSISTENT

IN CONCEPT

Varying your word choices with synonyms and colorful words may make speech sound more interesting, but for ELLs it adds another source of confusion. Oral academic language can be made more comprehensible for ELLs by using high-frequency words instead of less common ones and by repeating known words instead of using synonyms. Familiar and recognizable spoken words and phrases allow ELLs to focus more clearly on the concepts you are trying to convey. The more consistent your terminology and word patterns, the more readily your ELLs can process the content.

IN PRACTICE

Technique I
All students can benefit from exposure to a wide range of interesting vocabulary through the technique of association. Every time you use low-frequency words, pair them immediately with their more familiar synonym, as *autonomy* with *independence* and *emancipation* with *freedom*. Frequent pair repetition solidifies the association, and the unfamiliar word soon becomes readily recognized.

Technique II

Be consistent in the words you use to give oral directions for assignments and activities. Teachers are often unaware that they are using different words to give the same set of directions, as in the following:

Circle the word that best describes _____.

Draw a circle around the best word choice for _____.

Find the word that best fits each question and then circle it.

Choosing one word pattern to communicate these directions and using it on a regular basis simplifies oral input for ELLs.

Technique III

The words you speak in class should also be consistent with the words and phrases used in the students' textbooks. A brief examination of the words used in the textbook to give directions or to discuss a topic can help you decide which words and phrases to use in presenting and discussing the material. When you believe that directions written in the text seem overly complicated, like those in Figure 15.4, explain them through paraphrase and discussion. For ELLs, maintaining consistency of the words they hear in class and the words they read in their textbooks is another strategy to facilitate comprehension.

● FIGURE *15.4* Simplify Unclear Directions from the Textbook

If the textbook says:

Evaluate the following expression for the given value of the variable.

$A + 5 =$ For A = 2; A = 6.

Paraphrase to:

(Good)   Find A + 5 when A = 2.
          Find A + 5 when A = 6.

(Better)   If A = 2, then A + 5 = ?
           If A = 6, then A + 5 = ?

● FIGURE *15.5* Current Terminology May Be Difficult to Understand

Today's Terminology	Traditional Terminology
an extended constructed response	an essay
a brief constructed response	a paragraph
selected response questions	multiple-choice questions
making text-to-text connections	comparing books

Technique IV

"Translate" the current pedagogical jargon in your school district usage by pairing such terminology with more traditional forms of expression. Some widely used examples are shown in Figure 15.5. Use jargon if you must, but be sure that all your students know what the new words really mean.

STRATEGY 27 BECOME AWARE OF IDIOMATIC LANGUAGE

IN CONCEPT

Idioms and figurative speech make speech colorful and interesting. Language learners feel they are learning the "real English" when they learn idioms, and perhaps they are. Native speakers use them liberally in speech. Unfortunately, idioms and figurative speech also confuse ELLs because the meaning of the individual words, even when each word is well known, does not reflect the actual meaning of the whole message.

IN PRACTICE

Teachers use figurative language to get their students' attention. A teacher, wanting to check students' understanding of new material, might begin a question session with an enthusiastic opener, such as "Okay. I'm going to pitch some practice questions. Let's see who can hit a home run here!" It definitely adds an element of fun, but the ELLs in this classroom are likely to respond by looking around the room for a baseball and bat.

It is not possible to avoid using idioms and figurative speech, nor would you want that. Such language personalizes and flavors speech and often injects interest and humor. Developing an awareness of the idioms and figurative speech you use as you speak allows you the opportunity to paraphrase or explain your language choices in a simple way.

TEACHER TALK

The Objective: Enhance Your Words.

The Rationale

Why do families no longer listen to the radio as evening entertainment? Why is MTV so popular? The answer is that television enhances spoken words and music in ways that engage people. Enhancing words of instruction in the classroom will engage your students, too.

Adding visual elements to speech embeds it in context and facilitates comprehension of the oral language of instruction. Using strategies that move oral instruction from Cummins's Quadrant IV to Quadrant III makes it easier for ELLs to understand concepts and content.

STRATEGY 28 USE GESTURES

IN CONCEPT

Some people say they couldn't talk if their hands were tied behind their backs. Americans, and speakers of many other languages, use their hands to make gestures to help convey the meaning of their words. Hand gestures, along with facial expressions and body language, make speech easier to understand. Consider the difference in the ease of comprehension between watching a videotaped lecture and listening to the same lecture on audiotape. Gestures help embed the context of oral language.

IN PRACTICE

In classroom instruction, ELLs will become more involved if you make oral language as visual an experience as it can be. Make ample use of the gestures and facial expressions that come naturally. When you tell your students "There are three important things to remember," hold up three fingers for your students to see. Continue using one, two, and three fingers as you explain each piece of information. Point prominently to your first finger when you review by asking "What was the first thing we discussed?" Students form a visual picture that helps them retain the information.

Take advantage of any pictures or objects in the classroom that you can use to illustrate a particular word. Try pantomime to help explain a new or difficult term; it is a surefire way of getting the attention of all your students.

STRATEGY 29 USE VISUALS AND GRAPHICS

IN CONCEPT

Support your words with graphic representation. Seeing words and phrases in written form reinforces oral language and facilitates content comprehension.

IN PRACTICE

Technique I
Use the "chalk–talk" approach. Write key vocabulary words and phrases on the board or on an overhead transparency as you speak them. ELLs may not recognize spoken words, such as those in Figure 15.6, as the same ones that they know in their written forms. In some cases, the pronunciation is totally

• FIGURE *15.6* Pronunciation Puzzlers

sovereignty	epitome	tough
pneumatic	psychology	though
phlegm	posthumous	through
mnemonic	hegemony	thorough
choir	conscience	thought

unlike the spelling. In other instances, it may be a word previously encountered only in print that, when spoken, differs from a student's silent pronunciation. It may also be a word that is indistinguishable orally because its spelling is close to too many others, as in the last column of words in Figure 15.6. Seeing a word in writing as you speak it facilitates comprehension for ELLs students.

Technique II
Extend the chalk–talk approach beyond just writing words and phrases to include graphic organizers as a regular part of your teaching. Graphic organizers (discussed at length in Chapter 19) contextually embed oral language. They help ELLs see relationships and understand vocabulary and concepts in a linguistically simplified way.

Technique III
Incorporate pictures, photos, maps, graphs, tables, or anything else you may have on hand to help illustrate the meaning of your words. Draw a picture of an object—even stick figures and rough sketches are helpful. Refer to them as you talk. Remember the adage *One picture is worth a thousand words.* For language learners, this is a primary principle.

Technique IV
Supplement class lectures and discussions with filmstrips, slides, videotapes, DVDs, and CD-ROM programs. While these media types work well to create interest and decrease reliance on language, their soundtracks may present ELLs with some difficulties.

You can take any of several approaches to remedy the soundtrack difficulty. Consider finding some class time to allow ELLs a preview without sound. If this is not feasible, give students an outline or a list of key words and phrases to guide them as they watch.

Technique V
Encourage students to find and share content-appropriate Web sites on the Internet. You might maintain space on a bulletin board or chalkboard for students to write in new and interesting finds that support class content.

Technique VI

Bring in *realia* to explain and interest your students. Realia are authentic, real-world objects that illustrate a concept in ways that allow students to make meaningful connections to their own lives and to the world outside the classroom. Using bank deposit slips and check registers for a unit on banking or working with copies of actual floor plans to calculate square footage can motivate student learning. Suggest that students contribute their own realia—that may provide an interesting cultural experience for you and all your students.

STRATEGY 30   DEMONSTRATE YOUR WORDS

IN CONCEPT

Demonstration and modeling are effective ways to facilitate comprehension of the words of oral instruction. Students can "see" how to find an answer or solve a problem.

IN PRACTICE

Take your students through a step-by-step process to explain how to reach the end result. For each step, do a *think-aloud* to demonstrate *why* you choose to do it a certain way and why you choose *not* to do it in other ways. Ask out loud the questions you would normally ask yourself silently as you show the steps you take. For example, in a lesson about classifying objects, after asking the question, you might say something like "Now how will I know whether it is A or B? I have to think about. . . ." It is important to *not* make it seem too simple: Students need to realize that thinking, adjusting, and readjusting are a natural part of the learning process. Figure 15.7 shows some appropriate classroom applications of this strategy.

STRATEGY 31   BE DRAMATIC

IN CONCEPT

Dramatic lessons are memorable lessons. Make your lessons memorable by hamming them up.

IN PRACTICE

Dramatize, emote, role-play, pantomime. Have a good time! Come to class in a costume or an unusual outfit. Doing such things gives your students tacit permission to be dramatic, too. Groups of students may enjoy staging mini reenactments of events or acting out imaginary dialogs between historical or scientific figures. Students will remember the material and probably you, too.

> • FIGURE *15.7* Use Think-Aloud Demonstration to Show Process
>
> How to classify information
> How to sequence information
> How to summarize information
> How to locate information to answer a question
> How to highlight important information
> How to select the main idea and supporting details

CLASSROOM ROUTINE AND REVIEW

Routines create patterns of consistency, and review creates patterns of opportunity. Both lower levels of anxiety for the students in your classroom.

Routines lessen the need for wordy explanations that may confuse ELLs and, in doing so, raise their anxiety levels. Review offers students multiple opportunities for reinforcement of instructional information. Creating and using classroom routines can free up valuable extra minutes for review.

The Objective: Streamline Your Class Schedule.

The Rationale

Students often enter the classroom over a period of several minutes. Of course you're not going to start until everyone is in their seats and ready. How many minutes does it actually take until you are doing something instructional? (*Hint:* Students stall as long as possible.) Routines will remedy this situation.

STRATEGY 32 USE THE FIRST 5 MINUTES PRODUCTIVELY

IN CONCEPT

Students should know what to do immediately upon arrival and what is expected of them during the class period. Think about the ways you take attendance and correct homework. Techniques to streamline the process so it gets accomplished automatically and without your leadership will save valuable time at the beginning of each class period.

IN PRACTICE

Technique I
Designate a group captain (selected either on a regular rotation basis or as an academic reward) whose job is to take attendance and visually check completed homework assignments as soon as the students enter the room.

Technique II

The same group captain can next lead a discussion and comparison of the answers to the homework assignment. Among his or her responsibilities is to report to you any items that seemed problematic for the group or for which group members' answers differed. This gives you the option of spending valuable class time on only those items that need review, reinforcement, and possibly reteaching.

Students should have their homework clearly visible on their desks as you walk around the room to supervise and offer help during the homework discussion time. Group captains can also collect the papers for you if you want to see them every day.

Technique III

Teachers often wage an internal debate about whether and how often to collect homework. Collecting and correcting it on a daily basis adds another burden to teachers' already heavy workloads, but some teachers feel it may be the only way to ensure that all the students have actually completed the assignments.

An effective technique to resolve this situation is to do a homework check on random days of the week, anywhere from two to six days apart. The idea of this is to give the students just enough time to copy out the answers from the particular assignments you have listed on the board. If they've done their homework, it is an easy task to simply locate the items you request, rewrite them on a separate sheet, and submit them. If they have not done their assigned work, they will not be able to answer the questions and complete the required tasks in the allotted time. The details of this technique are illustrated in Figure 15.8.

STRATEGY 33 DISPLAY THE CLASS PLAN

IN CONCEPT

Routines involving lesson objectives create a sense of security through structure for your ELLs.

IN PRACTICE

Write lesson objectives, topics, and activities for the day or for the week on the board or in another prominent place so that ELLs (and other students) can use them for reference. Seeing what they will be doing next in class decreases the reliance on oral language input for ELLs, resulting in lower levels of anxiety and greater ability to focus on classroom tasks.

● FIGURE *15.8* Homework Check

1. Students fold a blank sheet of paper into four or six sections.
2. Students number each box one through four or one through six.
3. Teacher writes on the board four or six items to transfer to the appropriate box.

   Examples:
   Box 1. Tuesday, Question 5, page 138.
   Box 2. Wednesday, Question 2, page 151.

1. Tuesday, Q 5, P 138	2. Wednesday, Q 2, P 151
3. Thursday, Q 1, P 167	4. Friday, Q 3, P 189

4. Teacher allots only enough time to copy answers, not to respond or compute them.
5. Teacher collects and corrects the papers.

STRATEGY 34 POST THE HOMEWORK

IN CONCEPT

Teachers often run out of time at the end of the lesson. The homework assignment, usually the last piece of information in the class, often gets delivered in a hurried rush of words as students are packing up their books and getting ready to leave. For ELLs, this can be a confusing and difficult situation.

IN PRACTICE

Write homework assignments ahead of time in the same place everyday. The place you choose can be on a small section of the board, on chart paper, or on an overhead transparency. If you don't want your students to see the assignment at the beginning of class because they may be tempted to work on it during class time, keep it covered until an appropriate point in the lesson. The main objective is to avoid rushing it out orally as the bell is ringing. Make sure students know that homework information will appear in the same place every day. Your students can never use the excuse that they didn't hear you.

CLASSROOM ROUTINES AND REVIEW

The Objective: Get into the Routine of Review.

The Rationale

If background knowledge forms the building blocks of learning, then review is the cement that holds the learning together. It reinforces learning and makes it more solid. Mini-reviews during the lesson and a final review at the end benefit all students. Those who know will shine, and those who don't know will get another opportunity for learning. You get the opportunity to hear and correct any misconceptions. It's a win–win situation for everyone. Frequent review during and at the end of every class period far exceeds in value the minutes devoted to it.

STRATEGY 35 REVIEW WHILE YOU TEACH

IN CONCEPT

All students benefit from a quick review of content as the lesson progresses. Multiple mini reviews keep student attention and concentration focused throughout class time. For ELLs, in particular, repetition and review offer extra opportunities for language input that can reinforce and enhance their conceptual understanding.

IN PRACTICE

Technique I
As you teach, ask frequent questions so students can repeat, review, paraphrase, and summarize content. Those who know the material get a chance to reinforce their learning, and those who don't get the opportunity to hear the information again.

As often as every 5 or 10 minutes, ask appropriate questions:

So, what did we just cover?

Who remembers the reasons for _____?

Who can explain the process we just saw?

Why did we say _____ was important?

A good challenge is to ask simple yes/no questions that contain misinformation, such as "General Grant led the Confederacy's army, right?" Misinformation questions promote critical listening and encourage students to think before answering. You may find that your students like the idea of correcting your misstatements.

Technique II
One middle-school teacher treated review questions as a gamelike challenge. At any point in the lesson, she would announce, "Quick check!" The students became instantly alert in anticipation of the question and the opportunity to score bonus points. They loved it—perhaps your students will, too.

STRATEGY 36 END EACH LESSON WITH REVIEW

IN CONCEPT

Teachers, with the objective of utilizing every minute of class time for learning, often find themselves with no time at the end of class to conduct a review. With all good intentions, those who do this discard a critically important teaching strategy.

All students benefit from spending the last 3 to 5 minutes of class time in review. Every lesson needs closure, even those that will be continued the next day.

IN PRACTICE

Technique I
Just before class ends, either return to the brainstorming graphic for review or ask the simple question "So, what did we talk about today?" If important information is omitted, make your question more specific, as in "What about _____? What did we say about that?"

Technique II
In *Elbow Buddy Review* you ask your paired students to turn to their partners—their "elbow buddies"—and tell them a specific piece of information that you announce. Several ideas for this type of review are listed in Figure 15.9.

> ● FIGURE *15.9* Elbow Buddy Review
>
> "Turn to your elbow buddy and tell him or her. . . ."
>
> 2 causes of _____
>
> 3 substances that _____
>
> the definition of _____
>
> 3 reasons for _____
>
> 2 places that _____

Technique III

Partner Review pairs students who are designated as Partner A or B. (Use a simple technique to designate As and Bs, such as the student whose first name comes first alphabetically is partner A.) Using the same types of prompts as in Figure 15.9, ask Partner A to tell Partner B the items for review, alternating partners with each request for additional review items. To ensure that the information being exchanged between partners is correct and complete, you can ask students to share with the class what they just discussed with their partners.

Technique IV

Another way to review that is fast, effective, and fun is 3–2–1. At the end of the lesson, students write three facts they learned, two new words, and one item of particular interest, as shown in Figure 15.10.

The review format in Figure 15.11 offers the interesting addition of a "0" line for other aspects of the topic that students hope to learn in future lessons. You can combine this strategy with *Elbow Buddy Review* or *Partner Review*, using this as a follow-up written form after the oral partnered review. If you

> ● FIGURE *15.10* 3–2–1 Review
>
> 3 facts I learned today are:
>
> 1. _____
>
> 2. _____
>
> 3. _____
>
> 2 words I want to remember are:
>
> 1. _____
>
> 2. _____
>
> 1 thing I found very interesting is:
>
> 1. _____

● FIGURE *15.11* Variation on the 3–2–1 Review: Add a Zero

3 facts I learned today are:

1. _____

2. _____

3. _____

2 words I want to remember are:

1. _____

2. _____

1 thing I found very interesting is:

1. _____

0! I still don't know anything about _____ and I would like to!

---

use the *3–2–1* review by itself, you will get a more satisfactory result by doing it as a paired or small group activity, perhaps structuring it with a *Think–Write–Pair–Share* (Strategy 13, Chapter 14) approach.

Technique V

A different type of strategy involves using graphic organizers as review. Working again in pairs, students can use any of the graphic organizers discussed later in Chapter 19 to summarize and review information. *K–W–L* charts (Chapter 14, Figures 14.2–14.4) and learning logs (Chapter 18, Figures 18.10 and 18.11) also can be used for review. At some point, perhaps as a homework assignment, students can transfer the review items to the L section of their *K–W–L* charts to their learning logs.

STRATEGY 37 MAKE ACTIVE USE OF REVIEW NOTES

IN CONCEPT

As important as review is to reinforcing knowledge, it can become an even more powerful technique when students become aware that their daily reviews can help them in other ways.

IN PRACTICE

Have students keep their daily written reviews in a separate section of their notebooks or even in a completely separate review notebook. The review notes can be used daily to activate prior knowledge as you begin the next day's lesson on the same topic. Students can be encouraged to use their review notes to study for tests. These same notes can be used to link new information with previously learned material providing even more reasons to make review a regular class routine.

In Summary: Teaching the Lesson

It is apparent that good classroom instruction begins with speaking in a manner that facilitates comprehension for your ELLs. The challenge, however, lies in changing highly ingrained speech habits and mannerisms that may interfere with clarity. The first step in the process, and perhaps the hardest, is becoming aware of what you actually do.

An interesting way to start thinking about the way you use oral language in your classroom is to record—on videotape or audiotape—a lesson you teach. As you replay it, listen closely to your use of language, and select one or two areas you would like to improve. Choose the strategies you think would help and begin to incorporate them into your patterns of oral instruction. When those feel comfortable, try working on others, one or two at a time. Each modification you add enhances the clarity of your oral instruction for your ELLs.

A second part of good instruction involves classroom routine and review. For ELLs, predictable classroom routines and frequent content review lower anxiety and support language development at the same time that they facilitate comprehension of content. For teachers, routines save time, effort, and energy. They are clearly good for everyone. Try getting into your own routines for arrival, homework, review, and dismissal. You're going to like what happens.

Questions for Discussion

1. How do the strategies dealing with teacher talk and classroom routine and review reflect the *Guidelines for Practice* presented at the beginning of this chapter?
2. *If you are currently teaching a class,* audiotape or videotape a lesson in which you are actively teaching. Analyze the type of language you use and your pace of delivery. What advice would you give yourself to facilitate comprehension of your oral language for the ELLs in your classroom?

   If you are not currently teaching, get permission to audiotape or videotape a lesson in which the teacher is actively teaching. Analyze the recording as described above.

3. In pairs of one who is currently teaching and one who is not, compare and critique each other's analyses of the recorded lessons.

4. Prepare a text passage for reading aloud in class. After your reading, your colleagues will give you verbal feedback or a written critique.

5. Prepare a "Get-the-message-from-the-boldfaced-words" activity (Strategy 22). Read it to your peers in class. Did they get the message?

6. *If you are now teaching a class*, what routines do you think you could create to lower language input for your ELLs and, at the same time, make your class period more time efficient?

   If you are not currently teaching a class, arrange to observe a teacher and keep a written record, minute to minute, of classroom activities from the arrival of the first students through the final dismissal. In what ways do you think this teacher could benefit from creating routines?

References and Resources

Fillmore, L. W., & Snow, C. E. (2005). What teachers need to know about language. In P. A. Richard-Amato & M. A. Snow (Eds.), *Academic success for English language learners: Strategies for K–12 mainstream teachers* (pp. 47–75). White Plains, NY: Pearson Education.

Richard-Amato, P. A., & Snow, M. A. (2005). Instructional strategies for K–12 mainstream teachers. In P. A. Richard-Amato and M. A. Snow (Eds.), *Academic success for English language learners: Strategies for K–12 mainstream teachers* (pp. 197–223). White Plains, NY: Pearson Education.

chapter 16

Did They Get What I Taught? Checking Comprehension

THEORY TO APPLICATION: GUIDELINES FOR PRACTICE

- Use scaffolding strategies with ELLs to facilitate comprehension of the specialized academic language of content classrooms.
- Use scaffolding strategies to challenge ELLs to advance beyond their present state of independent activity, into the areas of potential learning in which content is learnable with the assistance of teachers and peers.
- Use scaffolding strategies that maintain a high level of cognitive challenge, but lower the language demand by embedding it in context.
- Provide opportunities for ELLs to negotiate conceptual understandings and to explore language usage through classroom interaction.
- Lower learner anxiety in the classroom to create students who are more willing to participate in class, to become risk takers in the learning process, and ultimately to become more successful learners.
- Provide opportunities for students to experience success in the classroom: Success in learning promotes more success by increasing learner motivation, interest, and self-confidence.

Checking Comprehension

You've taught the lesson. Now it's time to check comprehension: Do your students understand what you've taught?

With the goal of ensuring that their instruction has been understood, teachers almost always follow up the presentation section of a lesson with a question-and-answer session. The Q and A routine follows a traditional pattern: Teacher asks, teacher calls on student, student answers. If the response is incomplete, teacher calls on more students to add information. If the response is adequate, teacher moves on to the next question. It is always the same students who raise their hands to participate. Teachers' attempts to involve others in the class often result in uncomfortable silences.

The strategies in this chapter will help you expand student participation and increase the success of your question-and-answer sessions.

QUESTIONS, ANSWERS, AND PARTICIPATION IN THE CLASSROOM

The Objective: Formulate Questions in Ways that Encourage Participation.

The Rationale

Students hesitate to participate in class for a number of reasons, but the three most likely ones are they didn't understand the question; they don't know the answer; or they are fearful or shy about speaking in class. More students will willingly participate when you use strategies that involve selecting question types, offering assistance in answers, and lowering the affective filter.

STRATEGY 38 DON'T FALL INTO THE "DOES EVERYONE UNDERSTAND?" TRAP

IN CONCEPT

Teachers sincerely want to make sure that students *really* understand the new material that has just been taught. Teachers willingly seek to clarify, repeat, explain, give more examples, and correct misunderstandings before moving ahead. So at several points in the lesson, teachers stop to check student comprehension with questions such as these:

Does everyone understand?

Does anyone have any questions?

Does anyone need me to repeat any part of this?

OK, so everyone gets it, yes?

The fact is that no matter how little the students have actually understood—no matter how completely confused they are—they just don't raise their hands in response to such questions. And why don't they? The answer lies in the way the questions are phrased. In effect, what the students hear is "Will the one really dumb person in this class who didn't get this please raise your hand and publicly identify yourself?" Why would anyone want to do a thing like that? Better just to sit there and *feel* dumb than to raise your hand and have everyone *know* how dumb you really are! The unintended effect of these questions is exactly the opposite of the teacher's objective.

IN PRACTICE

How, then, can you word a question that will actually achieve your desired goal? Try this:

"It's question time. Who's got a question for me?"

These words make it sound like questions are a normal and expected part of every lesson.

You can reinforce your accepting attitude toward questions even further when you respond to a student's question with something very positive:

"That's a great question!"

"Thank you for asking that!"

"Good question!"

Responses like these actually make students feel *rewarded* for asking for clarification instead of penalized by drawing negative attention to themselves. You, too, will be rewarded by your students' responses when you change "Does everyone understand?" to "Question time. Who's got a question for me?"

STRATEGY 39 SELECT QUESTION TYPES

IN CONCEPT

Teachers' questions vary in difficulty depending on their conceptual and/or linguistic complexity. Selecting the types of questions you direct to your ELLs promotes their participation.

IN PRACTICE

Even those in the early stages of second-language acquisition may be willing and able to respond with answers requiring only a minimum number of words, especially if they can refer to key words and phrases that you have written previously on the board. Pattern your questions to elicit nonverbal, yes/no, either/or, or one-word responses, as in the examples shown in Figure 16.1.

● FIGURE *16.1* Select Questions for English Language Learners

Point to	Can you show us the location of Washington, DC, on the map?
Yes/no	Do Bedouins live on grassy plains?
Either/or	Is the Ukraine east or west of the major part of Russia?
Add more information	Who can give me another example of a deciduous tree?

It is tempting to ask lower-order questions, such as those in Figure 16.1, to the ELLs in your class because they are linguistically simple to answer. The drawback of these questions, however, is that they do not involve much thought processing. Responses to these types of questions call for only simple recall of information.

To become critical thinkers, students must engage in processing higher order questions that ask them to explain, analyze, synthesize, and evaluate information. It is not the cognitive level of these questions that may present a challenge for ELLs but rather the higher levels of language ability required to answer them.

The strategy of directing follow-up questions to ELLs is a technique that balances both linguistic and cognitive demands. ELLs can engage in complex thought processing while answering the following types of questions with relatively simple English:

Do you agree with Ilya's answer?

Why?

Why not?

Can you add anything to Shihan's answer?

STRATEGY 40 MAKE STUDENTS ACTIVE LISTENERS

IN CONCEPT

What happens immediately after the teacher calls on someone to give an answer? In most classes, all the other students simply turn off their thinking and listening until the teacher asks the next question. Students can be helped to become active listeners throughout the lesson.

IN PRACTICE

Encourage active listening by following up a student response with a request for another student to paraphrase or evaluate what was just said. Frequent follow-up questions, such as those in Figure 16.2, make students aware of

> • FIGURE *16.2* Follow-up Questions Encourage Active Listening
>
> "Brahim, can you tell me in your own words what Raoul just said?"
>
> "Rosalba, do you agree or disagree with what Raoul just said, and why?"
>
> "Irina, Raoul gave such a good answer. I think we all need to hear what he said again."

other students' thinking and problem-solving strategies. They also keep students tuned in and ready to respond.

The easiest follow-up question is simply "Do you agree with that answer?" Teachers routinely ask this question when the answer is wrong. The first time you try it when the answer is correct, you will witness a fascinating reaction. Students are accustomed to hearing "Do you agree with that answer?" exclusively as a means of correcting misinformation. The question renders students virtually speechless when you ask it as a follow-up to a *correct* question—after all, they've never encountered it used that way.

After you've used this questioning technique once or twice, remind students at the start of Q and A and discussion sessions that you will frequently ask them if they agree or disagree with other students' answers. Using this type of follow-up question as a regular part of your teaching will make your students active listeners. They are never "off the hook" because they know they may be called on to affirm or deny any student's answer.

STRATEGY 41 VARY WHOLE-CLASS RESPONSE TECHNIQUES

IN CONCEPT

When teachers want the whole class to answer a question, they most commonly use the choral response technique. The problem with this approach is that the teacher can never be sure who is answering correctly and who is not. The following three techniques allow ELLs to participate in a linguistically simple and nonthreatening manner. The entire class is actively involved and you, the teacher, get immediate feedback about the students' level of understanding.

IN PRACTICE

Technique I
Students make the *Thumbs Up/Thumbs Down* sign in response to a series of short yes/no questions. Thumbs in the mid-position can mean "sometimes" or "depending on circumstances" or even "I'm not sure."

Students can also hold up one to five fingers to indicate their responses to choices you've written on the board. Think of this as a sort of oral multiple-choice technique. It works particularly well for classification activities. If you see more than one response, you have the immediate opportunity to discuss the item and to clarify misunderstandings.

In this technique, as well as the ones that follow, students should not answer instantly. It is important that you allow enough wait time (see Strategy 45 later in this chapter) for all students to think the question through. Students respond only after you give the signal to do so.

Technique II

Before beginning a question or review session, students make *response cards* with content-specific words or symbols written on index cards or small squares of paper. Information on each card could be numbers, mathematical signs denoting processes, categories, identifying names, descriptive phrases, the words *yes* and *no*, or the symbols + for presence or − for absence of a quality. Students hold up the appropriate card or card combinations in response to your series of questions.

Technique III

Students use markers or dry-erase boards to write brief responses to your questions. At your signal, they hold up the boards for you to see. Students can work individually or in pairs. They love this strategy because it feels like the TV show *Jeopardy*.

You can get the dry-erase boards from large hardware and home improvement stores. These stores willingly donate the scrap ends from customers' custom cuttings to teachers who request them. Stores will save them up to make class sets and will generally trim them to size.

STRATEGY 42 "PRE-PAIR" TO RESPOND

IN CONCEPT

Students dread looking foolish in front of peers and often avoid answering teachers' questions for this reason. You can lower students' anxiety by offering them the opportunity of testing out an answer with a partner before stating it in front of the whole class.

IN PRACTICE

The *Pre-Pair* strategy invites students to check with a partner before volunteering an answer. After you pose a question to the class, allow 10 to 20 seconds for one member of prearranged pairs to tell the other member his or her ideas. One partner can be A and the other B, and you can specifically designate after each question whose turn it is to talk and whose to listen. At the end of the designated time, students can raise their hands to share an idea they had or one they heard.

STRATEGY 43   TRY "NUMBERED HEADS"

IN CONCEPT

Numbered Heads is a structured strategy that promotes student participation by allowing small groups of students to discuss possible responses before one group member is selected to answer. It is a strategy that offers extra linguistic support for ELLs and reinforces conceptual understanding for all students. It promotes student participation by building self-confidence and also increases student–student interaction. It is a source of authentic language input for language learners. Best of all, perhaps, students like it because it feels like a game.

IN PRACTICE

Students sit in groups of four. Each student has a designated number, one through four, decided by the members of each group (see Figure 16.3). After each question, the teacher gives the groups a brief period, from 20 seconds to 2 minutes, depending on the complexity of the question, to discuss their answers. When time is up, the teachers calls out a number—number three, for example. All the students designated number three raise their hands. The teacher chooses one number-three student to answer the question and continues calling on other number threes until enough information has been given. This procedure is repeated with each question.

● F I G U R E *16.3* Numbered Heads

A randomized process for choosing numbers works best here. Teachers can make a spinner with four quadrants, use numbered popsicle sticks or balls, or put numbered slips of paper in a box or paper bag. Psychologically, random drawings make students feel that no one number is being favored, neglected, or picked on. Even better, random drawings keep all students focused and on task for every question by removing the possibility that they won't be called on two or more times in a row.

STRATEGY 44   USE THINK–PAIR–SHARE

IN CONCEPT

Think–Pair–Share (a modification of Strategy 13, *Think–Write–Pair–Share*, in Chapter 14 to activate background knowledge) works equally well in question-and-answer sessions. Like *Numbered Heads*, the *Think–Pair–Share* strategy actively scaffolds learning by offering ELLs the opportunity to negotiate their conceptual understandings through interaction with peers. ELLs will experience less participation anxiety when they are able to test their content knowledge and language usage in the shelter of a small group setting.

IN PRACTICE

Prepare students by informing them that they will be using the *Think–Pair–Share* strategy prior to raising their hands to answer questions. During your Q and A sessions, allot 10 to 20 seconds for students to think about an appropriate response after you ask a question. Follow this "think time" with another 20 second segment during which students discuss the ideas they thought of with a partner or small group. Here again, students may find themselves more willing to participate because they can share either an idea that they had or one that they heard.

STRATEGY 45   ALLOW EXTRA WAIT TIME

IN CONCEPT

Wait time is the period of silence given to students to formulate an answer to a question. You probably first encountered the concept of wait time early in your teacher training classes. It would not be unusual if you have not given it much conscious thought since then.

Wait time is important because all students need time to sort out the meaning of the question and process the content required to answer it. Wait time is even more essential for ELLs because they have the additional layer of language processing to go through.

IN PRACTICE

Language learners benefit from wait times of 5 seconds for simple questions to as much as 10 to 20 seconds for more complicated questions. One way to ensure adequate time is to count slowly to yourself. The sound of silence may be uncomfortable to you at first, but extended wait times help lower the feelings of anxiety that often accompany being called on to produce an answer in a new language.

STRATEGY 46 GIVE CREDIT FOR TRYING

IN CONCEPT

Teachers hear wrong answers every day. How you respond to them can make the difference between students who are willing to participate and those who are not. Acknowledging incorrect answers with a pleasant, positive response takes at least some of the risk out of classroom participation.

IN PRACTICE

Try saying one of the following with sincerity and a smile when students offer misinformation:

> Good try.
> Almost.
> Thank you for trying.
> Not quite, but you're thinking.
> What an interesting (unusual) way to look at it.

Such responses lessen the stigma and anxiety of wrong answers and encourage continued attempts at participation. Wrong answers become an acceptable and normal part of learning.

STRATEGY 47 OFFER FACE SAVERS

IN CONCEPT

Offering your students a face-saving way to not answer a question also lowers anxiety levels. It lowers students' affective filters and makes them more willing to take academic risks in the classroom.

IN PRACTICE

Technique I

Make it an accepted practice for students in your class to exercise a *Pass* option. Students who cannot answer a question simply say "Pass," after which you can add "Fine. We'll get back to you later." Be sure that you do.

You might consider using actual pass tokens that sit on students' desks until redeemed at some point during the class period. Students have to return them by answering a later question or by contributing to the review at the end of the class.

Technique II

A second face-saving strategy is to allow students to call on another student for assistance. To make this an effective learning technique, the student you initially called on should paraphrase or repeat the information given by the student who assisted in answering the question.

STRATEGY 48 WATCH FOR STUDENT READINESS

IN CONCEPT

Sometimes you can sense that certain students would like to try to answer but can't quite bring themselves to raise their hands. This is a good time to *invite* their participation.

Start by making friendly eye contact and smiling at each of the students who seem reluctant to participate. Look closely at those students' faces when you direct a general question to the whole class. Call on them when you detect readiness, but ensure that they have positive early participation experiences by giving them positive feedback and assisting their efforts.

IN PRACTICE

Technique I

Smile and nod while you encourage ELLs to use visual aids to support their words. Point to anything in the classroom that might help them with their responses, particularly the key words and phrases you wrote on the board during the period of instruction. There may also be charts, pictures, or places on maps displayed on bulletin boards around the room that can help them complete their responses.

Technique II

Smile and nod as you expand their few words into more complete thoughts. Use your words to augment theirs, as in Figure 16.4. Follow up a one-word student response with "Good—tell me more" or "True, but tell me why you

● FIGURE *16.4* Expanding Students' Responses

Teacher Question	Student Response	Teacher Expansion
What is the name of the courts directly under the Supreme Court?	Circ . . . circa . . . circle courts.	Yes, the Circuit Court of Appeals. (Write the word *Circuit* on the board.)
Why do objects in motion continue to move in a vacuum?	No friction.	Exactly, a vaccum is a frictionless environment.
When would you use a bar graph and when a line graph?	Bar graph . . . to count . . . to put together . . . line for much change . . . long time.	Excellent! A bar graph shows data that can be counted and compared, and a line graph shows change over time.

think so." Affirming the correctness of the original answer gives students the confidence to continue.

Technique III

Smile and nod when you prompt students by supplying the word or phrase they are searching for or stumbling over. Fill in the missing word or phrase and perhaps they will be able to continue with their responses.

STRATEGY 49   FOCUS ON CONTENT

IN CONCEPT

When ELLs attempt to answer questions, keep your attention on the message, not on the medium. Focus on the *content* in the response rather than on the language used to express it.

IN PRACTICE

ELLs will participate more readily if their language usage and pronunciation are not constantly and overtly corrected. Instead, model correct usage, as shown in Figure 16.4, by rephrasing student answers using complete sentences with correct grammar, vocabulary, and pronunciation.

Restructuring responses should be a subtle, not obvious, form of correction. Too much overt correction raises students' affective filters and decreases their willingness to participate.

QUESTIONS, ANSWERS, AND PARTICIPATION IN THE CLASSROOM

The Objective: Fine Tune Your Awareness of Student Participation.

The Rationale

Successful learning takes place in classrooms that promote student participation. Teachers try to involve every one of their students in class discussions, but few really know if they actually succeed. The next strategy will fine-tune your awareness of student participation in your classroom.

STRATEGY 50 MONITOR YOUR INTERACTION PATTERNS

IN CONCEPT

Many teachers have a distinct *action zone* (Richards & Lockhart, 1996, p. 139), that is, a localized area of the classroom that they favor. This is the section of students toward whom they direct their instruction and discussion. Unconsciously, they look at and call on the students in this zone much more than the others.

IN PRACTICE

You can systematically determine if you have a particular action zone by videotaping a class you teach. (The suggestions in Figure 16.5 will ensure that you do not violate any privacy laws when you do the recording.) Making the videotape is easy if your school can provide an audiovisual team member to operate the camera as you teach. If that is not the situation, you can set the camera, focused on you, on a tripod in the rear of the room. Reviewing the videotape will help you determine whether you favor a particular section of the classroom. It will also allow you to observe your patterns of interaction. You may make some unexpected discoveries.

As you watch your videotape, look carefully at where you direct your attention and which students you actually call on. Use a class-seating chart to carefully note where you stand and who you look at as you teach. Note which students you call on and how many times. Your tallies may make you aware of an action zone and an interaction pattern you never knew you had.

Teachers have made many interesting discoveries from viewing themselves teaching. Some were surprised that they had called on several of their students so many times. Others saw that they had neglected to call on several very quiet students in the class, even though they were positive that they

> • FIGURE *16.5* Getting Permission to Videotape

Schoolwide Permission

Many schools routinely send home forms requesting permission to videotape for educational purposes. Parents sign and return the forms at the beginning of the school year. If your school does this, you are covered.

Individual Permission

If your school doesn't do this, you must request parental permission with a letter similar to this one:

Dear Parents,

In my ongoing pursuit of excellence in teaching, I would like your permission to videotape *myself* as I teach a lesson in our classroom. The focus will be exclusively on me and my teaching, and only I will view the tape. I will be observing myself as a teacher to become aware of any ways that I might improve the quality of instruction. My goal is to become the very best teacher I can be for your children, who will be the beneficiaries of this experience.

Thank you very much.

(Your Signature)

I give permission to videotape for this purpose only.

Parent's Signature _____

Student Name _____ Date _____

had actively involved every single student. Still others realized that they might improve student participation by working on smiling more and moving around the room.

Use the videotape to develop an awareness of other aspects of teaching discussed in this chapter. If you like what you see, give yourself a pat on the back. If, on the other hand, you feel you should find ways to increase student participation, you might try any of several techniques. A simple strategy that teachers use is to check off students' names on a class list or seating chart as you call on them. You can readily see participation patterns and frequency.

Another approach is to write students' names on popsicle sticks, place the sticks name side down in a cup, and randomly draw one after asking a question. (Use your teacher prerogative if you think the question may be too difficult for the name you draw by saying "Oops, I just called this name" or "Absent.") One teacher instituted a rule that all students who didn't participate during the lesson itself had to conduct the review at the end of the class. It was amazing how the participation in that class increased!

In Summary: Classroom Questions, Answers, and Participation

Teachers who strive to create a classroom environment that promotes and encourages participation invite students to become active learners. Active learners make better learners. Strategies that increase participation maximize potential for students to show what they know and to begin to experience feelings of academic success.

Questions for Discussion

1. How do the strategies dealing with classroom questions, answers, and participation reflect the *Guidelines for Practice* presented at the beginning of this chapter?
2. Research additional question types used in classrooms, such as rhetorical, inquiry based, closed, open ended. Give examples of all question types. Discuss the effect of each type of question on student participation.
3. How does lowering the affective filter promote classroom participation? Give some specific examples.
4. Compare a class you took in which you enjoyed participating with one in which you did not. Evaluate what the instructors did or did not do to encourage/discourage participation.
5. Respond to the following scenario individually if you are currently teaching a class and with a partner if you are not.

   You have just been assigned a student teacher and you want to start him/her out right. Write a list of at least five practices that encourage classroom participation and five practices that are sure to discourage participation.

References and Resources

Brown, H. D. (1994). *Teaching by principles: An interactive approach to language pedagogy* (pp. 157–169). Englewood Cliffs, NJ: Prentice Hall Regents.

Freeman, Y. S., & Freeman, D. E. (1998). *ESL/EFL teaching: Principles for success.* Portsmouth, NH: Heinemann.

Richards, J. C., & Lockhart, C. (1996). *Reflective teaching in second language classrooms.* Cambridge, England: Cambridge University Press.

chapter 17

Extending Comprehension: Textbook Vocabulary Strategies

THEORY TO APPLICATION: GUIDELINES FOR PRACTICE

- Use scaffolding strategies to challenge ELLs to advance beyond their present state of independent activity, into the areas of potential learning in which content is learnable with the assistance of teachers and peers.

- Use scaffolding strategies that embed the oral and written language of content material in a context-rich environment to facilitate learning for ELLs.

- Use scaffolding strategies with ELLs to facilitate comprehension of the specialized academic language of content classrooms.

- Use scaffolding strategies that maintain a high level of cognitive challenge, but lower the language demand by embedding it in context.

- Actively teach learning strategies to give students a "menu" of ways to process and learn new information.

If ELLs could tell you what part of their content classes they found the most challenging, the majority would say their textbooks. The written language in student textbooks combines the difficulties of highly abstract and cognitively demanding concepts with content-specific words and advanced academic vocabulary, all written in language appropriate to the grade for which they are intended. Fortunately, textbooks can be made more comprehensible to ELLs—and to native English-speaking students who read below grade level—through the creative application of scaffolding strategies. This chapter focuses on vocabulary strategies that facilitate comprehension of the textbook, and the next will focus on reading strategies.

New Vocabulary: Which Words to Teach?

Many ELLs believe that the key to understanding English lies in the vocabulary. It is difficult to argue against this point of view: Knowing what words mean is unquestionably critical to comprehension.

Textbooks and their accompanying teachers' editions do a creditable job of identifying and defining new vocabulary that appears in each chapter. These words are content specific or technical in nature, words students must learn if they are to understand the concepts that follow. If it were only these words that needed explanation, teachers and students would have an easy task.

Other than obvious technical or content-specific vocabulary in textbooks, four other categories of words may be unknown or misunderstood by ELLs. These are (1) synonyms, (2) idioms, (3) new usages of familiar words, and (4) just plain new words.

SYNONYMS

All writers use synonyms to add interest and variety to text. Indeed, it would be boring to read the same noun, adjective, or verb over and over in a piece of writing. While synonyms have the positive effect of adding flavor to writing, they also have the unintended negative effect of burdening ELLs with more unknown vocabulary. Consider the number of synonymous phrases we use to talk about the following simple arithmetic problem:

$$\begin{array}{r} 8 \\ -\ 5 \\ \hline \end{array}$$

Subtract 5 from 8.

5 from 8 equals ____.

Take 5 away from 8.

Take away 5 from 8.

How much less is 5 than 8?

How much is 8 less 5?

8 minus 5 equals ____.

What is the difference between 8 and 5?

At a more advanced level, think about the different words and phrases that are used to represent the concept of *freedom* in written texts. A search through several high school social studies textbooks produced this list:

liberty	liberation
independence	autonomy
sovereignty	emancipation
self-determination	self-government
self-sufficiency	self-reliance
home rule	

To make the situation even more confusing for ELLs, words and phrases used during class discussions may vary significantly from the wording used in the textbook. It's not hard to see why vocabulary is such a challenge.

IDIOMS

ELLs love to learn idioms because they feel, and perhaps rightly so, that if they understand idioms, they *really* know English. Idioms are more than the sum of their parts. These groups of words have meanings unrelated to knowledge of the actual words, and analyzing them on a word-by-word basis often produces some odd images. Visualize the literal meaning of the following widely used idiomatic expressions:

She really put her foot in her mouth.
It's raining cats and dogs.
I'm all ears.
He's got two left feet.

Idiomatic expressions are also used in academic writing. The phrases in Figure 17.1 are frequent idiomatic references in social studies textbooks. It is not difficult to imagine an ELL thinking "Why did they stand under a flag to fight?"

● FIGURE *17.1* Idiomatic References in Social Studies

About the Civil War	About the American Flag
a house divided fighting under the Confederate flag on the home front loss of lives	the Stars and Stripes Old Glory the Red, White, and Blue

NEW USAGES OF FAMILIAR WORDS

Think of the word *strike*. In what context might ELLs be familiar with this word? Did you think of baseball, perhaps bowling or fishing? Students will be familiar with these usages of the word *strike* from watching or participating in these activities or having parents who do.

Apart from sports, *strike*, as used in everyday conversation, has multiple meanings depending on the context in which it appears. Here are several:

Police thought the murderer would *strike* again.
He hoped a brilliant idea would *strike* him.
She tried unsuccessfully to *strike* up a conversation.
He tried again to *strike* the match.
She tried to *strike* a bargain.
   (Did she light any fires?)
The dog was *struck* by a car.
He was *struck* by the beauty of the sunset.
   (Was he hurt, too?)
We heard the clock *striking* midnight.
The similarity was *striking*.
   (And loud, too?)

In textbooks, however, the word *strike* appears in wholly different contexts. Think now of how it relates to these topics:

Industry: The workers went on *strike*.
Mining: The prospectors were hoping to *strike* gold.
Weather: Lightning can *strike* before a storm.
Military: The air *strike* was considered successful.

With good reason, ELLs will be confused by these multiple meanings and usages. You can help them by scanning the text for words that might be confusing or misunderstood because they would be more commonly known with a different meaning in a conversational or social context.

All subject domains have their own set of concept words, many of which fall into the category of familiar words used in new ways. Figure 17.2 lists examples from science, math, and social studies.

Imagine a student's puzzlement about how Sunday mass at church fits into science. Can you visualize the mental images that ELLs might form from the expressions *river bed* and *river bank*? Who got invited to those political parties? And what about those wings in government—where did they come from? Add

● FIGURE *17.2* Domain-Specific Usages of Familiar Words

Science	energy, mass, matter, force, kingdom
Math	table, round, root, mean, power, expression
Social Studies	river bed, river bank, interest rates, (political) parties, left wing, right wing

---

● FIGURE *17.3* A True Tale of Misunderstanding

A second-grade teacher of a self-contained ESL class was teaching a unit on Christopher Columbus and how he explored the Caribbean Islands and conquered the native Indian populations living there. She asked her class why they thought that Columbus, with so few men, was able to conquer the many thousands of native Indians who lived there. When none of them answered, she explained: "It's because Christopher Columbus and his men had arms, and the native Indians didn't have any."

Not yet realizing any misunderstanding, she continued the discussion by asking about the kind of life the Caribbean Indians had before being conquered by Columbus. One student answered, "Very hard," as all the others nodded their heads in agreement.

Surprised by this response, she asked, "How could it have been a hard life? They had beautiful warm weather, lots of food to eat—especially fruits and vegetables. They didn't need to wear a lot of clothing or build strong houses to keep out the cold. Why do you think they had a hard life?"

One student timidly offered an explanation: "Because they had no arms! How could they do anything?"

---

to this the further complication of a single word used to represent unrelated concepts in separate domains, as, for example, the word *root* in science and math.

It's easy to see why such words create confusion for ELLs. Figure 17.3 is a true story of a near perfect misunderstanding resulting from students knowing only the common usage of a word.

JUST PLAIN NEW WORDS

This is the catchall category—the least well defined, the most individualized, and the most challenging for the teacher. Words in this category are unknown to the learner and do not fit easily into the other categories. These are the words that are most often overlooked in vocabulary development. Following are some ideas to help you and your students determine and define words that may need some extra attention.

TEACHING AND LEARNING VOCABULARY

The Objective: Use Meaningful Strategies for Teaching and Learning Vocabulary

The Rationale

Knowing which words to teach is not the same as knowing how to teach them. Methodologies for teaching and learning vocabulary are often old-fashioned, uncreative, and unproductive.

The most widely used strategies for teaching vocabulary result in little long-term retention because they teach words in isolation. The traditional assignment of "Look the words up in a dictionary and use each in an original sentence" is rarely an effective approach. Students remember the words only as long as they must to pass a test. Similarly, activities such as word searches, scrambled words, matching tasks, or crossword puzzles do little to add to students' long-term retention and usage of new words, again because the words are used in isolation. Vocabulary teaching and learning strategies that approach words as they are used in context and are meaningful to students will result in more authentic and effective learning.

STRATEGY 51   SELECT STUDENTS TO BE YOUR VOCABULARY HELPERS

IN CONCEPT

Teachers can help their ELLs by asking the more advanced students to preview text chapters for ELLs, looking for potentially confusing vocabulary.

IN PRACTICE

Designated or volunteer students scan text looking for words and phrases used synonymously to refer to one or several central concepts or ideas, as well as for idiomatic usages and references. The resulting lists help to lighten the vocabulary load for ELLs as they read the chapter. Additionally, the students making the lists reinforce their vocabulary knowledge and can receive extra credit or bonus points for their efforts.

Although this strategy may at first seem to limit ELLs' vocabulary development, bear in mind that scaffolding strategies are used only until the learner no longer needs them. In this case, you are decreasing the language load so that ELLs can access the content in the textbook. During class instruction and discussion, however, you can feel comfortable using synonyms and idioms freely, pairing them with their more widely known word (see Strategy 56, later in this chapter).

STRATEGY 52   TURN YOUR STUDENTS INTO "LANGUAGE DETECTIVES"

IN CONCEPT

This is a wonderful strategy for students whose native language is Spanish or one of the other Latin root languages. This strategy works because of an event that took place in the year 1066.

• FIGURE 17.4 Comparing Conversational and Academic English

Conversational English	Academic English
Did you *meet* anyone at the store today? Get in *line*. Let's *build* a castle. The vacation *lasted* two full weeks. The salad was *enough* for two people.	The troops *encountered* no resistance. Arrange the numbers in *sequence*. The troops planned to *construct* a bridge. The people *endured* two centuries of tyranny. The supplies were *sufficient* for only a week.

In that year, the Normans from France conquered the Angles and Saxons living in what is now England. The conquerors' language, an early version of today's French, became the language of position and power. It also became the language of academia and the educated. The conquered Anglo-Saxons continued using their own language in everyday life, and a duality was created that still exists in the English that we use today.

Many academic words in English—the words that cut across all academic disciplines—come from the old Norman French, which has its roots in ancient Greek and Latin. The common words used in social, spoken English derive from Anglo-Saxon roots. So, we often speak and hear different words in conversation than we read and write in school, as illustrated in Figure 17.4.

IN PRACTICE

You can use this information to help your Spanish speakers, whose language is also based on Latin–Greek roots, to become *language detectives*. Spanish speakers can apply the database of their native language to textbook vocabulary by scanning texts for academic words with Spanish cognates, some examples of which are shown in Figure 17.5. They can even share their discoveries with the rest of the class. It becomes a win–win situation.

• FIGURE 17.5 Turn Your Spanish Speakers into Language Detectives

Academic Word	Spanish Word	Common Word
encounter	*encontrar*	meet
observe	*observar*	watch
maintain	*mantener*	keep
ultimate	*último*	last
equal	*igual*	same
entire	*entero*	whole
quantity	*cantidad*	amount

STRATEGY 53 HAVE STUDENTS DEVELOP A PERSONAL DICTIONARY

IN CONCEPT

Personal dictionaries benefit all students. They are valuable, easy-to-use tools for building vocabulary.

Personal dictionaries can be formatted in a variety of ways. No matter their form, they help students remember words that they find academically useful and/or personally meaningful or interesting.

IN PRACTICE

You or the students can select an organizing principle: subject specific, alphabetical, general/technical, or social/academic. Dictionaries can be written in English only or can include notations in students' native languages. ELLs at the beginner's level can use the format shown in Figure 17.6, the Vocabulary Circle. Additional possibilities for inclusion in the circle or as a column entry in personal dictionaries are native language translation, synonyms, or antonyms.

It may also be helpful to include a section for collocations: words that commonly appear in combination with the entry word. ELLs must learn these high-frequency word associations that come so naturally to native speakers who know, for example, that air can be heavy with humidity but thick with smoke, and thin, never slim or skinny, at high altitudes. Figure 17.7 offers additional examples of collocated usages in a format suitable for students to use.

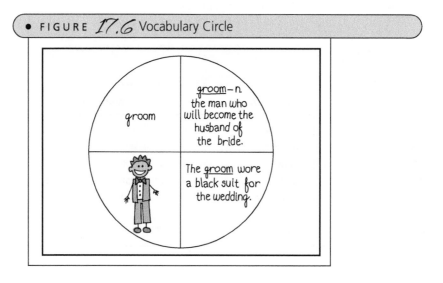

• FIGURE *17.6* Vocabulary Circle

● FIGURE *17.7* Examples of Collocations

New Word	Goes with . . .	But not . . .
bargain	fair bargain hard bargain	balanced, just firm, stiff, rigid
trick	clever trick dirty trick	bright, smart, intelligent dishonest, crooked
truce	uneasy truce	worried, nervous
rhetoric	empty rhetoric	vacant, blank, unoccupied
famine	severe famine	rigid, stern, strict, heavy
oath	solemn oath	serious, grave, somber

STRATEGY 54 DEMONSTRATE THE VALUE OF A STUDENT-FRIENDLY DICTIONARY

IN CONCEPT

Have you ever looked up a word in the dictionary and, after reading the definition, found you still had no idea of what the word meant? If that can happen to an educated native English language speaker, imagine what a challenge it would be for an ELL!

Dictionaries, which all students need, are essential for ELLs. Student dictionaries are available at beginner, intermediate, and advanced levels. In the Longman series of dictionaries, the vocabulary used in the definitions is based on the 2,000 most commonly used words in the English language. A side-by-side comparison of the definitions shown in Figure 17.8 leaves little doubt about which one is easier to understand.

Student dictionaries list multiple meanings of words as separate entries and use words in sentences. Additionally, they offer usage notes, synonyms, antonyms, examples, illustrations, and photographs. At the more advanced level, student dictionaries label words as approving or disapproving (think about the subtle differences between the words *thin/slim/skinny* or *childish/childlike*, for example), formal, literary or old-fashioned, informal, humorous, slang or nonstandard, and even offensive or taboo. Idiomatic expressions, collocations, usage notes, and frequency information for spoken and written words are also presented.

Students must become familiar with using the dictionary so that the task of finding a word definition no longer appears formidable. Dictionaries are wonderful resources but only if students feel confident enough to use them.

● FIGURE *17.8* Two Comparisons of Dictionary Definitions

Longman's Basic Dictionary	*Webster's Ninth Collegiate Dictionary*
landlady	landlady
"A woman who owns a building and rents it to others."	"A woman who is a landlord."
landlord	landlord
"Someone who owns a building and rents it to others."	"The owner of property (as land, houses or apartments) that is leased or rented to another; the master of an inn or lodging house (innkeeper)."

Longman's Advanced American Dictionary	*Oxford American Dictionary and Language Guide*
spurious 1 a spurious statement, argument, etc. is not based on facts or good reasoning and is likely to be incorrect: *A jury rejected the spurious claim that the police created evidence.* **2** insincere: *a spurious smile.*	**spurious 1** not genuine; not being what it purports to be; not proceeding from the pretended source *(a spurious excuse).* **2** having an outward similarity of form or function only.

Longman's Advanced American Dictionary (2000), p. 1408. Essex, England: Pearson Education Limited.

Longman Basic Dictionary of American English (1999), p. 162. Essex, England: Pearson Education Limited.

Merriam-Webster's Collegiate Dictionary, Eleventh Edition (2003), p. 699. Springfield, MA: Merriam-Webster.

Oxford American Dictionary and Language Guide (1999), p. 978. New York: Oxford University Press.

IN PRACTICE

Technique I

Play dictionary games to accustom your students to working with a dictionary. Figure 17.9 gives examples of items that might be included in this type of activity. Make the activity feel like a game by setting it up as a timed competition. Group students by tables or set one-half of the room against the other. Activities that are gamelike in nature get students instantly involved and motivated.

Technique II

While student dictionaries are valuable to students, they are perhaps even more valuable as aids to teachers. Use a student dictionary to make your vocabulary teaching clearer and more complete.

> ● FIGURE *17.9 Find It Fast!* The Dictionary Game
>
> Find synonyms for the word _____.
> Find the first and last word in the dictionary.
> Find a word on page _____ that means _____.
> Find the first adjective on page _____.
> Find an informal word on page _____.
> Find the third word on the page with the guide words _____ and _____.
> Find a word with more than one meaning on page _____.

In teaching, a word often comes up that requires some explanation. Keep a student dictionary at hand on your desk to take advantage of that teachable vocabulary moment. Using one will help you give your students a better definition of the word. Each time you reach for the dictionary, you are modeling an effective vocabulary strategy.

Every classroom should have at least one student dictionary. You and your students will find yourselves reaching for one on a regular basis.

STRATEGY 55   USE AN INTERNET WEB SITE TO DETERMINE WHICH WORDS TO TEACH

IN CONCEPT

A text analysis Web site can help you decide which words, of all the many in a text passage, you really need to teach. It is an awesome tool.

One such Web site, *The Compleat Lexical Tutor*, has been developed by the Université de Québec à Montréal. It is designed to create a vocabulary profile of any text you input. You can find it at this Web address: *http://www.lextutor.ca/vp/eng*. You can also use a search engine to find The Compleat Lexical Tutor by name.

The Lexical Tutor Web site presents you with a box to type or paste in the desired text. When you have completed inputting the text, click on the Submit-window button, and in a matter of seconds a color-coded vocabulary profile of the text appears on your computer screen. The color coding represents words of four different frequency types:

K1 (blue): the most frequent 1,000 word families

K2 (green): the second 1,000 most frequent word families

AWL (yellow): Academic Word List, or words that are common across all subject domains

Off-List Words (red): topic-specific, technical, and/or infrequently used words; also dates, place names, and names of people

IN PRACTICE

The easiest way to understand the wonders of this Web tool is to look at an actual example from a middle school social studies textbook, *World Explorer: People, Places, and Cultures* (Kracht, 2003, p. 35). Figure 17.10 shows the original passage as it appears in the textbook. After typing or pasting it into the Web page's textbox, the black-typed passage is returned, in a matter of seconds, color coded with a complete analysis of word counts and other linguistic data. Accompanying the passage is a vocabulary profile showing the actual listings of words in each of the four frequency categories. This vocabulary profile, summarized in Figure 17.11, gives you systematic information to help you locate specific words that your ELLs may find difficult.

The first piece of valuable information is that almost 78% of the words (184 of the 239) are in the K1 category. You can reasonably assume that these words are currently part of your ELL students' working vocabularies.

Examine next the words that fall into the other three categories, as listed in Figure 17.12. Of the 13 words listed in the K2 category, students may already know some words, such as *bend, cool, during, especially, ocean, storm, warm,* and *weather*. Now 5 words remain.

The Off-List category contains 12 words. This list, too, can be reduced by removing words such as *climate, Equator, hurricane, km,* and *tropics*, which will have been either included in the preselected vocabulary for the chapter or previously learned. Add the 7 words remaining in the Off-List category to the 5 K2 word families and the 4 academic word families (AWL), and the grand total of potentially unknown words for your ELLs is 16, listed in Figure 17.13, or less than 7% of the original 239 in the passage.

It should come as a comforting thought to know that your ELLs can handle over 90% of the words in this passage. Only the small number of remaining words are the ones you and your students need to focus on to increase their understanding of concepts. Vocabulary tools such as this Web site help you, the content teacher, narrow the challenge of "So many words, so little time." Try it—it's amazing.

TEACHING AND LEARNING VOCABULARY

The Objective: Integrate Vocabulary Development into Daily Instruction.

● FIGURE *17.10* Original text passage.

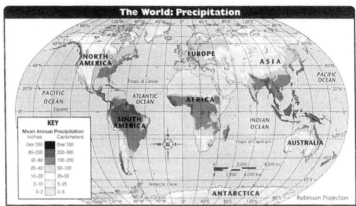

The World: Precipitation

KEY

Mean Annual Precipitation

inches	Centimeters
Over 200	Over 500
80–200	200–500
40–80	100–200
20–40	50–100
10–20	25–50
2–10	5–25
0–2	0–5

Robinson Projection

The Impact of Wind and Water

Without wind and water, the Earth would overheat. Together, wind and water moderate the effect of the sun's heat. Heat causes air to rise, especially near the Equator and over warm ocean water. Cold air sinks towards the surface away from the Equator. Wind blows from places where air is sinking towards places where air is rising. The Earth's rotation bends this flow to create circular wind patterns. So, depending on where you are in a circling weather system, the wind may be blowing north, south, east, or west.

The Earth's rotation also creates ocean currents, which are like rivers in the oceans. Some currents carry warm water from near the Equator toward the north and the south. Other currents carry cold water from the poles toward the Equator. Oceans also moderate the climate of nearby land just by their presence. Water takes longer to heat and cool than land. As a result, when the land has warmed during the summer, the nearby ocean remains cooler. Air blowing over the ocean becomes cool and then cools the land. In the winter, the opposite occurs.

Raging Storms   Wind and water can make climates milder, but they also create storms. Hurricanes are storms that form over the ocean in the tropics. Hurricanes rotate in a counter-clockwise direction around an "eye." They have winds of at least 74 miles (124 km) per hour and usually involve heavy rainfall. Tornadoes are just as dangerous, but they affect smaller areas. Their wind can range from 40 miles (67 km) per hour to over 300 miles (501 km) per hour and wreck anything in their path.

GEOGRAPHY The mean annual precipitation is the amount of rain or snow that falls in a region in an average year.   **Map Study** Which areas get the most precipitation? Which get the least?

LINKS TO Science

Smog Normally, air is cooler at higher altitudes. During a temperature inversion, however, a layer of warm air sits on top of the cooler air. The warm air traps pollution near the ground. This mixture of dangerous smoke and fog is called *smog.* The brown air seen in cities such as Los Angeles and Denver is smog caused by car exhaust.

CHAPTER 2   EARTH'S PHYSICAL GEOGRAPHY   35

From *Prentice Hall World Explorer: People, Places, and Cultures* by James B. Kracht © 2003 by Pearson Education, Inc., publishing as Pearson Prentice Hall, p. 35. Used by permission.

● FIGURE *17.11* Vocabulary Profile Summary

Category	Word Families	Tokens (Words)	Percentage (%)
K1 Words (1–1,000)	81	184	77.99
K2 Words (1,001–2,000)	13	28	11.72
AWL Words (academic)	4	6	2.51
Off-List Words	12	21	8.79
TOTALS	98	239	100.00

The Rationale

Just as words do not appear in isolation in the environment, so too should it be with vocabulary development. Substitute the once-a-week vocabulary lesson followed by a quiz with strategies that integrate vocabulary into every lesson you teach. Finding words in context and using them repeatedly in authentic applications aid long-term retention.

● FIGURE *17.12* K2, Academic, and Off-List Words

K2 Words	Academic Words	Off-List Words
bends	create	climate
cool	impact	clockwise
during	involve	counter
especially	occurs	currents
milder		Equator
moderate		hurricanes
ocean		km
opposite		overheat
patterns		poles
sinking		raging
storms		rotate/rotation
warm		tropics
weather		

● FIGURE *17.13* Which Words to Teach?

K2 Words	Academic Words (AWL)	Off-List Words

Teach:
  milder
  moderate
  opposite
  patterns
  sink
 	
Review:
  bends
	Teach:
	  create
	  impact
	  involve
	  occur
		Teach:
		  clockwise
		  counter
		  currents
		  overheat
		  poles
		  raging
		  rotate/rotation
		Review:
		  climate
		  Equator
		  hurricanes
		  km
		  tropics

STRATEGY 56   GET INTO A PAIR–DEFINE–EXPLAIN ROUTINE

IN CONCEPT

Young children acquire words from the environment at a staggering rate. Classroom strategies to expand vocabulary in ways similar to the natural acquisition of children are effective for long-term retention.

IN PRACTICE

As you teach, advance students' vocabulary development by sprinkling your instruction with interesting words and phrases, but *pair* the word or phrase with a high-frequency synonym, a definition or explanation, or a visual depiction. Students will learn new words naturally if you repeat them frequently, pairing them every time with an explanatory source. The more naturally you can work this pairing into your speech patterns, as in the examples in Figure 17.14, the more effective this technique will be.

● FIGURE *17.14* Extend Students' Vocabulary through the
Pair–Define–Explain Routine

"He committed an egregious error—a very bad mistake."
"The liquid becomes effervescent—bubbly, full of bubbles—when we stir it."
"The Pilgrims embarked on a long journey. They began . . . they started on a long trip."
"She was motivated by vengeance—she wanted to punish him, sort of get back or get
even with him."

STRATEGY 57   SET UP A WORD OF THE WEEK PROGRAM

IN CONCEPT

Learning new words involves more than just knowing their meaning; students also must be able to use words appropriately in authentic contexts. This is a fun strategy that promotes natural usage as it extends students' knowledge of vocabulary.

IN PRACTICE

Technique I

An entire school can make vocabulary growth a long-term goal. Each Monday morning, a word, along with its definition and several examples of usage, is announced as the Word of the Week. Words selected for this honor should be academic words that cross many disciplines. Students receive bonus points for using the word appropriately in any of their classes. Teachers, too, make every effort to use the word daily in natural and meaningful academic contexts. Students can show by a predesignated nonverbal signal that they recognize the word.

Technique II

As an individual class strategy, teachers can do a Word of the Day, choosing new and interesting words or recycling previously used words for reinforcement. Students try to use the day's word, orally and in written form, in class activities and homework assignments. Daily or weekly, students record the words in their personal dictionaries. You may also make it a practice to give extra bonus points to students who manage to use a former Word of the Day in class.

STRATEGY 58   MAKE YOUR STUDENTS INTO WORD WIZARDS

IN CONCEPT

Make vocabulary growth an ongoing objective in your classroom. Develop practices that encourage your students to become Word Wizards by using interesting words in class.

IN PRACTICE

Create a "word wall" board upon which students can write new words they come across in any form of media. Motivate students by making an ongoing game of it: Students win points for using a new word orally or in writing. Be ready to verbally recognize unusual vocabulary during class Q and A sessions, discussions, and conversations. Show your appreciation of uncommon or interesting words with comments that praise their usage. Ask students how they know the word. Make vocabulary one-upmanship work to everyone's advantage.

STRATEGY 59   PLAY VOCABULARY BINGO

IN CONCEPT

Bingo is a game that has been enjoyed by every generation of children. Many adults still like it. Make learning new vocabulary fun with a strategy that gives Bingo a twist.

IN PRACTICE

After handing out preprinted blank Bingo grids, tell your students to fill in the week's vocabulary words in any pattern on their papers. As caller, you randomly select words, but instead of saying the word, you pantomime, show or draw a visual, or give a verbal description, example, synonym, antonym, or—occasionally—the definition. By filling in their own grids, students cannot sulk over bad card choices or an unfair caller.

An additional twist to *Vocabulary Bingo* is that the winner must not just say the winning words but also may use them in a sentence. You can increase motivation and participation by using a team approach that invites team members to create the sentences.

In Summary: Teaching and Learning Vocabulary

True vocabulary growth is a long-term process. Students need a variety of approaches to develop the vocabulary that they need for academic success.

Students don't have to know the meaning of every word before they read a text passage. A great deal of vocabulary learning occurs as students engage in the reading process and afterward in discussion and assignments, especially when teachers make vocabulary learning a routine part of their classrooms.

Questions for Discussion

1. How do the strategies for teaching and learning vocabulary reflect the *Guidelines for Practice* presented at the beginning of this chapter?

2. Research the strategies for teaching vocabulary most commonly practiced in today's classrooms. Evaluate their effectiveness.

3. Prepare a list of additional domain-specific usages of familiar words, similar to the examples illustrated in Figure 17.2.

4. What strategies did you use in your years of schooling to learn vocabulary? How would you evaluate them? Do you believe you might have benefited from any of the vocabulary strategies discussed in this chapter?

5. What do you currently do when you find an unfamiliar word in a book you are reading? How often do you look it up in a dictionary? Do you remember the word and its meaning after you have looked it up? What strategies could you use if you really wanted to remember the word?

6. How often have you used a thesaurus? When was the last time you referred to one? What are the advantages and disadvantages of using a thesaurus?

References and Resources

Cobb, T. (n. d.). Why & how to use frequency lists to learn words. Retrieved August 9, 2006, from *www.lextutor.ca/research/rationale.htm.*

Folse, K. (2004). *Vocabulary myths: Applying second language research to classroom teaching.* Ann Arbor: The University of Michigan Press.

Kracht, J. B. (2003). *Prentice Hall world explorer: People, places, and cultures.* Upper Saddle River, NJ: Pearson Education.

Nation, P. (2001). *Learning vocabulary in another language.* New York: Cambridge University Press.

English Language Resources for Students and Teachers

For Beginners

Student Dictionaries

Oxford picture dictionary for the content areas. (2000). Oxford, England: Oxford University Press.
  Also available in English/Spanish version.
Vox Spanish and English student dictionary. (1999). Columbus, OH: McGraw-Hill, 1999.
Word by word picture dictionary. (1993). White Plains, NY: Pearson Longman.
  Also available in eight bilingual versions: English + Chinese, Haitian Kreyol, Japanese, Korean, Portuguese, Russian, Spanish, Vietnamese.

For High Beginners and Low Intermediates

Student Dictionary

Longman basic dictionary of American English. (1999). White Plains, NY: Pearson Longman.
  The three levels of the Longman Student Dictionary series use the Longman Defining Vocabulary, the 2,000 most common English words, to ensure that all definitions and sentence examples are easy to understand.

For Intermediates

Student Dictionary

Longman dictionary of American English (3rd ed.). (2002). White Plains, NY: Pearson Longman.

Thesaurus

Longman essential activator (2nd ed.). (2002). White Plains, NY: Pearson Longman.

Dictionary of Idioms

Longman pocket idioms dictionary. (2002). White Plains, NY: Pearson Longman.

For High Intermediates and Advanced

Student Dictionary

Longman advanced American dictionary. (2001). White Plains, NY: Pearson Longman.

Thesaurus

Longman language activator. (2002). White Plains, NY: Pearson Longman.

Dictionaries of Idioms

Longman American idioms dictionary. (2000). White Plains, NY: Pearson Longman.
Oxford idioms. (2001). Oxford: Oxford University Press.

Collection Dictionaries

BBI dictionary of English word combinations. (1997). Amsterdam, The Netherlands: John
   Benjamins Publishing.
LTP dictionary of selected collocations. (1999). Hove, England: Language Teaching
   Publications.
Oxford collocations dictionary for students of English. (2002). Oxford: Oxford University
   Press.

The TechConnection

http://www.wordcentral.com
      An online all-purpose dictionary.
http://www.math.com/students/references.html#dictionaries
      An online reference for math words and more.
http://www.clichesite.com/index.asp
      An online source for idioms, sayings, and proverbs.

chapter 18

Extending Comprehension: Textbook Reading Strategies

THEORY TO APPLICATION: GUIDELINES FOR PRACTICE

- Use scaffolding strategies to challenge ELLs to advance beyond their present state of independent activity, into the areas of potential learning in which content is learnable with the assistance of teachers and peers.
- Use scaffolding strategies that embed the oral and written language of content material in a context-rich environment to facilitate learning for ELLs.
- Use scaffolding strategies with ELLs to facilitate comprehension of the specialized academic language of content classrooms.
- Use scaffolding strategies that maintain a high level of cognitive challenge, but lower the language demand by embedding it in context.
- Actively teach learning strategies to give students a "menu" of ways to process and learn new information.
- Provide opportunities for ELLs to negotiate conceptual understandings and to explore language usage through classroom interaction.
- Lower learner anxiety in the classroom to create students who are more willing to participate in class, to become risk takers in the learning process, and ultimately to become more successful learners.
- Provide opportunities for students to experience success in the classroom: Success in learning promotes more success by increasing learner motivation, interest, and self-confidence.

$\mathcal{T}$eachers often have little control over which textbooks they use in their classrooms. In most school districts, teachers simply use the ones they are given and generally find them acceptable, as today's textbooks and ancillary materials tend to be user-friendly and engaging for students. ELLs, however, may view their texts with apprehension. Their English reading skills are not yet sufficiently developed to comprehend grade-level textbook materials. For them, reading content-area textbooks is often a frustrating experience. The amount of information may appear overwhelming. The time and effort they spend trying to make it understandable often bring few rewards and little satisfaction. Incorporating some of the strategies that follow will help make reading the class textbook more comprehensible for ELLs.

WORKING WITH YOUR TEXTBOOK

The Objective: Show Students How to Get the Most out of Their Textbooks.

The Rationale

The shift from learning to read to reading to learn occurs in third grade. From that point-on, teachers instruct students in learning the information within their textbooks but rarely in *using* their textbooks to make that learning easier. Few students instinctively develop the skills to use their textbooks in ways that could facilitate their comprehension.

STRATEGY 60   TEACH TEXTBOOK AIDS

IN CONCEPT

Textbook aids embed the written word in context. Hard as it may be to believe, however, students do not make the connection between textbook aids and the surrounding text. One student actually came to her teacher in mid-January and said, "Our textbook has a bilingual dictionary in the back! Did you know that?" There is no doubt that this student would have benefited had she been able to use this resource during the first half of the year.

Teachers must make students aware that textbook aids are included not to make the page look pretty (or, as one student suggested, so the author didn't have to write so many words) but to support students' efforts to understand the ideas that the printed words convey.

IN PRACTICE

Using textbook aids to facilitate comprehension is an important learning strategy and should be taught actively and explicitly at the beginning of the school year or whenever a new textbook is introduced. Use a class session to teach about the aids that your particular textbook offers (types of aids and their uses are described in the following paragraphs). Give explicit instruction or try a discovery approach: Give your students a list of aids and have them work in groups to identify and locate examples of each item in their textbooks. In either case, explain the purpose of each aid and how to use it to support students' understanding of the text. You can use the activity described in Figure 18.1 as an introduction to the lesson and, later, at the beginning of each new chapter. Or try a more radical approach, described in Figure 18.2, that one teacher used.

Remind students frequently to use textbooks aids as a pre-reading activity each time they encounter the text. The more students use textbook aids, the more they will recognize how valuable the aids are to text comprehension.

Table of Contents and Index. The table of contents and the index serve as shortcuts for locating specific information contained in a text. A simple technique to teach the usefulness of these aids is to give grouped students a list of topics and have them note the page number(s) in the text where information is given. They might also note whether they used the index or the table of contents to find the information. Try turning this practice activity into a game: Give it an intriguing name, like *Textbook Sleuths*, add a time limit, and make it a competition.

Chapter Titles, Section Headings, and Subsection Headings. Titles and headings should be considered *clues* to help students organize their thinking about the type of information that follows. Section and subsection headings usually contain key words or phrases that highlight important facts or concepts. Teach students to scan headings and make associations as a regular *pre-reading* activity.

Outlines and Questions. Content outlines or focus questions at the beginning of each chapter highlight forthcoming information. As a *pre-reading* activity, use these outlines and questions to direct students' attention to important concepts, ideas, and details presented in the chapter. Students can use outlines and questions during the reading to organize information and then as a *post-reading* strategy to check their comprehension and to engage in critical thinking.

● FIGURE *18.1* An Activity to Demonstrate the Values
of Textbook Aids

Write:	chapter title, headings, and subheadings on board
Ask:	"What is chapter about?"
Make:	brainstorming graphic
Tell:	students to open textbook to that chapter
Allot:	3 minutes to look over other textbook aids
Add:	more ideas to graphic
Use:	graphic as review at end of reading .

● FIGURE *18.2* True Tale: One Way to Teach
Textbook Aids

On the first day of school, Ms. Molvick, a middle-school science teacher, spent the period talking about the course that lay ahead. The class ended with a homework assignment to "Familiarize yourselves with your textbook." What the students heard, of course, was "No homework."

The next day as class began, Ms. Molvick told the students to clear their desks, take out a piece of paper, write their names at the top, and number a list 1 through 10. The students gave each other puzzled looks. A quiz? How could they have a quiz when they hadn't had any homework?

The first question on the quiz was "What is the name of your textbook?" Other questions followed:

What information is given at the beginning of each chapter?

What information is given at the end of each chapter?

How is new vocabulary presented in the text?

Does the text use margin notes or footnotes?

Does your textbook have a glossary?

Are any appendices included?

Ms. Molvick created the opportunity to teach a lesson on textbook aids when she corrected the quiz with the class. It was her way of ensuring that the students became well acquainted with their textbooks. The students in this science class learned a valuable lesson in class that day—about their textbook *and* about their teacher.

Summaries and Reviews. The summaries and reviews at the ends of sections and chapters highlight the key concepts presented in the body of the text. ELLs should know that the language used in reviews and summaries is generally more readable because the sentences are shorter and more concise. Teach your ELLs to read summaries and reviews *before* reading a textbook section or chapter. Pre-reading the summary/review sections helps all students organize their thinking about the content they are about to read in the text. It allows them to form a foundation that facilitates comprehension of the concepts and supporting details presented in the body of the text.

Glossaries. Textbook glossaries are a bonus feature for all students. For ELLs, they can be a lifeline. Make your students aware that the words or phrases highlighted by color or bolding in the body of the text are important to understanding the concepts. Show how these key words are explained in their textbooks: In a glossary at the end of the textbook, or written as notations in margins, or listed at the beginning or end of each chapter. Some textbooks include a bilingual glossary, but if yours does not, encourage your ELLs to make liberal use of *bilingual dictionaries* for additional clarification.

Text Organizers. Text organizers, and the aids that follow, are particularly valuable to ELLs because they offer a great deal of information in the fewest number of words. Text organizers call attention to key concepts by showcasing them in boxes, bulleted or numbered lists, and sentences written in bold or different colored ink. Students should be made aware that these elements indicate important information.

Graphics. Textbook graphics present information in chart, table, or diagram formats. They increase comprehensibility by visually contextualizing the printed words. ELLs can derive a great deal of information by learning to analyze the information displayed in these graphics.

Visuals. Visuals in textbooks are designed to appeal to students, to capture their attention, to offer them contextual support, and to enrich their understanding of concepts presented in the text. As with graphics, students should understand that they are not decoration or page fillers—indeed, real information is offered in the maps, pictures, and illustrations included in the text. ELLs and below grade-level readers should be encouraged first to scan visuals and graphics to activate or build background knowledge and then to use these features as an adjunct to the written text to help clarify meaning.

STRATEGY 61 TEACH READING IN REVERSE

IN CONCEPT

Reading in reverse is a scaffolding strategy that previews concepts to prepare students to mentally organize a forthcoming reading. It literally reverses the order of the traditional approach to an assigned textbook reading.

The standard pattern for reading generally looks like this:

- Teacher activates background knowledge.
- Students read the text.
- Students answer the questions in the text.
- Teacher discusses information in the text.
- Teacher applies information to real-life and/or past learning.

This widely practiced model, shown graphically in Figure 18.3, asks students to do the more difficult, dense part of the lesson first, before enough scaffolding is in place to support their attempts to read the text. Assigning students the text reading before the activities that embed the information in context means that students lack the strong foundational base to support their comprehension. There is a better way to do it.

The strategy of reading in reverse places the hardest part of the task at the end of the activity, rather than at the beginning. Students who complete these pre-reading steps have in place a strong scaffold for learning.

IN PRACTICE

Reverse the order of the reading, as illustrated in Figure 18.4. Step 1 is application: Relate the reading to real-life experiences or do something concrete to make it meaningful. Ideas to help you can often be found by looking at the application and extension sections at the end of the text chapter or in your teacher guide.

In Step 2, use discussion to introduce the topic and key concepts. This is the time to use the new vocabulary that will appear in the reading. Hearing new words spoken in authentic contexts (using the Pair–Define–Explain routine described in Strategy 56) prepares students for understanding when they encounter them in their written form.

Step 3 involves reading the summary and questions at the end of the chapter to focus student attention on "the big picture"—the main ideas and purpose of the reading. This is also the time to focus on the textbook aids. Preview the subheadings as a guide to the chapter's organization and the pictures and graphics for information.

In Step 4, students do the actual reading. At this point you return to the traditional model, following the reading sequentially with questions, class discussion, and real-life application. The strategy of reverse reading supports students' efforts and facilitates their comprehension of concepts as they read the textbook.

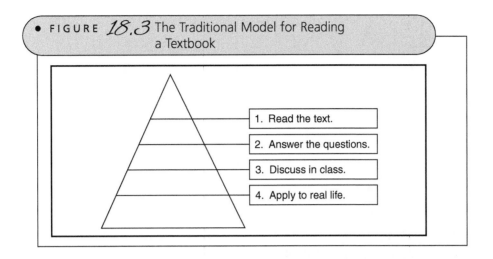

● FIGURE *18.3* The Traditional Model for Reading a Textbook

1. Read the text.
2. Answer the questions.
3. Discuss in class.
4. Apply to real life.

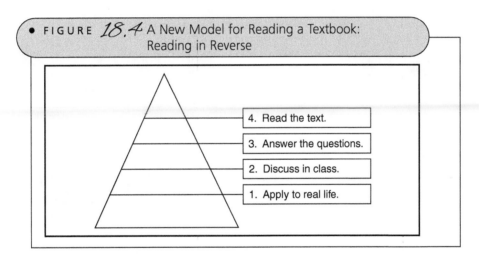

● FIGURE *18.4* A New Model for Reading a Textbook: Reading in Reverse

4. Read the text.
3. Answer the questions.
2. Discuss in class.
1. Apply to real life.

To demonstrate how this works with an actual reading, look now at the short reading "Nomads" in Figure 18.5.

As you read, think about the four-step process by focusing on these questions:

1. How would you introduce the topic of nomads? How would you relate this material to concrete, real-life experiences?
2. How would you apply these ideas to a class discussion of nomads?
3. How would you preview the reading?
4. How would you go about the reading itself?

Figure 18.6 offers ideas for each of the pre-reading steps. How do they compare with yours?

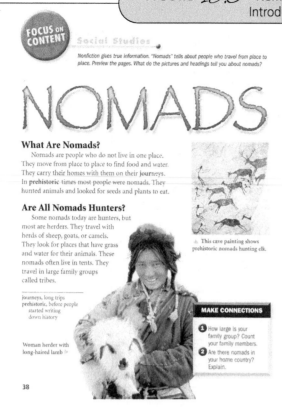

FOCUS ON CONTENT Social Studies

Nonfiction gives true information. "Nomads" tells about people who travel from place to place. Preview the pages. What do the pictures and headings tell you about nomads?

NOMADS

What Are Nomads?

Nomads are people who do not live in one place. They move from place to place to find food and water. They carry their homes with them on their **journeys**. In **prehistoric** times most people were nomads. They hunted animals and looked for seeds and plants to eat.

Are All Nomads Hunters?

Some nomads today are hunters, but most are herders. They travel with herds of sheep, goats, or camels. They look for places that have grass and water for their animals. These nomads often live in tents. They travel in large family groups called tribes.

journeys, long trips
prehistoric, before people started writing down history

Woman herder with long-haired lamb ▶

▲ This cave painting shows prehistoric nomads hunting elk.

MAKE CONNECTIONS

❶ How large is your family group? Count your family members.
❷ Are there nomads in your home country? Explain.

38

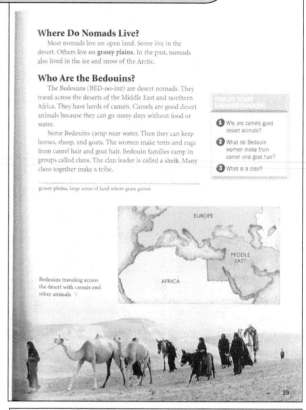

Where Do Nomads Live?

Most nomads live on open land. Some live in the desert. Others live on **grassy plains**. In the past, nomads also lived in the ice and snow of the Arctic.

Who Are the Bedouins?

The Bedouins (BED-oo-inz) are desert nomads. They travel across the deserts of the Middle East and northern Africa. They have herds of camels. Camels are good desert animals because they can go many days without food or water.

Some Bedouins camp near water. Then they can keep horses, sheep, and goats. The women make tents and rugs from camel hair and goat hair. Bedouin families camp in groups called clans. The clan leader is called a sheik. Many clans together make a tribe.

grassy plains, large areas of land where grass grows

❶ Why are camels good desert animals?
❷ What do Bedouin women make from camel and goat hair?
❸ What is a clan?

Bedouins traveling across the desert with camels and other animals ▼

39

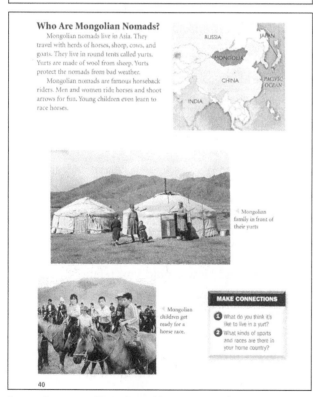

Who Are Mongolian Nomads?

Mongolian nomads live in Asia. They travel with herds of horses, sheep, cows, and goats. They live in round tents called yurts. Yurts are made of wool from sheep. Yurts protect the nomads from bad weather.

Mongolian nomads are famous horseback riders. Men and women ride horses and shoot arrows for fun. Young children even learn to race horses.

◀ Mongolian family in front of their yurts

◀ Mongolian children get ready for a horse race.

MAKE CONNECTIONS

❶ What do you think it's like to live in a yurt?
❷ What kinds of sports and races are there in your home country?

40

▲ Sioux hunters chasing buffalo

Are There Nomads in North America?

There are very few nomads left in North America. Before 1850, there were many nomads. The Sioux, for example, hunted buffalo on the plains. They used buffalo meat for food. They made tents and blankets from buffalo skins. The tents were called tepees.

The Inuit, who live in the most northern part of North America, were also nomads. In summer they lived in tents by the sea and fished. In winter they hunted seals and polar bears. They used small boats called kayaks. Today most Inuit live in towns or villages. They are no longer nomads.

▶ This tepee is made of buffalo skins.

❶ What animals did the Sioux hunt?
❷ What animals did the Inuit hunt in the winter?

◀ Inuit hunting in a kayak

41

● F I G U R E *18.6* Reading "Nomads" in Reverse

Step 1. Apply to real life.

Talk about:

- personal experience with moving.
- immigration experiences.
- experiences with frequent moves to seek employment, other reasons.
- migrant worker experiences.

Step 2. Discuss in class.

Talk about the following:

- Is moving from place to place "fun?" Why/why not?
- Does it feel different if the move is voluntary or forced?
- Compare leaving school, friends, and family behind to taking it all with you. (This is the time to introduce the word and the concept of *nomads*.)
- Look at pictures in the text to compare differences among nomad homes and students' homes.

Step 3. Read the questions—and the section and subsection headers.

Ask the following:

- What is this section about?
- What information will this section focus on?
- What is the main idea of this section?

Step 4. Read the text.

- Read one section at a time.
- Follow each section reading by discussing the questions in Step 3.

STRATEGY 62   READ TEXT IN SMALL SEGMENTS AND HIGHLIGHT MAIN IDEAS

IN CONCEPT

Today's textbooks are impressive in the amount of information they present, as well as in their size and weight. It is quite likely that, for students, they are intimidating. Students need strategies to break long text passages into smaller learnable segments. Techniques to do this can be used individually or in combination with each other and with reverse reading.

IN PRACTICE

Technique I

T-Notes, shown in Figure 18.7, are really a simplified form of an outline that ELLs can use as a reference while they are reading. The left column represents a main idea, and the right column lists supporting details and/or examples. You can ask for volunteers among your more advanced students to make and share sets of T-Notes. Everyone benefits from this technique: The ELLs have a clear outline to guide their reading, and the volunteers get extra credit while reinforcing their own understandings.

Figure 18.8 shows T-Notes for the first sections of the "Nomads" reading. For ELLs, the task of comprehending these concepts is facilitated by following the organized presentation and concise language of the outline as they read.

The T-Note format is user-friendly, easy to learn, and readily adaptable to multiple tasks. Figure 18.9 uses this format to outline a segment on water quality from the textbook *Focus on Earth Science* (Pearson Prentice Hall, 2001, pp. 333–336).

T-Notes serve as a reference and aid to learning not only during the reading process but also later as a review. Students can use them individually, in pairs, or in small groups to study for exams. T-Notes are a powerful strategy that helps to streamline the reading and learning process for ELLs and perhaps for other students in your classes.

Technique II

Learning logs are structured content journals based on reading assignments from the textbook. Students use them while they are attempting to complete assigned pages. Figure 18.10 shows two variations of a format for learning logs. The

---

● FIGURE *18.7* T-Note Format

Main Ideas	Details/Examples
1. _____	1. _____ 2. _____ 3. _____
2. _____	1. _____ 2. _____ 3. _____
3. _____	1. _____ 2. _____ 3. _____

positive phrasing of the last columns—phrases such as "Questions I Have," "Things I Want to Know," and "Clueless"—are more student friendly and less self-stigmatizing than the more traditional "What I Didn't Understand."

Because of the way that learning logs are structured, it is important to set aside a few minutes of class time to address the issues, questions, or difficulties that the students have noted in their logs. Students can meet in small groups to discuss their entries. They can help each other by exchanging understandings, answering each other's questions, and clarifying vocabulary. Encourage their independence, but offer your support as needed. Students should note in their logs the new understandings that result from these discussions.

Learning logs give language learners another way to become engaged in the process of negotiating knowledge and increasing their understanding of the text. The entries in students' learning logs also provide an excellent source of information for ongoing or summary review of the material. They can also serve teachers as an additional source of input for student assessment.

Learning logs, like T-Notes, are highly adaptable and can be used by students for a range of activities that go beyond text readings. In science, for example, the first column could be adapted for use with in-class exper-

● FIGURE *18.8* T-Notes for Reading: "Nomads"

Main Ideas	Details/Examples
1. Nomads are groups of people who . . .	1. move from place to place. 2. take homes with them. 3. move to find food and water.
2. Nomads are hunters or herders . . .	1. now most are herders. 2. travel with sheep, goats, camels. 3. look for grass and water for the animals. 4. travel in large family groups (tribes).
3. Nomads are people who live . . .	1. in the desert. 2. on grassy plains. 3. in ice and snow (long ago).
4. Bedouins are . . .	1. desert nomads. 2. travel across the Middle Last and northern Africa deserts. 3. herd camels. 4. family groups called clans. 5. sheik is leader of clan. 6. many clans make a tribe.

● F I G U R E *18.9* T-Notes for Science: Factors Affecting Water Quality

Main Ideas	Details/Examples
1. Appearance and taste	1. cloudiness 2. odor 3. color 4. minerals and chemicals
2. Acidity	1. measured in pH—0 to 14 2. pure water is neutral—pH of 7 3. lower pH = more acid 4. higher pH = more base
3. Hardness	1. based on 2 minerals—calcium and magnesium 2. hard water doesn't make suds 3. deposits from hard water clog water pipes and machines
4. Disease-causing agents	1. contamination from E. coli bacteria 2. comes from human and animal wastes
5. Standards of quality	1. set by the EPA 2. standards set concentration limits 3 concentration = amount of 1 substance in a certain amount of another substance 4. example: alphabet soup—number of letters per liter of soup

● F I G U R E *18.10* Two Formats for Learning Logs

Text Pages	What I Understood	New or Difficult Vocabulary	Questions I Want to Know

Text Pages	I Get It	I Think I Get It	I Don't Have a Clue

iments or demonstrations. In math, learning logs may be useful during lessons in which new concepts or applications are presented. In literature, learning logs can record characters as they are introduced or reactions to plot developments. In all subject areas, learning logs can be used when videos or other media are used to contextualize or enrich understandings. The uses of learning logs are limited only by the imagination and creativity of the teacher.

Technique III

Grouping students heterogeneously to discuss a text is another effective means to help ELLs understand main ideas and important concepts. (Rules for successful group work are addressed in Strategy 72 in Chapter 19.) The benefits of small group discussion of text are many.

Group work facilitates reading comprehension because the give and take of peer discussion embed the written words in context. ELLs—actually, *all* students—have the opportunity to clarify difficult or confusing concepts as they negotiate meaning. Working in groups lowers students' affective filters, allowing more learning to occur. Group discussion supports ELLs' language development by providing an authentic context to hear and use new vocabulary, and it readies students to participate in class discussion.

Technique IV

It has been well established that reading comprehension and retention rise when readers simultaneously see and hear information. Closed-captioned video has proven an effective technique for developing reading skills both for nonnative speakers and for preliterate native-speaking adults (Bean & Wilson, 1989; Goldman & Goldman, 1988; Neuman & Koskinen, 1992). Interestingly, one way that a good reader attempts to comprehend a difficult text is by reading the passage aloud. Hearing the printed words, even when reading them to yourself, assists in producing meaning.

ELLs also benefit from seeing and hearing text in other ways. They learn pronunciation of unfamiliar words. They may make new associations of words in their oral and written forms, words that they may know in spoken form but may not recognize in writing because they are spelled so differently from the way they are pronounced, like those in Figure 15.6 in Chapter 15. A final advantage concerns *homophones*, words that are pronounced the same but are spelled differently and have different meanings—*there*, *their*, and *they're*, for example—and homographs, words that are spelled the same but pronounced differently and have different meanings, as in *wind*, *lead*, and *bow*. Simultaneously seeing and hearing words like these in context may help students to understand and retain meanings and usages.

Again for extra credit, students in your class can read into a tape recorder entire chapters or important segments of the textbook. The bonus here again is that the readers are reinforcing their own learning while helping others (and helping themselves, too, with extra credit). Language learners can listen to the tape while reading the text, at home if possible or, if not, in school. Using this multimedia approach facilitates comprehension and offers ELLs greater access to important content concepts.

WORKING WITH YOUR TEXTBOOK

The Objective: Help Students to Become Competent Note Takers.

The Rationale

Few students are offered direct instruction in how to take notes. It is a skill students simply acquire and refine during their academic years. In today's educational environment, note-taking skills, like learning strategies, must become a part of classroom instruction. Like learning strategies, they are an essential key to academic success.

STRATEGY 63   TEACH NOTE-TAKING SKILLS

IN CONCEPT

As students advance through the grades, the importance of taking good notes intensifies. Students must take notes in an increasingly efficient and automatic manner. ELLs, in particular, need formats and techniques that put the most information into the fewest number of words. Explicit instruction in note-taking skills will help students become good note takers.

IN PRACTICE

Technique I
T-Notes are a useful format for teaching students the basics of note-taking skills. Prepare a set of T-Notes in which main ideas have already been listed in the left column as shown in Figure 18.11. Give your students an in-class or home assignment of completing the Details/Examples column. Students who are new to the use of T-Notes or those with low-level note-taking skills will benefit from seeing one or two items included in the Details/Examples column as a model of the type of information to look for. Once learned, T-Notes are an ideal format to record information from class instruction and text readings.

T-Notes can also be used to teach the concept of getting the main idea. In this instance, students' T-Notes show items in the Details column, and students must find the main idea that the details represent.

Technique II
Graphic organizers (discussed at length in Chapter 19) are an excellent device for note-taking because they visually convey large amounts of information in the fewest number of words. ELLs can use a web (see Figure 19.12 in Chapter 19) or a matrix (see Figure 19.18) to record the main ideas and supporting details of a reading. Other graphics that work well for note-taking are graphs, charts, maps, diagrams, timelines, and sequenced pictures, all illustrated in Chapter 19.

● F I G U R E *18.11* Use T-Notes to Teach Note-Taking Skills

Main Ideas	Details/Examples
1. Nomads are groups of people who	1. move from place to place 2. _____ 3. _____
2. Nomads are hunters or herders . . .	1. _____ 2. _____ 3. _____ 4. _____
3. Nomads are people who live (where?)	1. in the desert 2. _____ 3. _____
4. Bedouins	1. are _____ 2. travel _____ 3. herd _____ 4. _____ 5. _____ 6. _____

Technique III

Early in the school year, try teaching a lesson with the combined objectives of finding important information and taking notes. Start by photocopying a section of several pages from the students' textbook. Distribute the passage in class and read it with the students, section by section.

Start by asking the students to read only the first subsection. When students have finished their individual reading, re-read it aloud to them, stopping to explain your reasoning about what is important: how you recognize the details from the main ideas. Be sure to explain the *why* and *why not* behind your thinking.

As you finish discussing each subsection, show students how to highlight key words, phrases, and sentences from the photocopied passage with a highlighter pen. Repeat this read–discuss–highlight procedure with each successive subsection, encouraging greater student input as the lesson continues.

The next step in effective note taking is to teach students to condense the highlighted segments into a set of notes. Depending on the type of information, students can use T-Notes or any appropriate graphic. Model the wording of the notes you would make from the highlighted segments of the first subsection, demonstrating which words and phrases to omit or shorten. Be sure students understand the concept of *condensing:* Effective note takers do not copy each phrase or sentence from the text in its entirety.

Teach students that using abbreviations is another element of effective note taking. Explain to students the art of abbreviating commonly used words—*because, therefore, leading to, compared to,* for example. You can create a class set of abbreviations, and can encourage students to create their own—a practice they may not know is acceptable.

WORKING WITH YOUR TEXTBOOK

The Objective: Use Alternative Resources for True ELL Beginners.

The Rationale

Teachers often ask what to do in class with the true ELL beginner. How can a grade-level textbook be used by a newcomer who has just begun to learn English? The answer is as obvious as it is unsatisfying: An ELL at the earliest stage of language development cannot successfully use a grade-level textbook. Some approaches, however, may help students gain *some* knowledge of content while they are developing their English language skills.

STRATEGY 64   PAIR ELL BEGINNERS WITH VOLUNTEER BUDDIES

IN CONCEPT

In almost every class, certain students are the *nurturers.* These students can often be enlisted to work one on one with ELL beginners in a volunteer buddy system, a win–win situation for both sides. Beginners appreciate the help and support of a peer, and nurturers feel gratified and satisfied.

IN PRACTICE

Volunteer buddies can work together to use some of the strategies presented in previous sections of this chapter. A good place to start is with some of the less linguistically demanding textbook aids. Volunteer buddies can help as ELL beginners focus on getting information from charts, tables, diagrams, maps, pictures, and other illustrations. Buddies can also assist with vocabulary development by discussing cognates in the language detective activity, locating and explaining synonyms and idioms, and prompting generous use of personal and bilingual dictionaries. Most of all, volunteer buddies can offer support, encouragement, and perhaps even friendship.

You may think the buddy system would be most valuable if the buddy is one who is bilingual in English and the beginner's native language, or at least one at a more advanced level of English language development. While this type of pairing can be highly beneficial, it can also be fraught with risk by encouraging overtranslation of concepts and information from the readings. It may place an undue burden on the buddy and lead to the beginner's dependence on the translation and the translator. It can sometimes even slow the language learner's development of English reading skills. In reality, any willing student can offer enough help and support to make a difference.

STRATEGY 65   IN A PINCH, USE ALTERNATIVE TEXTBOOKS

IN CONCEPT

An approach of last resort for students at beginning levels of English language development is to obtain an alternate textbook for them as a supplement to your regular classroom textbook. If your school or district has no objection, you might consider using a text that is written either at a lower reading level or in the students' native languages. While this strategy may offer a small short-term advantage, it has a greater number of both short- and long-term disadvantages.

IN PRACTICE

Using an alternative textbook is stigmatizing, especially one written at a lower level. It sends a subtle, unintended message that those who use it are less capable than the others in the class. Using a native-language textbook may violate state laws concerning classroom use of a language other than English. Even if no legal issues are involved, students using native-language textbooks may become dependent on them to the point of not wanting to make any attempts at using the regular classroom text. Much like using a translator, it may ultimately impede the development of English language skills.

The use of native-language textbooks presents an additional difficulty. Your beginning ELLs may be from several language backgrounds. It is improbable that you could find suitable textbooks in each of the languages spoken by the beginners in your classroom. Is it fair to find native language textbooks only for some?

Despite the disadvantages of using alternative textbooks, however, it is important to note that—in some instances—native language resources can mean the difference between learning some content and learning none for ELLs, particularly for those entering U.S. schools in the middle of a school year and/or at the secondary school level.

There is no magic formula to help the true ELL beginners in your content class. These strategies are probably the best you can use for a while because, at the very least, they allow the student to learn some content and they show that you care.

In Summary: Working with Your Textbook

Reading the textbook is a daunting task for many students, ELLs and native speakers alike. Students arrive in your classes with differing levels of reading and language ability and differing sets of reading and literacy skills. They need a variety of strategies that show them how to interact with the text to derive meaning—techniques that embed written words in context and focus thinking on main ideas and supporting details. You can ease the challenge for your students by using the strategies in this chapter to scaffold their content learning as they learn English.

Questions for Discussion

1. How do the strategies for working with your textbook reflect the *Guidelines for Practice* presented at the beginning of this chapter?

2. Examine the textbooks you use in your classes to see which textbooks aids they contain. Plan a lesson to teach students how these aids can facilitate comprehension. How can you determine if students are already using these aids?

3. Using a textbook with which you are *not* familiar, examine a chapter following the steps in Figure 18.1. How successful do you believe you were in getting the gist of the chapter?

4. Read the "Nomads" passage again, this time focusing on types of problematic vocabulary discussed in Chapter 17. Look for words and phrases that might cause confusion: synonyms, idioms, and familiar words used in new ways.

5. Plan a Reading in Reverse lesson to introduce a reading or a new topic from a textbook. Select a reading or topic and follow the three preliminary steps to reading. Explain the reasoning behind your choices. Work individually if you are now teaching a class, or in pairs if you are not.

References and Resources

Cean, R. M., & Wilson, R. M. (1989). Using closed-captioned television to teach reading to adults. *Reading Research Instruction, 28*(4), 27–37.

Bortz, A., Padilla, M. J., Miaoulis, I., & Cyr, M. (2001). *Focus on earth science: Prentice Hall science explorer; California edition.* Upper Saddle River, NJ: Pearson Prentice Hall.

Daniels, H., & Semelman, S. (2004). *Every teacher's guide to content-area reading.* Portsmouth, NH: Heinemann.

Dornan, R., Rosen, L. M., & Wilson, M. (2005). Lesson designs for reading comprehension and vocabulary development. In P. A. Richard-Amato, M. A. & Snow (Eds.), *Academic success for English language learners: Strategies for K–12 mainstream teachers* (pp. 248–274). White Plains, NY: Pearson Education.

Echavarria, J., Vogt, M., & Short, D. J. (2000). *Making content comprehensible for English language learners: The SIOP model.* Needham Heights, MA: Allyn & Bacon.

Goldman, M., & Goldman, S. (1988). Reading with closed captioned TV. *Journal of Reading, 31*(5), 458.

National Captioning Institute (2003). *Using captioned television in reading and literacy instruction.* Retrieved March 20, 2006, from *http://www.ncicap.org/classroom.asp.*

Neuman, S., & Koskinen, P. (1992). Captioned television as comprehensible input: Effects of incidental word learning from context for language minority students. *Reading Research Quarterly, 27*(1), 95–106.

Peregoy, S. F., & Boyle, O. F. (2001). *Reading, writing, and learning in ESL: A resource book for K–12 teachers* (pp. 257–411). New York: Addison Wesley Longman.

The TechConnection

www.ncela.gwu.edu/practice/itc

The "In the Classroom" section of the National Clearinghouse for English Language Acquisition brings research and practice together for teachers of culturally and linguistically diverse learners, offering teaching tools and strategies that reflect principles of effective practice.

19

Reinforcing Learning: Activities and Assignments

THEORY TO APPLICATION: GUIDELINES FOR PRACTICE

- Use scaffolding strategies to challenge ELLs to advance beyond their present state of independent activity, into the areas of potential learning in which content is learnable with the assistance of teachers and peers.
- Use scaffolding strategies that embed the oral and written language of content material in a context-rich environment to facilitate learning for ELLs.
- Use scaffolding strategies that maintain a high level of cognitive challenge, but lower the language demand by embedding it in context.
- Provide opportunities for ELLs to negotiate conceptual understandings and to explore language usage through classroom interaction.
- Lower learner anxiety in the classroom to create students who are more willing to participate in class, to become risk takers in the learning process, and ultimately to become more successful learners.
- Provide opportunities for students to experience success in the classroom: Success in learning promotes more success by increasing learner motivation, interest, and self-confidence.

After the lesson is taught and the textbook is read, teachers assign in-class and at-home activities to reinforce and extend learning. For ELLs, these activities may present a challenge. For teachers, planning activities that are cognitively complex but linguistically simplified may present an equal challenge. Content teachers must look beyond the traditional activity types—question and answer, research reports, oral presentations—to strategies that engage ELL students in alternative means and products. The goal is to build rich conceptual understanding of content while keeping the language input and output as streamlined as possible.

ASSIGNMENTS TO PROMOTE STUDENT SUCCESS

The Objective: Good Assignments Begin with Good Directions.

The Rationale

Have you ever been a student in a class where you've been given directions that you didn't understand? You sat there with a growing sense of anxiety because you had absolutely no idea what to do. You looked around—had others already started working? Are you the only one who didn't get it? Perhaps you quietly asked several of your peers if they knew what you were supposed to do, only to discover that they didn't know either. By now you are all feeling considerably less capable than you felt just a few minutes ago. Anxiety is never a good way to begin an assignment.

STRATEGY 66   GIVE CLEAR DIRECTIONS

IN CONCEPT

Successful activities begin with clear directions. Students need to approach each assignment with a complete understanding of process and product. When you follow the simple, five-step plan summarized in Figure 19.1, you can be sure that your instructions will always be clearly understood by all your students.

IN PRACTICE

1. *Say* the directions. Explain them as explicitly as you possibly can. State what you want students to do in a simple, step-by-step manner. If the directions are complex, use the "one-step" approach: Tell students that after they complete the first step, you'll tell them what they'll be doing next.

2. *Write* the directions on the board, on chart paper, or on an overhead transparency. Written words reinforce spoken language and help language learners process what they are being asked to do. Keep the written directions on view so students can refer to them as needed during the assignment.

3. *Model* the process and the product. Demonstrate how to begin, and explain the choices you make to reach the final product. Show students what a finished product should look like. Show several possibilities of product if there will be variations. You may also want to show examples of excellent, acceptable, and poor products. Adding this visual element to your directions is essen-

```
● FIGURE 19.1 Clear Directions in Five Steps

    1. Say the directions clearly.
    2. Write them and leave them on view.
    3. Model the process and the product.
    4. Check comprehension.
    5. Ask for questions.
```

tial for your ELLs because it shortcuts your need for wordy explanation. It also gives all students a clear understanding of your expectations.

4. *Check* comprehension by asking the students to repeat, step by step, what they are expected to do. Start by asking "So, what's the first thing we're going to do?" Go through each step of the activity, adding detail or correcting as needed. Point to each step of the written directions as students review them orally.

It is important for the students themselves to explain each of the steps they are going to take to complete the project. After all, they are the ones who will be doing the activity.

5. *Ask* for questions. "Question time. Who's got a question for me?" Most likely they'll have none.

Clear directions start students out right. Using the five-step approach allows students to focus immediately and confidently on the work to be done—no lost time, no unnecessary anxiety. Students benefit from hearing detailed directions before every assignment, including homework. Good instructions give students the best chance of producing a satisfying result.

ASSIGNMENTS TO PROMOTE STUDENT SUCCESS

The Objective: Modify Whole Class Assignments to Make Language Comprehensible.

The Rationale

ELLs will be able to demonstrate that they understand content when the output required for the assignment matches their level of English language development. Modifying ELLs' assignments by lowering language demand does not mean that you are lowering your expectations.

Modifying assignments recognizes the difficulties that ELLs face in developing English language competency at the same time they are attempting to learn content in English. The types of modifications you choose should consistently challenge your ELLs with incrementally complex language. The strategies that follow are widely adaptable and can be applied to many homework tasks and in-class activities.

STRATEGY 67 OFFER A WORD BANK

IN CONCEPT

For assignments that require simple, short answers to a series of questions, consider using a word bank, especially with students who are in the early stages of English language development. Word banks are lists of content-related word or phrase choices. To correctly answer the assigned questions, students select items from the list. Including at least three extra words or phrases that relate closely to the topic encourages thoughtful consideration of answer choices and promotes critical thinking.

IN PRACTICE

Word banks work well with many straightforward questions used to check comprehension after textbook readings. They are also well suited to assignments that ask students to label, for example, parts of a diagram in science, such as that of the eye in Figure 19.2, or specific items on maps in social studies.

Word banks can be used as an additional support in combination with many of the following strategies. They allow ELLs to focus their attention on content by lowering the language demand.

STRATEGY 68 ASSIGN FEWER QUESTIONS

IN CONCEPT

Textbook chapters usually have a set of summary questions to check comprehension and to encourage students to think critically about the topic. An assignment that seems reasonable for your native English-speaking students may feel overwhelming to your ELLs. They will be able to respond better if you assign fewer questions, focusing on those that are either more conceptually important or less linguistically complex.

IN PRACTICE

Technique I
Textbook comprehension questions are written to check students' understanding of broad concepts and specific facts. Some questions are conceptually more central to the topic than others. By assigning only the more important questions, especially in combination with one or more other strategies presented in this chapter, your ELLs can focus their efforts on those that are most critical to their understanding.

● FIGURE *19.2* Diagram of the Eye

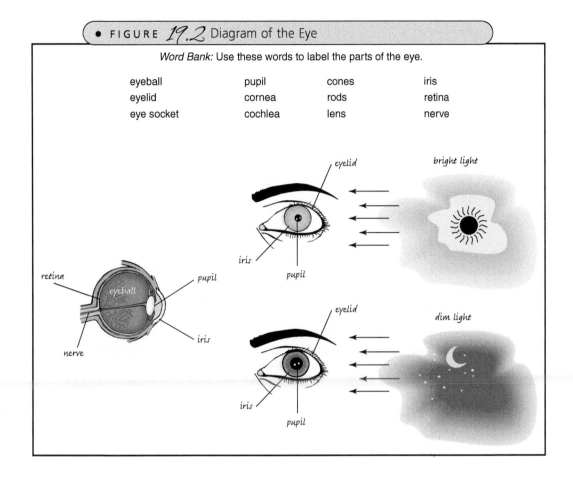

Word Bank: Use these words to label the parts of the eye.

eyeball	pupil	cones	iris
eyelid	cornea	rods	retina
eye socket	cochlea	lens	nerve

Technique II

The second approach is to select questions that are linguistically easier to complete. Questions vary in the amount and type of information required to answer them. Some questions can be answered adequately with a single word or short phrase while others require much longer, more linguistically complex responses. Again, especially for students in early stages of English language development, consider requiring written responses to only those questions that are linguistically simple to answer (perhaps even in combination with a word bank) and use one of the alternative assignments described later in this chapter for questions involving a longer, more complicated written answer.

STRATEGY 69 ALLOT EXTRA TIME

IN CONCEPT

Every assignment is twofold for ELLs: They must first decode the language and then deliver the content. They clearly need more time to get their work done.

IN PRACTICE

With this extra burden in mind, allow additional time for ELLs to complete readings and assignments. Remember that they are learning English at the same time that they are learning *in* English. More time makes content more learnable for them.

STRATEGY 70 SEPARATE CONTENT FROM LANGUAGE

IN CONCEPT

While you probably require the use of good grammar and complete sentences as a normal part of your regular assignments, remember that if your ELLs could write that way, they wouldn't be classified as ELLs. Separating content from language allows teachers to make more effective assessments of ELLs' understanding of content.

IN PRACTICE

Evaluate student assignments for accuracy of content information only. Look for key content words or phrases that signify some grasp of the topic under study and give credit for those. Accept grammar and spelling errors as long as the content is correct. Look for the positive—even by trying to pronounce an unreadable word phonetically to see if you can bring meaning to it. Using a simple rubric helps keep the focus on content. It's important to think about the message being sent, not about the *means* by which it is being sent.

STRATEGY 71 OFFER MODELS AND OUTLINES

IN CONCEPT

Many written assignments follow a relatively standardized type of paragraph structure. For these, consider giving the ELLs a model, an outline, or a preformatted page to follow. This strategy also appeals to native English-speaking students who find written work, in general, a challenge. Students—English speakers and learners alike—often feel more able to tackle an assignment when they don't have to begin with a completely blank page.

IN PRACTICE

Think about the kinds of written assignments you give. Most assignments ask students to classify, identify, list, explain, describe, predict, and compare and contrast in language much like that in Figure 19.3. For tasks such as these, student responses follow a basic pattern that can be modeled to lighten the linguistic burden. Figures 19.4 and 19.5 illustrate response models for questions in science and social studies, respectively.

Many types of written assignments lend themselves to modeled formatting. In science classes, for example, students often are required to write up experiments, demonstrations, or activities done in class. Figure 19.6 shows a format that students can use for this purpose. When the language and pattern of reports like these are prestructured, ELLs can concentrate on cognitively processing the content required for the response instead of first having to focus on creating the language to convey that content. Of equal importance, repeated exposure to formatted patterns teaches ELLs how to formulate appropriate responses when this scaffolding strategy is removed.

• FIGURE *19.3* Typical Writing Assignments that Can Be Modeled

- Describe the process by which _____ causes _____.
- Describe the factors that affect _____.
- Describe the characteristics of _____.
- Describe how _____ (changes) (uses) _____.
- Describe conditions that cause _____.
- Describe how _____ form _____.
- Name and describe (two) kinds of _____.
- List factors that affect _____.
- List and explain the main types of _____.
- Identify and explain the effects of _____.
- Explain why _____ is important to _____.
- Give examples of how _____ uses _____.

● FIGURE *19.4* Modeled Response to a Comprehension
Question: An Example from Earth Science

Question

Name and define the three major types of interactions among organisms.

Modeled Response

The first type of interaction is called _____.

This means _____.

The second type of interaction is called _____.

This means _____.

The third type of interaction is called _____.

This means _____.

● FIGURE *19.5* Modeled Response to a Comprehension
Question: An Example from Social Studies

Question

What was the goal of the Open Door Policy in China? Did it succeed?

Modeled Response

The goal of the Open Door Policy in China was to_____

_____. It (was, was not)

successful because _____

_____.

STRATEGY 72 DO MORE SMALL GROUP WORK

IN CONCEPT

ELLs can often do assignments in pairs or small groups that they would be unable to do individually. Group work is beneficial for many reasons.

Working in pairs or groups of three to four students promotes concept acquisition through social interaction. Small groups create a natural setting that encourages the negotiation of meaning in a nonthreatening environment. For ELLs especially, small groups offer the opportunity to use academic language in a meaningful way. ELLs can explore new vocabulary, attempt oral communication, and clarify knowledge through the exchange of information, examples, and comparisons with native English-speaking peers. Many students learn better by negotiating meaning with peers within the safety of small groups.

Partners or buddies act as resources for each other by enhancing each other's understanding. ELLs can work together to produce a pair product

● F I G U R E *19.6* Model for Write-up of Science Demonstration

Name of Experiment: _____

We wanted to show that _____

_____.

We used (materials) _____, _____, _____

_____, _____, _____, _____.

The first thing we did was _____

_____.

The second thing we did was _____

_____.

The third thing we did was _____

_____.

What happened was _____

_____.

This happened because _____

_____.

This shows that _____

_____.

while other students work individually. Students may be able to accomplish together an assignment that neither could complete alone. Think of it as an equation: *1 + 1 > 2*.

IN PRACTICE

Many teachers are reluctant to engage in frequent group work because they worry about loss of control. Following the set of basic rules in Figure 19.7 will maximize your chances for successful shared activities in your classroom.

1. Good group work starts with *selecting an appropriate task*. And what exactly is an appropriate task? It is one in which students must work together because each student in the group has only part of the information needed to reach the final product. Students must interact in a cooperative manner to figure out how to make all the pieces work together as a whole.

A good way to understand the concept of *appropriate task* is to examine a task that is definitely *not* appropriate. In this example of an unsuccessful group experience, the teacher tells the students that they are going to work in groups to review material from a content reading. Each student in the group gets a copy of a worksheet with five questions on it, along with directions to work together to answer the questions.

> ● FIGURE *19.7* Rules for Successful Group Work
>
> 1. Select an appropriate task.
> 2. Establish ground rules for group work.
> 3. Group students heterogeneously.
> 4. Give clear directions.
> 5. Announce a time frame for completion.
> 6. Monitor the groups as they work.
> 7. End with a whole-class sharing.

After several minutes of silence, one student asks the others in the group, "So what did you put for Question 1?"

As one student offers an answer, the others quickly write it down. Done this way, the task itself necessitates no negotiation of meaning, no communication or cooperation, no need to exchange any information. This is not group work; it is simply an individual task with students sitting in a group.

In good group work, students must rely on other group members' input and information to complete the task. Such tasks are challenging, creative, interesting, and widely adaptable for use in content classrooms.

Figure 19.8 illustrates an example of an appropriate task to review content information, about forest biomes in this instance. Students in each group receive individual envelopes containing information printed on slips of paper. In this type of group review, students work together to categorize items based on qualities or characteristics, arrange items sequentially, or classify items by types and subtypes.

Group tasks can also promote critical thinking, as shown in Figure 19.9. For this type of task, students use the items in their envelopes to make groupings based on as many different sets of similarities as they can think of. One student lists the groupings on paper so that items can be reused. During class discussion, students share lists and explain the basis for each set of groupings.

2. Good group work follows *a set of class rules* that have been generated through class discussion before the first group work session takes place. Students can be directed to offer rules that include these, among others: (1) Stay in your seat. (2) Use conversational voices. (3) Disagree politely (4) Stay on task.

Rules should be displayed prominently and permanently for teachers to direct students' attention to if needed during group sessions. Some strange quirk of human nature makes students less likely to argue with the statement "You're not following rule number two about using conversational voices" than with the perceived accusation "Your voices are way too loud."

3. Divide the class into *heterogeneous groupings*. All groups should reflect the general mix in your classroom. Each group should include diversity of

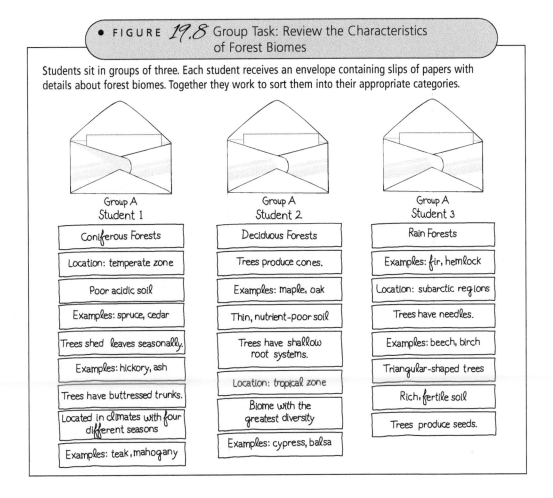

● FIGURE *19.8* Group Task: Review the Characteristics of Forest Biomes

Students sit in groups of three. Each student receives an envelope containing slips of papers with details about forest biomes. Together they work to sort them into their appropriate categories.

Group A Student 1	Group A Student 2	Group A Student 3
Coniferous Forests	Deciduous Forests	Rain Forests
Location: temperate zone	Trees produce cones.	Examples: fir, hemlock
Poor acidic soil	Examples: maple, oak	Location: subarctic regions
Examples: spruce, cedar	Thin, nutrient-poor soil	Trees have needles.
Trees shed leaves seasonally.	Trees have shallow root systems.	Examples: beech, birch
Examples: hickory, ash	Location: tropical zone	Triangular-shaped trees
Trees have buttressed trunks.	Biome with the greatest diversity	Rich, fertile soil
Located in climates with four different seasons	Examples: cypress, balsa	Trees produce seeds.
Examples: teak, mahogany		

gender, ability, language, and ethnicity. ELLs extend their zone of proximal development by working with more advanced peers, who themselves have the opportunity to reinforce and extend their own understandings.

4. Introduce the topic and task, and give *explicit directions*. Follow up with a *clarification check* to make sure students know exactly what to do. Use the five-step approach outlined in Strategy 68 in this chapter.

5. Give students a *time frame* for completing the task. People of all ages seem to focus better under the pressure of a deadline. Allocate the minimum amount of time you think the task will take, and announce frequently how many minutes remain to complete the work. If students groan about not being able to finish, you can always extend the time as needed.

6. *Monitor the task* by walking around the room as students work. Many students are more willing to seek clarification from their teachers in the security of small group settings. Consider this your golden opportunity to answer student questions and offer individual help.

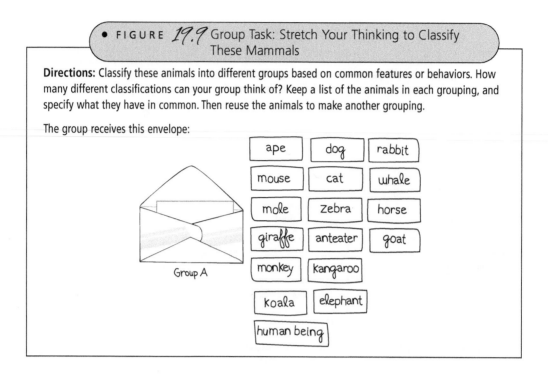

● FIGURE *19.9* Group Task: Stretch Your Thinking to Classify These Mammals

Directions: Classify these animals into different groups based on common features or behaviors. How many different classifications can your group think of? Keep a list of the animals in each grouping, and specify what they have in common. Then reuse the animals to make another grouping.

The group receives this envelope:

7. Bring *closure* to group work through whole class sharing. Even if the group work is ongoing, students should report how the session went and where their groups are now. This rewards students' natural curiosity to see the progress and products of the other groups.

If you'd like to do more group work in your classroom, follow these rules and start small. Start with paired assignments, such as grouping students to discuss answers to homework questions during the first few minutes of class, and build up to big group projects over time. You'll see that even small group activities bring big results.

STRATEGY 73 TRY PEER TUTORING

IN CONCEPT

ELLs can often complete an assignment with a little individualized assistance, and in every class certain students enjoy the role of peer tutor or peer coach. Peer tutoring pairs willing students with ELLs who can use a little extra help on an as-needed basis.

Peer tutoring—and group work in general—promotes language development, concept acquisition, and cognitive growth. It offers an opportunity for students to use academic language in a meaningful way in an authentic situation. It allows exchange of questions and clarification of knowledge in a lowered risk environment. It personalizes and adds a social element to learning and instruction. It can change students' attitudes toward content and to school in general. It ultimately raises students' feelings of self-confidence. In pair and small group work, one plus one really does add up to more than two.

IN PRACTICE

Peer tutoring helps in your classroom in several ways. First, pairing ELLs (and other students, too) who need extra help with peer coaches gives ELLs an opportunity for personalized attention from a more advanced student who is not the teacher.

Second, this strategy may also offer a rewarding solution for students who consistently complete individual assignments early and wait for others in the class to finish. Explaining concepts to others clarifies and expands tutors' conceptual knowledge and acts as a strong aid to retention.

A final benefit of peer tutoring is that you, the teacher, benefit from your small cadre of assistants who give you more flexibility to monitor all your students' understanding and progress.

ASSIGNMENTS TO PROMOTE STUDENT SUCCESS

The Objective: Develop Alternative Assignments.

The Rationale

Academic assignments must promote cognitive challenge. To meet the needs of ELLs' linguistic and conceptual development, teachers need to offer parallel, alternative assignments.

Alternative assignments engage ELLs in activities that maintain a high level of cognitive challenge and, at the same time, lower language demand. These assignments should be viewed as stepping stones on the path toward academic success in an English language environment. The goal is to move ELLs toward full participation in the mainstream assessments required of all students.

STRATEGY 74   USE DIAGRAMS, MAPS, AND CHARTS AS ASSIGNMENTS

IN CONCEPT

Students are often required to engage in factual descriptive content writing. ELLs can convey much of the same information alternatively through graphic or visual means.

IN PRACTICE

ELLs can label a diagram, map, chart, or drawing in place of expository writing. In subsequent assignments, they can add supplementary information in the form of more detailed descriptive words and explanatory phrases. Students can expand the drawings of the eye shown in Figure 19.2, for example, to include additional functional or descriptive data. For other types of diagrams, students can classify items by color coding or can indicate relationships among elements by adding arrows. Figure 19.10 uses separate drawings to label and explain a type of ocean movement.

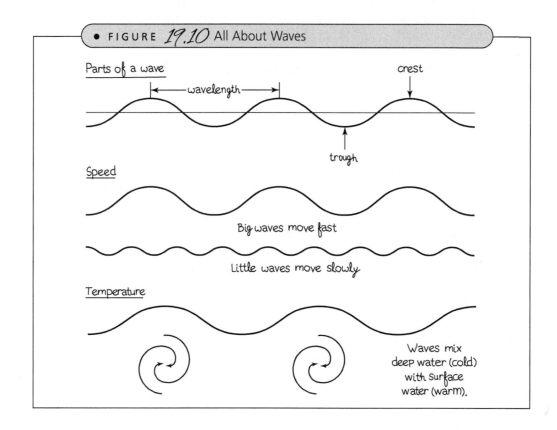

● FIGURE *19.10* All About Waves

● FIGURE *19.11* Sequence Pictures of a Science Experiment

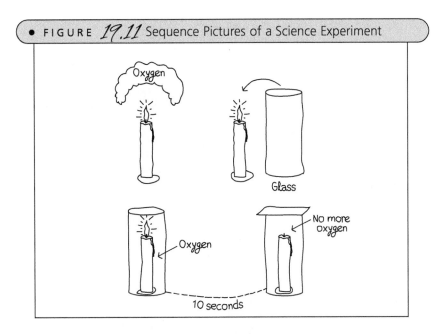

STRATEGY 75 USE SEQUENCED PICTURES AS ASSIGNMENTS

IN CONCEPT

ELLs can show their understanding by drawing or arranging a set of pictures. While other students are completing an assignment in standard paragraph form, language learners can be doing the same assignment through graphics.

IN PRACTICE

Sequenced pictures can depict steps or stages, or they can be as simple as *before* and *after*. After the pictures have been drawn or arranged, students can supplement the pictures with additional appropriate information.

Look at Figure 19.11, an assignment done as a series of sequenced pictures showing the process and results of an in-class science experiment. The student who did these drawings demonstrated a clear understanding of the experiment in a way that would have been unattainable in a written report.

Students whose English language skills are at the beginner level can label parts of each picture, with or without a word bank. Students at higher levels can add descriptive and explanatory words, phrases, and sentences.

STRATEGY 76 USE GRAPHIC ORGANIZERS AS ASSIGNMENTS

IN CONCEPT

It is likely that you make frequent use of graphic organizers as a routine part of your teaching. Now consider using them as alternative assignments for your ELLs.

Certain graphic organizers are widely adaptable, while others are more tightly structured. It is important to predetermine the most appropriate graphic format to convey the information that your other students will be expressing in written form.

Graphic organizers are interesting and easy for ELLs to work with. As an alternative assignment, they allow ELLs to convey a large amount of content information in a linguistically simplified form.

IN PRACTICE

Technique I

The graphic organizer with the widest application and greatest flexibility uses the concept of clustering or webbing, as illustrated in Figure 19.12. Students are able to give a maximum amount of information with only a minimum amount of language.

Cluster or web organizers are useful for explaining topics with multiple elements and for showing relationships among elements. Figure 19.13 uses a web to show details about the groups described in the "Nomads" passage in Chapter 18 (Figure 18.5).

Web organizers would work well in social studies, for example, to show the complex causes of World War II or factors influencing immigration to the United States in the early 1900s. In science, the web would be appropriate to categorize, classify, and describe types and subtypes of substances and structures.

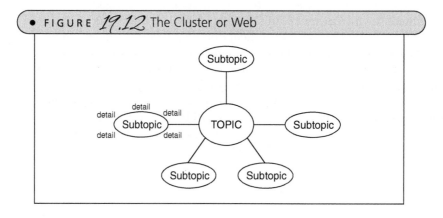

● FIGURE *19.12* The Cluster or Web

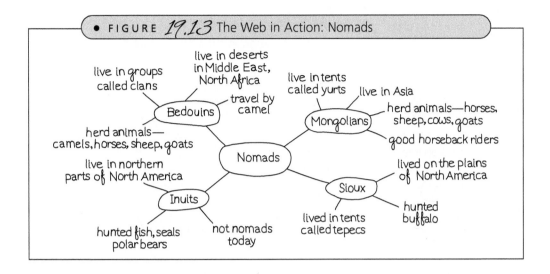

● FIGURE *19.13* The Web in Action: Nomads

Technique II

A more tightly controlled form of clustering is the problem-solving organizer, shown in Figure 19.14. It is a concept map designed to show multiple and sequential cause and effect. It is an effective graphic to explain more direct relationships and linear patterns.

The problem-solving organizer is structured around a central issue or problem. Figure 19.15 uses this format to graphically depict some causes of water pollution in the United States, the actions taken to deal with the problem, and the effects of these actions.

Language learners can use this type of organizer in science and social studies classes as an alternative to written reports on environmental and societal issues, such as those listed in Figure 19.16. The problem-solving organizer is an ideal way for students to express complex ideas and relationships in a linguistically simplified manner.

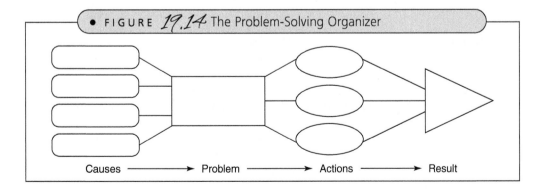

● FIGURE *19.14* The Problem-Solving Organizer

Causes ⟶ Problem ⟶ Actions ⟶ Result

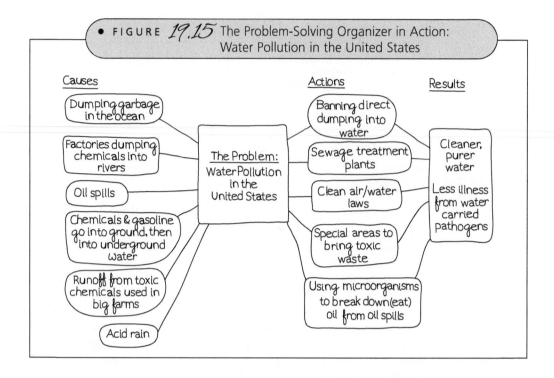

● FIGURE *19.15* The Problem-Solving Organizer in Action: Water Pollution in the United States

● FIGURE *19.16* Some Topics for Using Problem-Solving Organizers in Science and Social Studies

Environmental Issues	Societal Issues
Global warming	Slavery
Air or water pollution Recycling	Reconstruction of post-Civil War South
Endangered species	Rise of labor unions
Depletion of tropical rain forests	The Cold War
	Terrorism

Technique III

Venn diagrams are familiar to most teachers and students. They are used to show similarities and differences among concepts, events, people, or things. Figure 19.17 illustrates the Venn diagram in its most common form, comparing and contrasting two elements. Because students seem to enjoy expressing information in this graphic format, you may want to challenge them with a triple Venn diagram, as shown in Figure 19.18. Like other graphic organizers, Venn diagrams reduce language demand to single words and short phrases and allow ELLs to focus on the content.

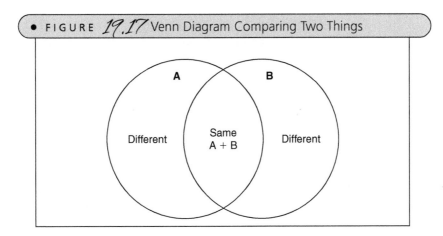

● FIGURE *19.17* Venn Diagram Comparing Two Things

Technique IV

Timelines show chronological sequences and temporal relationships graphically. Timelines can be drawn to record developments over periods of time as short as seconds or as long as many millennia. They can, for example, illustrate chemical change of matter within seconds, depict historical development over a single century, or show the evolution of man over hundreds of thousands of years. The timeline in Figure 19.19 shows the year that each department in the executive branch of U.S. government was created. In subsequent assignments, students can add additional information to explain the function and focus of each department.

Students can draw *parallel timelines* to compare two or more chains of related activity over simultaneous time periods, as in a timeline representing

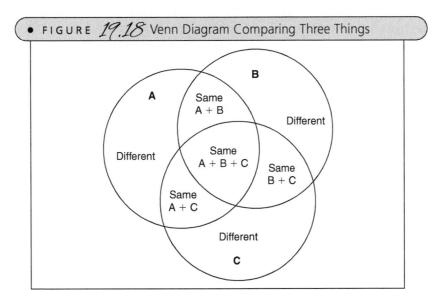

● FIGURE *19.18* Venn Diagram Comparing Three Things

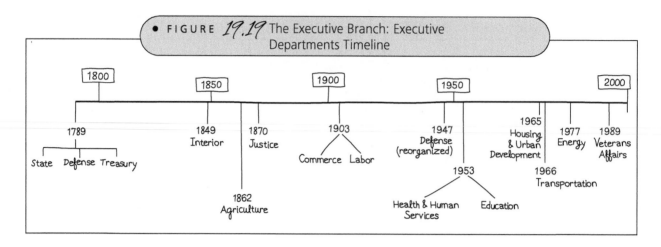

● FIGURE *19.19* The Executive Branch: Executive Departments Timeline

developments in land, sea, and air transportation from 1800 to 2000. Or students can expand a segment of a timeline to add greater detail to a short period within the longer timeline. Timelines are readily adaptable and simple to create. They convey a great deal of information in very few words, which makes them a valuable combination of qualities for language learning students.

Technique V

The *matrix,* as shown in Figure 19.20, is a form of attribute charting. It is a grid that visually compares key variables of a set of related items. Figure 19.21 shows a matrix that could be used in science lab to compare the characteristics and qualities of five different mineral substances. In social studies, the matrix is useful to compare, for example, the character and achievements of selected presidents, or demographic, geographic, and economic data of several countries or regions. Figure 19.22 illustrates the matrix used to graphically represent key information in the "Nomads" passage in Chapter 18 (Figure 18.5).

Information in the matrix grids can take a variety of forms. Students can fill boxes with a plus or minus sign to denote presence or absence of something, or insert a number to specify an exact amount or percentage. They can write in descriptive words or short phrases or can give specific representative names. The matrix is versatile and widely adaptable.

● FIGURE *19.20* The Matrix

Qualities → Items to Compare ↓	1	2	3	4	5
A					
B					
C					
D					
E					

STRATEGY 77 BUILD LANGUAGE FROM GRAPHICS

IN CONCEPT

Graphic organizers and other alternative assignments are productive means for ELLs, especially those in the early stages of English language development, to show what they know. However, if ELLs do only this type of written assignment, they will make slow progress in developing the language and literacy skills they need for academic success. Language learners must move from relying on graphics to building language by developing models, outlines, or formatted sentences to take them beyond graphics.

● F I G U R E *19.21* The Matrix in Science: Comparing Minerals

Specimen ↓	Luster	Cleavage	Hardness	Color	Other
A					
B					
C					
D					
E					

● F I G U R E *19.22* The Matrix in Social Studies: Nomads

Nomads	Hunter/ Herder	Country/ Area	Type of Land	Animals	Tents	Other
Bedouins						
Mongolians						
Sioux						
Inuits						

IN PRACTICE

All graphic organizers can be formatted to build language. Figure 19.23 presents examples of formatted models that students can use to convert information from their timelines to complete sentences. Figure 19.24 does the same for Venn diagrams.

Although the complexity of the problem-solving organizer requires a bit more ingenuity to create a simple format, Figure 19.25 shows a generic model that teachers can tailor to fit specific topics. Additionally, consider using the T-Notes discussed in Strategy 63 (Figure 18.7, Chapter 18) or the formatted models or outlines discussed in Strategy 71 in this chapter (Figures 19.4 to 19.6).

Using formats as an intermediary stage helps ELLs transition to more complex written expression at the same time that it offers models of good ways to do so. With enough practice and repetition, students can move from the model to effective independent writing. At this stage, they may still need assistance with certain academic words and phrases to write a complete answer. Posters on a bulletin board listing common words and phrases associated with writing in your discipline will be helpful to *all* students. Additionally, phrases to make writing more cohesive—for example, the lists of transition words shown in Figure 19.26—will provide support and help students become better writers.

● FIGURE *19.23* Using Timelines to Build Language

The First Step

In _____, _____ occurred.
     year   event

     _____ was invented by _____.
       product

     _____ was born.
       person

     _____ gained independence.
       country

The Next Step

_____ began in _____ and ended in _____.
Event   year   year

The Final Step

_____ began in the _____
Trend or movement   ordinal number (first/third/middle)

_____ of the _____.
period (decade/quarter/half)   _____century

● FIGURE *19.24* Using Venn Diagrams to Build Language

First Steps

To Compare:

(X) were _____, and (Y) were, too.

(X) were _____, and (Y) were _____, too.

To Contrast

(X) were _____, but (Y) were _____.

The Next Step

When we compare _____ to _____, we can see that some things are the same and some things are different.

The things that are the same are _____

_____

_____.

The things that are different are _____

_____

_____.

● FIGURE *19.25* Using the Problem-Solving Organizer to Build Language

First Steps

The problem was _____.

The causes were _____, _____,

and _____.

The actions taken were _____, _____,

and _____.

The result is _____.

The Next Step

The issue (problem) of _____ has (several, four, many, etc.) causes. The causes are _____

_____

_____

People (agencies, the government, etc.) have tried to deal with this issue (problem) by _____

_____

_____

These actions have (helped, not helped) because _____

_____

_____

The issue (problem) of _____ (has been resolved, needs more action, is unchanged, is growing, etc.).

● FIGURE *19.26* Transition Words for Writing Assignments

Showing Addition

First, first of all

Additionally, in addition

Also

Another reason

The most important reason

Finally

Showing Contrast

On the other hand

In contrast

However

But

Rather than

Giving Examples

For example

For instance

One example of this is _____.

Another example is _____.

Showing Chronological Order

First (second, etc.)

Next

Then

After that

Finally

Showing Similarity

Likewise

Similarly

In a similar way

Showing Cause and Effect

Cause	$\rightarrow\rightarrow\rightarrow$	Effect
X _____.	So,	Y _____.
X _____.	Consequently,	Y _____.
X _____.	As a result,	Y _____.
X _____.	Therefore,	Y _____.

—In Summary: Assignments that Promote Student Success

The assignment strategies you choose for your ELLs will depend on the combination of the content itself and the students' level of language development. Students need to start with simple tasks that are highly context-embedded before moving on to more complex ones. Remember that academic language develops slowly over a long period of time.

Modified and alternative assignment strategies allow students to demonstrate their understanding of content while they are building language skills. These assignments balance high levels of cognitive challenge with low levels of language demand so that language learners can begin to experience academic success. Even minimal changes, such as the inclusion of a word bank, can mean the difference between feelings of frustration and feelings of success.

Try to view assignments as your ELLs learners might see them. Anticipating areas of language difficulty and making appropriate modifications will go a long way in helping your language learners demonstrate their comprehension of the content you teach. The small investment of time and effort to put these ideas to work in your classroom will yield big returns for you and your students.

Questions for Discussion

1. How do the strategies dealing with assignments reflect the *Guidelines for Practice* presented at the beginning of this chapter?

2. All of the assignment strategies presented in this chapter encourage students to extend their understanding by maintaining high cognitive challenge while lowering linguistic demand. Many of them also support ELLs in other areas. Which of the assignment strategies do you think specifically raise learner self-confidence? Which raise student motivation? Which lower anxiety?

3. Choose an appropriate graphic organizer and use it to depict concepts presented in this chapter.

4. Working individually if you are now teaching or in pairs if you are not, choose an assignment and modify it for ELLs. Create several levels of modifications for beginners, intermediates, and advanced ELL students.

References and Resources

Brinton, D. M., & Master, P. (Eds.) (1997). *New ways in content-based instruction.* Alexandria, VA: TESOL (Teachers of English to Speakers of Other Languages), Inc.

Bromley, K., Irwin-De Vitis, L., & Modlo, M. (1995). *Graphic organizers: Visual strategies for active learning.* New York: Scholastic Professional Books.

Forte, I., Pangle, M. A., & Drayton, A. (2001). *ESL content-based language games, puzzles, and inventive exercises.* Nashville, TN: Incentive Publications.

The TechConnection

www.inspiration.com

An interactive site for grade-level graphic organizers, with common topics listed for the subject areas. You select the topic, and the program creates colorful graphic organizers.

Performance-Based Learning

—Why Performance-Based Learning?

MEGASTRATEGY 20
Maximize learning by basing performance on measurable outcomes

Teaching is both a humanistic endeavor and a science. It is a humanistic endeavor because many psychological and sociocultural factors must be balanced in order to evoke the highest-quality learning from each student. It is a science because the current emphasis on outcome-based learning is based on careful research on teaching and learning over the past one hundred years. Assumptions that underlie this approach are straightforward. To achieve learning, one must do the following:

1. Describe what students are expected to accomplish or perform.

2. Detail what kind of evidence will substantiate this performance.

3. Design learning activities that will accumulate the desired evidence.

Given the complicated social context of schools with English learners, and the students' pressures to acquire English as rapidly as possible, one can begin to appreciate the complex terrain in which teachers of English learners are employed. "What makes someone want to learn?" and "How can a teacher plan lessons that are driven by the learners' desires to learn?" are even more complex questions than previously thought.

Stakes are high. In a sense, the entire community is invested in the learning that takes place in a classroom, and the entire community suffers if the learning impetus of the young is misdirected, quashed, or squandered. As Einstein said, "The world we created today has problems which cannot be solved by thinking the way we thought when we created them." Teachers must help learners use psychological tools that are designed for contemporary minds.

What Is Performance-Based Learning?

English is taught for purposes of communication and/or academic achievement. Therefore, a classroom lesson usually contains some content, whether a communication skill or a content concept. Moreover, the current emphasis on students learning *how to learn* entails some learning strategy objective in each lesson. Additionally, because students are English learners, a third type of objective develops language. The objectives for an optimal lesson for English learners fall into three categories:

- Content (knowledge, skill, or disposition in a subject area or domain of communicative competence)

- Learning to learn (knowledge, skill, or learning strategy that teaches the student how to acquire or process information)

- Language (knowledge or skill in some facet of English)

How are these objectives chosen? Schools, school districts, or state agencies publish standards documents that spell out what students should know and be able to do. Curricular programs follow the goals put forth in the documents. A classroom teacher plans instruction using curriculum guides at the specific grade level. Units may be organized based on a theme or, if the course is text-driven, on chapters in the text (instructional planning is presented in greater detail later in this chapter). Units or chapters are further divided into specific lessons. Each lesson contains the essential content area objectives. The classroom teacher is responsible for presenting the material in an understandable way, arranging for students to participate in learning activities, and then measuring the extent of the student's mastery of the material. Thus, instruction and assessment are linked.

Objectives may include more than one content area. Both middle school and elementary school instruction increasingly feature thematic units that integrate basic skills and content areas (Short, 1991). The teacher considers the various tasks that language users must be able to perform in the unit (listening, speaking, reading, writing) and makes provision for learning the vocabulary and concepts needed in the discourse of the content areas involved.

The objectives chosen must be matched to a specific level of performance that students will demonstrate. This process is central to the contemporary focus on accountability because the specific performance expected of the student as a learning outcome can be directly linked to some standard for the performance. Together, these constitute *standards-based learning*.

Standards-Based Learning

At the 1989 Education Summit in Charlottesville, Virginia, President George H. W. Bush and the nation's governors proposed a long-term national education strategy (often referred to as Goals 2000). The call went out for national professional organizations to articulate clear, high standards for what students should know (content standards) and how well they should know it (performance standards). Then the states were supposed to establish delivery standards declaring what all schools must provide in order for students to achieve these standards. All students were henceforth to be measured at intervals (say, fourth, eighth, and tenth or twelfth grade). These standards and assessments together constituted a voluntary accountability system (Wolf, LeMathieu, & Eresh, 1992). This emphasis on standards led to the No Child Left Behind Act of 2002.

TESOL STANDARDS

> **MEGASTRATEGY 20.1**
>
> Align instruction with local, state, and national standards

The organization TESOL, Inc., responded to the call for professional standards by adopting the PreK–12 English Language Proficiency Standards (see Box 20.1). The document serves as a complement to other standards documents and specifies the proficiency that English learners need in order to become fully fluent in English. Using these standards, teachers give students an opportunity to acquire these skills and knowledge. Assessment is a way of ensuring that students are making progress and that instructional activities are used wisely. The use of standards helps ensure that assessment is purposeful and systematic so that educators can agree on the expectations and content of English-language instruction and be certain that the school successes of English learners are clearly documented.

The standards do not prescribe instructional practices that match the proficiency goals. These aspects are covered in five useful volumes: *Integrating the ESL Standards into Classroom Practice: Grades Pre-K–2* (Smallwood, 2001); *Integrating the ESL Standards into Classroom Practice: Grades 3–5* (Samway, 2001); *Integrating the ESL Standards into Classroom Practice: Grades 6–8* (Irujo, 2001); *Integrating the ESL Standards into Classroom Practice: Grades 9–12* (Agor, 2001); and *Scenarios for ESL Standards-Based Assessment* (TESOL, 2001).

Box 20.1　TESOL STANDARDS FOR PRE-K–12 STUDENTS

The English-language proficiency standards are broad statements encompassing the range of language competencies required of all English learners for success in the classroom.

Standard 1:　English language learners communicate for social, intercultural, and instructional purposes within the school setting.

Standard 2:　English language learners communicate information, ideas, and concepts necessary for academic success in the area of language arts.

Standard 3:　English language learners communicate information, ideas, and concepts necessary for academic success in the area of mathematics.

Standard 4:　English language learners communicate information, ideas, and concepts necessary for academic success in the area of science.

Standard 5:　English language learners communicate information, ideas, and concepts necessary for academic success in the area of social studies.

SOURCE: Teachers of English to Speakers of Other Languages (2006a, p. 2).

Together, these volumes contain curricular units that demonstrate how classroom teachers organize standards-based instruction.

PROGRAM STANDARDS

Standards are also available that assist in the evaluation of programs for English learners. *Program Evaluation: English as a Second Language* (Edwards & Fitzpatrick, 2002) offers guidelines for defining the expectations for student learning, analyzing student performance, identifying priorities for improvement, and collecting and using evidence of instructional and organizational effectiveness. Using the principles provided in this document, schools can formulate plans to improve their education of English learners.

INSTRUCTION ALIGNED WITH TESOL STANDARDS

In the kindergarten unit "Making Bread Together" (James, 2000), ESL students develop social interaction skills together with academic skills in an inclusion model, in which ESL instruction takes place in the mainstream classroom taught by the kindergarten teacher together with the ESL specialist. The content objectives are based on the science theme of the four main food groups: Students learn to (1) identify different kinds of bread around the world and (2) describe the four food groups. The learning objective is that students work in small groups to complete assignments. The language objectives are that students will (1) respond orally to a story in print, (2) practice oral language, and (3) develop listening skills. The learning activities include story retelling, storybook reading, making a book, making a bread chart and collage, listening to and reading a story using the computer, graphing using dry cereal, and taking a field trip to a bakery. Assessment matches the objectives.

"The Most Beautiful Place in the World" is an instructional unit based on the book by the same title (Cameron, 1988) about a young boy in Guatemala who longs to attend school and learn to read (Levine, 2000). Levine found that the Spanish words, foods, and other cultural aspects incorporated in the novel were particularly appropriate for her class, who were all from Spanish-speaking families. The unit also integrated social studies curricular goals as students studied map locations, compass directions, and cultural comparisons. To fulfill language arts goals, they read for comprehension and enjoyment, read for specific information, predicted and inferred from text, answered questions using oral and written sentences, and acquired academic vocabulary. To meet affective goals, they learned to listen to and show respect for peers, help one another learn, and feel secure and successful. To achieve study skills goals, they learned specific techniques to learn vocabulary.

At the middle school level, Sillivan (2000) used the unit "Mastering the Art of Persuasion: Marketing and the Media" to culminate a yearlong ESL/ language arts course. Students worked their way through a standards chart that stipulated the language functions and critical thinking skills used in persuasive media-based writing (creating print, radio, and television advertising). Students analyzed and created print ads, critiqued radio ads, and wrote and evaluated their own ad copy. Rubrics were used throughout the unit so that students could evaluate their own work as well as that of their peers.

In a high school intermediate/advanced ESL/social studies class using specially designed academic instruction in English (SDAIE), standards-based instruction was incorporated into the unit "Exploring World Religions" (Riles & Lenarcic, 2000). Students developed a word web journal to define religion, used reading passages and journals to discuss religion, and conducted library and Internet research to identify important religious figures. Final portfolios were used to archive students' essays and other writings. Throughout the unit, note-taking skills, outlines, time lines, maps, games, and other knowledge technologies were incorporated into group research, oral presentations, paragraph writing, and grammar work.

ENGLISH-LANGUAGE DEVELOPMENT STANDARDS

The TESOL standards do not define what students should know or be able to do in each level of proficiency. Nor does this document provide educators with directions and strategies to assist English learners. In contrast, California has prepared *English Language Development (ELD) Standards* (California Department of Education, 1999a) to ensure that English learners develop proficiency in both the English language and the concepts and skills contained in the English-Language Arts (ELA) Content Standards (California Department of Education, 1999b) (see Box 20.2 for first-grade ELA standards). Like the ELA standards, the California *ELD Standards* are organized into areas of reading, writing, and listening/speaking. The California English Language Development Test (CELDT) is aligned with the standards as a placement and achievement test. Using the ELD and ELA standards, teachers can work with students through a developmental framework that stipulates the requirements of each proficiency level. Other standards—standards for effective pedagogy—are available from the Center for Research on Education, Diversity, and Excellence (CREDE) (1999).

INCORPORATING STANDARDS INTO LESSON PLANS

A standard becomes useful to teachers only when they can identify when the standard has been met or progress is being made toward meeting it (Jametz, 1994). Moreover, when schools communicate performance standards to students, the students know what is considered important for them to be able to do and can more easily judge where they stand within the full range of performance expectations. Assessment should provide information on what students already do well and pinpoint what they still need to learn. In this way, assessment can provide information about what aspects of instruction need to be redesigned so that both student and teacher performance improves (Jametz, 1994).

Box 20.2 GRADE 1: ENGLISH-LANGUAGE ARTS CONTENT STANDARDS

Reading

1.0 Word Analysis, Fluency, and Systematic Vocabulary Development

Students understand the basic features of reading. They select letter patterns and know how to translate them into spoken language by using phonics, syllabication, and word parts. They apply this knowledge to achieve fluent oral and silent reading.

Concepts about Print

1.1 Match oral words to printed words.
1.2 Identify the title and author of a reading selection.
1.3 Identify letters, words, and sentences.

Phonemic Awareness

1.4 Distinguish initial, medial, and final sounds in single-syllable words.
1.5 Distinguish long- and short-vowel sounds in orally stated single-syllable words (e.g., *bit/bite*).
1.6 Create and state a series of rhyming words, including consonant blends.
1.7 Add, delete, or change target sounds to change words (e.g., change *cow* to *how*; *pan* to *an*).
1.8 Blend one to four phonemes into recognizable words (e.g., /c/ a/ t/ = cat; /f/ l/ a/ t/ = flat).
1.9 Segment single syllable words into their components (e.g., /c/ a/ t/ = cat; /s/ p/ l/ a/ t/ = splat; /r/ i/ c/ h/ = rich).

Decoding and Word Recognition

1.10 Generate the sounds from all the letters and letter patterns, including consonant blends and long- and short-vowel patterns (i.e., phonograms), and blend those sounds into recognizable words.
1.11 Read common, irregular sight words (e.g., *the, have, said, come, give, of*).
1.12 Use knowledge of vowel digraphs and *r*-controlled letter-sound associations to read words.

1.13 Read compound words and contractions.
1.14 Read inflectional forms (e.g., *-s, -ed, -ing*) and root words (e.g., *look, looked, looking*).
1.15 Read common word families (e.g., *-ite, -ate*).
1.16 Read aloud with fluency in a manner that sounds like natural speech.

Vocabulary and Concept Development

1.17 Classify grade-appropriate categories of words (e.g., concrete collections of animals, foods, toys).

2.0 Reading Comprehension

Students read and understand grade-level-appropriate material. They draw upon a variety of comprehension strategies as needed (e.g., generating and responding to essential questions, making predictions, comparing information from several sources). The selections in *Recommended Readings in Literature, Kindergarten through Grade Eight* illustrate the quality and complexity of the materials to be read by students. In addition to their regular school reading, by grade 4, students read one-half million words annually, including a good representation of grade-level-appropriate narrative and expository text (e.g., classic and contemporary literature, magazines, newspapers, online information). In grade 1, students begin to make progress toward this goal.

Structural Features of Informational Materials

2.1 Identify text that uses sequence or other logical order.

Comprehension and Analysis of Grade-Level-Appropriate Text

2.2 Respond to *who, what, when, where,* and *how* questions.
2.3 Follow one-step written instructions.
2.4 Use context to resolve ambiguities about word and sentence meanings.
2.5 Confirm predictions about what will happen next in a text by identifying key words (i.e., signpost words).

(continued)

$\mathcal{B}$ox 20.2 CONTINUED

2.6 Relate prior knowledge to textual information.

2.7 Retell the central ideas of simple expository or narrative passages.

3.0 Literary Response and Analysis

Students read and respond to a wide variety of significant works of children's literature. They distinguish between the structural features of the text and the literary terms or elements (e.g., theme, plot, setting, characters). The selections in *Recommended Readings in Literature, Kindergarten through Grade Eight* illustrate the quality and complexity of the materials to be read by students.

Narrative Analysis of Grade-Level-Appropriate Text

3.1 Identify and describe the elements of plot, setting, and character(s) in a story, as well as the story's beginning, middle, and ending.

3.2 Describe the roles of authors and illustrators and their contributions to print materials.

3.3 Recollect, talk, and write about books read during the school year.

Writing

1.0 Writing Strategies

Students write clear and coherent sentences and paragraphs that develop a central idea. Their writing shows they consider the audience and purpose. Students progress through the stages of the writing process (e.g., prewriting, drafting, revising, editing successive versions).

Organization and Focus
1.1 Select a focus when writing.
1.2 Use descriptive words when writing.

Penmanship
1.3 Print legibly and space letters, words, and sentences appropriately.

2.0 Writing Applications (Genres and Their Characteristics)

Students write compositions that describe and explain familar objects, events, and experiences. Student writing demonstrates a command of standard American English and the drafting, research, and organizational strategies outlined in Writing Standard 1.0.

Using the writing strategies of grade 1 outlined in Writing Standard 1.0, students:

2.1 Write brief narratives (e.g., fictional, autobiographical) describing an experience.

2.2 Write brief expository descriptions of a real object, person, place, or event, using sensory details.

Written and Oral English Language Conventions

The standards for written and oral English language conventions have been placed between those for writing and for listening and speaking because these conventions are essential to both sets of skills.

1.0 Written and Oral English Language Conventions

Students write and speak with a command of standard English conventions appropriate to this grade level.

Sentence Structure
1.1 Write and speak in complete, coherent sentences.

Grammar
1.2 Identify and correctly use singular and plural nouns.
1.3 Identify and correctly use contractions (e.g., *isn't, aren't, can't, won't*) and singular possessive pronouns (e.g., *my/mine, his/her, hers, your/s*) in writing and speaking.

Punctuation
1.4 Distinguish between declarative, exclamatory, and interrogative sentences.
1.5 Use a period, exclamation point, or question mark at the end of sentences.

Box 20.2 CONTINUED

1.6 Use knowledge of the basic rules of punctuation and capitalization when writing.

Capitalization

1.7 Capitalize the first word of a sentence, names of people, and the pronoun *I.*

Spelling

1.8 Spell three- and four-letter short-vowel words and grade-level-appropriate sight words correctly.

Listening and Speaking

1.0 Listening and Speaking Strategies

Students listen critically and respond appropriately to oral communication. They speak in a manner that guides the listener to understand important ideas by using proper phrasing, pitch, and modulation.

Comprehension

1.1 Listen attentively.
1.2 Ask questions for clarification and understanding.
1.3 Give, restate, and follow simple two-step directions.

Organization and Delivery of Oral Communication

1.4 Stay on topic when speaking.

1.5 Use descriptive words when speaking about people, places, things, and events.

2.0 Speaking Applications (Genres and Their Characteristics)

Students deliver brief recitations and oral presentations about familiar experiences or interests that are organized around a coherent thesis statement. Student speaking demonstrates a command of standard American English and the organizational and delivery strategies outlined in Listening and Speaking Standard 1.0.

Using the speaking strategies of grade 1 outlined in Listening and Speaking Standard 1.0, students:

2.1 Recite poems, rhymes, songs, and stories.
2.2 Retell stories using basic story grammar and relating the sequence of story events by answering *who, what, when, where, why,* and *how* questions.
2.3 Relate an important life event or personal experience in a simple sequence.
2.4 Provide descriptions with careful attention to sensory detail.

SOURCE: © 1999 by the California Department of Education.

What Is the Best Use of Assessment?

Assessment means more than scoring high marks on a test, getting good grades, or satisfying the accountability demands of an external authority. Assessment plays a vital role in supporting and enhancing learning. Performance assessment has received attention in contemporary educational practice because of its close association with outcome-based education (OBE) and standards-based education. The goal of these educational reforms is to make schools, teachers, and students accountable for learning. This trend has brought assessment issues to the fore.

Assessment is a process for determining the current level of a learner's performance or knowledge. Assessment for the purpose of placement informs educators about the strengths and needs of the language learner so that students can be appropriately instructed. Classroom instruction that is directly linked to placement tests for English learners permits teachers to begin using effective instructional practices as soon as students enter the classroom. Ongoing assessment informs parents and school authorities of the student's progress and ensures continuous progress. In the current climate of standards-driven instruction, the results of assessment may also be used to assess the effectiveness of the teacher's instruction.

*MEGA*STRATEGY 20.2
Understand the purposes and functions of assessment

Various evaluation methods have been used with English learners. Some are required by government programs and legal mandates; others, more informal, are devised by classroom teachers. If it is to be a valid part of education, assessment should be used not merely for labeling and placing students but also for designing instruction that advances students' understanding and abilities. Testing must therefore be an integral part of learning, helping students to seek meaning and use a second language to fulfill academic and personal goals.

THE CHANGING NATURE OF ASSESSMENT

Three major factors have converged to intensify the focus on new forms of assessment. First, advances in cognitive psychology have led educators to recognize the complex nature of learning. Assessment must be diverse to capture this complexity accurately and fairly (cf. Shuell, 1986). Second, many educators have acknowledged that multiple-choice, standardized achievement tests do not measure the complexity of learning processes despite the fact that educators are increasingly pressured to use such measures to document school improvement (Wiggins, 1989; Guskey, 1994). Third, tests are increasingly being used to measure the success of school reform and to document accountability. Tests used as criteria should be dependable and credible measures of student learning (Linn, 2000).

Traditional views of testing were based on the behaviorists' belief that knowledge can be analyzed into small skill units that could be taught, measured, and reinforced separately (Shepard, 2000). Objective tests, administered uniformly to all students, were believed to represent scientific measurement of learning.

Classroom assessment based on constructivist, cognitive, and sociocultural theory, in contrast, offered a radically different focus. Rather than seeing the capacity to acquire knowledge as an inborn skill, Vygotsky and his colleagues argued that knowledge is based on a set of cognitive structures that are created through a dynamic, socially based process of meaning making. As a result of this view, thinking and problem-solving skills have come to the fore. Assessment is still used to report to others on students' ability, but it also provides direct feedback to learners so that they can take responsibility for self-correction and improvement.

Standardized testing will probably persist because of the economic and political investment in the type of assessment that compares students with one another. Too often, however, social and economic pressures from testing overshadow the curriculum and the affective goals of schooling. The judgments resulting from this testing may affect students' present adjustment to school and their future academic and social successes, effectively undermining their ability to plan their own learning strategies, activities, and use of time and resources (O'Malley & Pierce, 1996).

Overall, assessment used wisely can become a source of insight, helping to achieve high standards for schooling. Involving students and teachers in collaborative, informative assessment makes the process more authentic and equitable, and "makes it possible to hold students to higher standards because the criteria are clear and reasonable" (Wiggins, 1992, p. 30).

ASSESSMENT AND NO CHILD LEFT BEHIND

The No Child Left Behind Act (2001) requires that all students be "proficient" in reading and mathematics by the school year 2013–14. Beginning in 2005–06, all public school students in grades 3 through 8 must be tested annually, using state achievement tests. This group includes English learners, who must be assessed in a valid and reasonable manner that includes reasonable accommodations and, to the extent practicable, testing in the primary language. Those students who have completed thirty months of schooling must, however, be tested in English reading (special exemptions can be applied for on a case-by case basis, and students living in Puerto Rico are automatically exempted). States must establish baseline proficiency goals to which yearly progress is compared.

In the current climate of standards-driven instruction, the results of assessment are often used to assess the effectiveness of the teacher's instruction. Often, funds are augmented for schools that show increased test scores or, conversely, withheld from schools in which test scores have not risen over a given period. Under NCLB, schools that fail to make acceptable yearly progress (AYP) for two years in a row are subject to corrective action. This is "high-stakes" assessment—the reputation and resources of schools and teachers rest on students' test performance.

The increased emphasis on accountability testing results in increased pressure on teachers of English learners to prepare students to succeed on standardized tests. This pressure does not take into consideration the difficulty that English learners experience. The pressure for students to perform well on these tests may detract from time spent on language development activities. Educators have argued that these nationally standardized tests penalize English learners, causing schools with large percentages of English learners to rank comparatively poorly on school achievement indices (Groves, 2000).

Haycock (2001) has documented that students at risk of failure are more likely to have insufficient resources; less experienced teachers, who are not prepared for the subjects they teach; and a watered-down curriculum, combined with low expectations for student achievement. This calls into question whether state standards and assessments can achieve educational equity.

One effect of high-stakes testing is the attempt to exclude English learners from testing when scores would penalize schools:

> School officials in Port Chester, N.Y. would rather neither Dayana nor Israel [third graders from Latino immigrant families] takes the New York State English-language-arts test when it is given statewide. They say they do not want such children to be embarrassed by their scores. But they also do not want those scores [to count when] 90 percent of fourth graders score well enough to be regarded as proficient readers.
>
> But that statistic is not a true reflection of the district because so many students from immigrant families [had] been exempted from taking the test. . . . [L]ast June, the U.S. Department of Education required all students in school for more than a year to take regular tests.
>
> That was bad news for Port Chester. Officials here now predict that the proportion of proficient students will drop into the 70s . . . and their schools will be branded in need of improvement and suffer penalties. (Berg, 2006)

The difficulties for English learners inherent in NCLB legislation have galvanized professional organizations in the run-up to its reauthorization in 2007. TESOL, Inc., has issued a Statement of Principles and Preliminary Recommendations for the Reauthorization of the Elementary and Secondary Education Act (2006b), including a request that clear guidance be provided for testing accommodations for English learners as well as provision that local educational agencies be permitted to determine when English learners must be tested in reading, math, and science. The National Council of Teachers of English (NCTE) has issued a statement reflecting the changes requested in the No Child Left Behind Act when it is reauthorized. It should:

> support policies that reward rather than punish teachers who choose to work in the nations' most challenging schools; abandon impoverished assessment systems and support the development of multiple tools that measure the complexity of student literacy and learning; and shift the focus from packaged reading programs to initiatives that support teachers' expertise in educating all children to read and write. (Harris, 2006, p. 1)

What Is Performance-Based Assessment

Outcome-based performance assessment is designed to provide information about students' proficiency (Marzano, 1994), including the ability to analyze and apply as well as simply recognize or recall information. Performance-based testing procedures can be based on tasks that students are asked to do, including essays, demonstrations, computer simulations, performance events, and open-ended problem solving. Collectively, these measures are referred to as *authentic assessments*, because they are related to a student's ability to think knowledgeably about real-life problems.

In an example of performance-based assessment, a beginning English learner might be given clues to a treasure hunt to practice the vocabulary associated with schoolroom objects (eraser, chalk, globe). The teacher might observe the student's ability to collect all the relevant items in an informal assessment. The performance assessment is authentic, because the student actually needs to learn the names of common classroom objects and where to find them.

An ideal performance test for reading would be one that contained materials similar to that found in real books, rather than one that reproduced paragraphs written with a controlled vocabulary. The person administering the test would be the concerned adult who is usually present to help (the teacher or classroom parent volunteer). The test would be observational and interactional, but scores would also be valid and reliable, and available for comparison and reporting purposes. The test would be diagnostic in order to offer a picture of the student's reading strengths and weaknesses. Ideally, it would be motivating and fun so that students, by taking it, would be encouraged to read more (Bembridge, 1992).

The benefits of performance-based assessments are the match of assessment with instruction and the satisfying feedback provided to the teacher and learner alike about areas of satisfactory attainment and areas of needed improvement. Assessment is an integral part of the instructional process, rather than an "add-on" at the end (Guskey, 1994). At the same time, it provides evidence that a standard of quality has been accomplished. Performance-based assessment is directly related to classroom performance and permits teachers to design and offer the extra mediation that students may need as determined by the assessment.

Performance rubrics are often used to assign grades to performance-based assessment. Students have these available as they begin the task. The results from the task constitute the evaluation product, and in addition, the process itself is assessed. Students, together with the teacher, make judgments about the progress being made in language (Hancock, 1994). Multiple measures may be used for assessment, incorporating nontraditional domains such as the arts and thus providing a wide range of evidence on which to evaluate a student's competence. Some of these methods are discussed below.

Methods of Assessment

Before taking a closer look at performance-based assessment as a method, let us survey a broad range of assessment types and take a closer look at some terms that are used to compare types of assessment. This examination may assist in identifying what separates performance assessment from other approaches.

ASSESSMENT TERMS

The assessment literature has developed a rich vocabulary of concepts. Allen, Noel, and Rienzi (2001) offer a glossary of terms (see Table 20.1).

● TABLE 20.1 Assessment Glossary

Type of Assessment	Definition
Traditional measurement	Students exhibit how well they have achieved an objective by taking traditional tests, such as multiple-choice tests.
Performance measure	Students exhibit how well they have achieved an objective by doing it, such as reciting a poem.
Authentic assessment	The assessment process is similar to or embedded in relevant real-world activities, such as debugging a computer program or providing community service.
Quantitative assessment	Assessment results are summarized in a numerical score.
Qualitative assessment	Assessment results are described verbally and may involve counts of categories (such as those for scoring rubrics or rating scales).
Embedded assessment	Assessment activities are embedded within classwork. Students generally receive grades on this work; some or all of the work also is used to assess specific program learning objectives.
Formative v. summative assessment	Formative assessment is designed to give feedback to improve what is being assessed. Summative assessment provides an evaluative summary. For example, a student paper receives a C+ (summative), and formative information is written in the margins to help the student improve.

SOURCE: Adapted from Allen, Noel, & Rienzi (2001, p. 5). Used with permission.

STANDARDIZED AND LESS STANDARDIZED ASSESSMENT

Methods for assessing a performance can be *standardized* (students are scored according to a predetermined outcome) and *less standardized* (scoring is flexibly tailored to the product). A combination of assessment (standardized and less standardized) provides a cross-check of student capabilities. For example, a teacher uses a structured observation checklist to circulate among students while they are working and monitors specific skills, such as emergent literacy, word identification, and oral reading (Miller, 1995). The advantage of a standardized assessment is its speed of scoring through the use of predetermined questions and answer keys.

Less standardized, open-ended assessment, on the other hand, may be more labor-intensive and subjective, although with effort, acceptable agreement can be achieved among a group of assessors. Generally speaking, open-ended assessments may feature longer problem-solving exercises, assignments that involve performances or exhibitions, and/or portfolios that contain student work gathered over a longer period of time, such as a semester. Despite the potential drawbacks of open-ended assessment, it can furnish valuable information about students' abilities.

STANDARDIZED PROFICIENCY TESTS

Several large-scale standardized proficiency tests are available for English learners. For example, the ESL curriculum in the United Kingdom uses a standard—the Graded Tests—produced by a national examination board to determine ESL/EFL proficiency and readiness for entry into British universities. The Test of English as a Foreign Language (TOEFL), developed by the Educational Testing Service in Princeton, New Jersey, is a similar test used for nonnative speakers of English who wish to study at universities and colleges in the United States. The benefits of standardized tests include speed in administration and convenience in scoring.

Norm-referenced standardized tests compare student scores against a population of students with which the test has been standardized. Examples of norm-referenced tests are the Language Assessment Scales (LAS), a test designed to measure oral language skills in English and Spanish, and the Woodcock-Muñoz Language Assessment. Results from these assessments are used for multiple purposes, including student placement, school accountability, and program improvement. *Criterion-referenced* standardized tests are used principally to find out how much of a clearly defined domain of language skills or materials students have learned. The focus is on how the students achieve in relation to the material, rather than to one another or to a national sample. In an ELD program with many levels, students may be required to pass criterion-referenced tests to progress from one level to the next.

TEACHER- AND STUDENT-CREATED RUBRICS

Instructionally sound assessment requires more than implementing meaningful tasks and standards. Teachers must develop the capacity to analyze student work, as well as the leadership ability to train students to do this analysis. Together, teachers and students need to practice self-assessment on a daily, ongoing basis so that students can regularly make judgments about their own progress as learners, with the teacher's help.

A rubric is a scoring guide that provides criteria to describe various requirements or levels of student performance. The use of rubrics helps to score student work more accurately, quickly, fairly, and reliably and can lead to shared standards among faculty about what constitutes quality in a response. Rubrics give students a better idea about the qualities their work should exhibit and help them to understand the meaning behind the grades they are given. If the students are given the rubric in advance or if they help to create it, they can self-assess their work before completion and offer feedback to their peers.

Developing a rubric first requires decoding what criteria define "quality performance." Next, samples of work must be assembled that demonstrate a range of quality, according to a three-, four-, or five-point scale. Following this step, samples of student work need to be separated into the quality levels represented by the rubric. If the rubric does not permit adequate separation of the work, it may need to be revised. Finally, reliable samples of good, average, and poor work can be shown to students to help them understand the quality levels.

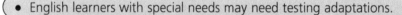

● English learners with special needs may need testing adaptations.

Some teachers work with students to analyze the standards required for the task and design rubrics together with the students, thus underscoring the importance of the specific criteria. With the evaluative criteria as well as the standards in mind, students are more likely to complete work they can honor (Perrone, 1994). Particularly important is finding a measure to infer individual performance if the task is based on group performance (Baker, 1994).

Having a role in determining and describing the evaluation criteria also helps students who may be underprepared for regular learning. The emphasis for them is not only on how they can attain high standards, but also on which strategies will be necessary (Dole, 2001). Planning the evaluation criteria with students in advance helps teachers become aware if the rubric should include revised criteria for those at beginning levels of English acquisition.

TEACHER-CONSTRUCTED TESTS

Teacher-constructed tests can assess skills in reading comprehension, oral fluency, grammatical accuracy, writing proficiency, and listening. Although they may not be as reliable and valid as tests that have been standardized, the ease of their construction and administration and their relevance to classroom learning have made them a popular basis for awarding grades. Tests can be either highly convergent (one right answer required) or open-ended (many answers possible). Many teachers can have a tendency to devise tests that call for specific items of grammar or vocabulary rather than requiring students to use judgment and skillful language. Different types of tests have different advantages and disadvantages (see Table 20.2).

PORTFOLIO ASSESSMENT

The purpose of portfolio assessment is to maintain a long-term record of students' progress, to provide a clear and understandable measure of student productivity, to improve student self-esteem through demonstrating progress and accomplishment, to recognize different learning styles, and to provide an active role for students in self-assessment (Gottlieb, 1995). Portfolios may include writing samples (compositions, letters, reports, drawings, dictation); student self-assessments; audio recordings (retellings, oral think-alouds); photographs and video recordings; semantic webs and concept maps; and/or teacher notes about students (Glaser & Brown, 1993).

No matter what kind of a portfolio system is developed, some common questions arise: What goes into the portfolio? Who decides? Who "keeps" the portfolio, and where? How are the contents of the portfolio used for grading? (B. Johnson, 1996). A *best-works* portfolio might feature the works of which the student is most proud, with reflective writing or audiotaping from the student explaining why the particular works were chosen. A *selection* portfolio contains work samples, for example, what a student considers the most difficult

● TABLE *20.2* Advantages and Disadvantages of Various Types of Tests

Test Type	Advantages	Disadvantages
Multiple choice	Easy and reliable to score using answer key.	Evaluates only recognition knowledge.
True/False	Quick selection from two alternatives; easy to score.	Questions may be easy to misunderstand.
Matching items	Appropriate for content such as vocabulary/definitions.	One error can lead to others.
Short-answer and fill-in-the-blank	Students must generate the answer.	Scoring may be difficult to standardize, leading to unreliability.
Essay	Requires students to organize and synthesize their knowledge.	Students may find writing difficult, and answers are more difficult to score, leading to unreliability.
Oral	Students must speak.	Oral responses are difficult to judge as accurate without strict criteria.
Self-assessment	Students take ownership of the process and may become more motivated to improve.	Students may over- or underestimate their products or performances.

SOURCE: Adapted from Farrell (2006, pp. 126–131).

task. A *process* portfolio might contain evidence of developmental work. Each portfolio might contain a table of contents, reflective entries that discuss the work from the student's perspective, and copies of rubrics that explain why certain works received the grades they did. Pierce (1998) and Wolfe-Quintero (1998) offer practical guidelines on planning and implementing portfolio assessment for ESL students.

Portfolios can be used in an ELD program to record students' progress in reading, oral language, and writing. The reading assessment component might begin with an initial reading assessment and include group and individual checklists to document reading-related behaviors. The oral assessment might document the results when students are asked to invent a story, to listen or retell, and to produce spontaneous speech. The writing assessment component features rough drafts as well as final copies.

Portfolio records about students should be descriptive (what the child does when learning). Once every few weeks, the teacher reviews these records and makes interpretations, taking notes about a student's strengths and weaknesses and making tentative conclusions that plan ways to help the student succeed. These reflections and insights are the basis for an emerging understanding about that student (Barr et al., 2007).

In many classrooms, students use technology to archive digital portfolios that can store both words and images. Using a digital portfolio requires that both students and instructor have the equipment and the means to enter and retrieve documents. O'Bannon and Puckett (2007) outline the format and contents of such a portfolio. Barrett (2000) emphasizes that neither the media nor the contents of a portfolio create learning; it is the student's reflection and thought during and after the process—without this, a multimedia presentation is merely a digital scrapbook.

TEACHER OBSERVATION AND EVALUATION

Teachers are in the best position to diagnose needs and document student progress. As students interact and communicate using language, an observant teacher can record how a collaborative group works together or how students use oral language. These observations may extend across all areas of the curriculum and in all types of interactional situations. Observations may be formal (e.g., miscue analysis) or informal. They may be based on highly structured content or on divergent and creative activities. Multiple observations show student progress (Crawford, 1993).

GRADING

A variety of approaches have been used to assign grades to English learners. Some teachers of English learners assign a traditional A–F grade scale in accordance with grade-level expectations. Performance standards are not lowered for ELD students, although assignments are adjusted to meet the students' language levels. Alternatively, a pass/fail grade scale is used to avoid comparing English learners with English-proficient classmates. A modified A–F grade scale may used for ESL classes, with A–F grades given based on achievement, effort, and behavior and report card grades modified by a qualifier signifying work performed above, at, or below grade level.

STUDENT SELF-ASSESSMENT AND PEER ASSESSMENT

Many teachers have used self-assessment and peer assessment (including student portfolios) to help students take responsibility for their own learning. As part of the reflection on their learning, students can include in the portfolio a letter to the teacher that describes the areas in which they achieved the most growth over a stipulated period, what are now their strongest and weakest areas and why, what their plan is for improving their weakest area, and what grade they would give themselves and why. This task is supplemented by a learning log in which students evaluate their practice and make plans for future effort (McNamara, 1998a). McNamara recommends that teachers offer three types of feedback to this log: *cheerleading feedback*, in which the teacher celebrates, suggests, or offers encouragement; *instructional feedback*, in which the teacher suggests strategies or materials; and *reality-check feedback*, in which the teacher helps students to set more realistic goals or soften their self-criticism.

Student self-assessment can take several forms. Students can discuss their progress with one another, write reflection logs, use checklists and inventories, and participate in reading and writing conferences to determine their progress and needs for growth. They can ask themselves the following questions: What did I learn? What did I do well? What am I still confused about? What do I need help with? What do I want to learn more about? What am I going to work on next (Gottlieb, 2007)?

Brown (1998) offers a rich source for self- and peer assessments in ESL/EFL, including assessment of group work, oral presentation, natural communication, interviews, and so forth. O'Malley and Pierce (1996) provided a useful compendium of assessments for educators, including self- and peer assessments.

OTHER TYPES OF TESTS

Not all testing is performance based. Several types of tests are reviewed below, along with some cautions about the use of assessment. Proficiency tests determine a student's level of performance; diagnostic and placement tests provide information to place students in the appropriate level of academic or linguistic courses; achievement tests assess the student's previous learning; and competency tests assess whether a student can be promoted or advanced. Teachers and school administrators sometimes have a choice about which tests are used and for what purposes, but often tests are mandated by state authorities. It is usually up to teachers to develop effective grading procedures and communicate assessment results to students, parents, and other educators (Ward & Murray-Ward, 1999).

Proficiency Tests. Proficiency tests measure overall ability in English. By definition, proficiency tests are not authentic measures of language skill; they are designed to be independent of the curriculum and do not measure the extent to which a student has worked to acquire meaning. Educators should be cautious about using proficiency tests to predict academic or vocational success because language is only one element among many that contribute to success (Alderson, Krahnke, & Stansfield, 1987).

Diagnosis and Placement Tests. Diagnosis and placement tests are proficiency tests that are used to determine the academic level or the grade level into which students need to be placed. In addition to identifying students who are English learners and determining the level of proficiency, placement tests can be used to monitor the progress of English learners in acquiring English and to assist in transferring students to mainstream classrooms.

Achievement Tests. Achievement tests measure a student's success in learning specific instructional content. A curriculum-based achievement test is given after instruction has taken place and contains only material that was actually taught. However, many contemporary standardized achievement tests are not aligned with specific curricular content. Teachers who understand the needs of English learners can adjust their instruction to balance lesson planning with the need to prepare students to perform well on standardized achievement tests.

Competency Tests. Competency tests are achievement tests that are used to identify students who can be promoted or graduate. Some states have provisions that modify or exempt testing for English learners until they are ready for standardized testing. Other states offer modifications in the testing such as extended time, a separate site, small-group testing, or testing supervised by a familiar person.

Identification, Assessment, and Placement of English Learners in the Schools

Many states have specific laws and provide procedural guidelines regarding identification procedures for English learners; others do not have state laws but do provide guidelines for assessment. Many states also have procedures for redesignating students and for placing them in mainstream classes. Generally speaking, when students enroll in school, if they are identified as needing ELD services, they are placed in suitable programs, if available. Ideally, students are given placement tests that correspond directly to an instructional plan that can be implemented immediately by a classroom teacher. Once in a program, students are then periodically reevaluated for purposes of reclassification.

IDENTIFICATION PROCEDURES FOR ENGLISH LEARNERS

A variety of methods are used to identify English learners needing services. The *home-language survey* is a short form administered by school districts to determine the language spoken at home, but students can be identified by other measures. Among these are registration and enrollment information;

staff observation; and interviews or referrals made by teachers, counselors, parents, administrators, or community members (Cheung & Solomon, 1991).

Cheng (1987) recommended other ways to gain information about students' language abilities that can be helpful in making placement decisions: Observe students in multiple settings (classroom, home, and playground); obtain history (medical, family, previous education, immigration experience, home languages); interview current or previous classroom teachers for information about learning styles and classroom behavior; seek information from other school personnel (counselor, nurse); and ask the student's parents to characterize a student's language and performance skills in the home and the community. Educators who draw from a variety of information sources can see the students' needs in a broader context and thus design a language program to meet these needs.

ASSESSMENT FOR PLACEMENT

Ideally, once students are identified, bilingual staff conduct an assessment to determine placement. In addition, parents and students should be given an orientation about the assessment and placement process and informed about the services of the school system.

Some districts place students using the LAS to measure oral language skills in English and Spanish. Another frequently used proficiency test is the Bilingual Syntax Measure (BSM), which measures oral proficiency in English and/or Spanish grammatical structures and language dominance. The Basic Inventory of Natural Language (BINL) determines oral proficiency in English by means of pictures that are used to elicit natural speech; spoken sentences are analyzed for fluency, average length of utterance, and level of syntactic complexity.

A more comprehensive instrument is the English Language Development Monitoring Tool, employed by Hacienda La Puente Unified School District in California, based on the California English-Language Development Test (CELDT). The placement instrument travels with the student, permitting a smooth transition from ELD services to mainstream instruction.

Even after administering placement tests and gathering information, appropriate academic placement may be difficult. Placement tests measure only language proficiency; they are not informative about a student's academic background, which may vary from strong to weak depending on the subject area. Placement by age can also be a problem. Students may need much more time in the system to learn English, but placement in an earlier grade may lead to social adjustment problems. Teacher-devised checklists and observational data from the classroom can be used to confirm or adjust student placement (Lucas & Wagner, 1999).

REDESIGNATION AND EXIT PROCEDURES

School districts use specific criteria to determine when English learners have attained the language skills necessary to succeed in an English-only classroom. This reclassification (redesignation or exiting) process may use multiple criteria (Rico, 2000), which include, but are not limited to, measures of speaking, comprehension, reading, and writing as well as evidence that students can participate meaningfully in the general program. Some districts organize bilingual education advisory committees to ensure ethnic parent representation and participation in implementing redesignation criteria that are reliable, valid, and useful. Norm-referenced tests—or standardized, criterion-referenced tests using national norms or district, regional, or state nonminority norms—are often employed for purposes of reclassification. The establishment of minimum score levels as criteria for proficiency is often a political issue because the higher the score that must be attained, the longer the students will remain in a primary-language class.

In summary, the decisions about identifying and placing English learners are as follows: When a student enrolls in a school district, administer the home-language survey. If the student has a primary language other than English, administer an English-language proficiency test. If the student is an English learner, administer achievement and placement tests in English and in the primary language. If the student is eligible for support services, notify parents of options and proceed with placement (Gottlieb, 2006).

Limitations of Assessment

Tests play a large role in placing and reclassifying English learners. Often pressure is applied for programs to redesignate students as fluent English speakers in a short period of time, perhaps before they are ready. Continuing support—such as tutoring, follow-up assessment, and primary-language help—is often not available after reclassification. Standardized tests, though designed to be fair, are not necessarily well suited as measures of language ability or achievement for English learners. In fact, both the testing situation and the test content may be rife with difficulties and bias for EL students.

DIFFICULTIES IN THE TESTING SITUATION

The context in which a test is administered needs to be examined to understand how students may be affected. Factors within the context of testing such as anxiety, lack of experience with testing materials, time limitations, and lack of rapport with the test administrator may cause difficulties for culturally and linguistically diverse students.

All students experience test anxiety, but this anxiety can be compounded if the test is alien to the students' cultural backgrounds and experiences. Allowing students to take practice exams may familiarize them with the test formats and reduce test anxiety. Moreover, students may take longer to answer individual questions because they need more time for mental translation and to formulate a response. Some students may need a time extension or should be given untimed tests.

When testers and students do not share the same language or dialect, the success of the testing may be reduced. Students who ostensibly speak the same primary language as the test administrator may not share certain dialectic features, reducing their understanding as a result. Students may not verbalize freely if they are shy or wary about test taking, feel defensive about teachers' negative stereotypes, or resent the testing situation itself. Students from some cultural groups may not feel comfortable making eye contact with a test administrator. Those from cultures that discourage individuals from displaying knowledge may not be quick to answer questions and may be reluctant to guess unless they are certain they are right. They may be embarrassed to volunteer a response or receive positive feedback about their performance (Cloud, Genesee, & Hamayan, 2000).

Tests, particularly achievement tests, may have bias that affects the performance of English learners. *Language-specific bias* is created when a test developed for use with one language is simply translated into another language; the translation may fail to furnish equivalent vocabulary items. *Geographic bias* happens when test items feature terms used only in particular geographic regions. *Dialect bias* occurs when certain expressions are used that are relevant only to certain dialect speakers. *Cultural bias* may be present when English learners understand test items derived from mainstream culture differently or not at all. Many students are completely unfamiliar with common European American food items, sports, musical instruments, nursery rhymes, or children's stories. Test content may represent *class bias*; for example, *vacuum cleaner* may be a term familiar only among the middle class.

CAUTIONS ABOUT TESTING

Tests are an influential part of the U.S. schooling system and are used in every classroom. When choosing standardized tests, teachers can consider the following guidelines to help them determine the benefits and limitations of the test: Does the test correspond to the task that it measures? Is the score a true measure or fair sample of the student's ability? How can the score be supplemented with other information? Is the testing driving the curriculum? Is the test being used unfairly to compare students and schools with one another (Worthen & Spandel, 1991)?

Researchers have the following recommendations for effective practice in the assessment of English learners (August & Pease-Alvarez, 1996; Navarrete & Gustke, 1996):

- Test both content knowledge and language proficiency in the native language and in English.
- Use a variety of techniques to measure content knowledge and skills (e.g., portfolios, observations, anecdotal records, interviews, checklists, exhibits, students' self-appraisals, writing samples, dramatic renditions, and criterion-referenced tests).
- Be sure that the teacher is aware of the purpose of the assessment (e.g., whether the test is intended to measure verbal or writing skills, language proficiency, or content knowledge).
- Take students' backgrounds into account, including their educational experiences and parents' literacy.
- Add context to assessment tasks by incorporating familiar classroom material (brief quotations, charts, graphics, cartoons, works of art) as a stimulus and including questions for small-group discussion and individual writing.
- Mirror learning processes with which students are familiar, such as the writing process and reading conferences.
- Match administration procedures to classroom instructional practices (e.g., cooperative small groups, individual conferences, and assessment in the language of instruction).
- Give students extra time to complete or respond to assessment tasks, making accommodations such as simplifying directions in English and/or paraphrasing in the student's native language, as well as permitting students to use dictionaries or word lists.
- Maintain a positive outlook. Regardless of a teacher's personal opinion about standardized tests, it is only fair to children that teachers assume a positive attitude. Teachers who are tense and grim may negatively affect test scores.

A final comment about standardized testing raises questions about the long-term effects of testing on culturally and linguistically diverse students:

> What effect does the unrelenting emphasis on standardized literacy testing have on students' perception of the purposes and possibilities of literacy? By extension, what effect does testing have on their perception of the possibilities for themselves as readers and writers? Many concerns about identity and standardized testing have been framed in terms of race and social class; . . . teachers and researchers have argued that standardized testing works not from a set of objective standards somehow as constant as the North Star but from a set of cultural conceptions about literacy that are neither objective nor static. Students whose race or social class is not a part of the dominant culture often face more complex challenges in meeting the standards of that dominant culture. (Williams, 2007, pp. 70–71)

Academic Expectations

How can English learners achieve the highest possible performance? Without question, there is a connection between teacher expectations for English learners and their subsequent school success, or lack of it. The next section examines teacher expectations for student performance. Overall, the effect of teacher expectations amounts to a de facto ongoing assessment of students' worth and capabilities. Addressing these expectations and how they operate is therefore an integral part of examining the role of performance outcomes in the achievement of English learners.

HOW TEACHER EXPECTATIONS ARE FORMED AND COMMUNICATED TO STUDENTS AND HOW STUDENTS RESPOND

> **MEGASTRATEGY 20.3**
>
> Expect the highest performance possible in the time available.

How can teachers communicate positive expectations in order to increase the academic achievement of these students? How do teachers form expectations about student achievement and communicate these during instruction? How do students react?

Students may perform at levels consistent with the teacher's expectations. Although the expectation may have no basis in fact, the student's behavior comes to match the expectation. This effect can be positive (a teacher overestimates a student's abilities, and the student is stimulated to perform well), or it can be negative (a teacher expects very little from a student and communicates this expectation so clearly that student performance is affected adversely).

Jussim (1986) offered a general framework for the operation of expectancy effects: Teachers develop expectations, teachers treat students differently depending on their expectations, and students react to this differential treatment in ways that confirm the expectations. According to Jussim, expectation operates through a set of mediating factors, described as follows.

Teachers Form Expectations. Teachers first form expectations about students based on prejudgments (a student's reputation, inferences from information in cumulative files, experience with older siblings, or anecdotes from other teachers); racial and cultural stereotypes; scores from placement or standardized tests; observations of a student's classroom performance compared against memories of previous successful and unsuccessful students; and naive predictions and fallacies, such as exaggerating the salience of a few examples of behavior. Together, these factors create an image in a teacher's mind about the likely success or failure of a student.

Teachers' beliefs about students' capabilities can be modified as new information is collected if teachers alter their expectations in the light of subsequent evidence. When a student's performance is consistent with expectations, these expectations will be confirmed. When student performance does not fit expectations, though, it may take many instances of behavior contrary to a teacher's expectations to change a teacher's beliefs about the ability of a student (Brophy, 1983). Teachers with flexible expectations readily revise their impressions when direct information about student achievement is available (Brophy, 1983).

Differential Treatment of Students. Expectations and treatment of students are linked. This linkage provides an understanding of the operation of the expectation effect in classroom teaching, both at the psychological level (teachers' actions and reactions) and at the situational level (sociocultural features of schooling).

Attributions may explain why students of whom teachers have high expectations receive positive attention. Teachers tend to prefer students who are attentive, cooperative, and conscientious, and who time their questions, interruptions, requests, and misbehavior appropriately. They perceive that high-performing students hold similar academic values to their own, and they tend to spend more time with those students to whom they attribute the most potential payoff for their instructional investment. This may explain why teachers spend more time coaching "highs" with more cues and prompts; offer them more feedback, prompts, and response opportunities; are less accepting of poor-quality answers from such students; and design more challenging assignments for them. This closer communication is a factor in students' academic success.

Tracking and ability grouping are ways in which schools make differential curricula available to students in accordance with their beliefs about student ability. In the United States, middle-income students are more often tracked in average and higher groups, whereas low-income and minority students are found in disproportionate numbers in lower-ability groups (Sleeter & Grant, 1987). Students who are placed in low-ability groups may be systematically denied access to "high-status" knowledge, which includes the academic skills, content, attitudes, and experiences that are inculcated into well-educated members of society.

The social context of the learning environment permeates teachers' expectations. A teacher's behavior must be consonant with the motivational climate of school. If the discipline climate in the school is punitive, a less punitive discipline style on the part of the teacher may be perceived as weak. Conversely, if school discipline is lax, the teaching staff may fail in efforts to create high expectations for homework completion. Students participating in a resistance culture may see teachers' motivational efforts as evidence of weakness or react in a hostile manner to teacher demands (see Díaz-Rico, 1993). A school climate featuring fierce academic competition may exacerbate feelings of helplessness and depression on the part of some students. In these contexts, teachers may find it necessary to adapt to the context and behave as expected, opt out and seek a context more suitable to their teaching styles and values, or become advocates for a school climate more supportive of all learners.

Students' Reactions. Differential treatment received by students alters the potential for achievement. Being called on less and having attempts to speak cut short reduces the chance to think spontaneously and to articulate ideas. If teachers attribute poor performance to students' lack of ability, this assessment is communicated to students, who are likely to lower their level of aspiration.

Teachers can influence students' attributions of the cause of their academic success and failure. When teachers respond to a student's mistakes with pity, praise, or unsolicited help, that student is more likely to attribute the errors to lack of ability. In contrast, a critical, corrective response from the teacher conveys the message that the student is capable of success.

Minority-group students may sometimes be victims of well-meaning pity from teachers who "ease up" on requirements so that students will "experience success" and "feel good about themselves." This attitude, however well meaning, may also communicate the message, "You don't have the ability to do this, so I will overlook your failure." This targeting of minority-group members for pity, praise in the event of failure, or unsolicited help may cause the internalization of low self-esteem and is a subtle form of racial discrimination that detracts from academic motivation. Rather than pitying or excusing students who need additional academic support, teachers can teach them how to learn and hold them accountable.

Attention, participation, and cooperation on the part of students may *cause* positive or negative teacher evaluation or *result* from it. Decreased motivation may follow lowered expectations, and lower motivation may in turn lead to lowered performance, which serves to confirm teacher expectations. Cooperation and participation may be enhanced by an understanding of students' differing ability to understand the participation expectations and perform in ways that are consonant with the culture of the classroom.

STUDENT CONTROL OVER CLASSROOM LEARNING

Teachers can reduce the negative effects of teacher-induced achievement by reducing the frequency of teacher-directed lessons and providing an opportunity for more peer interaction and support. This approach allows students' voices to be heard in determining the topics of interest, contributing to these topics, and choosing with whom to work cooperatively. Those students who need more individual attention should be encouraged to attend teacher-led study sessions at predetermined times.

INTERCULTURAL COMMUNICATION OF EXPECTATIONS

Differences in the cultures of the teacher and the student may cause miscommunication of expectations. Language and word choice are other factors that make intercultural communication challenging. Words that may seem harmless in one context may have a negative connotation within a subculture; teachers have to be careful both to use appropriate terms of address and reference when communicating with students and to be aware of which terms used in the classroom might have an incendiary effect.

Student response to teacher expectations seems to be highly influenced by cultural background and home discourse patterns. Some cultures encourage students to set internal standards of worth, and peer pressure devalues dependence on teachers for approval.

Expecting high achievement from English learners and communicating these expectations require specific educational programs that draw attention to the hidden curriculum of the school, quality dialogue between teachers and students, diverse learning styles, the use of the community as a resource, and a commitment to democratic ideals in the classroom (Gollnick & Chinn, 2006).

"Culturally relevant teaching" is one approach to intercultural communication (Ladson-Billings, 1994). Prospective teachers may need to be observed closely and objectively so they can be offered feedback on practices that encourage classroom equity. Prospective teachers may also need to participate in sessions that raise self-awareness of racism in practice in the classroom (see Díaz-Rico, 1998, 2000). New forms of instruction are necessary that promote equity, and new forms of communication must be developed that allow teachers to believe in their students' capacity for high achievement and to communicate that belief to the students.

Planning Instruction

Effective teaching makes a strong connection between goals and outcomes. A teacher who sets precise, well-delineated objectives, plans instruction to teach the targeted skills clearly, and then carefully assesses the results can usually count on most of the students achieving the desired objectives. Does this sound like pedagogical science? Despite the seductive clarity of this approach, it is based on the underlying assumption that good teaching causes learning. The reality of the teaching–learning connection is much more complex. Students who are not involved in the process of setting goals miss out on the opportunity to desire to learn.

> **MEGASTRATEGY 20.4**
>
> Plan cooperatively and flexibly for maximum student involvement and achievement

The desire to learn, like other kinds of desires, has a specific object. A person who desires, desires *something*—usually something tangible, like a new car, a better house, a video game. People can be socialized to desire intangibles, such as victory in a soccer game, more power at work, or high grades at school. But the desire to learn is a tricky intangible, because learning is destabilizing. In Piaget's terms, learning causes disequilibration. Many people dislike learning; they wish to be satisfied by a life in which every question has an answer and every problem has a simple solution. But the central question that drives high-quality teaching is one that in itself is complex, ill defined, and unsettling: What makes someone want to learn? How can a teacher plan lessons based on the learners' desires to learn?

CONSTRUCTIVIST PLANNING

The teacher might ask that question, but the learner must answer. Cognitive, constructivist teaching asks, "What is interesting here? What about this subject provokes us? What makes us wonder? Why do we care?" Structures such as K-W-L help teachers bring students' knowledge and interests into the planning cycle. In the long run, the learner is fully engaged only when there is a sense of co-ownership of the learning process so that the learner has a sense of involvement and shared control. This situation is not easy to achieve.

When curriculum and content standards are set by external governing agencies, neither students nor teachers have complete freedom to study what they will. In most school districts, the grade-level curriculum is predetermined, and standards of content mastery are distributed to the teacher before the start of the school year. Co-planning, co-monitoring, and co-evaluation are the hallmark of co-ownership of the instructional process. How can they fit with a standards-driven curriculum?

In its most inclusive sense, a lesson is a plan that affords or allows learning. *Affordance* means that a student can acquire a new concept as a part of a sociocultural process, the activity system that makes this acquisition possible (Van Lier, 2000). The teacher's role is to help the learner to design and perform learning, set learning in motion, identify important problems and make them comprehensible, and set up times and places to showcase discovery and report results. This is the best use of instructional planning.

THE DIRECT TEACHING MODEL

The seven-step lesson plan is a popular one, stemming from the days of direct teaching. In this model, the teacher determines the objectives of the lesson; teaching then begins with an anticipatory set, in which the teaching materials are displayed and students are told the key topics to be covered. Next, direct instruction takes place, in which the teacher presents information and models the activity that constitutes the learning. Guided instruction follows, as the teacher continues to model and guide students before they engage in independent practice. At this point, there may be supplementary activities before the evaluation/summary/closure (Molina, Hanson, & Siegel, 1997).

MODIFYING THE DIRECT TEACHING MODEL

Critics of the direct instruction model see a lack of student "ownership" of the design and implementation of this kind of lesson. However, the seven-step model does not have to be teacher-driven. For example, the teacher might involve students in thematic planning before the start of the unit of instruction. The anticipatory set can be used as a means of bringing forth prior knowledge. Direct teaching can be done by students or the teacher, or it can be a very brief stage setting forth instructions for a prolonged practice phase. Students might choose among several different activities to achieve the objective. Finally, students can self-assess or peer-assess in addition to undergoing teacher assessment.

In the long run, however, two major paradigm shifts (learning-centered instruction and standards-based instruction) have made the direct teaching model useful only for small, turnaround lessons that demonstrate a specific skill. Project-based learning—with its extended time frame, complex set of skills to be acquired, and highly visible set of outcomes—is a more robust and authentic model of learning that makes the direct instruction model seem artificial.

Matching Performance and Assessment

MEGASTRATEGY 20.5
Set criteria for effective performance and assess attainment of those criteria

Teachers who have been given the opportunity to think carefully about the connection between assessment and learning understand that learning goals, lesson plans, classroom activities, and evaluations of student learning must be consistent (Jametz, 1994). Most teachers know that they need to plan stimulating, intellectually challenging tasks for students. Performance-based assessments cannot by themselves bring about significant changes in learning unless classroom instruction improves.

SETTING OBJECTIVES

The cycle of planning begins with a rich question that "stirs up" swirls of interest. Together the teacher and learner plan how questions that arise can be addressed. A lesson can be guided by clear objectives that focus instruction; but lessons can also be layered, overlapping, and confusing, with objectives that are hard to grasp, control, and divide into pieces. The teacher helps to refine goals, discover means, set time lines, and define performances that will help students showcase their learning. In this process, content, learning, and language objectives go hand in hand as language is used to acquire information and perform written or spoken outcomes.

After teachers and students have determined objectives, they can plan to use many means, such as illustrating, dramatizing, creating songs, or rewriting stories to demonstrate their performance. The learning tasks then become ways to transform information into knowledge, ways that meet the standards that have been set. A variety of ways can be used to employ students' language skills on both formal and informal occasions: learning centers; dramatic, visual, or oral presentations; readers theater; or slide, video, or computer-based audiovisual shows. Re-presentation of knowledge is an important means by which teachers assess student learning and pinpoint areas for reteaching, expansion, and/or modification. In this manner, assessment becomes a part of the learning cycle.

Authentic tasks provide a richer means of assessing English learners than traditional paper-and-pencil tests. In one community college English class that had been in session one block away from the World Trade Center when it crumbled, students gathered when class resumed to speak of their shock and horror. The class debated what type of writing project they could initiate that would serve as a collection of their thoughts and reactions and convey their response to the tragedy (Abdoh, 2001). This situation is typical of the power of student-determined goals. Obviously, a teacher-imposed project would not sustain the full measure of their emotions and desire to make meaning, yet the teacher can work with them to evoke and refine their work.

Lessons are performance based when the objective is stated in measurable terms: What is the student expected to be able to do, or perform, when the objective is mastered? Therefore, the wording of the objective is active, as in the following samples:

- Students will survey a variety of weather charts.
- Students will ask for and give opinions and advice.
- Students will describe a sequence of events.

TASKS AS OBJECTIVES

In *task-based learning* (Nunan, 1989), the goal or objective is linked to the learning activities through *tasks*. A task is "a piece of classroom work which involves learners in comprehending, manipulating, producing, or interacting in the target language while their attention is principally focused on meaning rather than on form" (p. 10). Communication and learning tasks are the central building blocks of a lesson plan. Additional elements, such as a focus on form, may be included as lesson supplements.

Tasks have one central characteristic: They rehearse communicative events that take place in the real world, using language that appears naturally in these events. The social function—perhaps learning to extend an invitation—serves as a goal or performance indicator to be attained.

A classroom lesson involves a clear connection between the objectives, activities, and assessment. After the objectives have been determined, activities are designed that will accomplish these objectives. Tasks are linked to the objectives of the lesson by means of task chains.

TASK CHAINS

A task chain is a linked series of actions that accomplishes a specific objective, performed by the learner under the supervision of the teacher. Tasks are linked thematically to the objective. They may involve a variety of language modes, such as listening and speaking, reading, writing, and critical thinking.

The tasks may consist of a mix of short activities across various modalities. In the previous example, extending an invitation, tasks could be the following: Practice in pairs using sentences containing invitation gambits ("How about . . ."; "Are you free Friday afternoon . . ."); a listening activity followed by comprehension questions; a writing activity ("Write four sentences that could function as invitations to go roller skating on Saturday morning"); or a role play. Alternatively, the task chain could consist of one complex task built from several steps.

In the curriculum *Atlas* (Level 2, Unit 3, "Old Friends"), the first unit goal is to "Talk about Friends" (see Nunan, 1995, pp. 25–27). Task Chain 1 ("Close Friends") is designed to accomplish this goal. Several of the tasks in Task Chain 1 are summarized as follows (some tasks have been omitted):

Task 1. (Pair work). Circle which of the words below (eleven adjectives are given) that describe your best friend.
(Pair work). Think of three friends and make statements about them using words from the list.

Task 2. Listen to the tape-recorded conversation in which Tony is talking about his best friends. Using the given chart, circle the names he mentions and write the correct occupation beside each name.

Task 4. (Group discussion). What does Tony do? Is this an unusual occupation for a man? What about in your country? Do men do this type of job? What jobs do men rarely do? Women?

Task 6. Think of three friends and then complete the chart. (The chart has five columns: "Name," "Things You Do Together," "Things You Talk About," "Occupation, " and "Where You Met.")
(Pair work). Use the chart to talk about your friends with a partner.

ASSESSING THE TASK CHAIN

The success of a task chain is evaluated in several ways, through assessment activities at the end of the chain or through a final assessment at the end of the lesson. Using assessment, the teacher is able to measure directly the extent to which students have mastered the objective. Based on this information, the teacher can choose to reteach the task to all or some of the students, or the class can move forward to the next objective.

Figure 20.1 offers a set of criteria for assessing an instructional plan based on task chains. Each objective of the plan is assessed during the task chain or at the end. The tasks themselves are supported by four kinds of materials. *Posters* offer large, whole-class presentation of information; *focus sheets* offer information that can be used as a component of instruction but are not written on by students during the lesson and can be collected for reuse; *worksheets* are completed during the lesson; and *assessment sheets* are used as the test and scored by the teacher or by peers. This can include peer- or self-assessment sheets.

Figures 20.2 through 20.4 show how a TPR-based lesson features some of these components.

● FIGURE *20.1* MA in Education, TESOL Option Program Outcome Assessment Criteria for Instructional Plan, Standards-Based

Candidate _____   Assignment: A B C D E
Component of Plan_____   **Point Value/Critique**

Introductory Information   _____/**10**
• Unit/lesson has relevant and appropriate title.
• Level, characteristics of students are specified.
• Materials are listed.
• Provision is made for involving students.

Performance Indicators   _____/**10**
• Specific
• Feasible in time allotted
• Indicate adequate content
• Matched to TESOL, ELD, district standards

Task Chains   _____/**10**
• Content is supported using focus sheets or other source
   materials; matched to performance indicator.
• Activities are relevant; adequate to attain indicator; matched to
   performance indicator.
• Activity is supported using worksheets or other practice materials.
• Focus sheets and worksheets are referenced and source(s) cited.

Assessment   _____/**10**
• Formative assessment is relevant and adequate to measure
   attainment of indicator; performance criteria are specified.
• Summative assessment is supported using assessment sheets or
   other materials.
• Assessment sheets are referenced and source(s) cited.

Format   _____/**10**
• Consistent format is used throughout.
• Appearance is professional, word-processed.
• Titles of supporting materials match presentation in lesson plan.

TOTAL   _____/**50**

● FIGURE *20.2* Demonstration Instructional Plan: Making Flowers from Tissue Paper

Level: Adult—Speech Emergence

Performance Indicators:

Learning Strategy Objective	**1.** To sequence written directions using context cues
Language Objective	**2.** To acquire vocabulary for simple sensorimotor actions
Content Objective	**3.** To make flowers from tissue paper

Warm-Up: Pass out tissue paper flowers and ask who knows how to make one. If someone knows, recruit him/her as assistant in Task Chain **3**.

TESOL Standard: Standard 1. English language learners communicate for social, intercultural, and instructional purposes within the school setting.

Task Chain 1. *Sequencing written directions using context cues*

1. Instructor explains task: Sequence written directions using context cues.
2. Pair students. Each pair receives an envelope with directions on how to make a tissue paper flower (Focus Sheet 1, cut up). Each pair sequences the strips to re-create the proper sequence of instructions.
3. When sequencing task is completed, instructor shows solution on overhead (transparency of Focus Sheet 1).
4. Pairs self-assess their versions for accuracy, reordering if necessary. (Pairs keep directions spread out before them.)

Task Chain 2. *Acquiring vocabulary for simple sensorimotor actions*

1. Each pair chooses ten new words from the directions.
2. First pair writes their ten new words on board. Second pair writes their ten words; if one of their words is already on the board, they put a check beside it, writing only words that have not appeared already.
3. When enough pairs have written their words, instructor takes ten words with the highest number of checks as vocabulary. These are circled on transparency and pronounced together. Students act out sensorimotor actions.
4. Students put strips back in envelopes and return them to instructor.

Task Chain 3. *Making flowers from tissue paper*
1. Instuctor demonstrates how to make a flower following directions on transparency (see Focus Sheet 1), accentuating (acting out) verbs that are circled as vocabulary items.
2. Students choose tissue paper colors and follow instructions from overhead.
3. Students process-check against models of partially made flowers.

Final Assessment: *Making flowers from tissue paper*

1. Using the Assessment Sheet, students check their awareness of sequence, knowledge of vocabulary, and context for sensorimotor actions. Scoring: 18–20, Flower; 15–17, Bud; 12–15, Leaf; 8–11, Stem; below 7, Root.

● FIGURE *20.3* Focus Sheet 1: Sequencing Written
Directions Using Context Clues

1. Select six sheets of tissue paper, each 10 inches by 15 inches.
2. Stack neatly. For variety, the four on top should be color A, the other two color B.
3. Stack all six layers together and fold into accordion pleats. The pleat should be 10 inches long. Each pleat should measure about 1.5 inches wide.
4. Fold the pleated strip in half at the 5-inch point.
5. Pinch and wrap tightly in wire. The result should look like a bow tie.
6. Shape ends of petals by making either curved or pointed cuts at both ends of tissue paper "bow." For curved petals, cut a semicircle at each end of the bow tie. For pointed petals, cut a triangle at the ends.
7. With fingertips, stretch folds outward to shape tissue paper into a bowl.
8. Delicately fluff out the petals, using a gentle touch to separate the layers of tissue.
9. Holding the floral tape in one hand, wind the tape around the wire stem in a spiral, working from the center of the bow to the end of the wire.

FORMATIVE ASSESSMENT

As students are engaged in the activity system, the teacher can help them maintain momentum and solve ongoing problems through formative assessment. This process involves progress checks that help students evaluate their efforts in light of their goals and stay on track with benchmark performance measures. The teacher may require formal weekly progress reports, ask for partial products at predetermined times, or set deadlines for circulation of rough drafts. Rich documentation of the progress of an ongoing project helps to create a final product that is not overly dependent on one final spurt of activity that can cause tension and frustration. These requirements help students avoid procrastination and keep their projects moving forward.

SUMMATIVE ASSESSMENT, CULMINATING PERFORMANCE, AND METALEARNING

A final performance on a certain day—a play with other students as audience, an exhibit for parents, or a publication with a printer's deadline—helps students to understand the real world of promise and fulfillment. The excitement that these events generate helps to provide community pressure and support for achievement. Despite the satisfaction these culminating events offer, the substance of assessment remains with the content standards that have been achieved. Peer evaluation, self-evaluation, and teacher evaluation together identify the final wisdom: What did the project achieve? What was learned about the content? What was learned about the process? And, most exciting, what is still not known? What remains to be discovered? This summative assessment is the basis for metalearning, learning about improving learning.

● FIGURE *20.4* Assessment Sheet: Making Flowers from Tissue Paper

I. *Awareness of Sequence.* Number these steps in the correct order.

_____ Pinch and wrap in wire.
_____ Wind the tape around the wire stem.
_____ Fold the pleated strip in half.
_____ Stretch folds outward.
_____ Fluff out the petals.
_____ Fold in accordion pleats.
_____ Select paper.
_____ Stack neatly.
_____ Cut ends of petals.

II. *Vocabulary for Simple Sensorimotor Actions.* Draw a circle around the words that describe an action that takes place in the directions above.

wire	pinch	outward
wrap	pleated	cut
stem	strip	around
wind	tape	stretch
petal	half	out
pleats	fold	ends
select	accordion	paper
fluff	neatly	stack

III. *Context for Sensorimotor Actions.* Write "Yes" if the **bold** word is used correctly in the sentence. Write "No" if it is not.

1. _____ We **wrap** gifts in gift wrap paper.
2. _____ **Wind** the turkey in the oven.
3. _____ **Stack** the clean clothes.
4. _____ **Stretch** your legs before running.
5. _____ **Fluff** the dirt under the bed.
6. _____ We can use an **accordion** to play music.

Monitoring and Adjusting Instruction

Formative evaluation can permit much valuable ongoing readjustment of the learning process. The responsibility for this monitoring is shared between teacher and learners, but much of the responsibility for adjustment falls on the learner.

Teachers exercise patience in helping students to monitor and adjust their learning to meet the desired performance standards; vanquish the students' habits of sloth or procrastination, if that is a problem; conquer the students' lack of faith in themselves by providing encouragement, structure, and guide-

> **MEGASTRATEGY 20.6**
>
> Adjust instruction to attain performance criteria

lines; overcome students' impatient desire to improve instantly, as they perhaps try and fail several times before succeeding; help students to accept the disappointment of failure if there is some aspect of a complex problem that eludes solution; or make themselves available during the basic struggle to use English as a means of expression.

Not all learning is successful. Sometimes problems that are worth addressing are beyond comprehension, and sometimes problems that are comprehensible are simply not interesting. Most teachers do everything possible to facilitate successful learning. In the last analysis, however, it is not the teacher's job to rescue students from disappointment or failure; these are a part of authentic learning. Sometimes the metalearning—the wisdom about learning—that takes place comes after the learning has taken place, in a process of reflection and hindsight.

The teacher, who is the storehouse of success and failure, can take into consideration the struggles and triumphs of one year's students in order to modify instruction the next time. What is exciting about teaching is the opportunity for metalearning—that is, learning better and better how to learn. This goal is not easily achieved, for one must look clearly at the failure that took place as well as the success. Without failure there is no learning; there is only the "already known." For in the last analysis, errors—when assessment shows these clearly and precisely—are the best teachers, providing the opportunity for failure to be converted to wisdom.

Show What You Know

1. Describe the relationship between objectives and assessment.

2. Define *objective* in ELD or EFL teaching. Give four examples appropriate to your target teaching level, one each in reading, writing, listening, and speaking.

3. Define *task chain* in ELD or EFL teaching. Give a title to the task chains that match each of the four objectives described above.

4. Give one example of a series of tasks that fulfill one of the task chains titled above.

5. Describe a formative assessment that could be used to monitor task performance on the task chain described in #4.

6. Describe a summative assessment that could be used to monitor task performance on the task chain described in #4.

mylabschool
Where the classroom comes to life!

Video Workshop: "Using Student Self-Assessment to Evaluate Communication Skills"

This video demonstrates the use of student self-assessment to critique oral performance. As you watch, think about ways to apply performance-based assessment to improving English learners' oral skills.

To access the video, log on to MyLabSchool at www.mylabschool.com, enter Assignment ID **ETV18** into the **Assignment Finder,** and select the video entitled "A Communication Exercise." Watch the video, complete the first two questions that follow, and e-mail your responses to your professor for credit.

Glossary of Acronyms

English language learner or *ELL* is the term used consistently in this text. However, many other terms are in general usage.

The acronyms listed here are used in various school districts in the United States and by state and federal education agencies. The terms refer to individuals, classes, programs, concepts, and agencies.

Individuals

LEP	Limited English proficient
NEP	Non-English proficient
PEP	Partially English proficient
FEP	Fluent English proficient
NES	Non-English speaker
LES	Limited English speaker (or speaking)
FES	Fluent English speaker (or speaking)
EL	English learner
ELL	English language learner
NNS	Non-native speaker
NS	Native speaker
LMS	Language minority student

Classes and/or Programs

EFL	English as a foreign language
ESL	English as a second language
ESOL	English for speakers of other languages
EAL	English as an additional language
ELD	English language development
ELA	English language arts
SDAIE	Specially designed academic instruction in English
SEI	Structured English immersion
SEIP	Structured English immersion program
SI	Sheltered instruction
ESP	English for specific (or special) purposes
EOP	English for occupational purposes
EAP	English for academic purposes

IEP	Intensive English program
LCD	Linguistically and culturally diverse
CLAD	Cross-cultural, language and academic development

Concepts

BICS	Basic interpersonal communication skills
CALP	Cognitive academic language proficiency
ELP	English language proficiency
L1	First (native) language
L2	Second (target) language
SLA	Second language acquisition

Agencies

CABE	California Association for Bilingual Speakers
CAL	Center for Applied Linguistics
CREDE	Center for Research on Education, Diversity, and Excellence
NABE	National Association for Bilingual Speakers
NAME	National Association for Multicultural Education
NCBE	National Clearinghouse of Bilingual Education
OBEMLA	Office of Bilingual Education and Minority Languages Affairs (*now defunct*)
OELA	Office of English Language Acquisition, Language Enhancement, and Academic Achievement for Limited English Proficient Students
TESOL	Teaching (or Teachers of) English to Speakers of Other Languages

349